Equality's Guardians

Equality's Guardians

How Courts Conceptualize Equal Protection and Non-Discrimination Guarantees

Edited by

NIELS PETERSEN
Professor of Public Law, University of Münster, Germany

OXFORD
UNIVERSITY PRESS

OXFORD
UNIVERSITY PRESS

Great Clarendon Street, Oxford, OX2 6DP,
United Kingdom

Oxford University Press is a department of the University of Oxford.
It furthers the University's objective of excellence in research, scholarship,
and education by publishing worldwide. Oxford is a registered trade mark of
Oxford University Press in the UK and in certain other countries.

Published in the United States of America by Oxford University Press
198 Madison Avenue, New York, NY 10016, United States of America.

British Library Cataloguing in Publication Data
Data available

Library of Congress Control Number: 2025934322

ISBN 9780198961093

DOI: 10.1093/9780198961109.001.0001

Printed and bound by
CPI Group (UK) Ltd., Croydon, CR0 4YY

MIX
Paper | Supporting
responsible forestry
FSC® C013604

The manufacturer's authorised representative in the EU for product safety is
Oxford University Press España S.A., Parque Empresarial San Fernando de Henares,
Avenida de Castilla, 2 – 28830 Madrid (www.oup.es/en or product.safety@oup.com).
OUP España S.A. also acts as importer into Spain of products made by the manufacturer.

This project has received funding from the European Research Council (ERC) under the European Union's
Horizon 2020 research and innovation program (grant agreement No 817652).

To Salwa, the love of my life, and Charlotte, the spark of endless joy

Preface

This book is the result of a collaborative research project. The project was part of the ERC Consolidator Grant "Correcting Inequality through Law" that has received funding from the European Research Council (ERC) under the European Union's Horizon 2020 research and innovation programme (grant agreement No 817652) and was based at the University of Münster. The project had three aims, which are all addressed in this book. First, it intended to give a sense of the diversity of equality case law in different jurisdictions by assessing the case law of different apex courts, that is, supreme courts, constitutional courts, and international human rights courts and tribunals. In total, we analyzed 18 different jurisdictions from all inhabited continents, including selected international and supranational courts and quasi-judicial institutions. Second, the project sought for an explanation of this diversity, considering that the underlying equality and non-discrimination norms are quite similar in their wording across different jurisdictions. Third, it aimed at making a normative assessment on whether certain models of equality and non-discrimination are superior to competing approaches.

A comparative project spanning 18 different jurisdictions demands an enormous effort. It does not only require significant resources to analyze the case law of these different jurisdictions but also different language skills and an understanding of the different legal cultures from which the analyzed jurisdictions stem. For this reason, I would not have been able to do the project on my own. Instead, the ERC grant allowed me to assemble a diverse group of junior researchers with different backgrounds, different language skills, and from different regions of the world. These researchers are Helina Stiphanos Teka, Jasmin Beck, Joanna Mrozinska, Shubhangi Roy, Tainá Garcia Maia, and Wei-Ju Huang, who each authored different chapters in this book that concerned the jurisdictions which they have analyzed.

Certainly, such an approach involves risks. Junior researchers lack the experience of more established academics. Furthermore, we did not have one team member per jurisdiction so that almost all of us had to work on jurisdictions with which they were initially unfamiliar. It is common for such large-scale comparative projects to ask established experts from each jurisdiction to write a chapter on "their" jurisdiction, yet we deliberately took a different approach. Having a research team allowed us closer cooperation and exchange on the overall project and it ensures that the final product is more coherent. Every member of the team bought into the same analytical framework that involved a tedious empirical analysis of apex court judgments according to a preconceived coding scheme, which would have been almost impossible to achieve with a group of assembled jurisdictional experts.

In order to mitigate the mentioned risks, we put in place several safeguards. First, I tried to ensure the diversity of the research team in the hiring process by hiring team members with a background in one or two of the analyzed jurisdictions. The team members came from Brazil, Ethiopia, India, Liechtenstein, Poland, and Taiwan. Some of them have completed internships or fellowships at relevant international human rights courts. Second, we invited international experts from the analyzed jurisdictions for a workshop in Münster where these experts commented on the drafts of each jurisdictional chapter. Third, some members of the team had research stays at target jurisdictions, and we had informal conversations with various experts from the different jurisdictions even outside the mentioned workshop. Furthermore, all chapters written by junior researchers went through at least three rounds of revisions, taking into account extensive comments from the invited experts and myself. Furthermore, I revised my own chapters based on comments from the jurisdictional experts as well as comments from the team or other colleagues with whom I discussed the project.

Therefore, we owe a great deal of thanks to many colleagues who read and commented on sample chapters, gave conceptual or contextual input, and generally contributed their ideas. These colleagues include Vicente Benitez-Rojas, Faisal Bhaba, Jacco Bomhoff, Gráinne de Búrca, Aparna Chandra, Konstantin Chatziathanasiou, Sujit Choudhry, Erin Delaney, James Fowkes, Carlos Gaio, Michaela Hailbronner, Samuel Issacharoff, Neha Jain, Abdi Jibril Ali, Tarunabh Khaitan, Malcolm Langford, Sonia Lawrence, Nora Markard, Marjorie Marona, Jud Mathews, Janet McLean, Sophia Moreau, Jaclyn Neo, Arie Rosen, Anna Śledzińska-Simon, Richard Stacey, Emanuel Towfigh, Joseph Weiler, Chin-Wen Wu, and Gentian Zyberi. I am deeply grateful to these colleagues and friends for having contributed their time and ideas to the project.

Finally, I equally owe thanks to the many research assistants who supported the project either through the coding of cases, by assisting in the organization of the workshop, or in various other ways. These include Paula Aguilar Sievers, Olivia Bernhörster, Ingo Borgdorf, Parya Darafshan, Paul Leonard Enderle, Johanna Fischer, Felix Fouchard, Eileen Friederichs, Julia Gosing, Eva Marie Janke, Helena Kaim, Dilan Kilic, Antonia Lawrenz, Luca Katharina Lichter, Annkathrin Lindert, Nele Meier, Joshua Okeke, Konrad Schilling, Theo Schütz, Paula Schrage, Sophie Schwab, as well as my excellent assistant Petra Fentner. I am extremely grateful for their assistance.

Contents

Contributors

Jasmin Beck is a PhD candidate at the University of Münster and research assistant at the Center for Interdisciplinary Labor Law Studies at Europa-Universität Viadrina Frankfurt (Oder). She was a trainee at the European Court of Human Rights from March to July 2019 and holds an MA in International Law and the Settlement of Disputes from the United Nations-mandated University for Peace, a BA in Law and Development Studies from SOAS University of London, and a BLaw from UniDistance Suisse.

Tainá Garcia Maia is a postdoctoral research fellow at the Center for Human Rights of the University Erlangen-Nuremberg. She holds a PhD from the University of Münster and the Federal University of Minas Gerais and an MPhil in the Theory and Practice of Human Rights from the University of Oslo. Her research focuses on human rights in international and comparative constitutional law, poverty and equality law, sociolegal studies, and law and politics, with an emphasis on Latin American institutions.

Wei-Ju Huang is a PhD Candidate at the University of Tübingen. She holds an LLM from National Taiwan University. Her research focuses on EU Law, Public Law, and the legal control of monetary policy. Her research was financially supported by the scholarship for studying abroad of the ministry of education (Taiwan), the scholarship for doctoral thesis of Chiang Ching-kuo foundation for international scholarly exchange (Taiwan), and the Taiwanese Overseas Pioneers Grants of the ministry of technology (Taiwan).

Joanna Mrozińska is a PhD candidate at the University of Münster. She holds a Master's degree from the University of Silesia in Katowice and an LLM in EU Law from the College of Europe. She is a member of the Polish Bar Association.

Niels Petersen is Professor of Public Law, International Law, and EU Law at the University of Münster. He holds a PhD from Goethe University in Frankfurt/Main and an MA in Quantitative Methods in the Social Sciences from Columbia University. His research focuses on international human rights and domestic fundamental rights, the sources of international law, the decision-making of courts, and the use of empirical methods in comparative constitutional law. He was the principal investigator of the ERC consolidator grant "Correcting Inequality through Law" and is author of the book *Proportionality and Judicial Activism* (CUP 2017).

Shubhangi Roy is a postdoctoral research fellow at the Institute for Law and Economics at the University of Hamburg. She holds a PhD from the University of Münster and an LLM from the University of Chicago. Her research focuses on the role of legal institutions in development and social change. She is author of the book *When Do People Obey Laws*, which was awarded a prize for the best PhD thesis in law from the University of Münster.

Helina Stiphanos Teka is a PhD candidate at the University of Münster. She holds an LLM in International Humanitarian Law from the University of Essex and an LLB from Addis Ababa University.

Abbreviations

art/arts	article/articles
ACHR	American Convention on Human Rights
AfrCtHPR	African Court of Human and Peoples' Rights
AJCL	American Journal of Comparative Law
ANC	African National Congress (South Africa)
APSR	American Political Science Review
CCP	Chinese Communist Party
CJEU	Court of Justice of the European Union
CEDAW	Convention on the Elimination of All Forms of Discrimination against Women
CERD	Convention on the Elimination of All Forms of Racial Discrimination
CESCR	Committee on Economic, Social and Cultural Rights
COBs	concluding observations (UNHRCttee)
CoE	Council of Europe
COIDA C	ompensation for Occupational Injuries and Diseases Act 1993 (South Africa)
CUP	Cambridge University Press
DDP	Democratic Progressive Party (Taiwan)
ECHR	European Convention on Human Rights
EuConst	European Constitutional Law Review
ECtHR	European Court of Human Rights
EEA	Employment Equity Act (South Africa)
EJIL	European Journal of International Law
ELJ	European Law Journal
EU	European Union
EUChFR EU	Charter of Fundamental Rights
GC	Grand Chamber
GFCC	German Federal Constitutional Court
HRCttee	UN Human Rights Committee
IACommHR	Inter-American Commission on Human Rights
IACtHR	Inter-American Court of Human Rights
ICCPR	International Covenant on Civil and Political Rights
ICESCR	International Covenant on Economic, Social and Cultural Rights
ICU	intensive care unit
ISA	Internal Security Act (Singapore)

IVF	*in vitro* fertilization
JL	Journal of Law
KMT	Kuomintang (China; Taiwan)
LR	Law Review
MCNS	Military Council of National Salvation (Poland)
NAACP	National Association for the Advancement of Colored People (United States)
NGO	nongovernmental organization
NLUD	National Law University Delhi
NZBORA	New Zealand Bill of Rights Act
OUP	Oxford University Press
PAP	People's Action Party (Singapore)
para	paragraph
PCT	Polish Constitutional Tribunal
s/ss	section/sections
SC	Supreme Court
SEBCs	socially and educationally backward classes
STF	Federal Supreme Court (Brazil)
TEU	Treaty on European Union
TFEU	Treaty on the Functioning of the European Union
UK	United Kingdom
UKHL	United Kingdom House of Lords
UKSC	United Kingdom Supreme Court
UN	United Nations
US	United States

1

Mapping Equality Case Law Around the World—Conceptual Preliminaries

Niels Petersen

In recent years, equality has become a central focus point in the public discussion. There is concern about rising inequality within societies.[1] This development has been identified as a major reason for the rise of populism that threatens the stability of liberal democracies across the world.[2] While social inequality is a significant concern, there are other kinds of inequality that figure prominently in the public debate. The Black Lives Matter movement in the United States has highlighted the continuing problem of racial inequality,[3] and the so-called gender pay gap is an example of the persistence of gender inequality.[4]

Solutions to these problems are usually sought in the political arena. However, equality is also a legal concept. Most fundamental rights catalogues in constitutions or international human rights treaties contain equality or non-discrimination guarantees. This book seeks to analyze how and to what extent courts, making use of constitutional or treaty-based equality guarantees, contribute to reducing inequality. For that purpose, we have analyzed the equality case law of apex courts of 18 different jurisdictions. These courts comprise national domestic constitutional and supreme courts from many different regions of the world as well as five international courts and quasi-judicial institutions.

Equality clauses in national constitutions and international human rights treaties come in roughly three forms.[5] First, some norms are framed as general equality clauses that do not focus on prohibited grounds of distinction, such as

[1] Seminally Thomas Piketty, *Le capital au XXIe siècle* (Editions du Seuil 2013).

[2] See eg Ganesh Sitaraman, *The Crisis of the Middle-Class Constitution: Why Economic Inequality Threatens Our Republic* (Alfred A. Knopf 2017).

[3] See eg Christopher J Lebron, *The Making of Black Lives Matter: A Brief History of an Idea* (OUP 2017).

[4] See eg Francine D Blau and Lawrence M Kahn, "Analyzing the Gender Pay Gap" (1999) 39 Quarterly Review of Economics and Finance 625; Sebawit G Bishu and Mohamad Alkadry, "A Systematic Review of the Gender Pay Gap and Factors That Predict It" (2017) 49 Administration & Society 65.

[5] Monika Florczak-Wator, "Equality Rights" in Wolfgang Babeck and Albrecht Weber (eds), *Writing Constitutions, Vol 2: Fundamental Rights* (Springer 2024) 247, 256; Brun-Otto Bryde and Michael Ashley Stein, "General Provisions Dealing with Equality" in Mark Tushnet, Thomas Fleiner, and Cheryl Saunders (eds), *Routledge Handbook of Constitutional Law* (Routledge 2012) 287, 288–89.

Niels Petersen, *Mapping Equality Case Law Around the World—Conceptual Preliminaries* In: *Equality's Guardians*. Edited by: Niels Petersen, Oxford University Press. © Niels Petersen 2025. DOI: 10.1093/9780198961109.003.0001

the equal protection clause of the Fourteenth Amendment of the US Constitution or Article 24 of the American Convention on Human Rights (ACHR). Secondly, there are non-discrimination clauses, specifying the prohibited grounds of distinction. Some of these contain an exhaustive list of prohibited grounds, such as section 19 of the New Zealand Bill of Rights Act in combination with section 21 of the New Zealand Human Rights Act, while others have an open-ended list, such as Article 14 of the European Convention on Human Rights (ECHR). Thirdly, there are several mixed models that combine general equality clauses with more specific non-discrimination clauses. Examples are section 15 of the Canadian Charter of Rights and Freedoms or Article 3 of the German Constitution.

While the wording of different equality norms is fairly similar, we hypothesize that the legal doctrines that have been developed by courts in order to operationalize equality vary quite significantly.[6] We examine the equality doctrines that have been developed by courts in order to observe the understanding of equality that is underlying these doctrines. The book predominantly has two aims. First, it provides a mapping of equality doctrines, showing the doctrines employed by courts, the kind of inequalities that are intended to be remedied by these doctrines, and the degree of deference that is afforded to the legislature. Second, it seeks an explanation for why these doctrines have emerged in the form that we currently observe: Why do some courts focus primarily on racial or sex inequality, while others also target social inequality or minor inequities of legislation?

These two research questions aim to contribute to the international discussion on equality and non-discrimination. However, they also hold lessons for the broader comparativist discourse. On the one hand, our hypothesis regarding the significant variance of legal equality doctrines would stand, if confirmed, in stark contrast to the influential "global model of constitutional rights" narrative in comparative constitutional law scholarship.[7] This global model, characterized by a two-step analysis of fundamental rights with the proportionality test at its core, is, arguably, not reflected in the equality doctrines, which are more diverse and based on different influences than the doctrines operationalizing civil rights and liberties.[8] On the other hand, the book also makes a contribution to the discussion on the "migration of constitutional ideas."[9] While it is largely accepted that the migration of constitutional concepts is not equivalent to a mere copying of doctrines but

[6] See Florczak-Wator (n 5) 248.

[7] The term stems from Kai Möller, *The Global Model of Constitutional Rights* (OUP 2012).

[8] On this discussion, see more specifically Niels Petersen, "Gibt es ein 'globales Modell' der Grundrechte?" in Carsten Bäcker, Martin Borowski, and Jan-Reinard Sieckmann (eds), *Grundlagen der demokratischen Verfassung: Festschrift für Robert Alexy zum 80. Geburtstag* (Mohr Siebeck, forthcoming 2025).

[9] Frederick Schauer, "On the Migration of Constitutional Ideas" (2005) 37 Connecticut LR 907; Sujit Choudhry, "Migration as a New Metaphor in Comparative Constitutional Law" in Sujit Choudhry (ed), *The Migration of Constitutional Ideas* (CUP 2006) 1.

that there are always local adaptations,[10] there are still gaps in understanding the mechanisms of this local adaptation. By exploring the reasons why courts adapt different doctrines for putting into operation largely shared constitutional language in the field of equality, the book explores factors that shape judicial choices about doctrine.

The starting point of our analysis is the observation that equality is a "fundamentally ambiguous" concept.[11] The uncertainty about the meaning of equality finds its expression in Peter Westen's critique of equality as an "empty idea"[12] (Section 1). If one agrees with the gist of Westen's critique, the doctrinal operationalization of the various equality norms contained in national constitutions and international human rights treaties becomes crucial for shaping the content of legal equality. I will present four models of equality that are used as blueprints for the analysis of the judicial case law (Section 2). These four models mainly differ according to the degree of deference that they grant to the legislature. The least deferential model has a substantive understanding of equality. Under this model, courts require the legislature to adopt positive measures in order to correct existing structural inequalities. A second model understands equality as a guarantee of reasonableness, where courts review the reasonableness of legislation and executive action. A third model, equality as non-discrimination, focuses on discrimination based on certain suspect criteria of distinction, while the final model grants significant deference to the political branches. The third part specifies the research questions, the methodology and the research hypotheses of this book (Section 3). Section 4 contains a detailed description of the research design. It explains the selection of jurisdictions, the analysis of the individual case law and the process for identifying reasons for why a specific doctrine was established before discussing some of the methodological challenges. Section 5 concludes by providing an overview of the structure of the book.

1. The problem: formal equality as an empty formula

In an influential article, Peter Westen argued that equality was an "empty idea."[13] According to the Aristotelian, formal notion of equality, like cases should be treated alike and unlike cases should be treated differently. While this operationalization of equality seems intuitively plausible *prima facie*, Westen pointed out that

[10] See eg Jacco Bomhoff, *Balancing Constitutional Rights: The Origins and Meanings of Postwar Legal Discourse* (CUP 2013).

[11] Wojciech Sadurski, *Equality and Legitimacy* (OUP 2008) 99.

[12] Peter Westen, "The Empty Idea of Equality" (1982) 95 Harvard LR 537.

[13] ibid. See also Dennis M Davis and Karl E Klare, "Transformative Constitutionalism and the Common and Customary Law" (2010) 26 South African Journal on Human Rights 403, 439–41, who argue—more generally—that legal concepts are never self-defining but need to be made real.

individuals and situations are never identical in all possible respects.[14] Instead, we have to identify criteria to determine whether two individuals or situations are sufficiently "alike" in order to deserve like treatment. This determination does not follow from the standard of equality itself. Instead, we have to refer to external standards of justice in order to establish whether two cases are comparable, that is, they are "alike."[15]

Let us consider a simple example to clarify the idea. If we want to design an egalitarian tax standard, we have at least three choices: Firstly, it is possible to impose the same absolute amount of taxes on every citizen; secondly, we can apply the same tax rate to all citizens so that the amount of due taxes varies with income but always constitutes the same share of the citizen's income; thirdly, one can differentiate the tax rates and apply higher rates to individuals with higher incomes. Arguably, all three standards are consistent with the idea of formal equality. In order to choose between these three standards, we have to resort to an external standard of justice. In particular, we have to decide whether the ability to pay should be a relevant consideration or whether it all comes down to the ability to benefit from specific services provided by the state as a result of taxation.

Westen's observation has led to a discussion on the essence of equality norms. Some scholars argue that equality does not have an independent moral value.[16] Westen, for example, believes that the protection of individual liberties is sufficient to safeguard equality.[17] Nevertheless, most legal scholars reject the conclusion that equality is tautological. While formal equality may often be dependent on external standards of justice, it arguably has independent normative force in some situations as there are measures that clearly violate formal equality regardless of any external normative standards.[18] Furthermore, Westen's argument reduces the concept of equality to formal equality while not taking into account substantive conceptions.

Yet the precise meaning of equality is contested and there is intense discussion regarding making the concept concrete. Many authors tie equality—sometimes explicitly, sometimes implicitly—to conceptions of dignity.[19] Jeremy Waldron

[14] Westen (n 12) 544.

[15] ibid 557.

[16] ibid; Joseph Raz, *The Morality of Freedom* (Clarendon Press 1988) 217–44; Christopher J Peters, "Equality Revisited" (1997) 110 Harvard LR 1210; Uwe Steinhoff, "Against Equal Respect and Concern, Equal Rights, and Egalitarian Impartiality" in Uwe Steinhoff (ed), *Do All Persons Have Equal Moral Worth?—On Basic Equality and Equal Respect and Concern* (OUP 2014) 142.

[17] Westen (n 12).

[18] Kent Greenawalt, "How Empty Is the Idea of Equality?" (1983) 83 Columbia LR 1167; Kent Greenawalt, "'Prescriptive Equality': Two Steps Forward" (1997) 110 Harvard LR 1265.

[19] In a similar vein, some scholars deny that there is a close connection between the concepts of equality and non-discrimination, see Elisa Holmes, "Anti-Discrimination Rights Without Equality" (2005) 68 Modern LR 175. Others argue that non-discrimination norms rather served the preservation of individual autonomy, see Sophia Moreau, "What is Discrimination?" (2010) 38 Philosophy & Public Affairs 143; Sophia Moreau, "In Defense of a Liberty-based Account of Discrimination" in Deborah Hellman and Sophia Moreau (eds), *Philosophical Foundations of Discrimination Law* (OUP 2013) 71.

argues that equality is about granting each individual his or her equal self-worth.[20] Similarly, Deborah Hellman sees non-discrimination norms as norms protecting against demeaning actions.[21] Iyiola Solanke frames anti-discrimination law as a protection against stigma,[22] while Benjamin Eidelson argues that discrimination is wrong if it expresses disrespect for the personhood of those that are disfavored.[23]

Sophia Moreau developed a pluralist theory of discrimination in her recent book.[24] She argues that the wrong of discrimination can express itself in three different ways—if people are unfairly subordinated, if their deliberative freedom is infringed, or if they are denied access to a basic good. Sandra Fredman puts a strong focus on substantive equality in her book on discrimination law.[25] She develops a four-dimensional model of substantive equality, according to which equality should redress existing disadvantage, promote dignity and worth, enable political and social inclusion, and recognize difference.[26] Finally, there are several scholars who have argued that non-discriminations norms serve the protection of groups that are systematically or structurally disadvantaged.[27] Such structural disadvantage may be caused by biases, discriminatory preferences, or inaccurate negative stereotypes.[28]

In continental Europe, there are many theoretical accounts of equality that try to defend the formal approach to equality and are opposed to substantive notions. For example, French legal scholars often adhere to the notions of republicanism and universalism and argue that these advocate for a formal understanding of equality.[29] Similarly, many German legal scholars equally promote formal notions of equality.[30] Such approaches are often reluctant to accept positive measures, such as quotas for minorities or disadvantaged groups.[31]

[20] Jeremy Waldron, *One Another's Equals: The Basis of Human Equality* (Harvard University Press 2017) 66–83.

[21] Deborah Hellman, *When Is Discrimination Wrong?* (Harvard University Press 2008); Deborah Hellman, "Equality and Unconstitutional Discrimination" in Hellman and Moreau (eds) (n 19) 51.

[22] Iyiola Solanke, *Discrimination as Stigma: A Theory of Anti-discrimination Law* (Hart 2017).

[23] Benjamin Eidelson, *Discrimination and Disrespect* (OUP 2015).

[24] Sophia Moreau, *Faces of Inequality: A Theory of Wrongful Discrimination* (OUP 2020).

[25] Sandra Fredman, *Discrimination Law* (3rd edn, OUP 2022).

[26] ibid 29–45. See also Sandra Fredman, "Substantive Equality Revisited" (2016) 14 I.CON 712.

[27] Owen M Fiss, "Groups and the Equal Protection Clause" (1976) 5 Philosophy & Public Affairs 107; Cass R Sunstein, "The Anticaste Principle" (1994) 92 Michigan LR 2410; Catherine Barnard and Bob Hepple, "Substantive Equality" (2000) 59 Cambridge LJ 562; Hugh Collins, "Discrimination, Equality and Social Inclusion" (2003) 66 Modern LR 16; Tarunabh Khaitan, *A Theory of Discrimination Law* (OUP 2015).

[28] Larry Alexander, "What Makes Wrongful Discrimination Wrong?—Biases, Preferences, Stereotypes, and Proxies" (1992) 141 University of Pennsylvania LR 149; Sujit Choudhry, "Distribution vs. Recognition: The Case of Anti-Discrimination Laws" (2000) 9 George Mason LR 145.

[29] See the critical accounts of this prominent strand of thinking in France in Jeremie Gilbert and David Keane, "Equality vs. Fraternity? Rethinking France and Its Minorities" (2016) 14 I.CON 883; Stéphanie Hennette-Vauchez and Elsa Fondimare, "Incompatibility between the 'French Republican Model' and Anti-Discrimination Law? Deconstructing a Familiar Trope of Narratives of French Law" in Barbara Havelková and Mathias Möschel (eds), *Anti-Discrimination Law in Civil Law Jurisdictions* (OUP 2019) 56.

[30] See Stefan Huster, *Rechte und Ziele—Zur Dogmatik des allgemeinen Gleichheitssatzes* (Duncker & Humblot 1993); Simon Kempny and Philipp Reimer, *Die Gleichheitssätze* (Mohr Siebeck 2012).

[31] See eg Huster (n 30) 323–39.

This discussion on the meaning of equality is predominantly theoretical. When it makes use of judicial decisions, the cited cases are often used as a source of inspiration or anecdotal support for the advanced concept. If we find a systematic analysis of the case law, this is usually restricted to specific jurisdictions. Furthermore, the focus of the international discussion is predominantly the case law of the US Supreme Court and of other common law jurisdictions.[32] Our book takes the reverse approach. It starts with empirical observations and broadens the perspective beyond the United States and common law jurisdictions. It analyzes how different courts deal with the challenge of making the notion of equality concrete and what doctrines these courts have developed to operationalize equality norms. In the following, I would like to start by sketching four different models of equality that should serve as basis and reference point for the analysis of the judicial case law.

2. Four models of equality

When courts operationalize equality, they must also address, at least implicitly, the relationship between the judiciary on the one hand and the legislature and the executive on the other. If the meaning of equality is contested, its realization is also a political matter. One may therefore wonder to which extent questions of redistribution, the determining of likeness, or the establishment of positive measures to support vulnerable groups that have suffered disadvantages in the past should be left to the political branches. Courts, therefore, have to determine how much deference they afford to legislature and executive.

We hypothesize that courts find different answers to the question of deference. Furthermore, we assume that the level of deference that courts apply is expressed in different conceptions of equality.[33] As a frame of analysis, we have established four basic models of equality. These models have a descriptive purpose and do not imply a normative assessment of these approaches. Certainly, the four basic models that are presented in this section are only rough models that do not account for smaller variations. Furthermore, the borders between the different models are not always clear-cut. Nevertheless, the models allow us to classify jurisdictions by focusing on certain important characteristics.

[32] There are certainly exceptions, see eg Barbara Havelková and Mathias Möschel, "Introduction: Anti-Discrimination Law's Fit into Civil Law Jurisdictions and the Factors Influencing It" in Barbara Havelková and Mathias Möschel (eds), *Anti-Discrimination Law in Civil Law Jurisdictions* (OUP 2019) 1 (who predominantly focus on the implementation of EU anti-discrimination legislation in civil law jurisdictions).

[33] For a framework of conceptualizing deference, see Cora Chan, *Deference in Constitutional Adjudication* (OUP 2024), who identifies six devices for exercising deference: burden of proof, standard of proof, standard of review, giving of weight to views, choice of interpretation, and choice of remedy. In this framework, our differentiation would predominantly concern the standard of review that is applied, but we are not measuring the doctrinal "input" but rather the "output" of the case law.

The first model understands equality as reasonableness and grants a rather low level of deference. According to this model, courts interpret equality as formal equality and thus implicitly or explicitly refer to external standards of justice when interpreting constitutional equality clauses even if these standards are not contained in the constitution. As a consequence, legislative choices with equality implications are fully reviewable by courts, and any differentiation needs to be justified.

The second model is the equality as non-discrimination approach. This approach is more deferential than the equality as reasonableness approach because it does not target all inequalities but only differentiations based on specific suspect criteria. Therefore, the different treatment of various individuals or social groups is predominantly the choice of the legislature and not of courts. However, legislative discretion finds its limits when the regulation disadvantages vulnerable groups defined by "suspect" criteria.

The third model understands equality as substantive equality. In contrast to the second model, it not only corrects active discrimination of vulnerable groups but requires the legislature to enact positive measures to address structural inequalities that disadvantage vulnerable groups. This model is less deferential than the equality as non-discrimination approach. In comparison to the equality as reasonableness approach, it depends on how the model is put into practice. Finally, the fourth model is a deferential approach, according to which the legislature has the prerogative to determine the meaning of equality. Consequently, legislative choices are invalidated only in exceptional cases on equality grounds.

2.1 The equality as reasonableness approach

The first approach is the equality as reasonableness approach. The starting point is a formal conception of equality, according to which like cases should be treated alike. Consequently, any differentiation of like cases, regardless of whether it is based on a suspect classification or not, would be a *prima facie* equality concern. This would include for example distinctions between employees and public servants or between pharmacies and other shops within train stations. Certainly, not all differentiations concerning like cases are automatically a violation of equality. Rather, the equality as reasonableness approach usually consists of two steps. In the first step, the court analyzes whether there was a differential treatment. In a second step, the court then examines whether the differential treatment was justified.

Normatively, this approach poses two challenges. First, courts have to decide when cases are alike or not alike. Equality does not contain any standards in order to decide what factors to take into account when determining "likeness."[34] Courts

[34] Westen (n 12) 544.

can take a rather generous approach, but that only pushes the problem to the justification analysis. This leads us to the second challenge, the standard for the justification analysis. Such a standard cannot be derived from the equality norm itself. Therefore, courts have to find an external normative standard to determine whether an unequal treatment can be justified. One doctrinal tool to which courts can resort in the justification analysis is the proportionality test. But proportionality usually requires a balancing of competing values in the last step,[35] and it is not entirely clear how they should resolve the conflict between equality and competing public aims that are the basis for the unequal treatment.

2.2 The equality as non-discrimination approach

The equality as non-discrimination approach tries to remedy the deficiencies of the equality as reasonableness approach by focusing on suspect classifications. According to this approach, not every unequal treatment is *per se* problematic. Instead, unequal treatments only require a stringent justification if they are based on a suspect classification. This resolves the likeness challenge posed by Peter Westen. The focus of the analysis is not on whether there are two individuals who are sufficiently alike so that they must be treated equally but rather on whether a distinction was based on a "problematic" differentiation, such as race, sex, or religion. If a distinction is based on race, such a distinction is problematic regardless of whether the concerned individuals are otherwise alike or not. Certainly, not all distinctions based on a suspect classification are automatically a violation of equality. Courts also need to perform a justification analysis. However, there is a presumption of illegality, which reduces the problem of finding a normative standard of justification that loomed so prominently in the equality as reasonableness approach. However, while the equality as non-discrimination approach resolves some of the challenges that plague the equality as reasonableness approach, it also leads to a number of new challenges. In the following, I would like to discuss four of these: the identification of suspect criteria, the treatment of indirect discriminations, the normative evaluation of positive measures and affirmative action, and, finally, the potential under-inclusiveness of the equality as non-discrimination approach.[36]

[35] On balancing, see eg the diverse accounts and critiques of Bernhard Schlink, *Abwägung im Verfassungsrecht* (Duncker & Humblot 1976); T Alexander Aleinikoff, "Constitutional Law in the Age of Balancing" (1987) 96 Yale LJ 943; Aharon Barak, *Proportionality—Constitutional Rights and their Limitations* (CUP 2012); Niels Petersen, *Proportionality and Judicial Activism* (CUP 2017); Jamal Greene, "Rights as Trumps" (2018) 132 Harvard LR 28; Alec Stone Sweet and Jud Mathews, *Proportionality Balancing and Constitutional Governance* (OUP 2019); Mordechai Kremnitzer, Talya Steiner, and Andrej Lang (eds), *Proportionality in Action* (CUP 2020).

[36] For a further challenge, see Aileen McColgan, *Discrimination, Equality and the Law* (Hart 2016) 52–54 (arguing that the grounds-based non-discrimination approach essentializes group characteristics, ignoring that they result from social constructions).

2.2.1 Identifying suspect criteria

The first challenge is to determine what actually constitutes a "suspect" criterion. Several national constitutions and international human rights treaties contain non-discrimination clauses that explicitly list criteria of distinction that are considered to be suspect. However, most of these non-discrimination clauses have open-ended lists, to which courts have added other criteria that are not explicitly mentioned. For example, sexual orientation is today widely considered to be a suspect criterion, even though it is not contained in the non-discrimination clauses of most of the older human rights catalogues.[37] Furthermore, the Fourteenth Amendment of the US Constitution does not explicitly mention any suspect criteria. Nevertheless, the US Supreme Court has identified certain criteria of distinction that merit more rigid scrutiny.[38]

This has led to an intense discussion on what constitutes a suspect criterion.[39] The most elaborate attempt can be found in Tarunabh Khaitan's seminal monograph on the *Theory of Discrimination Law*.[40] According to Khaitan, a criterion can be considered as suspect under two conditions: First, it has to make a distinction between different groups between which we can observe a significant advantage gap; second, the classifying characteristic is either immutable or reflects a fundamental choice.[41] The first condition relates to the vulnerability of a specific group.[42] Non-discrimination norms are not meant to remedy all inequalities. Instead, they are an expression of legal and judicial deference by focusing only on the most egregious inequalities that usually have structural reasons. A group is vulnerable if it has been subject to discrimination in the past and if this past discrimination arguably leads to a lower social status in the present.[43] This vulnerability is usually the result of a lack of political power of this particular group.[44] Because race

[37] See eg *Salgueiro da Silva Mouta v Portugal* ECHR 1999-IX 309, para 28; *L. and v. v Austria* ECHR 2003-I 29, para 45; *Vallianatos v Greece* ECHR 2013-VI 125, para 77 and *Atala Riffo v Chile* (IACtHR, February 24, 2012), paras 83–93.

[38] On the details, see Chapter 2.2.1.

[39] See eg John Hart Ely, *Democracy and Distrust. A Theory of Judicial Review* (Harvard University Press 1980) 135–79; Jack M Balkin, "The Constitution of Status" (1997) 106 Yale LJ 2313; Sunstein (n 27); Khaitan, *A Theory of Discrimination Law* (n 27) 49–62.

[40] Khaitan, *A Theory of Discrimination Law* (n 27) 49–62.

[41] ibid 50.

[42] Vulnerability is traditionally conceived as a group concept, see, seminally, Fiss (n 27). For the purposes of our analysis, we will adhere to the traditional understanding as it is also underlying much of the analyzed case law. Yet, it should be pointed out that there are also alternative understandings of vulnerability, see eg Martha Albertson Fineman, "The Vulnerable Subject: Anchoring Equality in the Human Condition" (2008) 20 Yale Journal of Law and Feminism 1; Martha Albertson Fineman, "The Vulnerable Subject and the Responsive State" (2010) 60 Emory LJ 251; Lourdes Peroni and Alexandra Timmer, "Vulnerable Groups: The Promise of an Emerging Concept in European Human Rights Convention Law" (2013) 11 I.CON 1056.

[43] See Fiss (n 27) 144–45; Hellman, *When Is Discrimination Wrong?* (n 21) 14–15; Sunstein (n 27) 2433.

[44] See Sadurski, *Equality and Legitimacy* (n 11) 142–43; Wojciech Sadurski, *Constitutional Public Reason* (OUP 2022) 251–52, who argues that a differentiation should be considered suspect if it targets a "politically powerless group" and contributes to an "existing pattern of social disadvantage." See also Victoria Miyandazi, *Equality in Kenya's 2010 Constitution: Understanding the Competing and*

has been an obvious cause for suppression in the past and present, it is undisputed as a suspect criterion. By contrast, eye color is not a suspect criterion because there is no disadvantage gap between blue- and green-eyed individuals except to the extent that eye color correlates with race.

The second condition serves the purpose of restricting the protection of the non-discrimination guarantee to structural minorities—in contrast to those who end up in the minority because of decisions made.[45] Decisions taken democratically always result in some winners and some losers. However, not all those who lose out as a result of decisions made democratically should be protected by equality guarantees, even if they end up losing continuously. Certain political ideologies may have a hard time finding majority support and therefore suffer from an "advantage gap." Yet this does not make them worthy of protection from discrimination. A group of Marxists wanting to erect a society according to Marxist principles does not deserve legal support after the conception of society is rejected by the democratic process. Instead, physical immutability focuses on individual characteristics, like skin color or origin that the concerned individual cannot change so that she cannot simply move to the majority camp even if she wanted to.[46] However, physical immutability as such is too narrow a criterion.[47] There are some characteristics that are a fundamental part of one's identity but could be changed in theory.[48] One can change one's own religion or even sex, yet religion is a part of your identity that is usually protected by a fundamental right, the freedom of religion, so that an involuntary change is normatively undesirable. Similarly, your sex is also an essential part of your identity and the costs of changing it are significant.

Certainly, these two conditions do not allow for a clear-cut distinction between suspect and non-suspect criteria. The vulnerability of a group is only a matter of degree. Furthermore, one can debate in some cases whether a classifying characteristic reflects a fundamental choice. Therefore, one may reasonably disagree on whether individual criteria should be considered as suspect or not.

2.2.2 Dealing with indirect discriminations

A second challenge is the treatment of indirect discriminations. The distinction between direct and indirect discrimination is not always clear-cut.[49] One can either

Interrelated Conceptions (Hart 2021) 66 (arguing that vulnerable groups deserve "special protection because of its group members' lack of access to the political process").

[45] On this distinction, see Jeremy Waldron, "The Core of the Case Against Judicial Review" (2006) 115 Yale LJ 136, 1397–98, who uses the term "topical" instead of structural minority.

[46] See Balkin (n 39) 2366.

[47] Catherine Albertyn and Janet Kentridge, "Introducing the Right to Equality in the Interim Constitution" (1994) 10 South African Journal on Human Rights 149, 168; Miyandazi (n 44) 61–63.

[48] Khaitan, *A Theory of Discrimination Law* (n 27) 58–59.

[49] Tarunabh Khaitan, "Indirect Discrimination" in Kasper Lippert-Rasmussen (ed), *The Routledge Handbook of the Ethics of Discrimination* (Routledge 2017) 30, 34; Andy Yu, "Direct Discrimination and Indirect Discrimination: A Distinction with a Difference" (2019) 9 Western Journal of Legal

focus on discriminatory intent or distinguish based on whether the distinction in question is, on its face, based on a suspect ground.[50] For our purposes, we define indirect discrimination as differentiations which are not explicitly based on a suspect criterion; that is, on their face they are neutral but may have a disparate impact on a vulnerable group.[51] For example, a rule granting more favorable pension terms to full-time employees than to part-time employees appears to be neutral on its face.[52] However, it becomes problematic when the majority of full-time employees are men, while the majority of part-time employees are women because it *de facto* disadvantages the latter, a group which already faces many disadvantages in the work context.

It is undisputed that the reach of non-discrimination guarantees has to extend beyond direct discriminations.[53] Otherwise, it would be possible to circumvent prohibitions of discrimination by designing schemes that differentiate based on apparently neutral criteria that are highly correlated with a suspect criterion.[54] If a racial minority receives a worse education because of structural discrimination than those of another race that forms the majority, distinctions based on educational achievement may effectively exclude many members of the racial minority without mentioning race explicitly.

It is disputed, however, to what extent a rule that has a negative impact on a vulnerable group can be considered an indirect discrimination. Is a rule that, in principle, pursues a legitimate aim discriminatory if it disproportionately benefits members of a non-vulnerable social group? For example, is a rule that gives subsidies to technology startups discriminatory if it mostly benefits men because the latter are overrepresented in this field, compared to the startup scene in general? How should we treat a rule that gives preference to veterans for public service positions if the vast majority of veterans are men?[55]

There are two main approaches to this problem. On the one hand, courts can focus on discriminatory intent.[56] This has the advantage of providing apparently clear limits. Not every rule that has a remote disparate impact on a vulnerable

Studies 1, 3; Neha Jain, "Manufacturing Statelessness" (2022) 116 American Journal of International Law 237, 278.

[50] Yu (n 49) 3.

[51] For the problem on how to determine the existence of a disparate impact, see Khaitan, "Indirect Discrimination" (n 49) 32–34.

[52] See Case 170/84 *Bilka-Kaufhaus* [1986] ECR 1607.

[53] See Hugh Collins and Tarunabh Khaitan, "Indirect Discrimination Law: Controversies and Critical Questions" in Hugh Collins and Tarunabh Khaitan (eds), *Foundations of Indirect Discrimination Law* (Hart 2018) 1, 4; Anna Katharina Mangold, *Demokratische Inklusion durch Recht* (Mohr Siebeck 2021) 242–46.

[54] See Reva Siegel, "Why Equal Protection No Longer Protects: The Evolving Forms of Status-Enforcing State Action" (1997) 49 Stanford LR 1111 (for an elegant elaboration of this point).

[55] See *Personnel Administrator of Massachusetts v Feeney* 442 US 256 (1979).

[56] This is the approach of the US Supreme Court, see *Wash v Davis* 426 US 229 (1976); *McCleskey v Kemp* 481 US 279 (1987).

group is automatically an indirect discrimination. However, intent is often difficult to prove, in particular when it comes to decisions of collective bodies, such as the legislature.[57] Furthermore, this approach implies a normative choice that unintentional indirect discriminations are normatively irrelevant—even if they might be caused by implicit biases or stereotypes—and thus enables the legislature to entrench already existing structural discrimination of minorities.[58] On the other hand, courts can focus on mere disparate impact.[59] However, in this case, they have to determine where to draw the line. Does any—even random or accidental—negative effect on a vulnerable group constitute an indirect discrimination? In judicial practice, the question is usually discussed in the justification analysis. However, relegating the question to what extent indirect discrimination should be permissible to the justification analysis does not give an answer: It does not give us a standard on how to balance principally legitimate policy reasons against the disparate impact on a vulnerable group. Instead, the answer may instead depend on the normative reason for which we consider nonintentional indirect discriminations to be problematic.[60]

2.2.3 Positive measures and affirmative action

Another challenge of the equality as non-discrimination approach is the treatment of positive measures that are supposed to benefit a vulnerable group at the expense of the majority group in society. Prominent examples are affirmative action quotas for African Americans for university admission in the United States or quotas for female members of corporate boards or female job applicants. Under the equality as non-discrimination approach, one may wonder whether such measures constitute discrimination at all. There is a controversial discussion on whether non-discrimination guarantees should be applied symmetrically.[61]

[57] Ely (n 39) 138. On different ways to prove discriminatory intent, see Aziz Z Huq, "What is Discriminatory Intent?" (2018) 103 Cornell LR 1211, 1265–84.

[58] But see John Gardner, "Discrimination: The Good, the Bad, and the Wrongful" (2018) 118 Proceedings of the Aristotelian Society 55, 60–61, who proposes a middle ground according to which an action is discriminatory if it was taken *because of* the suspect criterion without requiring intentionality. This would also cover implicit biases and stereotypes.

[59] See Collins and Khaitan (n 53) 11.

[60] ibid 17; Gerald L Neuman, "Questions of Indirect Discrimination on the Basis of Religion" (2021) 34 Harvard Human Rights Journal 177. On the potential reasons for why indirect discrimination should be considered problematic, see the excellent account of Mangold (n 53) 242–46.

[61] See Fiss (n 27); Neil Gotanda, "A Critique of 'Our Constitution is Color-Blind'" (1991) 44 Stanford LR 1; Kenji Yoshino, "Assimilationist Bias in Equal Protection: The Visibility Presumption and the Case of 'Don't Ask, Don't Tell'" (1998) 108 Yale LJ 485; Sadurski, *Equality and Legitimacy* (n 11) 111–24; Khaitan, *A Theory of Discrimination Law* (n 27) 61–62; McColgan (n 36) 70–100. See also Jack M Balkin and Reva Siegel, "The American Civil Rights Tradition: Anticlassification or Antisubordination" (2003) 2 Issues in Legal Scholarship 1, who distinguish between an "antisubordination" and an "anticlassification" principle. This distinction has important implications for the question of symmetric application even if it is not limited to this question but also has consequences for the treatment of indirect discriminations.

Let us consider an example to grasp the intuition behind this discussion: Sex is a suspect criterion because women have been and often still comprise a group that suffers from a significant disadvantage gap. However, does this mean that men should not be protected by constitutional non-discrimination guarantees? This discussion is complicated by the fact that some rules may nominally disadvantage men, but are the result of traditional gender stereotypes. For example, pension benefits that are only paid to widows but not to widowers after the death of a public servant nominally disadvantage men, but are based on the stereotype of men as (exclusive) breadwinners of the family.

If the aim of non-discrimination clauses is the protection of vulnerable groups, one can argue that these clauses should be interpreted asymmetrically.[62] Not all distinctions based on sex or race would constitute discriminations, but only those that disadvantage groups that were already previously disadvantaged. Consequently, positive measures benefiting racial minorities or women would not constitute discrimination in the first place. Opponents of such an asymmetric interpretation of non-discrimination clauses argue that distinctions based on race or other suspect criteria are problematic *per se*.[63] Race or sex should simply not be a consideration on which public authorities base their decisions. Furthermore, it would make group identities more salient and thus be an obstacle to the formation of a common societal identity.[64] However, even if one interprets non-discrimination clauses symmetrically, this does not mean that positive measures constitute an automatic violation of equality. Instead, such measures may be justified. The problem is, again, one of finding the right standard to determine when positive measures should be justified.

2.2.4 Under-inclusiveness

Finally, the equality as non-discrimination approach is sometimes criticized for its under-inclusiveness.[65] Unequal treatment may be normatively problematic even beyond differentiations based on suspect criteria. This concerns, for example, regulatory distinctions which are either irrational or due to capture of the legislature. However, it is difficult to extend the equality as non-discrimination approach beyond distinctions based on suspect criteria without—at the same time—inviting all the problems of the equality as reasonableness approach. A more limited extension would focus on arbitrary state action: If differentiations are not directly or indirectly based on a suspect criterion, they only violate the equality guarantee

[62] See Fiss (n 27); Yoshino (n 61); Khaitan, *A Theory of Discrimination Law* (n 27) 61–62.

[63] See *Regents of the Univ of Cal v Bakke* 438 US 265, 360–61 (1978). For a critique of the *per se* approach, see Sadurski, *Equality and Legitimacy* (n 11) 111–24.

[64] See Hennette-Vauchez and Fondimare (n 29) 58–62 (describing the resistance to substantive equality in the French legal and political discourse).

[65] See Erwin Chemerinsky, "The Rational Basis Test is Constitutional (and Desirable)" (2016) 14 Georgetown Journal of Law & Public Policy 401; Greene (n 35) 43–47.

if they are arbitrary. Yet arbitrariness is an elusive concept. It alludes to situations where the unreasonableness of a decision is obvious, plain for everyone to see. However, where to draw the line between obviously arbitrary state action and state action that is merely arguably unreasonable is often in the eye of the beholder.[66]

2.3 The positive equality approach

The positive equality approach resembles the equality as non-discrimination approach in its focus on vulnerable groups. However, it does not only target active discrimination but also requires positive measures to address structural inequalities. While the admissibility of positive measures is also a focal point of the discussion regarding equality as non-discrimination, the latter debate is concerned with whether and to what extent the legislature is allowed to enact positive measures to support vulnerable groups. By contrast, the positive equality approach goes one step further and examines to what extent the legislature and the executive are legally *required* to enact a positive measure to protect vulnerable groups. Such measures can reach from requiring the state to protect women against gender-based violence[67] over ensuring the workplace safety of vulnerable members of society[68] to requiring the legislature to expand social programs.

While the requirement and the extension of positive measures figure prominently in the positive equality approach, the court's approach to invalidating existing measures is less clear. Because of the focus on vulnerable groups, it has certainly resemblances to the equality as non-discrimination approach. Therefore, one could expect that a court following this model would predominantly focus on invalidating differentiations based on suspect classifications. This would make the model both more and less deferential than the equality as reasonableness approach. It would be more deferential because it generally does not invalidate measures not involving a suspect classification. At the same time, it would also be less deferential because it asks the state to adopt positive measures, while the equality as reasonableness approach usually concentrates on invalidating existing measures. However, one can also imagine an even less deferential version of the positive equality model if the court combines the features of the model with the equality as reasonableness approach when it comes to reviewing existing state measures. This would certainly be the least deferential of our four models.

66 Calvin Massey, "The New Formalism: Requiem for Tiered Scrutiny" (2004) 6 University of Pennsylvania Journal of Constitutional Law 945, 954.

67 See *Maria da Penha Maia Fernandes* v *Brazil* Report No 54/01 Case 12.051 (IACommHR, April 16, 2001).

68 See *Workers of the Fireworks Factory in Santo Antônio de Jesus and their Families v Brazil* (Preliminary objections, merits, reparations, and costs) (IACtHR, July 15, 2020).

Regardless of how the positive equality approach is conceptualized in detail, it also has certain drawbacks. To its credit, it is the closest judicial implementation of the idea of substantive equality by acknowledging that substantive equality does not only require an abstention from unequal treatment but also a positive promotion of disadvantaged groups. Judicial intervention to achieve substantive equality may be most necessary if the legislature continuously fails to tackle the issue of structural discrimination in society. Consequently, certain positive obligations will be rather uncontroversial: Few people will object when courts require states to enact positive measures to protect women against gender-based violence.

However, as a broader approach, the derivation of positive obligations from fundamental rights runs into the danger of courts substituting for the legislature.[69] In the context of EU integration, scholars have made a fundamental distinction between regulative and redistributive measures.[70] It is argued that the legitimacy of regulative decisions can be strengthened if they are taken by independent experts, such as independent regulatory agencies or courts.[71] By contrast, redistributive decisions are inherently political that should be decided by the political process.[72] Positive measures derived from equality predominantly fall into the latter camp. They are redistributive because they give benefits to certain social groups to the detriment of other groups in society. Furthermore, there may be various strategies to combat structural discrimination, which each involve their own trade-offs. For example, one can debate whether racial or gender quotas are a recommendable mechanism to correct past wrongs and to fight extant structural discrimination. They have the disadvantage of making the suspect criterion salient as a selection criterion and may thus entrench their importance even more. Additionally, positive measures are naturally exclusive. They support certain vulnerable groups and minorities, for example African Americans, while excluding others, for example Asian Americans or Latinos, that are also less privileged than the majority society. Therefore, one may wonder whether courts are the adequate institutions to impose such positive measure or whether their discussion and enactment should not better be left to the legislature.[73]

[69] See eg Ernst-Wolfgang Böckenförde, "Grundrechtstheorie und Grundrechtsinterpretation" (1974) 27 Neue Juristische Wochenschrift 1529.

[70] See Michael Zürn, *Regieren jenseits des Nationalstaats: Globalisierung und Denationalisierung als Chance* (Suhrkamp 1998) 224–25.

[71] Giandomenico Majone, "Independence vs. Accountability? Non-Majoritarian Institutions and Democratic Government in Europe" in Joachim Jens Hesse and Theo AJ Toonen (eds), *The European Yearbook of Comparative Government and Public Administration* (Nomos 1994) 117, 118–19.

[72] Zürn (n 70) 225.

[73] But one can think of justifying court intervention to impose positive measures in the political process as corrections of political market failures. On this concept, see Ely (n 39) 105–79; Petersen (n 35) 13–37.

2.4 The deferential approach

The fourth and final approach is a deferential approach that rarely challenges executive or legislative action on equality grounds. The rationale behind this approach is that—considering the difficulties to determine what equality actually is—it should be up to the legislature to give meaning to the concept of equality. This approach avoids the conceptual problems that both the equality as reasonableness and the equality as non-discrimination approaches encountered. Instead, there is a strong presumption that state action is in accordance with equality so that courts do not have to determine when two situations are sufficiently alike to be considered a problem under the constitutional equality guarantee. The courts are also mostly relieved from defining suspect classifications or asking how to deal with indirect discriminations.

However, this approach has significant drawbacks. It basically makes judicial review of measures of the legislature or the executive ineffective. Instead, it trusts the political branches to make an unbiased determination of the meaning of equality. But even in liberal and democratic societies that is not always a safe assumption. Political decisions may be influenced by implicit stereotypes or biases or even perpetuate existing structural discrimination, in particular, if vulnerable minorities are underrepresented in the political decision-making process. In these situations, courts play an important role in correcting malfunctions of the political process.[74] However, an overly deferential approach denies them the ability to assume such a role as equality's guardians.

2.5 Summary

This section has described four models of equality—a formal equality as reasonableness approach, an equality as non-discrimination approach, a positive equality approach requiring the state to adopt positive measures to address structural inequality, and a deferential approach that leaves the determination of the meaning of equality to the political branches. None of the four approaches is without challenges: The interpretation of equality as reasonableness struggles to determine likeness and to establish normative standards for the justification analysis; the equality as non-discrimination approach has to define the concept of suspect criterion of distinction and find a strategy to deal with indirect discriminations; the positive equality approach affords very little deference to the legislature and might assume a role for courts that is better left to politics; and the deferential approach gives up the role of the court as an effective guardian of the political process. This

[74] See n 73.

section was not meant to provide answers on these conundrums. Instead, it intended to highlight the normative frictions: It is precisely because none of the four approaches is without weaknesses that it will be interesting to observe how courts deal with these challenges in operationalizing equality, what approach they choose, and to examine why they choose this approach.

When classifying the case law according to the proposed models we have to be aware that the distinction between the different models is often fleeting. For example, the equality as reasonableness approach can encompass elements of the equality as non-discrimination approach. A court that reviews the rationality of the legislature and the executive will usually also correct measures making distinctions based on suspect criteria to the extent that the latter distinctions lack a rational justification. Similarly, even if a court often requires the legislature to enact positive measures, the majority of its case law will still deal with cases that challenge distinctions that were made by the legislature or the executive. Finally, adhering to these models is a matter of degree. Even a deferential court may occasionally invalidate a measure based on the equality guarantee. Similarly, a court that largely follows the equality as non-discrimination approach may sometimes strike down a distinction that did not involve a suspect classification. Therefore, our analysis looks at the main emphasis of the equality case law.[75]

3. Research questions, methodology, and hypotheses

The empirical study has two aims. On the one hand, it wants to take stock of the different approaches that courts apply when operationalizing equality. In that sense, it provides a mapping of equality doctrines. This mapping will be based on the four equality models introduced here. We will show to which model of equality the doctrine of an analyzed court corresponds. On the other hand, our study tries to identify reasons for why courts adopt a specific doctrine: Why are some courts more deferential than others when conceptualizing equality? Certainly, it is unlikely that we will find monocausal explanations for doctrinal developments. Nevertheless, the analysis should allow us to draw conclusions about the factors that are more or less likely to influence the doctrinal development.

The reasons why courts adopted a particular doctrine cannot be directly observed.[76] Therefore, we have to observe secondary indicia and draw inferences regarding causality. The analysis relies on a multiple case studies method that combines a cross-case comparison with an in-depth contextual analysis of the individual cases. The cross-case comparison uses the variation between cases in order

[75] For a more detailed discussion, see Chapter 20, section 1.1.

[76] See Alan M Jacobs, "Process Tracing and the Effects of Ideas" in Andrew Bennett and Jeffrey T Checkel (eds), *Process Tracing: From Metaphor to Analytical Tool* (CUP 2015) 41, 52.

to explain the emergence of equality doctrines. For this purpose, the cases are drawn from different regions as well as different legal traditions and feature courts with varying institutional strengths as well as different kinds of equality clauses.

Still, the total number of case studies is too small to rely merely on the cross-case comparison for causal inferences. For this reason, the cross-case comparison is complemented by a process tracing approach that makes use of the context for each individual case.[77] This contextual analysis is used to identify the most likely of several competing explanations. The contextual information can consist of the reasoning and the factual as well as historical circumstances of key decisions or the historical development of the equality doctrine. For example, the development of the equal protection doctrine in the United States tells us that the drafting history was not the only driving force because many of the factors that lead to heightened scrutiny cannot be explained by this history.[78]

There are several factors that could explain differences in equality doctrines, and the analysis is supposed to identify the explanatory factors that are the most important. In particular, I intend to include the following variables into the analysis.

3.1 Wording of the constitutional norm

The first factor is the wording of the constitutional norms. It is now largely accepted that abstract legal norms cannot completely determine concrete decisions about the law.[79] Yet, this does not automatically mean that legal norms and legal doctrine do not have a constraining effect.[80] The extent of this constraining effect is subject to debate in the empirical literature on judicial decision-making.[81] If the wording

[77] On process tracing, see Alexander L George and Andrew Bennett, *Case Studies and Theory Development in the Social Sciences* (MIT Press 2005); Andrew Bennett, "Process Tracing and Causal Inference" in Henry E Brady and David Collier (eds), *Rethinking Social Inquiry: Diverse Tools, Shared Standards* (Rowman & Littlefield 2010) 207; Andrew Bennett and Jeffrey T Checkel, "Process Tracing: From Philosophical Roots to Best Practices" in Andrew Bennett and Jeffrey T Checkel (eds), *Process Tracing: From Metaphor to Analytical Tool* (CUP 2015) 3. For process tracing in the context of legal research, see also Katerina Linos and Melissa Carlson, "Qualitative Methods for LR Writing" (2017) 84 University of Chicago LR 213, 231–37.

[78] See Chapter 2, section 4.1.

[79] Seminally Immanuel Kant, *Kritik der reinen Vernunft* (first published 1781, Suhrkamp 1983) A 130–47.

[80] Davis and Klare (n 13) 441.

[81] See Mark J Richards and Herbert M Kritzer, "Jurisprudential Regimes in Supreme Court Decision Making" (2002) 96 American Political Science Review 305; Saul Brenner and Marc Stier, "Retesting Segal and Spaeth's Stare Decisis Model" (1996) 40 American Journal of Political Science 1036; Stefanie A Lindquist and David E Klein, "The Influence of Jurisprudential Considerations on Supreme Court Decision Making: A Study of Conflict Cases" (2006) 40 Law & Society Review 135; Michael A Bailey and Forrest Maltzman, "Does Legal Doctrine Matter? Unpacking Law and Policy Preferences on the US Supreme Court" (2008) 102 American Political Science Review 369; Michael A Bailey and Forrest Maltzman, *The Constrained Court: Law, Politics, and the Decisions Justices Make* (Princeton University Press 2011).

was the only determining factor, courts interpreting a general equality clause would instead resort to a formal concept of equality, while courts facing a non-discrimination clause would prefer an interpretation of equality as a guarantee of non-discrimination. However, it is unlikely that the text completely determines the doctrinal choices because it leaves judges considerable room of discretion. Usually, non discrimination clauses contain open-ended lists of prohibited grounds. That means that courts can easily resort to criteria of distinction that are not contained in the list. At the same time, the example of the US Supreme Court shows that courts can also use a discrimination-based concept of equality to interpret a general equality clause.

> ***Hypothesis 1:*** *The wording of the equality or non-discrimination clause has an influence on the concept of equality that is adopted by the apex court, but is—by far—not the only determining factor.*

3.2 Drafting history und context

Secondly, the drafting history and the contextual purpose of the equality and non-discrimination clause may play a role if the specific clause was enacted to correct a societal wrong prevalent at the time of drafting. For example, the Fourteenth Amendment of the US Constitution was drafted after the American Civil War in order to guarantee racial equality to African American citizens.[82] This may have influenced the interpretation of the doctrine and be a reason why race plays such a prominent role in the US equality jurisprudence. Similarly, one could think of discrimination based on caste in the Indian or on ethnicity in the South African context as factors influencing the interpretation of equality. The constraining effect of the drafting history will probably differ between jurisdictions. In some jurisdictions, it might provide a strong frame for the judicial operationalization of equality, while the effect is negligible in other jurisdictions.

> ***Hypothesis 2:*** *The effect of the drafting history and context will differ quite significantly between jurisdictions. In some jurisdictions, the purpose and drafting history of the equality clause will have a strong influence on the shape of the doctrine.*

[82] John P Frank and Robert F Munro, "The Original Understanding of 'Equal Protection of the Laws'" (1950) 50 Columbia LR 131, 136–42.

3.3 Institutional strength

Thirdly, judges are constrained by the institutional strength of their court.[83] The stronger the position of a court is, the less deferential it can be toward the legislature. It is well known that courts are not able to implement their own decisions. Therefore, they are—to a certain extent—dependent on the cooperation of the legislature and the executive. The greatest strength of courts vis-à-vis the political branches is their legitimacy.[84] If courts have a high level of public acceptance, they gain in institutional strength and do not jeopardize their position if they afford less deference to the legislature.

According to this hypothesis, a strong court would adopt a formal concept of equality as reasonableness or even a positive equality approach, while granting little deference to the legislature. This would allow the court to impose positive measures on the legislature or correct legislation even in the absence of structural deficits. A less strong court would adopt a concept of equality focusing on suspect classifications and apply medium-level deference. Interventions in cases in which there is a glaring societal imbalance require less moral justification and might therefore be more easily acceptable, while the court would refrain from intervening in cases that do not involve structural injustices. Finally, courts with little institutional strength vis-à-vis the legislature and the executive would adopt a formal concept of equality, giving deference to the legislature regardless of whether the distinction was based on a suspect classification or not.

> ***Hypothesis 3:*** *The institutional strength of a court influences the adopted concept of equality. The stronger the court, the less deference it grants—all other factors being equal—to legislature and executive.*

3.4 Judicial ideology

Another factor influencing the equality doctrine that courts choose is the prior conception of equality of its judges. This conception of equality may have different

[83] Martin Shapiro, *Courts: A Comparative and Political Analysis* (University of Chicago Press 1981); Alec Stone Sweet, "Constitutional Politics: The Reciprocal Impact of Lawmaking and Constitutional Adjudication" in Paul Craig and Carol Harlow (eds), *Lawmaking in the European Union* (Kluwer 1998) 111; Karen J Alter, *Establishing the Supremacy of European Law: The Making of an International Rule of Law in Europe* (OUP 2001); Georg Vanberg, *The Politics of Constitutional Review in Germany* (CUP 2005).

[84] Lee Epstein, Jack Knight, and Olga Shvetsova, "The Role of Constitutional Courts in the Establishment and Maintenance of Democratic Systems of Government" (2001) 35 Law & Society Review 117, 125; Vanberg (n 83) 49–53; Clifford James Carrubba, "A Model of the Endogenous Development of Judicial Institutions in Federal and International Systems" (2009) 71 Journal of Politics 55, 65.

sources. It may be based on philosophical convictions or political ideology.[85] For example, judges with an ideology focused on social justice might care more about social inequality than libertarian judges and therefore favor a model emphasizing positive equality. Some judges might be more inclined to protect particular minorities or vulnerable groups and thus adopt a discrimination-based conception of equality, while other judges deem liberty more important than equality and prefer a more deferential approach. It is assumed that judges try to adopt a doctrine that comes closest to their prior conception of equality. Notwithstanding, the overall effect will probably be weak in most jurisdictions: Judges face the constraints mentioned in the first three hypotheses and, furthermore, have to compromise with their colleagues on the bench.

> ***Hypothesis 4:*** *Judges try to adopt an equality doctrine that comes closest to their prior conception of equality, but the overall effect on the jurisprudence will be rather weak in most jurisdictions.*

3.5 Legal tradition

Finally, legal tradition may influence the shape of the equality doctrine.[86] In his book on legal traditions, Patrick Glenn defines them as "a loose conglomeration of data, organized around a basic theme or themes."[87] Therefore, traditions are not exclusive or incommensurable. Instead, they may overlap and share common characteristics and traits.[88] Nevertheless, they are also characterized by differences. One of the traditional distinctions in the comparative literature is between civil law and common law traditions. There is a discussion on the importance of this distinction in the judicial practice, in particular in the field of constitutional law.[89] Nevertheless, it seems to be a potential explanatory factor that we should at least take into account. But there are other influences that shape legal traditions. These might be historical path dependencies, such as a colonial history, or shared

[85] On the influence of political ideology on judicial decisions, see Jeffrey A Segal and Albert D Cover, "Ideological Values and the Votes of US Supreme Court Justices" (1989) 83 American Political Science Review 557; Jeffrey A Segal and others, "Ideological Values and the Votes of US Supreme Court Justices Revisited" (1995) 57 Journal of Politics 812; Jeffrey A Segal and Harold J Spaeth, *The Supreme Court and the Attitudinal Model Revisited* (CUP 2002); Thomas Brennan, Lee Epstein, and Nancy Staudt, "The Political Economy of Judging" (2009) 93 Minnesota LR 1503.

[86] On the concept of legal tradition, see eg H Patrick Glenn, *Legal Traditions of the World: Sustainable Diversity in Law* (5th edn, OUP 2014); Jaakko Husa, "Legal Culture vs. Legal Tradition—Different Epistemologies" (Maastricht European Private Law Institute Working Paper No 2012/18).

[87] Glenn (n 86) 15.

[88] See the discussion of Husa (n 86) 13–17.

[89] See Ran Hirschl, *Comparative Matters: The Renaissance of Comparative Constitutional Law* (OUP 2014), 233; András Jakab, Arthur Dyevre, and Giulio Itzcovich, "Conclusion" in András Jakab, Arthur Dyevre, and Giulio Itzcovich (eds), *Comparative Constitutional Reasoning* (CUP 2017) 761.

supranational institutions. Furthermore, courts might adhere to concepts important for the national identity, such as the notion of republicanism in France.[90] Or courts may be influenced by the diversification of society through immigration and may be more sensitive to problems of minority identities than judges in more homogenous societies.[91]

Hypothesis 5: *The legal tradition has an influence on the shape of the equality doctrine. The strength varies from jurisdiction to jurisdiction.*

3.6 The influence of international, supranational, and foreign courts

A final factor that may shape equality doctrines is the influence of international, supranational and foreign courts. This is most obvious in the case of a supranational court, such as the Court of Justice of the European Union (CJEU). The CJEU has developed a significant body of anti-discrimination law. As secondary EU legislation has to be implemented in the legal orders of the EU member states and EU law enjoys primacy over domestic legal orders of EU member states,[92] we can expect that domestic courts of EU member states are influenced by the case law of the CJEU. Similarly, we can expect domestic apex courts to be influenced by the case law of relevant regional human rights courts. European courts are likely to be influenced by the European Court of Human Rights (ECtHR), while Latin American courts are expected to take into account the case law of the Inter-American Court of Human Rights (IACtHR). This will not lead to total homogenization. Research on the relationship between the ECtHR and domestic apex courts shows that the latter try to accommodate the ECtHR's jurisprudence, while refraining from accepting an absolute primacy of Strasbourg's rulings.[93] Finally, we may also observe a "migration of constitutional ideas"[94] between jurisdictions

[90] See Hennette-Vauchez and Fondimare (n 29).

[91] cf Dagmar Schiek, Lisa Waddington, and Mark Bell, "A Comparative Perspective on Non-discrimination Law" in Dagmar Schiek, Lisa Waddington, and Mark Bell (eds), *Cases, Materials and Text on National, Supranational and International Non-Discrimination Law* (Hart 2007) 15–17; Jule Mulder, "Cultural Narratives and the Application of Non-Discrimination Law" in Barbara Havelková and Mathias Möschel (eds), *Anti-Discrimination Law in Civil Law Jurisdictions* (OUP 2019) 31, 32.

[92] See Case 6/64 *Costa v ENEL* [1964] ECR 585; Case 11/70 *Internationale Handelsgesellschaft* [1970] ECR 1125, para 3; Case 106/77 *Simmenthal* [1978] ECR 629, paras 21–26; Case 149/79 *Commission v Belgium* [1980] ECR 3881, para 19; Joined Cases C-46 and 48/93 *Brasserie du Pêcheur and Factortame II* [1996] ECR I-1029, para 33; Case C-473/93 *Commission v Luxemburg* [1996] ECR I-3207, para 38; Case C-213/07 *Michaniki* [2008] ECR I-9999, paras 62–69. The practice of primacy of EU law in the domestic legal orders is not as straightforward as the case law of the Court of Justice suggests. For a survey of how domestic apex courts treat the status of EU law in their domestic legal orders, see Niels Petersen and Patrick Wasilczyk, *The Primacy of EU Law and the Polish Constitutional Court Judgment* (European Parliament 2022).

[93] Nico Krisch, "The Open Architecture of European Human Rights Law" (2008) 71 Modern LR 183.

[94] Schauer (n 9); Choudhry (n 9).

even if these are not standing in a hierarchical relationship. Foreign influences might be due to regional proximity, imports of legal transplants, the authority of the influencing court, or the foreign education of a significant number of judges.[95]

4. The research design

The study on which this book is based performed an empirical analysis of the case law of eighteen different jurisdictions. For each jurisdiction, we analyzed the case law of the apex court regarding the constitutional equality clause—or, in the cases of international tribunals, the equality clause of the respective international human rights treaty. In the following, I will describe different aspects of the research design in more detail. First, I will describe and justify the selection of the various jurisdictions that form part of the project (4.1). Second, I will explain how the analysis of the different jurisdictions was put into practice and which variables were taken into account (4.2). Finally, I will discuss some of the methodological difficulties that the study encountered (4.3).

4.1 Selection of jurisdictions

In total, the study comprised 18 different jurisdictions for the analysis. The jurisdictions that will be analyzed include six common law jurisdictions (United States, Canada, UK, New Zealand, India, Singapore), seven civil law jurisdictions (Brazil, Colombia, Germany, France, Poland, Taiwan), one jurisdiction with roots both in common and civil law (South Africa), and five international and supranational courts and tribunals (IACtHR, ECtHR, United Nations Human Rights Committee, African Court on Human and Peoples' Rights, CJEU).

These jurisdictions were selected for several reasons. First, we selected cases from different legal traditions (common law/civil law) and different geographical regions in order to control for influences that are caused by a shared legal tradition or shared institutions. Secondly, there is some variation regarding the wording of the constitutional equality guarantees. Some norms are designed as general equality norms, others as non-discrimination norms, and some show a mixture of both. This allows us to test to what extent the wording of the norm influences the shape of the equality doctrine.

Thirdly, we included both domestic apex courts and international judicial bodies into the analysis. It is now largely recognized that domestic and international

[95] On the latter point, see eg David S Law and Wen-Chen Chang, "The Limits of Global Judicial Dialogue" (2011) 86 Washington LR 523, 563.

courts face similar institutional constraints.[96] The inclusion of international courts has two advantages: On the one hand, this choice allows us to extend the regional diversity; on the other hand, it gives the study some variation with regard to institutional strength as international courts and tribunals on average have a weaker institutional position than domestic courts because they receive less public attention than their domestic counterparts.

4.2 Analysis of jurisdictions

In order to construct the sample for the analysis, we analyzed the case law of the apex court for each of the jurisdictions. In exceptional cases, we also looked at other courts if the jurisprudence of the apex court was not sufficiently rich. For example, we analyzed the case law of the Court of Appeal next to the Supreme Court in New Zealand because the former has issued the final decision for the majority of equality cases. The same strategy was followed in Singapore, where we analyzed the case law of the Court of Appeal and the High Court, which together form the Singapore Supreme Court. In most jurisdictions, the sample comprised the entire equality case law. However, in some jurisdictions, we had to restrict ourselves to the analysis of a representative selection of cases because of the sheer volume of the equality case law. If this was the case, the contribution regarding the concerned jurisdiction explains in more detail how the sample was constructed.

Once the sample was established, each case of the sample was analyzed and hand-coded according to a pre-established coding scheme. This analysis and coding was predominantly done by the researcher responsible for the specific chapter. In jurisdictions with a high volume of cases, the researchers were supported by research assistants who coded the cases according to the same coding scheme. In order to ensure inter-coder reliability, all researchers and research assistants were in constant exchange to discuss specific coding choices in problematic cases. Furthermore, the researchers also randomly checked the coding of cases performed by research assistants.

The coding comprised a number of different variables. These were, *inter alia*, the name of the case and the year in which it was decided; whether the court found an equality violation; whether the challenged distinction was based on a suspect criterion; the concrete suspect criterion in question (if there was any); the subject area of the challenged measure (eg criminal law, tax law, etc); whether the challenge concerned a statute, a decision by the executive, or a judicial decision;

[96] Jeffrey K Stanton and Will H Moore, "Judicial Power in Domestic and International Politics" (2011) 65 International Organization 553; Tom Ginsburg, "Political Constraints on International Courts" in Cesare Romano, Karen Alter, and Yuval Shany (eds), *The Oxford Handbook of International Adjudication* (OUP 2014) 483, 486.

whether the distinction amounted to an indirect discrimination; and whether it was an affirmative action measure. In some jurisdictions, we also coded additional variables if this was indicated because of the available information or the nature of the analyzed court's case law.

When coding the different variables, we used our own assessments of the cases: Whether a distinction was considered to be based on a suspect criterion or whether it involved an indirect discrimination depended on the evaluation of the coder, not the court. While one might debate this decision, it made it easier for us to compare results across jurisdictions because we could work with one concept of suspect classification instead of jurisdiction-specific conceptions. A detailed description of the code book with all coded variables, their definition, and how they performed in real-life situations can be found in Annex 1. The results of the analysis can be found in the data repository of the University of Münster.[97]

4.3 Potential selection biases

While we constructed representative samples of the case law we cannot exclude a selection effect because of the nature of judicial proceedings and the docket and publication practices of the analyzed courts.[98] When trying to establish a representative sample of court cases, there are several problems. First, courts may publish only a fraction of the cases that they actually decide. For example, the German Federal Constitutional Court publishes all decisions that it takes when sitting as a full Senate with eight judges. However, decisions that are taken by Chambers of three judges are published only selectively. As a consequence, merely 1–2% of all cases that come to the Court are actually published. Whether a case rejecting a constitutional complaint is published is mostly within the discretion of the judge-rapporteur. There are no publicized criteria determining the publication of a decision.

Second, some courts have explicit docket control. For example, the US Supreme Court has had complete control over its docket since 1988, that is, it can choose the cases it wants to decide without restrictions.[99] Similarly, the Supreme Court of Canada exercises discretionary docket control.[100] It can be assumed that the Court

[97] <https://data-management.uni-muenster.de/datastore> accessed April 16, 2025.

[98] On this problem, see, generally, George L Priest and Benjamin Klein, "The Selection of Disputes for Litigation" (1984) 13 Journal of Legal Studies 1; Tonya L Putnam, "Courts without Borders: Domestic Sources of U.S. Extraterritoriality in the Regulatory Sphere" (2009) 63 International Organization 459, 472–73.

[99] David Fontana, "Docket Control and the Success of Constitutional Courts" in Tom Ginsburg and Rosalind Dixon (eds), *Comparative Constitutional Law* (Edward Elgar 2011) 624, 626.

[100] Bruce Ryder and Taufiq Hashmani, "Managing Charter Equality Rights: The Supreme Court of Canada's Disposition of Leave to Appeal Applications in Section 15 Cases, 1989–2010" (2010) 51 Supreme Court LR 505, 507–08.

will usually choose cases which are controversial or "problematic." Therefore, cases which are inadmissible or clearly unfounded will be underrepresented in the sample. This may lead to the impression that certain types of equality challenges are more successful than they actually are.

Third, choices of the parties of a potential case may also lead to a selection bias. If a challenger believes that a case will be unsuccessful under the current equality doctrine of the apex court, she is less likely to bring the case to a court at all. In addition, members of certain minorities may be less likely to get sound legal advice or to have the necessary resources to bring a case to court. Finally, equality cases may be crowded out by other fundamental rights or alternative institutional resolution mechanisms. For example, many constitutions contain a guarantee of freedom of religion. For this reason, religious discrimination cases might be dealt with under the freedom of religion clause and not under the prohibition of discrimination. We have to keep these potential selection biases in mind when we draw conclusions from the analysis of the case law. However, this issue will be addressed more specifically in the individual country reports as the situation regarding docket control and the publication of cases differs across jurisdictions.

5. Structure of the book

The remainder of this book is organized based on jurisdictions. There is one chapter for each analyzed jurisdiction. The chapters are organized by regions. It starts with the analysis of the North and South American jurisdictions, including the IACtHR, continuing to Europe, Africa, and Asia as well as the South Pacific. Lastly, it analyzes the practice of the UN Human Rights Committee. Each chapter will briefly describe the constitutional equality norm and the equality doctrine that the analyzed apex court has developed in order to put the norm into practice. Then it will present and discuss the results of the empirical analysis, trying to classify the jurisdiction according to our four models of equality. Finally, it tries to explain the shape of the specific doctrine. After the jurisdictional chapters, the book's final chapter concludes and presents the overall results of our study.

2
United States

Niels Petersen

1. Introduction

The equality clauses of the US Constitution are contained in the Fifth and the Fourteenth Amendments. The more prominent Fourteenth Amendment was introduced in 1868 after the Civil War. According to section 1 of the Amendment, no state shall "deny to any person within its jurisdiction the equal protection of the laws." If we just focus on the wording of the norm, it seems that the provision contains a general equality clause that does not highlight particular suspect characteristics, yet the US Supreme Court has developed a highly complex doctrine, in which the question whether a distinction is based on a suspect criterion plays a crucial role. The Fourteenth Amendment is only binding on the states, not on federal authorities. For the latter, equal protection is guaranteed by the Fifth Amendment. While the norm does not explicitly mention equality, the US Supreme Court reads an equal protection guarantee into the due process guarantee contained in the provision.[1]

The following analysis will proceed in three steps. The first part introduces the doctrine of tiered scrutiny that the Supreme Court applies to implement the equal protection clause. It also looks at the treatment of two special situations—indirect discrimination and affirmative action. The second part then presents the results of an empirical analysis of all equal protection cases of the Supreme Court in the 54 years from 1970 to 2023. It shows that the level of scrutiny applied by the Court is highly predictive of whether the latter finds a violation of the equal protection clause. Yet, a closer analysis draws a more nuanced picture. Even if the Court does not apply strict scrutiny, challenges of distinctions based on suspect classifications have a rather high success rate. At the same time, the success rate for distinctions based on race or sex is lower than one might expect considering the heightened standard of scrutiny triggered by these classifications. The third part attempts an explanation for this observation. It argues that it is to some extent due

[1] *Bolling v Sharpe* 347 US 497 (1954). On the reading an equal protection clause into the Fifth Amendment, see Peter J Rubin, "Taking Its Proper Place in the Constitutional Canon: Bolling v. Sharpe, Korematsu, and the Equal Protection Component of Fifth Amendment Due Process" (2006) 92 Virginia LR 1879.

Niels Petersen, *United States* In: *Equality's Guardians*. Edited by: Niels Petersen, Oxford University Press.
 DOI: 10.1093/9780198961109.003.0002

to strategic considerations but also to the ideology of the deciding judges. The final part concludes.

2. The equality doctrine of the US Supreme Court

2.1 Doctrine of tiered scrutiny

The US Supreme Court has developed a doctrine of tiered scrutiny to implement the equal protection clause. According to this doctrine, the Court differentiates between three tiers of scrutiny. The more problematic the distinction, the higher the burden of justification for the state. The first tier is strict scrutiny. The Court applies strict scrutiny for differentiations based on race[2] and national origin[3] or if the distinction concerns a fundamental right.[4] If strict scrutiny is applied, a measure can only be justified if it is necessary or narrowly tailored to serve a compelling state interest.[5] The second tier is intermediate scrutiny. This standard of review is applied for distinctions based on sex[6] and for discrimination against nonmarital children.[7] Such a distinction can be justified if it is "substantially related" to "important governmental objectives."[8] For all other distinctions, the Court applies the rational basis test. There are different formulations of this test, but according to one common conception, the equal protection challenge is unsuccessful "if there is any reasonably conceivable state of facts that could provide a rational basis for the classification."[9] This standard of review is very deferential and only rarely leads to the invalidation of a norm.[10]

2.2 Indirect discrimination and affirmative action

Two issues of the US equal protection doctrine deserve specific attention because they are controversial in legal scholarship—the treatment of indirect discriminations and affirmative action cases. With regard to indirect discriminations, the Court held in *Washington v Davis* that it was not sufficient to show that a norm had a disparate impact.[11] Instead, the Court only applies strict scrutiny if it could

[2] *McLaughlin v Florida* 379 US 184, 196 (1964).
[3] *Graham v Richardson* 403 US 365, 371–72 (1971).
[4] *Shapiro v Thompson* 394 US 618, 634 (1969).
[5] *See Palmore v Sidoti* 466 US 429, 432–33 (1984). For a nuanced description of the doctrine of strict scrutiny, see Richard H Fallon, "Strict Judicial Scrutiny" (2007) 54 UCLA LR 1267, 1302–15.
[6] *Craig v Boren* 429 US 190 (1976).
[7] *Clark v Jeter* 486 US 456, 461 (1988).
[8] *Craig v Boren* (n 6) 197.
[9] *FCC v Beach Communications, Inc* 508 US 307, 314 (1993).
[10] Erwin Chemerinsky, "The Rational Basis Test is Constitutional (and Desirable)" (2016) 14 Georgetown J Law & Public Policy 401, 402.
[11] *Wash v Davis* 426 US 229 (1976).

be proven that the distinction had a discriminatory purpose.[12] Even evidence of structural discrimination is not sufficient to trigger strict scrutiny. In *McCleskey v Kemp*, the Black defendant produced compelling evidence of structural discrimination of Black suspects in death penalty cases,[13] yet the Court required the defendant to demonstrate "that the defendants in *his* case acted with discriminatory purpose."[14] Furthermore, the Court requires that the discriminatory purpose is causal for the measure.[15] Even if it is shown that a discriminatory purpose was a motivating factor in the decision, the Court would still only apply the rational basis test if the authority can show that the same decision would have resulted even without the discriminatory motivation.[16] If a party cannot prove discriminatory purpose, this does not automatically mean that the norm in question has not violated the equal protection clause. Instead, the Court applies the rational basis standard. However, there is not a single case of alleged race discrimination in which the Court has denied discriminatory purpose and still found a violation of equal protection.

The issue of affirmative action was initially contentious. In *Regents of the University of California v Bakke*, Justice Powell applied strict scrutiny to affirmative action.[17] However, there were subsequent cases in which the majority of the Court applied intermediate scrutiny[18] or left the issue undecided.[19] Yet in most cases, the Court applies strict scrutiny to affirmative action measures.[20] This does not mean that the Court automatically holds all affirmative action measures to be a violation of the equal protection clause. Rather, there are quite a few cases in which the Court has applied strict scrutiny and still upheld the challenged measure.[21] Still, in the majority of affirmative action cases in which the Court has applied strict scrutiny, it has declared the challenged measure unconstitutional.[22]

12 ibid 239. On legislative intent, see Richard H Fallon, *The Nature of Constitutional Rights* (CUP 2019) 124–54.
13 *McCleskey v Kemp* 481 US 279 (1987).
14 ibid 292 (emphasis in original).
15 See *Pers Adm'r of Mass v Feeney* 442 US 256 (1979).
16 *Village of Arlington Heights v Metropolitan Housing Development Corp* 429 US 252 (1977).
17 *Regents of the Univ of Cal v Bakke* 438 US 265, 289–91 (1978).
18 See *Metro Broad v FCC* 497 US 547, 564–65 (1990).
19 See *Fullilove v Klutznick* 448 US 448, 491–92 (1980); *United States v Paradise* 480 US 149, 166 (1987).
20 See *Wygant v Jackson Bd of Education* 476 US 267, 274 (1986); *Richmond v JA Croson Co* 488 US 469, 493 (1989); *Adarand Constructors v Pena* 515 US 200, 222 (1995); *Gratz v Bollinger* 539 US 244, 257 (2003); *Grutter v Bollinger* 539 US 306, 321 (2003); *Parents Involved in Cmty Sch v Seattle Sch Dist No 1* 551 US 701, 720 (2007); *Fisher v Univ of Tex* 570 US 297 (2013); *Fisher v Univ of Tex II* 579 US 365 (2016); *Students for Fair Admissions, Inc v President and Fellows of Harvard College* 600 US 181 (2023).
21 See *Fullilove* (n 19); *United States v Paradise* (n 19); *Grutter v Bollinger* (n 20); *Fisher II* (n 20).
22 See *Wygant* (n 20); *Richmond v JA Croson Co* (n 20); *Adarand Constructors* (n 20); *Gratz v Bollinger* (n 20); *Parents Involved in Cmty Sch* (n 20); *Fisher* (n 20); *Students for Fair Admissions* (n 20).

3. Empirical analysis of the equal protection case law

3.1 Generating and analyzing the sample

The empirical analysis is based on an examination of all equal protection cases before the US Supreme Court under the Fifth and the Fourteenth Amendments since 1970. The sample of analyzed cases was created by searching the US Supreme Court Cases, Lawyer's Edition database of LexisNexis. The search term was "equal protection" and the timeline comprised all cases from January 1, 1970 until December 31, 2023. The year 1970 was chosen as a starting point because the decade of the 1970s was the period during which today's form of the Supreme Court's equality doctrine largely emerged. In a second step, the data was cleaned manually because not all results of this search indeed concerned constitutional equal protection cases. The analyzed sample of remaining cases contained a total of 270 cases. These were analyzed and coded according to the criteria introduced in the introductory chapter. It is important to note that the criterion of distinction referred to the alleged criterion, not the criterion on which the Court based its decision. Consequently, a case was still coded as involving racial discrimination if the concerned party claimed a disparate impact but the Court ultimately denied the existence of discriminatory purpose. However, such cases were captured by a binary variable that indicated that the concerned party had alleged an indirect discrimination but that the Court has rejected the application of strict scrutiny for the lack of discriminatory purpose.

3.2 Level of scrutiny perspective

Our empirical analysis shows that the level of scrutiny indeed influences the probability that the Court will find an equal protection violation. However, as other studies have shown, strict scrutiny does not automatically lead to a violation of the equal protection clause.[23] Instead, the success rate in our sample of 63 cases, in which the Court applied strict scrutiny, is 91.80%. All cases in which the Court did not find a violation despite applying strict scrutiny are affirmative action cases.[24]

If the Court applies intermediate scrutiny, the success rate is still high, but slightly lower than under strict scrutiny. In the 32 cases of our sample, the Court

[23] See in particular Adam Winkler, "Fatal in Theory and Strict in Fact: An Empirical Analysis of Strict Scrutiny in the Federal Courts" (2006) 59 Vanderbilt LR 793.

[24] See *Fullilove* (n 19); *United States v Paradise* (n 19); *Grutter v Bollinger* (n 20); *Fisher II* (n 20). See also *United Jewish Organizations, Inc v Carey* 430 US 144 (1977) (which did not concern affirmative action in the strict sense but allowed the creation of a Black majority district using explicit racial consideration in implementation of s 5 of the Voting Rights Act). Contrary to the latter, see *Wisconsin Legislature v Wisconsin Elections Com'n* 595 US 398 (2022), where the Court refused to regard the creation of an additional Black majority electoral district as justified under the Voting Rights Act.

found a violation in 78.12% of cases. Yet, there are a substantive number of cases in which the Court did not find a violation despite applying intermediate scrutiny. One group of cases is related to distinctions based on sex. These cases usually concern provisions that favor women over men; in other words, cases in which the vulnerable group had an advantage.[25] Two of the cases involved rules governing citizenship, where it was easier for children of female US citizens to acquire US citizenship than for children of male US citizens.[26] Two cases dealt with distinctions based on whether the parents were married at the time of birth. Here, the Court held that under certain circumstances it can be justified to distinguish between children of a married couple and nonmarital children if at least some nonmarital children also receive the benefit.[27] Finally, there is one affirmative action case regarding racial classifications, in which Justice Brennan, delivering the opinion of the Court, applied intermediate scrutiny.[28]

Finally, when the Court resorts to the rational basis test, it only finds a violation of the equal protection clause in 13.82% of a total of 113 cases. Most of the successful cases concern a distinction that is arguably based on a suspect criterion but which do not trigger a heightened standard of review. There are two cases of sex discrimination before the latter was classified as a criterion eliciting intermediate scrutiny.[29] Furthermore, there are other arguably suspect criteria, for which the Court never formally accepted a heightened form of scrutiny. These comprise residency,[30] sexual orientation,[31] disability,[32] property ownership,[33] and indignancy.[34] Finally, there are a small number of cases in which the Court found a violation of the equal protection clause even though no suspect classification was involved. Arguably, all of these cases concern arbitrary administrative and legislative action.[35] For example, in *Willowbrook v Olech*, the municipality demanded much higher costs for connecting the applicant to the municipal water supply than it had for similarly situated neighbors.[36] Yet, the boundaries between what the

[25] See *Califano v Webster* 430 US 313 (1977); *M v Superior Court* 450 US 464 (1981); *Heckler v Mathews* 465 US 728 (1984).

[26] See *Miller v Albright* 523 US 420 (1998); *Tuan Anh Nguyen* 533 US 53 (2001).

[27] See *Mathews v Lucas* 427 US 495 (1976); *Lalli v Lalli* 439 US 259 (1978).

[28] *Metro Broad* (n 18) 564–65.

[29] See *Reed v Reed* 404 US 71 (1971); *Stanton v Stanton* 421 US 7 (1975).

[30] See *Zobel v Williams* 457 US 55 (1982); *Metro Life Ins Co v Ward* 470 US 869 (1985); *Williams v Vermont* 472 US 14 (1985); *Hooper v Bernalillo County Assessor* 472 US 612 (1985).

[31] See *Romer v Evans* 517 US 620 (1996); *Pavan v Smith* 582 US 563 (2017).

[32] See *Jackson v Indiana* 406 US 715 (1972); *City of Cleburne v Cleburne Living Ctr* 473 US 432 (1985).

[33] See *Phoenix v Kolodziejski* 399 US 204 (1970); *Quinn v Millsap* 491 US 95 (1989).

[34] See *Mayer v Chicago* 404 US 189 (1971); *Lubin v Panish* 415 US 709 (1974).

[35] See *Lindsey v Normet* 405 US 56 (1972); *Eisenstadt v Baird* 405 US 438 (1972); *United States Dep't of Agric v Moreno* 413 US 528 (1973); *O'Brien v Skinner* 414 US 524 (1974); *Logan v Zimmerman Brush Co* 455 US 422 (1982); *Allegheny Pittsburgh Coal Co v County Com* 488 US 336 (1989); *Willowbrook v Olech* 528 US 562 (2000).

[36] *Willowbrook* (n 35).

judges consider arbitrary and what they still consider to be rational are unclear.[37] Furthermore, it seems that the US Supreme Court has applied an even more restrictive standard in more recent cases so that it is doubtful whether the Court would still even review distinctions on arbitrariness.[38]

This perspective suggests that the level of scrutiny indeed has a significant influence on the success rate of cases. There is no perfect correlation. Strict scrutiny is not "fatal in fact" as Gerald Gunther assumed for the strict scrutiny analysis of the Warren Court.[39] Yet, there is a significant chance that the Court finds a violation of the equal protection clause if it applies strict scrutiny. On the other side of the scale, the rational basis test is not completely toothless.[40] However, the chances of success are less than one in seven. Therefore, we find a significant correlation between the level of scrutiny and the chances that the Court finds a violation of the equal protection clause.

3.3 Suspect classifications perspective

The last section looked at the success rate of different levels of scrutiny. It showed that the chance of success is higher, the stricter the scrutiny. This section takes a different perspective. It looks at the success rate of cases based on the existence of a suspect classification: How likely is it that a challenged measure violates the equal protection clause if it makes a distinction involving a suspect classification? To be clear, the concept of suspect classification is not a concept used by the US Supreme Court. Instead, we look at characteristics of distinction that can arguably be classified as suspect according to the discussion in the introductory chapter.[41]

If we apply such a frame of analysis, the picture looks slightly different than in the analysis focusing on tiers of scrutiny. It suggests that the chance of success for distinctions involving suspect classifications is mostly above 50%, regardless of whether the suspect classification in question triggers heightened scrutiny or not (see Table 2.1). By contrast, the success rate is only 15.93% in cases which do not involve a suspect classification.

These results invite a few comments and caveats. For a start, it has to be acknowledged that Table 2.1 shows a static picture that somewhat obscures the dynamism

[37] See Fallon, *The Nature of Constitutional Rights* (n 12) 103. See also Chemerinsky (n 10) 410–16 (arguing for a more structured rational basis test).

[38] See *Armour v City of Indianapolis* 566 US 673 (2012).

[39] Gerald Gunther, "In Search of Evolving Doctrine on a Changing Court: A Model for a Newer Equal Protection" (1972) 86 Harvard LR 1, 8.

[40] See Gale Lynn Pettinga, "Rational Basis with Bite: Intermediate Scrutiny by Any Other Name" (1987) 62 Indiana LJ 779; Robert C Farrell, "Successful Rational Basis Claims in the Supreme Court from the 1971 Term Through Romer v. Evans" (1999) 32 Indiana LR 357, 411–15; Raphael Holoszyc-Pimentel, "Reconciling Rational Basis Review: When Does Rational Basis Bite?" (2015) 90 NYU LR 2070; Katie R Eyer, "The Canon of Rational Basis Review" (2018) 93 Notre Dame LR 1317.

[41] See Chapter 1, section 2.2.1.

Table 2.1 Success rate in equal protection cases based on suspect classification

Criterion	Violation	No violation	Violation pct	Total
Not suspect	18	95	15.93	113
Race	36	24	60.00	60
Citizenship	7	3	70.00	10
Sex	15	11	57.69	26
Illegitimacy of birth	10	5	66.67	15
Residence	8	7	53.33	15
Religion	1	0	100	1
Disability	2	1	66.67	3
Sexual orientation	4	0	100	4
Property	3	3	50.00	6
Indignancy	7	10	41.18	17
Total	111	159	41.11	270

and shifts in the development of the equal protection doctrine. This is most obvious for the characteristic of indignancy. A glance at the table suggests that this is a vibrant characteristic inviting a significant number of important cases. However, all cases in the table stem from the 1970s when the issue was indeed controversial among the judges. Today, the Supreme Court does not decide such cases anymore, suggesting that the chances of success of such a case brought today are close to zero.

Keeping this in mind, the analysis nevertheless offers some interesting insights. On the one hand, suspect classifications that trigger intermediate or strict scrutiny all have a success rate of well above 50%. At the same time, the success rate is lower than one might expect. In particular, the success rate of only 60% for cases involving alleged racial discrimination appears rather striking. The reasons for this low success rate are twofold. On the one hand, the category also comprises affirmative action cases. As we have seen earlier, the challenge of affirmative action is sometimes unsuccessful even if the Court applies strict scrutiny.[42] While there are good reasons to debate whether affirmative action is the right answer to correct past discrimination, there is a strong argument to be made that positive measures

[42] See n 22.

to support a vulnerable group are less problematic than measures that entrench the structural disadvantages of this group.

Yet even without affirmative action, the success rate in cases of racial discrimination improves only slightly to 63%. Therefore, the results are mainly driven by a different dynamic. The sample of all race discrimination cases also involves cases of alleged indirect discrimination. Therefore, most of the race discrimination cases in which no violation was found concern cases in which the majority of the US Supreme Court argued that it could not find a discriminatory purpose. Certainly, one may debate whether these cases should be classified as race discrimination cases. After the US Supreme Court adopted strict scrutiny for racial distinctions in *McLaughlin v Florida*,[43] however, discrimination practices have become more subtle and sophisticated. Direct discrimination today is exceedingly rare because it is unlikely to withstand legal scrutiny. Only 7 of the 60 cases concerning racial discrimination concerned direct discriminations and no affirmative action. At the same time, the US Supreme Court imposes a high burden of justification for finding that a measure was based on discriminatory purpose.[44] Just showing a discriminatory effect is not sufficient.[45] If we leave out indirect discrimination and affirmative action cases, the success rate becomes 100%.

Yet, the question whether an indirect discrimination is actually based on discriminatory purpose can be extremely controversial. This becomes clear if we look at the number of dissenting opinions in indirect discrimination cases. Almost 30% of cases involving indirect racial discrimination have been decided with four dissenting votes (12 out of 41). This is a significantly higher share than for equal protection cases overall, where only 20.9% of cases have been decided with four dissenting votes (56 out of 268). At the same time, the number of uncontroversial cases without dissenting votes is significantly lower in indirect racial discrimination cases than in equal protection cases overall (14.63% compared to 30.6%).

Some commentators have claimed that the US Supreme Court's treatment of affirmative action cases and indirect discrimination leads to paradoxical results: While positive measures aiming at correcting the disadvantages of past discrimination trigger strict scrutiny, many of the measures that are an expression of structural disadvantages for the vulnerable group pass the court's scrutiny because it cannot be proven that they were based on discriminatory intent.[46] The numbers

[43] *McLaughlin* (n 2) 196.

[44] See *McCleskey* (n 13) 291–96.

[45] *Wash v Davis* (n 11) 239.

[46] See Reva Siegel, "Why Equal Protection No Longer Protects: The Evolving Forms of Status-Enforcing State Action" (1997) 49 Stanford LR 1111, 1143; Ian F Haney López, "Equal Protection as Intentional Blindness" in Anne Richardson Oakes (ed), *Controversies in Equal Protection Cases in America* (Ashgate 2015) 67. See also Michael Klarman, "An Interpretive History of Modern Equal Protection" (1991) 90 Michigan LR 213, 312 (noting the inconsistency, arguing "[i]f strict scrutiny cannot be justified to ensure that facially neutral laws producing disparate racial impacts are licitly motivated, why is it necessary to safeguard against malevolently motivated racial preferences masquerading as benevolent ones?").

offer support to this critique. While the success rate in indirect discrimination cases is higher than in affirmative action cases, the difference is not all that large: In affirmative action cases, the challenge of the positive measure has had a success rate of 50% (7 out of 14), while the success rate in indirect discrimination cases has been 63.41% (26 out of 41). However, it has to be borne in mind that indirect discrimination is arguably more problematic than affirmative action,[47] suggesting that the marginal difference in success rates underlines the problem rather than alleviates the raised concerns.

In the field of sex discrimination, most of the cases in which an alleged discrimination did not lead to a violation of the equal protection clause concern asymmetric measures; that is, cases in which men claimed to be discriminated.[48] Two cases in which equal protection was denied concerned an alleged indirect sex discrimination in which the Court did not find a discriminatory purpose.[49] Finally, there are two cases related to the criteria for receiving US citizenship through birth abroad. In these cases, the Court held that it was justified to have more favorable requirements to get US citizenship for children of female US citizens than for children of male US citizens because it was easier to prove parentage of the mother than of the father.[50]

Discrimination based on national origin usually triggers strict scrutiny, yet the success rate is also far from perfect. Seventy percent of all cases in which a measure based a distinction on national origin were successful. The three cases in which the US Supreme Court held that the distinction based on citizenship was justified all concerned access to public service or distinctions involving the exercise of sovereign power where the Court only applied rational basis review.[51] Finally, the success rate for cases that distinguish according to the marital status of the parents at birth is 66.67%. The cases in which the Court did not find a violation usually concern distinctions in which a benefit that is granted to marital children is also given to some nonmarital children but not to all.[52] They predominantly fall into a time when the question of the right standard of scrutiny for distinction based on the legitimacy of birth was not yet settled. In many of the cases in which the Court ultimately does not find a violation, it applied the rational basis test[53] or left the standard of scrutiny open.[54]

[47] See Aileen McColgan, *Discrimination, Equality and the Law* (Hart 2016) 74–75.

[48] See *Kahn v Shevin* 416 US 351 (1974); *Schlesinger v Ballard* 419 US 498 (1975); *Califano v Webster* (n 25); *M v Superior Court* (n 25); *Rostker v Goldberg* 543 US 57 (1981); *Heckler v Mathews* (n 25). Certainly, rules seemingly favoring women are not always unproblematic because they often entrench problematic gender stereotypes, see Klarman (n 46) 308.

[49] See *Geduldig v Aiello*, 417 US 484 (1974); *Feeney* (n 15).

[50] See *Miller v Albright* (n 26); *Tuan Anh Nguyen* (n 26).

[51] See *Foley v Connelie* 435 US 291 (1978); *Ambach v Norwick* 441 US 68 (1979); *Cabell v Chavez-Solido* 454 US 432 (1982).

[52] See *Labine v Vincent* 401 US 532 (1971); *Mathews v Lucas* (n 27); *Fiallo v Bell* 430 US 787 (1977); *Quilloin v Walcott* 434 US 246 (1978); *Lalli v Lalli* (n 27); *Parham v Hughes* 441 US 347 (1979).

[53] See *Labine v Vincent* (n 52); *Fiallo v Bell* (n 52); *Parham v Hughes* (n 52).

[54] See *Quilloin* (n 52).

Furthermore, there are many cases in which the Supreme Court does not automatically apply a heightened standard of scrutiny even though the distinction in question was arguably based on a suspect criterion.[55] Even in these cases, however, the success rate is significantly higher than the baseline success rate. The most prominent example is sexual orientation: Even though the Supreme Court has not classified sexual orientation as a suspect category triggering a heightened standard of review, it has found a violation of equal protection in 100% of cases.[56] But sexual orientation is not the only example. The Supreme Court has also found violations in the majority of cases involving distinctions based on residency,[57] religion,[58] and disability.[59] In cases concerning the possession of property,[60] the success rate is either 50% or not far below. In legal academia, this has spurred a discussion on whether there are actually different levels of scrutiny within the rational basis test—a very deferential version and a more searching one, coined rational basis test "with bite."[61]

Considering these numbers, it is tempting to conclude that it does not matter which level of scrutiny the Supreme Court applies to a distinction based on a suspect classification. Instead, Table 2.1 suggests that the most important distinction is between cases that involve a suspect classification and cases which do not. However, we have to apply two substantial caveats to these findings. First, the overall number of cases in most categories is very low. Except residency and indignancy, all categories that do not trigger heightened scrutiny comprise six cases or fewer. The category of religion consists only of one case, marriage of two cases, and disability of three cases. Second, the results might be driven by a substantial selection bias.[62] On the one hand, the Supreme Court has had complete control over its docket since 1988; that is, it can choose the cases it wants to decide without restrictions.[63] Therefore it may be that it just chooses not to decide the cases involving discrimination based on religion or disability that would be unsuccessful in any case. On the other hand, the selection bias might also result from choices of the parties to a dispute. It might be that the potential victims do not

[55] For a list of suspect criteria triggering heightened scrutiny, see Chemerinsky (n 10) 405–06.

[56] See *Romer v Evans* (n 31); *United States v Windsor* 570 US 744 (2013); *Obergefell v Hodges* 576 US 644 (2015); *Pavan v Smith* (n 31).

[57] See *Dunn v Blumstein* 405 US 330 (1972); *Memorial Hospital v Maricopa County* 415 US 250 (1974); *Zobel v Williams* (n 30); *Metro Life Ins Co v Ward* (n 30); *Williams v Vermont* (n 30); *Hooper* (n 30); *Attorney Gen of New York v Soto-Lopez* 476 US 898 (1986); *Saenz v Roe* 526 US 489 (1999).

[58] See *Cruz v Beto* 405 US 319 (1972).

[59] See *Jackson v Indiana* (n 32); *Cleburne Living Ctr* (n 32).

[60] See *Phoenix v Kolodziejski* (n 33); *Hill v Stone* 421 US 289 (1975); *Quinn v Millsap* (n 33).

[61] See Gunther (n 39) 12; Pettinga (n 40); Miranda Oshige McGowan, "Lifting the Veil on Rigorous Rational Basis Scrutiny" (2012) 96 Marq LR 377; Holoszyc-Pimentel (n 40).

[62] See George L Priest and Benjamin Klein, "The Selection of Disputes for Litigation" (1984) 13 Journal of Legal Studies 1; Tonya L Putnam, "Courts without Borders: Domestic Sources of U.S. Extraterritoriality in the Regulatory Sphere" (2009) 63 International Organization 459, 472–73.

[63] David Fontana, "Docket Control and the Success of Constitutional Courts" in Tom Ginsburg and Rosalind Dixon (eds), *Comparative Constitutional Law* (Edward Elgar 2011) 624, 626.

bring the cases before the courts because they fear they will be unsuccessful if the latter applies only the rational basis test.

3.4 Making tiered scrutiny flexible

Despite these caveats, the picture that has emerged in the previous section demands an explanation. While the tiered scrutiny doctrine of the US Supreme Court seems to favor predictability over flexibility, the preceding analysis has shown that the doctrine is more flexible and less predictable than it appears *prima facie*. If we look more closely, we can identify several mechanisms in the application of the doctrine that give room for such flexibility. Predominantly, there are three mechanisms for permitting flexibility. The first concerns the choice of the standard of review where the Court is not always consistent. The second concerns indirect discrimination cases. In cases in which there is a disparate impact, the Supreme Court requires discriminatory intent in order to apply heightened scrutiny. Whether discriminatory intent can be proven is usually decisive: If the Court applies strict scrutiny, it almost always finds a violation; if it applies the rational basis standard, the reviewed measure is mostly upheld. The final mechanism allowing flexibility is the rational basis test itself. In some cases, in particular when a suspect classification is involved, the rational basis test is more searching than in other instances so that challenges may also be successful even if the Court only applies the rational basis standard.

The first mechanism for flexibility concerns the choice of the standard of review. The standard of review is less certain than might appear *prima facie*. For some suspect classifications, the Court switched between different standards of review at least initially before the matter was later settled. For example, in the early sex discrimination cases, the US Supreme Court sometimes applied intermediate or "heightened" scrutiny,[64] in one case even strict scrutiny,[65] while in other cases it relied on the rational basis test.[66] Similarly, the Court also applied the rational basis test in some of the early cases concerning extramarital birth.[67] Finally, the treatment of affirmative action was initially highly controversial within the Court. In *Regents of the University of California v Bakke*, only Justice Powell applied strict scrutiny.[68] There are some subsequent cases in which the majority of the Justices applied intermediate scrutiny to affirmative action measures.[69]

[64] See *Weinberger v Wiesenfeld* 420 US 636 (1975); *Craig v Boren* (n 6).

[65] See *Frontiero v Richardson* 411 US 677 (1973).

[66] See *Reed v Reed* (n 29); *Kahn v Shevin* (n 48); *Geduldig v Aiello* (n 49); *Schlesinger v Ballard* (n 48); *Stanton v Stanton* (n 29).

[67] See *Labine v Vincent* (n 52); *Weber v Aetna Casualty & Surety Co* 406 US 164 (1972); *Fiallo v Bell* (n 52); *Parham v Hughes* (n 52).

[68] See *Bakke* (n 17) 289–91.

[69] See *Metro Broad* (n 18) 564–65.

But initial insecurity about the right standard is not the only reason to apply different standards of scrutiny to the same suspect classification. In some cases, the Supreme Court intentionally applies different levels of scrutiny to the same suspect classification. In the case of national origin, the Court applies only rational basis review to differentiations concerning state power while it applies strict scrutiny in other situations.[70] Sometimes, the Court also leaves the standard of review open. In these cases, the Court takes a decision without explicitly revealing the standard of review that it applies or even adhering to the traditional doctrinal formulae that mark the different standards. Finally, there is also insecurity with regard to the definition of fundamental rights. According to the traditional doctrine, strict scrutiny is not only triggered through certain suspect classifications but also by the existence of fundamental rights. However, the content and extent of these fundamental rights is not always well defined.[71]

The second mechanism for flexibility concerns the proof of discriminatory purpose in indirect discrimination cases. As we have seen earlier, many of the unsuccessful sex or race discrimination cases are cases in which the concerned party claimed a disparate impact but could not, according to the opinion of the Court, prove discriminatory purpose. However, as we have seen, the treatment of these indirect discrimination cases is often highly controversial.[72]

The final mechanism is the rational basis test itself. While the success rate of cases in which the rational basis test is applied, is significantly lower than for strict or intermediate scrutiny, the Court still finds a violation of equal protection in about one out of every seven cases. In the literature, this has led to a discussion whether the Court actually applies different standards within the rational basis test: the usual rational basis test and one rational basis test "with bite."[73] Our analysis finds some support for this hypothesis. In particular, the Court finds violations of equal protection if the challenged distinction is based on a suspect classification even if the latter does not formally trigger a heightened standard of scrutiny.[74]

3.5 Conclusion

Our empirical analysis has shown that the doctrine with which the US Supreme Court implements the equal protection clauses of the US Constitution is more

[70] See *Foley v Connelie* (n 51); *Ambach v Norwick* (n 51); *Cabell v Chavez-Solido* (n 51).

[71] See Gary S Goodpaster, "The Constitution and Fundamental Rights" (1973) 15 Arizona LR 479.

[72] There are also similar examples with regard to sex discrimination. See eg *Geduldig v Aiello* (n 49) (with three dissents of JJ Brennan, Douglas, and Marshall).

[73] See eg Gunther (n 39) 18–24; Pettinga (n 40); McGowan (n 61); Kenji Yoshino, "Why the Courts Can Strike down Marriage Restrictions under Rational Basis Review" (2013) 37 NYU Review of Law & Social Change 331, 333–34; Holoszyc-Pimentel (n 40); Fallon, *The Nature of Constitutional Rights* (n 12) 103.

[74] Similarly Pettinga (n 40) 801; McGowan (n 61); Yoshino (n 73) 335.

complex than appears *prima facie*. If we try to characterize the case law, the Supreme Court clearly follows a nondiscrimination model. The chances of success are quite significant if the challenged distinction is based on a suspect classification, while rather low in cases in which no suspect classification is involved. Yet there are a few cases in which a challenge is nevertheless successful. These arguably concern arbitrary administrative action, for which the rational basis test provides a screening mechanism of last resort.[75] But even here, the Supreme Court has recently become more restrictive.[76] In any case, it does not change the overall evaluation of a doctrine that is mostly focused on discrimination based on suspect criteria.

4. Explanation of the doctrine

What are the reasons for this development? If we only look at the wording of the Fourteenth Amendment which guarantees the "equal protection of the laws," the pattern looks rather surprising. The wording would have suggested an approach focused on equality as reasonableness rather than on nondiscrimination, yet the preceding analysis has shown that the equality jurisprudence of the US Supreme Court rather focuses on nondiscrimination. Neither the identification of specific suspect classifications nor the concrete shape of the tiered scrutiny approach has a concrete basis in the text of the Fourteenth Amendment. There are several reasons for this observation, which we will explore more in detail in the following. The dominant narrative points to the historical origins of the equal protection clause, which was drafted after the Civil War and was supposed to grant equality to Black citizens. However, this explanation tells only part of the story. A second reason for the current shape of the doctrine lies in the concrete challenge that the Supreme Court faced when it developed the doctrine. After the breakdown of the *Lochner* jurisprudence in the late 1930s, it needed to replace the *Lochner* approach with a new doctrine. First, it reverted to a deferential rational basis test before identifying instances that deserved heightened scrutiny. Finally, the ideology of the Judges who were serving on the Supreme Court also played a role. This concerns, in particular, the approaches of the court regarding affirmative action and indirect discrimination.

[75] See n 34.

[76] See n 38 and accompanying text.

4.1 Historical origin of the Fourteenth Amendment

According to a widespread narrative, the doctrine of the Supreme Court regarding the equal protection clause can be traced back to the historical origin of the norm. The Fourteenth Amendment was drafted after the Civil War in the so-called reconstruction era. While the wording of the norm prohibits states to "deny to any person within its jurisdiction the equal protection of the laws" and does not mention race or color, it was clear that the drafters particularly intended to guarantee racial equality.[77] This interpretation is also confirmed in the early cases before the Supreme Court. In the Slaughterhouse Cases in 1873, the Court argued:

> We doubt very much whether any action of a State not directed by way of discrimination against the Negroes as a class, or on account of their race, will ever be held to come within the purview of this provision. It is so clearly a provision for that race and that emergency [the Black Codes], that a strong case would be necessary for its application to any other.[78]

Only a few years later, in *Strauder v West Virginia*, the Supreme Court also highlighted the special importance of the Fourteenth Amendment for racial equality. The Court argued that the equal protection clause declared "in regard to the colored race, for whose protection the amendment was primarily designed, that no discrimination shall be made against them by law because of their color."[79]

The historical origin of the norm may be a starting point for its interpretation but it does not fully explain the subsequent doctrinal development or the concrete shape and differentiation of the current doctrine. Despite the early focus on racial equality, today's version of the strict scrutiny analysis that is triggered by distinctions based on race did not emerge before the 1960s.[80] Instead, the Court mostly retreated from protecting Black people between the 1870s and 1920s.[81] Most infamously, the Court denied equal protection to Black citizens in *Plessy v Ferguson* in 1896 by authorizing segregation through its "separate but equal" doctrine,[82] which was not overruled before *Brown v Board of Education* in 1954.[83] Furthermore, the historical origins only partially explain the extension of heightened scrutiny to other suspect criteria, like national origin, sex, or legitimacy of birth. In particular, the drafters of the Fourteenth Amendment agreed at the time

[77] John P Frank and Robert F Munro, "The Original Understanding of 'Equal Protection of the Laws'" (1950) 50 Columbia LR 131, 136–42.
[78] *Slaughterhouse Cases* 83 US (16 Wall) 36, 81 (1873).
[79] *Strauder v West Virginia* 100 US 303, 307 (1880).
[80] Fallon, "Strict Judicial Scrutiny" (n 5) 1275–78.
[81] Robert M Cover, "The Origins of Judicial Activism in the Protection of Minorities" (1982) 91 Yale LJ 1287, 1295.
[82] *Plessy v Ferguson* 163 US 537 (1896).
[83] *Brown v Bd of Education* 347 US 483 (1954).

that the clause should not protect against sex discrimination.[84] Finally, the historical account does not account for the emergence of a rational basis test "with bite" for distinctions based, for example, on sexual orientation, nor for the treatment of indirect discrimination or affirmative action.[85] Therefore, we have to find additional factors that may explain the doctrine in its current shape.[86]

4.2 Strategic explanation

Another explanation for the development of the current shape of the equal protection doctrine is strategic. The doctrine evolved because it provided a solution to a concrete challenge that the Supreme Court faced when it started to develop today's equal protection jurisprudence. In the first decade of the 20th century, the Supreme Court was infamous for its so-called *Lochner* jurisprudence,[87] which mostly targeted economic regulation.[88] *Lochner* is often seen as the epitome of judicial activism and faced severe political resistance in the 1930s.[89] When the *Lochner* doctrine broke down,[90] the Court reverted to a deferential rational basis test.[91] But the Court realized early that there were some constitutional interests that deserved more stringent protection.[92] One prominent early sign was the famous footnote four in the *Carolene Products* case where Justice Stone delivering the opinion of the Court left open "whether *prejudice against discrete and insular minorities* may be a special condition, which ... may call for a correspondingly *more searching judicial inquiry*."[93]

A few years later, in *Korematsu*, the Court toiled again with the idea of establishing heightened scrutiny for certain kinds of classifications. It argued "that all legal restrictions which curtail the civil rights of a single racial group" must be subjected "to the most rigid scrutiny."[94] However, the Court only paid lip service to

[84] Ruth Bader Ginsburg, "Sex Equality and the Constitution" (1978) 52 Tulane LR 451, 452.

[85] See Klarman (n 46) 308–16 (for affirmative action).

[86] See Fallon, *The Nature of Constitutional Rights* (n 12) 122 ("[N]early across the board, the Constitution's text and original history provide a starting point for judicial identification, analysis, and protection of constitutional rights, but little more").

[87] *Lochner v New York* 198 US 45 (1905).

[88] See Sujit Choudhry, "The *Lochner* Era and Comparative Constitutionalism" (2004) 2 I.CON 1, 4–5.

[89] ibid 2; Sujit Choudhry, "Worse than Lochner?" in Colleen M Flood, Kent Roach, and Lorne Sossin (eds), *Access to Care, Access to Justice: The Legal Debate Over Private Health Insurance in Canada* (University of Toronto Press 2005) 75, 77. See also Ronald Dworkin, *Freedom's Law: The Moral Reading of the American Constitution* (Harvard University Press 1996) 82 (calling *Lochner* the "whipping boy" of US constitutional law).

[90] *West Coast Hotel v Parrish* 300 US 379 (1937); *NLRB v Jones and Laughlin Steel Corp* 301 US 1 (1937).

[91] Fallon, "Strict Judicial Scrutiny" (n 5) 1287.

[92] Klarman (n 46) 223; Fallon, "Strict Judicial Scrutiny" (n 5) 1288.

[93] *United States v Carolene Products Co* 304 US 144 (footnote 4) (1938) (emphasis added).

[94] *Korematsu v United States* 323 US 214 (1944).

the notion of rigid scrutiny for race-based distinctions and applied a very deferential standard of review to the internment of Japanese Americans during the Second World War for security reasons.[95] But the Court slowly became more consequential in its subsequent jurisprudence. In *Bolling v Sharpe*, a companion case to *Brown*, it argued that race-based classifications "must be scrutinized with particular care"[96] and held that segregated public schools in the District of Columbia violated the implicit equal protection clause of the Fifth Amendment. Finally, the Court arrived at a version of the strict scrutiny test in 1964 in *McLaughlin v Florida*[97] that mostly corresponds to the version that is still applied to race-based classifications today.[98]

Yet the Court did not restrict heightened scrutiny to race-based classifications. Instead, it extended the classifications that deserve a more searching form of judicial review also to other distinctions, such as national origin, sex, and legitimacy of birth. This category is even larger if one also considers the cases in which the Court presumably applied the rational basis test "with bite." This is in line with the *Carolene Products* footnote, which referred to "discrete and insular minorities" in general, mentioning in particular religious and national minorities next to racial ones.[99]

4.3 Ideology of judges

While the contextual explanation gives a plausible account of the big picture, it is not the only factor that played a role. Instead, judicial ideology was also influential in teasing out the concrete shape of the doctrine. While the Supreme Court showed signs of applying a different standard of review for certain preferred rights in 1950s,[100] this did not translate into a consistent doctrine. This was mostly because the liberals on the Court lacked a consistent fifth vote. The situation changed in 1962, when Arthur Goldberg joined the Court, replacing Felix Frankfurter.[101] This allowed the Court to establish the strict scrutiny doctrine in *McLaughlin v Florida* and subsequent cases. In 1969, when Warren Burger and Harry Blackmun joined the Supreme Court, the Court reverted to a conservative majority.[102] This did not lead to a fundamental revision of the equal protection doctrine.[103] The Burger Court implemented smaller changes. It stopped the extension of preferred rights seen in the 1960s.[104] Furthermore, the switch arguably also influenced the

95 Klarman (n 46) 232; Fallon, "Strict Judicial Scrutiny" (n 5) 1276–77.
96 *Bolling v Sharpe* (n 1) 499.
97 *McLaughlin* (n 2) 196.
98 Klarman (n 46) 255; Fallon, "Strict Judicial Scrutiny" (n 5) 1277.
99 *Carolene Products* (n 93) (footnote 4).
100 Fallon, "Strict Judicial Scrutiny" (n 5) 1290.
101 ibid 1291.
102 Klarman (n 46) 282–316.
103 Gunther (n 39) 10–12.
104 ibid 12–15.

treatment of indirect discriminations and affirmative action in *Washington v Davis* and *Bakke*.[105] This development of the equal protection doctrine by the Court's majority made reliance on indirect discriminations more difficult while easing the path for challenges to affirmative action programs—both developments that were resisted by the more liberal judges on the Court. Some authors suggest that this development is the expression of an anti-egalitarian mindset opposed to substantive equality among the majority of judges.[106] This suggests that ideology had a significant influence on its concrete shape of the equal protection doctrine even if it might not have been the main driver of its basic structure.

5. Conclusion

The US Supreme Court has developed a tiered scrutiny approach to implement the equal protection clauses of the Fifth and Fourteenth Amendments. The tier is determined by whether a distinction is based on specific suspect classifications. Our analysis has shown that there is a high correlation between the tier that the Supreme Court chooses for its analysis and the likelihood that it will find a violation of the equal protection clause. The likelihood of an equal protection violation is highest when the Court applies strict scrutiny, closely followed by cases in which it applies intermediate scrutiny. While the likelihood for a case to succeed if the Court applies the rational basis standard is above zero, it is still a rather long shot—the odds being about one in seven.

However, if we change the perspective of our analysis, we see that there is also a high likelihood of success if distinctions are challenged that do not belong to the traditional triggering distinctions leading either to a strict or intermediate scrutiny analysis. This is the case, for example, for distinctions based on residency, religion, disability, or sexual orientation. We must be careful not to draw definitive conclusions because the numbers of analyzed cases are rather small. Still, the pattern suggests that the Supreme Court follows a nondiscrimination approach to equal protection. It polices distinctions based on suspect criteria while being deferential with regard to all other distinctions where the Court only intervenes occasionally in cases of arbitrary administrative action.

There is no monocausal explanation for the current shape of the doctrine. Instead, several factors played together. The starting point is the historical origin of the Fourteenth Amendment in the reconstruction period which suggests that racial equality was a primary motivation for the drafters of the norm. However,

[105] Klarman (n 46) 295–99 and 308–16.

[106] For example, Jamal Greene, "The Elephant in the Room" in Francisca Pou-Giménez, Laura Clérico, and Esteban Restrepo-Saldarriaga (eds), *Proportionality and Transformation: Theory and Practice from Latin America* (CUP 2022) 309, 320–21.

this is not the only factor. Instead, the doctrine played a strategic function for the Court. After the breakdown of the *Lochner* jurisprudence, the Court first applied a very deferential rational basis test, and yet it saw the necessity to afford more stringent protection to certain preferred rights. The introduction of strict scrutiny offered the opportunity to police distinctions based on suspect classifications, such as race while applying a deferential standard for all other distinctions. Finally, judicial ideology played a role as well in shaping the concrete implementation of the doctrine.

3
Canada

Niels Petersen

1. Introduction

The Canadian equality guarantee is contained in section 15 of the Canadian Charter of Rights and Freedoms.[1] The provision constitutes both an equality and a non-discrimination clause. It guarantees the right to "equality before and under the law" and to "equal protection and equal benefit of the law . . ., in particular, without discrimination based on race, national or ethnic origin, colour, religion, sex, age or mental or physical disability." Furthermore, paragraph 2 of section 15 contains an explicit justification clause for positive measures. Finally, measures that infringe section 15 are subject to the general limitation clause in section 1 of the Charter, even though this clause has only played a minor role in the equality case law of the Canadian Supreme Court.

In its jurisprudence, the Supreme Court has developed a rather complex doctrine that has evolved quite significantly since its earliest inception in 1989. As our analysis will show, this doctrine focuses exclusively on the non-discrimination part of section 15, even though the Court has added some suspect classifications to the ones explicitly mentioned in the norm. The following analysis will proceed in three steps. First, it will trace the development of the equality doctrine in the Canadian jurisprudence. Second, it will present the results of an empirical analysis of the Canadian case law, showing that the Supreme Court is rather restrictive even in cases involving a suspect classification. The third part examines the reasons for the particular shape of the Canadian equality doctrine.

2. The equality doctrine of the Supreme Court of Canada

2.1 Development of the Doctrine

The equality doctrine of the Supreme Court of Canada operationalizing section 15 of the Canadian Charter has evolved quite considerably since its earliest inception

[1] Canadian Charter of Rights and Freedoms, Part I of the Constitution Act, 1982, being schedule B to the Canada Act 1982, ch 11.

Niels Petersen, *Canada* In: *Equality's Guardians*. Edited by: Niels Petersen, Oxford University Press.
 DOI: 10.1093/9780198961109.003.0003

in *Andrews*.[2] In *Andrews*, the Court was concerned with a citizenship requirement as prerequisite for entering into the legal profession. Justice McIntyre, writing for the majority of the Court regarding section 15(1), defined discrimination as a

> distinction . . . based on grounds relating to personal characteristics of the individual or group, which has the effect of imposing burdens, obligations, or disadvantages on such individual or group not imposed upon others.[3]

If the Court found a discrimination, it could be justified under section 1 of the Charter. In *Andrews*, the majority of the Court held that the citizenship requirement was not justifiable.[4]

In three equality cases, that were all decided in 1995,[5] frictions in the interpretation of section 15(1) emerged among the different Justices of the Supreme Court.[6] In order to return to a unified approach, the Court developed a new doctrinal formula in *Law v Canada* in 1999.[7] The formula developed in *Law* consists of a three-step test.[8] First, the Court asks whether there was a difference in treatment, and second, whether this distinction was based on the grounds explicitly mentioned in section 15(1) or on analogous grounds. While these two initial steps reflect the approach in *Andrews*, the innovation was the third step, in which the Court asked whether the distinction was discriminatory. In order to evaluate the discriminatory character, the Court referred to four contextual factors.[9] The Court stressed that the main purpose of the non-discrimination guarantee was preventing the violation of essential human dignity through the imposition of disadvantage, stereotyping, or political or social prejudice.[10]

In the legal literature, this new approach in *Law* was severely criticized.[11] Commentators stressed, in particular, the indeterminateness of the concept of

[2] *Law Society of British Columbia v Andrews* [1989] 1 SCR 143.

[3] ibid 174 (per McIntyre J).

[4] ibid 151–58 (per Wilson J).

[5] *Miron v Trudel* [1995] 2 SCR 418; *Egan v Canada* [1995] 2 SCR 513; *Thibaudeaux v Canada* [1995] 2 SCR 627.

[6] On this development, see Christopher D Bredt and Adam M Dodek, "Breaking the Law's Grip on Equality: A New Paradigm for Section 15" (2003) 20 Supreme Court LR 33, 38–40; Jennifer Koshan and Jonnette Watson Hamilton, "The Continual Reinvention of Section 15 of the Charter" (2013) 64 University of New Brunswick LJ 19, 27–29.

[7] *Law v Canada (Minister of Employment and Immigration)* [1999] 1 SCR 497.

[8] ibid 548–49 (per Iacobucci J).

[9] ibid 534–41.

[10] ibid 529.

[11] See eg Debrah M McAllister, "Section 15—The Unpredictability of the Law Test" (2003) 15 National J of Constitutional Law 3; Bredt and Dodek (n 6) 45–48; Daphne Gilbert, "Time to Regroup: Rethinking Section 15 of the Charter" (2003) 48 McGill LJ 627; Daphne Gilbert and Diana Majury, "Critical Comparisons: The Supreme Court of Canada Dooms Section 15" (2006) 24 Windsor Yearbook of Access to Justice 111; Sophia Moreau, "Equality Rights and the Relevance of Comparator Groups" (2006) 5 J of Law & Equality 81; Mary Eberts and Kim Stanton, "The Disappearance of the Four Equality Rights and Systemic Discrimination from Canadian Equality Jurisprudence" (2018) 38

human dignity so that the doctrine gave little guidance to courts deciding concrete cases.[12] Furthermore, they criticized the formalistic application of difference-in-treatment analysis of the first step.[13] In some of the post-*Law* cases, the Supreme Court had adhered to an understanding, according to which there could only be one "correct" comparator group,[14] which imposed a significant burden on the plaintiff.[15]

In reaction to this criticism,[16] the Supreme Court modified its doctrine again in *Kapp*[17] and *Withler.*[18] The Court simplified the test and condensed it into two steps.[19] First, the Court asked whether the challenged measure makes a distinction based on an enumerated or analogous ground. In a second step, it analyzes whether there was a discrimination by perpetuating prejudice or stereotyping. Yet this refined approach also drew criticism in the literature.[20] Compared with other jurisdictions following a non-discrimination approach, the Canadian Supreme Court explicitly required an additional element, perpetuating prejudice or stereotyping, for a discrimination claim to be successful.[21] As a consequence, the Supreme Court continued to relax this requirement. In *Taypotat*, the Court reformulated the second step of the *Kapp* test and now required that the challenged measure had "the effect of reinforcing, perpetuating or exacerbating [the] disadvantage" of the concerned group.[22] This focus on disadvantage in lieu of stereotyping and prejudice has been confirmed in *Fraser* and several later decisions.[23]

National J of Constitutional Law 89. But see also the defense of the SCC's approach in *Law* by Donna Greschner, "Does Law Advance the Cause of Equality?" (2001) 27 Queen's LJ 299.

[12] Bredt and Dodek (n 6) 45–47; Peter W Hogg, "What Is Equality? The Winding Course of Judicial Interpretation" (2005) 29 Supreme Court LR 39, 56–57; R James Fyfe, "Dignity as Theory: Competing Conceptions of Dignity at the Supreme Court of Canada" (2007) 70 Saskatchewan LR 1, 11; Rory O'Connell, "The Role of Dignity in Equality Law: Lessons from Canada and South Africa" (2008) 6 I.CON 267, 285.

[13] Bredt and Dodek (n 6) 47–48; Gilbert and Majury (n 11); Moreau (n 11).

[14] See eg *Granovsky v Canada (Minister of Employment and Immigration)* [2000] 1 SCR 703, 731–32; *Hodge v Canada (Minister of Human Resources Development)* [2004] 3 SCR 357, 366–78; *Auton (Guardian ad item of) v British Columbia (Attorney General)* [2004] 3 SCR 657, 678–80.

[15] See in particular the analysis of Moreau (n 11).

[16] See *R v Kapp* [2008] 2 SCR 484, 504.

[17] ibid 502.

[18] *Withler v Canada (Attorney General)* [2011] 1 SCR 396, 410.

[19] *Kapp* (n 16) 502.

[20] See eg Jennifer Koshan and Jonnette Watson Hamilton, "Meaningless Mantra: Substantive Equality after Withler" (2011) 16 Review of Constitutional Studies 31.

[21] Peter W Hogg, *Constitutional Law of Canada* (Carswell, student edition 2020) para 55.29.

[22] *Kahkewistahaw First Nation v Taypotat* [2015] 2 SCR 548, 557. See also *Quebec (Attorney General) v A* [2013] 1 SCR 61, 217 (arguing that a proof of the perpetuation of "prejudicial or stereotypical attitudes" was not necessary).

[23] See *Quebec (Attorney General) v Alliance du personnel professionnel et technique de la santé et des services sociaux* [2018] 1 SCR 464, 484; *Fraser v Canada (Attorney General)* [2020] 3 SCR 113, 162; *R v Sharma* 2022 SCC 39 para 31.

2.2 Indirect discrimination and positive measures

The Canadian Supreme Court has acknowledged early in its case law that differentiations having a disparate impact on vulnerable groups can constitute a discrimination even if there is no differentiation based on a suspect characteristic.[24] Unlike the US Supreme Court, the Supreme Court of Canada has always insisted on treating indirect discriminations under the same framework as direct discriminations.[25] In particular, it has not required a discriminatory purpose.[26] Nevertheless, the general approach of the Court towards section 15 has imposed a significant burden on appellants bringing an indirect discrimination case to the Court under the *Law* and *Kapp* frameworks.[27] On the one hand, the Court asks the appellant to prove that the disparate impact is indeed caused by the measure challenged under the equality provision.[28] On the other hand, the Court also applied its requirement that discrimination perpetuates stereotyping or prejudice to disparate impact cases.[29] For example, in *BC Health Services*, the Court denied the discriminatory character of observed adverse effects because "the evidence [did not] disclose that the Act reflects the stereotypical application of group or personal characteristics."[30] Similarly, in *Hutterian Brethren*, the Court argued that the distinction in question did not arise "from any demeaning stereotype."[31]

While this second requirement has been eased significantly in *Taypotat*,[32] the appellant still has to show that a statute has a disparate impact on a disadvantaged group.[33] Only after the appellant has shown disproportionate impact and disadvantage does the burden of proof shift to the government to show that the

[24] See *Andrews* (n 2) 165 (per McIntyre J). For a discussion of the case law regarding disparate impact, see Jonnette Watson Hamilton and Jennifer Koshan, "Adverse Impact: The Supreme Court's Approach to Adverse Effects Discrimination under Section 15 of the Charter" (2015) 19 Review of Constitutional Studies 191.

[25] *Fraser* (n 23) 151–52.

[26] *Andrews* (n 2) 174; *Fraser* (n 23) 159.

[27] Watson Hamilton and Koshan (n 24) 193–94; Sonia Lawrence, "The Admittedly Unattainable Ideal: Adverse Impact and Race under Section 15" in Law Society of Upper Canada (ed), *Canada at 150: The Charter and the Constitution* (Irwin Law 2018) 547, 551–60. See also Andy Yu, "Direct Discrimination and Indirect Discrimination: A Distinction with a Difference" (2019) 9 Western J of Legal Studies 1, 20 (warning of the danger that judges implicitly assume that discriminatory intent is necessary even though they reject the concept explicitly); Denise G Réaume, "The Relevance of Relevance to Equality Rights" (2006) 31 Queen's LJ 696, 703 (arguing that much the critique of the interpretation of section 15 is due to the fear that the relevance requirements collapses into an inquiry into the subjective intentions of the legislature).

[28] See *Symes v Canada* [1993] 4 SCR 695, 764–65 (per Iacobucci J). For a detailed discussion of what constitutes proof of disparate impact, see *Fraser* (n 23) 152–59.

[29] See Watson Hamilton and Koshan (n 24) 215–16.

[30] *Health Services and Support-Facilities Subsector Bargaining Association v British Columbia* [2007] 2 SCR 391, 470.

[31] *Alberta v Hutterian Brethren of Wilson Colony* [2009] 2 SCR 567, 617.

[32] *Taypotat* (n 22) 557; *Alliance du personnel professionnel et technique de la santé et des services sociaux* (n 23) 484; *Fraser* (n 23) 152 and 162.

[33] *Sharma* (n 23) para 31.

discriminatory effect can be justified under the general justification clause of section 1 of the Charter.[34] Yet most indirect discrimination cases do not even get to this last step. An example is the recent case of *R v Sharma*, in which the majority of the Court rejected the challenge of a statute that restricted the availability of a milder sentencing regime for certain offences.[35] The appellant had argued that the exclusion of these offences constituted indirect race discrimination because of the high incarceration rate of indigenous individuals. However, the majority, while acknowledging the "indigenous incarceration crisis,"[36] claimed that the appellant had failed to prove a disproportionate impact of the specific impugned provision.[37] Yet the disproportionate impact will often be difficult to prove for the appellant because the relevant data is usually in the possession of the government.

Positive measures that privilege disadvantaged groups are explicitly allowed under Canadian law. According to section 15(2) of the Canadian Charter, the equality clause does not preclude any law that has as its object the amelioration of conditions of disadvantaged individuals or groups. This paragraph has been introduced in reaction to the *Bakke* decision of the US Supreme Court[38] and is, thus, an explicit authorization of affirmative action measures.[39] Doctrinally, there was initial uncertainty as to where to situate the discussion on the admissibility of ameliorative measures.[40] Under the *Law* framework, section 15(2) was largely insignificant because ameliorative measures did already not constitute a discrimination.[41] Instead, the Court considered section 15(2) largely to act as an interpretative aid to section 15(1).[42] However, in *Kapp*, the Court gave the exception clause in section 15(2) independent force.[43] It argued that section 15(2) could shield ameliorative programs from scrutiny under section 15(1) if certain conditions were fulfilled,[44] which the Court specified in *Cunningham*.[45] At the same time, the Court stressed that an ameliorative program that benefits one disadvantaged group did not necessarily have to encompass all disadvantaged groups for the conditions to be fulfilled.[46]

[34] *Fraser* (n 23) 163–64.
[35] *Sharma* (n 23).
[36] ibid para 3.
[37] ibid paras 66–83.
[38] *Regents of the Univ of Cal v Bakke* 438 US 265 (1978).
[39] Walter Surma Tarnopolsky, "The Equality Rights in the Canadian Charter of Rights and Freedoms" (1983) 61 Canadian Bar Rev 242, 257.
[40] On the development of the doctrine, see Jena McGill, "Ameliorative Programs and the Charter: Reflections on the Section 15(2) Landscape since R v Kapp" (2017) 95 Canadian Bar Rev 213.
[41] See *Law* (n 7) 539–40.
[42] See also *Lovelace v Ontario* [2000] 1 SCR 950, 1009–11.
[43] *Kapp* (n 16).
[44] ibid 518.
[45] *Alberta v Cunningham* [2011] SCR 670, 691–92.
[46] ibid 690–91.

3. Empirical analysis of the equality case law

3.1 Generating and analyzing the sample

The empirical analysis of the Canadian equality case law is based on an examination of all equality cases decided by the Supreme Court of Canada under section 15 of the Canadian Charter of Rights and Freedoms. The sample consists of 71 cases from 1989 to the end of 2023. The first analyzed case is *Andrews*,[47] the first equality case of the Court under section 15 of the Canadian Charter, while the last case is *R v Sharma* from November 4, 2022.[48] The cases were identified by executing a search for "section 15" or "s. 15" and "Canadian Charter" in the database of the Supreme Court of Canada.[49] This sample was subsequently cleaned manually because not all hits concerned equality cases. A case was only considered to be an equality case if the majority of the Court engaged in a substantive discussion of a potential violation of section 15(1) of the Canadian Charter and decided that section 15(1) was either violated or not violated. If the Court mentioned section 15 without making a substantive pronouncement on a potential violation of the norm, or if the Court thought that the analysis of section 15 was precluded, these cases were not included in the sample. After the construction of the sample, all cases contained therein were analyzed, and the variables were coded according to the coding scheme discussed in the introductory chapter.[50]

3.2 The results of the analysis

Previous empirical studies of the Canadian equality case law have demonstrated that equality claims are less likely to be successful than claims under the liberty provisions of the Charter.[51] In an empirical assessment, Bruce Ryder, Cidalia Faria, and Emily Lawrence found that the success rate of equality claims under the Charter stood at 27.9%, thus lower than the general success rate of Charter cases, which were found by other studies to be around 33–35%.[52] Our study, which includes observations over a longer time period comes to similar results: We

[47] *Andrews* (n 2).

[48] *Sharma* (n 23).

[49] <https://decisions.scc-csc.ca/scc-csc/en/nav.do> accessed 20 January 2025.

[50] See Chapter 1, section 4.2.

[51] Bruce Ryder, Cidalia Faria, and Emily Lawrence, "What's Law Good For? An Empirical Overview of Charter Equality Decisions" (2004) 24 Supreme Court LR 1, 10.

[52] ibid. For studies on the general success rate of Charter cases, see Patrick J Monahan and Nadine Blum, "Constitutional Cases 2002: An Overview" (2003) 20 Supreme Court LR 3, 6–7; Frederick Lee Morton, Peter H Russell, and Troy Riddell, "The Canadian Charter of Rights and Freedoms: A Descriptive Analysis of the First Decade, 1982–1992" (1994) 5 National J of Constitutional Law 1; J. Patrick Kelly, "The Charter of Rights and Freedoms and the Rebalancing of Liberal Constitutionalism in Canada, 1982–1997" (1999) 37 Osgoode Hall LJ 625.

Table 3.1 Success rate of equality claims over time

Framework	Andrews 1989–1999	Law–Kapp 1999–2014	Taypotat 2015–2021
No of Cases	29	34	8
Success rate	20.7%	23.5%	50%
Success rate cases with suspect classifications	30%	28.6%	50%

find a success rate of 25.7% for equality cases under section 15 of the Canadian Charter (18 out of 70 cases). However, there is an interesting twist: Ryder, Faria, and Lawrence also found that the success rate was higher under the *Law* framework from 1999 than under the previous *Andrews* framework.[53] Our analysis also shows a slight increase of the success rate following *Law* and later its reformulation in *Kapp* (see Table 3.1).

However, we must add two qualifications. First, while there were lots of successful cases in the early years that were part of the analysis of Ryder, Faria, and Lawerence, the success rate declined significantly over time. After 2003, there was only one successful section 15 claim under the *Law* and *Kapp* framework.[54] Furthermore, there was a significant number of cases that did not involve a suspect classification under *Andrews*. When it became clear that the Court did not pursue a formal approach to equality, the number of such cases decreased considerably.[55] If we disregard the formal equality cases that do not involve a suspect classification, the success rate under *Law* is slightly lower than under the original *Andrews* approach (28.6% vs. 30%, see Table 3.1). Finally, Ryder and Hashmani found in an analysis from 2010 that the grant of applications for leave to appeal in section 15 cases declined significantly from 1999 onwards.[56] Therefore, the increase of the success rate under *Law* is most likely due to a selection effect. If we take into consideration the decrease of the leave-to-appeal rate and of cases without suspect classification, the actual success rate rather declined under the *Law* framework.

[53] Ryder, Faria, and Lawrence (n 51) 10–12.

[54] *Canada (Attorney General) v Hislop* [2007] 1 SCR 429.

[55] Before *Andrews*, a formal understanding of equality in section 15 had been advocated in an important textbook of Canadian constitutional law, see Peter W Hogg, *Constitutional Law of Canada* (2nd edn, Carswell 1985) 799–801. It would have also been in line with the prior case law of Canadian courts under the Canadian Bill of Rights, see Hogg (n 25) para 55.15.

[56] Bruce Ryder and Taufiq Hashmani, "Managing Charter Equality Rights: The Supreme Court of Canada's Disposition of Leave to Appeal Applications in Section 15 Cases, 1989–2010" (2010) 51 Supreme Court LR 505, 511–12.

A significant change in the success rate came in 2015 with the reformulation of the doctrine in *Taypotat* and the doctrinal shift from stereotyping to disadvantage in the second step of the analysis regarding section 15.[57] While the Court found no violation of section 15 in *Taypotat*, the success rate raised to 50% for the period after the decision (four out of eight, including *Taypotat*). Certainly, we have to be careful not to overinterpret these numbers. The overall number of cases is small, and the higher success rate may also be due to a selection effect if appellants brought fewer cases to the Supreme Court due to the low chances of success.[58]

If we turn away from the mere historical success rate and focus on the shape of the Canadian equality case law, the data reveals some interesting findings. The Court clearly does not follow an equality as reasonableness approach. There are 15 cases in which the alleged discrimination was not based on a suspect classification. In all these cases, the Supreme Court did not find a violation of section 15 of the Canadian Charter.[59]

But even if we look only at the cases that involve a suspect classification, the success rate is rather low—in particular if compared to other jurisdictions. For all cases involving a suspect classification, the success rate is 32.1% (18 out of 56). This rate varies quite significantly, depending on the type of suspect classification (see Table 3.2). The most promising categories are sexual orientation (66.7%), sex (46.2%), and disability (44.4%). Residency status also has a success rate of 50%, albeit with only two cases. All other categories have rather low success rates. This concerns, probably unsurprisingly, age (10%) and marriage (25%), but also categories like nationality (25%) or religion (0%). Most surprising is probably that the success rate for distinction based on race—the prototypical suspect classification—also stands at 0% (zero out of seven cases).[60]

If we dig deeper, some patterns emerge. In the cases concerning distinctions based on race, three cases concerned positive measures that were supposed to ameliorate the position of a vulnerable group.[61] Here, the Court emphasized that positive measures did not necessarily have to benefit all potentially vulnerable groups in the same way.[62] This concerned, in particular, cases where the legislature had made a

[57] *Taypotat* (n 22) 557.

[58] However, the trend is confirmed by an analysis of lower court decisions by Alicija Puchta, which shows that the success rate for cases not applying the prejudice and stereotype requirement is considerably higher, see Alicja Puchta, "Quebec v A and Taypotat: Unpacking the Supreme Court's Latest Decisions on Section 15 of the Charter" (2018) 55 Osgoode Hall LJ 665, 692–96.

[59] *Gauthier v Quebec (Commission de Protection du Territoire Agricole)* [1989] 1 SCR 859; *Reference Re Workers' Compensation Act, 1983 (Nfld.)* [1989] 1 SCR 922; *R v Turpin* [1989] 1 SCR 1296; *Edmonton Journal v Alberta (Attorney General)* [1989] 2 SCR 1326; *Rudolph Wolff & Co v Canada* [1990] 1 SCR 695; *R v S (S)* [1990] 2 SCR 254; *R v Généreux* [1992] 1 SCR 259; *R v Finta* [1994] 1 SCR 701; *Delisle v Canada* [1999] 2 SCR 989; *Therrien (Re)* [2001] 2 SCR 3; *Siemens v Manitoba* [2003] 1 SCR 6; *R v Malmo-Levine; R v Caine* [2003] 3 SCR 571; *Health Services* (n 30); *Baier v Alberta* [2007] 2 SCR 673; *Ontario (Attorney General) v Fraser* [2011] 2 SCR 3.

[60] For an attempt to explain the absence of successful race discrimination cases, see Lawrence (n 27).

[61] *Lovelace* (n 42); *Kapp* (n 16); *Cunningham* (n 45).

[62] *Cunningham* (n 45) 690–91.

Table 3.2 Success rate depending on the type of suspect classification

Suspect criterion	No. of cases	Success rate
Sex	13	46.2%
Race	7	—
Nationality	4	25%
Religion	1	—
Residence	2	50%
Disability	9	44.4%
Age	10	10%
Sexual orientation	6	66.7%
Marital status	4	25%
Total	56	32.1%

distinction between different groups of Indians and not extended the conferred benefits in the same way to all of these groups. In *Ermeskin Indian Band*, the Court held that the investment strategy of the Crown in cases in which it was a trustee for royalties belonging to Indian bands did not violate the equality clause.[63] The Court argued that different investment strategies had different advantages and disadvantages so that it was difficult even to identify a disadvantage.[64] At least, the exclusion of certain investments did not constitute discrimination because it was not based on stereotyping.[65] Finally, in three cases, the appellants alleged an indirect discrimination based on race.[66] In all three cases, the Court found that the appellants had not proven a disparate impact of the challenged regulation on their ethnic group.[67]

In the case of sex discrimination, the majority of unsuccessful cases concerned alleged indirect discriminations. In these cases, the Supreme Court argued that the appellants had failed to prove a disparate impact of the challenged measure on women.[68] In two further cases, the appellants were men who alleged a discrimination compared to women. But men were not considered to be a vulnerable group.[69] The final case concerned a Newfoundland Act that was supposed to raise

63 *Ermeskin Indian Band and Nation v Canada* [2009] 1 SCR 222.
64 ibid 283.
65 ibid 283–86.
66 *Taypotat* (n 22); *Ewert v Canada* [2018] 2 SCR 165; *Sharma* (n 23).
67 *Taypotat* (n 22) 557–59; *Ewert* (n 66) 204; *Sharma* (n 23) paras 66–83.
68 *Symes* (n 28); *Native Women's Assn. of Canada v Canada* [1994] 3 SCR 627; *Thibaudeau* (n 5); *Vancouver Society of Immigrant and Visible Minority Women v MNR* [1999] 1 SCR 10.
69 *R v Hess; R v Nguyen* [1990] 2 SCR 906; *Weatherall v Canada (Attorney General)* [1993] 2 SCR 872.

women's wages in order to close the gender pay gap.[70] When the pay raise was suspended by the Newfoundland legislature because of a severe economic and fiscal crisis, the suspension was challenged by a Labor Union. However, the Canadian Supreme Court held that the suspension, while constituting a discrimination, was justified under the limitations clause of section 1 of the Canadian Charter.[71]

The Court also had to decide a considerable number of cases regarding distinctions based on disability. The success rate in this category is similar to the one concerning sex discrimination (44.4%).[72] However, the pattern of unsuccessful cases is slightly more difficult to explain. In *Rodriguez*, the Court deemed the prohibition of assisted suicide justified because it protected the life of vulnerable individuals.[73] *Eaton* concerned a decision in an individual case, where the Court denied a discrimination of a mentally disabled child who was put in a special education class after a Committee had assessed that an integrated setting was not in the child's best interest.[74] In *Winko*, the Court had to examine a provision in the criminal code that established a special scheme for mentally disabled convicts when determining whether the latter could be released and held that this scheme struck the right balance between taking into account the individual circumstances of the concerned convicts and the protection of the public.[75]

The most controversial decisions of the Court regarding disability were *Granovsky* and *Auton*.[76] In *Granovsky*, the appellant had a work-related accident that made him temporarily disabled in 1980.[77] In 1993, the condition deteriorated to an extent that he became permanently disabled. When he applied for a disability pension under the Canada Pension Plan, his request was denied because he had failed to make sufficient contributions in the previous ten years. The appellant claimed that this regulation was discriminatory because he was unable to make the contributions precisely because of his initially temporary disability. The Court held that section 15(1) was not violated because the provision did not "[demean] persons with temporary disabilities, or [cast] . . . doubts on their worthiness as human beings."[78] In *Auton*, the Court held that the denial of payment for a specific

[70] *Newfoundland (Treasury Board) v NAPE* [2004] 3 SCR 204.

[71] ibid 404–29. For a critical discussion of this case, see Sonia Lawrence, "Equality and Anti-Discrimination: The Relationship between Government Goals and Finding Discrimination in Section 15" in Peter Oliver, Patrick Macklem and Nathalie Des Rosiers (eds), *Oxford Handbook of the Canadian Constitution* (OUP 2017) 815, 833–35.

[72] The successful disability cases are *Eldridge v British Columbia (Attorney General)* [1997] 3 SCR 624; *Vriend v Alberta* [1998] 1 SCR 493; *Quebec (Commission des droits de la personne et des droits de la jeunesse) v Montréal (City); Quebec (Commission des droits de la personne et des droits de la jeunesse) v Boisbriand (City)* [2000] 1 SCR 665; *Ontario (Attorney General) v G* [2020] SCR 629.

[73] *Rodriguez v British Columbia (Attorney General)* [1993] 3 SCR 519.

[74] *Eaton v Brant County Board of Education* [1997] 1 SCR 241.

[75] *Winko v British Columbia (Forensic Psychiatric Institute)* [1999] 2 SCR 625.

[76] For criticism of these decisions, see eg Gilbert and Majury (n 11) 119–32 (with further references).

[77] *Granovsky* (n 14).

[78] ibid 740.

medical treatment for autistic children was not discriminatory even though similar treatments for other disabilities had been financed by the health insurance.[79] The Court argued that the government was justified in waiting because the therapy in question was still emergent at the time and the Court thought that it was not treated less favorably than other emergent therapies.[80]

Lastly, let us add a few observations regarding indirect discriminations. The success rate of indirect discrimination cases is 35.7% and thus slightly higher than the success rate of suspect classifications in general.[81] In most of the unsuccessful indirect discrimination cases, the Court held that the appellant had not proven a disparate impact of the challenged measure on a vulnerable group.[82] In *Hutterian Brethren*, the Court had to deal with a universal photo requirement for driver's licenses, which was rejected by members of a particular colony for religious reasons.[83] The Court rejected the argument that this requirement constituted an indirect discrimination based on religion because it "ar[ose] not from any demeaning stereotype but from a neutral and rationally defensible policy choice."[84] Finally, in *Rodriguez*, the Court held that the prohibition of assisted suicide did not constitute a discrimination based on disability even though it predominantly affected individuals who were unable to commit suicide themselves.[85] Justice Sopinka, writing for the majority, assumed that section 15 was infringed[86] but argued that the infringement was justified under section 1 of the Charter.[87]

In summary, the Supreme Court of Canada follows an equality as non-discrimination approach. While the success of equality cases involving suspect classifications is significantly lower than in other jurisdictions, this might partly be due to the circumstances. The racial discrimination issues faced by the US Supreme Court when trying to dismantle Jim Crow laws in the 1950s and 1960s are fundamentally different from the problems coming to the Canadian Supreme Court, which often had to decide about measures providing positive benefits to vulnerable groups. Furthermore, many of the cases coming to the Canadian Supreme Court were age discrimination or disability cases—both factors of distinction

[79] *Auton* (n 14).
[80] ibid 681–82.
[81] The successful indirect discrimination cases are *Eldridge* (n 72); *Vriend* (n 72); *British Columbia (Public Service Employee Relations Committee) v BCGSEU* [1999] 3 SCR 3; *Alliance du personnel professionnel et technique de la santé et des services sociaux* (n 23); *Fraser* (n 23).
[82] *Symes* (n 28); *Native Women's Assn. of Canada* (n 68); *Thibaudeau* (n 5); *Vancouver Society of Immigrant and Visible Minority Women* (n 68); *Taypotat* (n 22); *Ewert* (n 66); *Sharma* (n 23) paras 66–83.
[83] *Hutterian Brethren* (n 31).
[84] ibid 617.
[85] *Rodriguez* (n 73).
[86] ibid 612–13.
[87] ibid 613–15.

which would not be considered suspect under US constitutional law. Moreover, we have also seen that age discrimination cases have a significantly lower success rate in other jurisdictions.[88] Yet we also must note that the doctrine developed by the Canadian Supreme Court has some peculiar elements, in particular the stereotyping requirement that was dominant under the *Law-Kapp* framework. Whether this requirement had an influence on the success rate is difficult to disentangle. While the success rate increased significantly after the doctrinal modification in *Taypotat*, the number of cases is still too small to attribute this effect merely to the doctrinal change.

4. Explanation of the doctrine

When we look for explanations of the shape of the Canadian equality case law, the US influence looms large. Certainly, on the face, the doctrines look quite different. The US Supreme Court applies a system of tiered scrutiny with three different levels of scrutiny, which largely determine the success rate of equality cases.[89] By contrast, the Canadian Supreme Court has developed a rather complex test with several steps that went through various mutations since its inception in *Andrews* in 1989.[90] Yet while the shape of the doctrine differs, we can still observe a significant influence. The US doctrine has been shaped quite considerably by the famous footnote 4 of the *Carolene Products* case.[91] The reference to "discrete and insular minorit[ies]" served as justification for the heightened scrutiny in cases in which distinctions were based on a suspect classification.[92]

This concept of "discrete and insular minorit[ies]" also played a crucial role in the early decisions of the Canadian Supreme Court. In *Andrews*, Justice Wilson referred to the work of the US legal theorist John Hart Ely and argued that non-citizens are a vulnerable group because they lack political power.[93] He also held that non-citizens were a "discrete and insular minority," which is why they deserved protection under section 15(1) even though citizenship was not explicitly enumerated as a suspect classification.[94] In later decisions the Court often used the concept to exclude appellants from the protection of section 15(1). In several decisions, the appellants could not invoke a discrimination under section 15(1) because the Court argued that they were not members of a "discrete and insular

[88] See Chapter 20, section 2.1.
[89] See Chapter 2, section 3.2.
[90] See section 2.1 earlier.
[91] *United States v Carolene Products Co* 304 US 144 (footnote 4) (1938).
[92] See Chapter 2, section 4.2.
[93] *Andrews* (n 2) 152 (per Wilson J).
[94] ibid.

minority."[95] This idea was formalized in *Law* by the introduction of the contextual factors and the reference to human dignity and later in *Kapp* by the emphasis of perpetuating prejudice and stereotyping.

These developments also seem to have been driven in opposition to doctrinal developments in the United States with regards to affirmative action. The drafters of the Charter have included an explicit US counter-model in section 15(2) of the Charter by prescribing that affirmative action programs are not precluded by section 15(1). However, the Supreme Court of Canada did not rely heavily on section 15(2) in its case law. Instead, it already designed its doctrine concerning section 15(1) of the Charter to avoid that privileged groups could challenge positive measures aiming at correcting structural disadvantages of vulnerable groups.[96] Through this asymmetrical interpretation of the equality clause, the Court wanted to stay true to the spirit of the *Carolene products* footnote. While *Law* did not cite the US Supreme Court explicitly, it referred to "discrete and insular minorities" on several occasions. Justice *Iacobucci* mentioned the concept when describing one of the contextual factors that he introduced[97] and also relied on it when justifying that the age discrimination did not violate the appellant's human dignity.[98]

Furthermore, there was also influence in the treatment of indirect discrimination cases. Again, the Canadian Supreme Court did not adopt the central tenets of the US doctrine but instead saw the US development as a warning sign, from which it wanted to distance itself. Instead of referring to the US cases developing the criterion of discriminatory intent as a central requirement for indirect discrimination,[99] it cited one of the US Supreme Court's earlier cases, which was adopted prior to the establishment of today's more rigid doctrine. This decision was *Griggs v Duke Power Co*,[100] a labor case which was decided under the Civil Rights Act and was cited prominently in several Canadian cases concerning indirect discriminations.[101] At the same time, the Supreme Court explicitly rejected the requirement of a discriminatory intent in indirect discrimination cases.[102]

[95] See eg *Turpin* (n 59) 1333 (per Wilson J); *Rudolf Wolff* (n 59) 702 (per Cory J); *Généreux* (n 59) 275 (per Lamer CJ).

[96] Jim Hendry, "The Idea of Equality in Section 15 and Its Development" (2002) 21 Windsor Yearbook of Access to Justice 153, 184. See also Lawrence (n 71) 828–29.

[97] *Law* (n 7) 537.

[98] ibid 555 ("Relatively speaking, adults under the age of 45 have not been consistently and routinely subjected to the sorts of discrimination faced by some of Canada's *discrete and insular minorities*," emphasis added).

[99] See *Wash v Davis* 426 US 229 (1976); *McCleskey v Kemp* 481 US 279 (1987).

[100] *Griggs v Duke Power Co* 401 US 424 (1971).

[101] See *BCGSEU* (n 81) 19; *Quebec (Attorney General) v A* (n 22) 219; *Taypotat* (n 22) 557–58; *Fraser* (n 23) paras 32–38, 53–55, 70–71.

[102] *Andrews* (n 2) 174; *Fraser* (n 23) 159.

Finally, the Canadian Supreme Court has been sensitive to criticism in the Canadian constitutional law scholarship.[103] This is particularly evident in *Kapp*, where the Court extensively referred to the criticism voiced in the literature before modifying the doctrine applied to the section 15 analysis.[104] Furthermore, criticism of the legal literature also led the Court to relax the stereotyping requirement in the jurisprudence following *Taypotat*. While the Court did not explicitly refer to academic critique in *Taypotat* itself, it was certainly aware of the criticism that was voiced against the *Kapp* framework.[105] Additionally, the Court undertook an extensive review of the literature in the recent *Fraser* case, which consolidated the doctrinal changes initiated in *Taypotat*.[106] The relaxation of the requirements for a discrimination claim in the recent case law is closely linked to the personality of Justice Rosalie Silberman Abella, who was the judge rapporteur in *Taypotat* and many of the subsequent equality decisions up until *Fraser*.[107] After she left the court, it remains to be seen whether this development will continue.

Finally, the overly stringent test required by the Supreme Court of Canada also led to a significant decrease in equality cases over the last two decades. Appellants have instead explored alternative avenues to pursue their interests, such as framing equality cases as liberty cases or to bring cases under provincial human rights codes.[108] This probably explains the low number of equality cases that we have seen in recent years.

5. Conclusion

The Canadian Supreme Court has developed a quite complex doctrine concerning the equality guarantee in section 15 of the Canadian Charter of Rights and Freedoms. While the jurisprudence still fits the equality as non-discrimination model, the Supreme Court is considerably more restrained when correcting the legislature and the executive than comparable courts in other common law jurisdictions. The data shows an increase in the success rate since 2015 after the decision of *Taypotat*.[109] Yet the sample is still too small to be certain whether this

[103] This was a point that was also confirmed by former Justice Rosalie Silberman Abella in the discussion during a symposium in her honor that was held at the University of Toronto on Friday, September 23, 2022.

[104] See *Kapp* (n 16) 504–05.

[105] See, in particular, Koshan and Watson Hamilton (n 20). The article was later cited in *Fraser v Canada (Attorney General)* [2020] 3 SCR 113.

[106] *Fraser* (n 23) 142–65 (per Abella J).

[107] *Taypotat* (n 22); *Alliance du personnel professionnel et technique de la santé et des services sociaux* (n 23); *Centrale des syndicats du Québec v Quebec (Attorney General)* [2018] 1 SCR 522; *Fraser* (n 23).

[108] See Peter W Hogg, "Equality as a Charter Value in Constitutional Interpretation" (2003) 20 Supreme Court LR 113 (arguing that many equality claims have been decided under other Charter rights). This claim is supported by Ryder and Hashmani (n 56) 519–25.

[109] *Taypotat* (n 22).

trend is durable and due to the doctrinal modifications. When we look for an explanation of the shape of the Canadian doctrine, the US influence is particularly strong. However, the Canadian court rather refers to the early developments in US jurisprudence after the *Carolene Products* case and the strong emphasis on vulnerable groups. At the same time, the Court also tried to immunize its equality test against the developments that occurred after the conservative turn in the US Supreme Court in the 1970s. However, this immunization arguably overshot the target so that the Supreme Court recently changed course. Whether this doctrinal shift can revive the section 15 jurisprudence remains to be seen.

4

European Court of Human Rights

Jasmin Beck

1. Introduction

The right to equality within the Council of Europe (CoE) is guaranteed through Article 14 of the European Convention on Human Rights (ECHR, the Convention)[1] and Article 1 of Protocol No 12 to the ECHR (P12).[2] While the Convention is binding on all member states,[3] P12 entered into force in 2005 and has been signed by 37, but ratified by only 20 of the 46 CoE member states.[4] Consequently, the European Court of Human Rights (ECtHR, the Court) has found very few violations under P12.[5]

The main difference between the two sources of the right to equality is that the prohibition of discrimination enshrined in Article 14 ECHR is limited in scope to cover discriminations relating to "[t]he enjoyment of the rights and freedoms set forth in [the] Convention." In contrast, Article 1 of P12 serves as a general prohibition of discrimination in "[t]he enjoyment of any right set forth by law" (paragraph 1). The term "law" primarily relates to national law.[6] International law may fall under Article 1(1) of P12, too, but the provision does not give the Court jurisdiction "to examine compliance with rules of law in other international instruments."[7]

[1] Convention for the Protection of Human Rights and Fundamental Freedoms, November 4, 1950 (entry into force: September 3, 1953, European Treaty Series No 005).

[2] Protocol No 12 to the ECHR, November 4, 2000 (entry into force: April 1, 2005, European Treaty Series No 177).

[3] CoE, Chart of signatures and ratifications of Treaty 005, <https://www.coe.int/en/web/conventions/full-list?module=signatures-by-treaty&treatynum=005> accessed January 20, 2025.

[4] CoE, Chart of signatures and ratifications of Treaty 177, <https://www.coe.int/en/web/conventions/full-list?module=signatures-by-treaty&treatynum=177> accessed January 20, 2025.

[5] As per December 31, 2020, violations of art 1 of P12 have been found in six cases against Bosnia and Herzegovina: *Sejdić and Finci v Bosnia and Herzegovina* [GC] ECHR 2009-VI 273; *Zornić v Bosnia and Herzegovina* App no 3681/06 (ECtHR, July 15, 2014); *Šlaku v Bosnia and Herzegovina* App no 56666/12 (ECtHR, May 26, 2016); *Pilav v Bosnia and Herzegovina* App no 41939/17 (ECtHR, June 9, 2016); *Baralija v Bosnia and Herzegovina* App no 30100/18 (ECtHR, October 29, 2019); *Pudarić v Bosnia and Herzegovina* App no 55799/18 (ECtHR, December 8, 2020). Except in *Baralija*, the Court in substance based its findings on *Sejdić and Finci*.

[6] Explanatory Report to Protocol No 12 to the ECHR, Rome, November 4, 2000 (European Treaty Series No 177) para 22.

[7] ibid para 29.

Jasmin Beck, *European Court of Human Rights* In: *Equality's Guardians*. Edited by: Niels Petersen, Oxford University Press. © Jasmin Beck 2025. DOI: 10.1093/9780198961109.003.0004

Despite the difference in scope between Article 14 ECHR and Article 1 of P12, the definition of discrimination enshrined in the two provisions is identical.[8] Both refer to "sex, race, color, language, religion, political or other opinion, national or social origin, association with a national minority, property, birth or other status" as grounds of discrimination.

With this background in mind, the following section explains the analysis performed by the Court when dealing with non-discrimination cases. This introduction to the Court's equality and non-discrimination doctrine is followed by a presentation of the results of the empirical analysis of the ECtHR's jurisprudence, before the chapter closes with some final remarks.

2. The Court's equality and non-discrimination doctrine

The test of the Court for Articles 14 ECHR and 1 of P12 goes back to the seminal *Belgian Linguistics* case.[9] This test consists of the following three steps: First, the Court asks whether a claim falls within the ambit of another article of the ECHR or of one of its Protocols; second, it requires a difference in treatment based on a specific ground; third, it analyzes whether there was an objective and reasonable justification. The first step is only relevant where the Court analyzes a claim under Article 14 ECHR. While this constitutes a formal difference between the two equality norms, Judge Bratza pointed out in his concurring opinion in *Zarb Adami* that the Court had consistently adopted a wide interpretation of the term "within the ambit."[10] In particular in the more recent case law of the Court, the two norms do not differ that much in practice.[11]

The second step requires the Court to decide on a relevant aspect of the case which is used to compare the case to, or to distinguish it from, another specific situation or case. This aspect, "ground," or "status" can be any "identifiable, objective or personal characteristic."[12] The term "other status" in particular, has "generally been given a wide meaning, and [its] interpretation has not been limited to

[8] ibid para 18. The Court has already followed this approach in several cases, see eg *Sejdić and Finci* (n 5) para 55; and *Pilav* (n 5) para 40.

[9] *Case Relating to Certain Aspects of the Laws on the Use of Languages in Education in Belgium v Belgium* (1968) Series A no 6 (*Belgian Linguistics case*). In *I.B. v Greece* ECHR 2013-V 81, para 10, the Court also pronounced upon affirmative action: Justification for a difference in treatment would exist where "legal inequalities tend only to correct factual inequalities."

[10] *Zarb Adami v Malta* ECHR 2006-VIII 305, para 7 (Bratza J concurring).

[11] Niels Petersen, "The Principle of Non-discrimination in the European Convention on Human Rights and in EU Fundamental Rights Law" in Yumiko Nakanishi (ed), *Contemporary Issues in Human Rights Law* (Springer 2018) 129. See also Ruth Rubio-Marín and Mathias Möschel, "Anti-Discrimination Exceptionalism: Racist Violence before the ECtHR and the Holocaust Prism" (2016) 26 EJIL 881, 883 (with further references). For a description of the Court's initial formal approach to equality, see Alexandra Timmer, "Toward an Anti-Stereotyping Approach for the European Court of Human Rights" (2011) 11 Human Rights LR 707, 710–11.

[12] See eg *Carvalho Pinto de Sousa Morais v Portugal* App no 17484/15 (ECtHR, July 25, 2017) para 45.

characteristics which are personal in the sense that they are innate or inherent."[13] For example, in *Inze*, the Court found that "children born in and children born out of wedlock" were placed in similar situations in respect of their inheritance rights.[14] Therefore, the respondent government was required to put forward "[v]ery weighty reasons"[15] for maintaining these differentiations in law.

The third step, the justification analysis, consists predominantly of a proportionality test. An important element of the Court's proportionality test is the "margin of appreciation doctrine" which the Court has developed in order to limit its jurisdiction vis-à-vis the member states' domestic spheres. In *Rasmussen*, the Court argued that

> [t]he scope of the margin of appreciation will vary according to the circumstances, the subject-matter and its background; in this respect, one of the relevant factors may be the existence or non-existence of common ground between the laws of the Contracting States.[16]

Consequently, the margin of appreciation is narrower when there is a consensus on the issue in question among the majority of the member states of the CoE.[17] Where such consensus has only recently developed, the Court refers to the Convention as "a living instrument, to be interpreted in the light of present-day conditions."[18] For example, in *Inze*, the respondent state's margin of appreciation was narrowed by the 1975 European Convention on the Legal Status of Children born out of Wedlock that had been ratified by the respondent state.[19] Furthermore, the Court has identified certain subjects in which it generally grants CoE member states a wide margin of appreciation, such as education, while in others, such as racial segregation, this margin is drastically limited.[20]

In areas in which the margin of appreciation is wide, the Court considers that "the national authorities are in principle better placed than the international judge to appreciate what is in the public interest."[21] By contrast, a narrow margin of appreciation requires the respondent state to put forward "very weighty reasons" to justify a difference in treatment in otherwise similar situations.[22] The margin of

[13] *Aleksandr Aleksandrov v Russia* App no 14431/06 (ECtHR, March 27, 2018) para 18; *Khamtokhu and Aksenchik v Russia* App no 60367/08 (ECtHR, January 24, 2017) para 61; similarly, *Carson v UK* [GC] ECHR 2010-II 407, para 70; *Clift v UK* App no 7205/07 (ECtHR, July 13, 2010) para 56.

[14] *Inze v Austria* App no 8695/79 (ECtHR, October 28, 1987) para 41.

[15] ibid.

[16] *Rasmussen v Denmark* App no 8777/79 (ECtHR, November 28, 1984) para 40.

[17] This was first alluded to in *Marckx v Belgium* (1979) Series A no 31, para 41, and later confirmed eg in *Kiyutin v Russia* App no 2700/10 (ECtHR, March 10, 2011) para 65.

[18] Among many: *E.B. v France* App no 43546/02 (ECtHR, January 22, 2008) para 92.

[19] *Inze* (n 14) para 41.

[20] *D.H. v Czech Republic* [GC] ECHR 2007-IV 241, para 139.

[21] *Stec v UK* [GC] ECHR 2006-VI 131, para 52.

[22] The grounds of discrimination and subject areas indicating a narrow or wide margin of appreciation are listed in Table 4.1.

appreciation may also be narrow when the distinction concerns criteria explicitly mentioned in Articles 14 ECHR and 1 of P12, such as birth, or for certain grounds covered by the term "other status," such as sexual orientation[23] or disability.[24] By contrast, the Court grants a wider margin of appreciation to the respondent state for certain other grounds, such as marital[25] or immigration[26] status.

In indirect discrimination cases, the Court's analysis has two parts: First, the applicant is required to establish a disproportionate adverse impact on a protected group of a policy or measure. Discriminatory intent is not required.[27] Reliable and significant statistical evidence of a disparate impact is usually considered sufficient by the Court.[28] However, disparate impact can also be proven without statistical evidence.[29] Furthermore, if the knowledge of the situation lies wholly or predominantly with the authorities, the Court generally applies less strict evidential rules[30] or even places a burden on the respondent state "to provide a satisfactory and convincing explanation."[31] If the Court finds that the applicant established "a rebuttable presumption that the effect of a measure or practice is discriminatory,"[32] the burden of justification shifts to the respondent state. It is then up to the government to objectively and reasonably justify the difference in treatment caused by the disparate impact of a policy or general measure.[33]

3. Empirical analysis of the ECtHR's jurisprudence on Article 14 ECHR and Article 1 of P12

3.1 Selection of cases and limitations

For the present analysis, I selected all violations and non-violations which the Commission,[34] a Committee,[35] a Chamber or the Grand Chamber (GC) found

[23] *X v Poland* App no 20741/10 (ECtHR, 16 Sep 2021) para 70.
[24] *Glor v Switzerland* ECHR 2009-III 1, para 84.
[25] *Şerife Yiğit v Turkey* App no 3976/05 (ECtHR, 2 Nov 2010) para 72.
[26] *Hode and Abdi v UK* App no 22341/09 (ECtHR, 6 Nov 2012) para 48.
[27] *D.H.* (n 20) para 184.
[28] ibid para 188.
[29] ibid.
[30] ibid para 186.
[31] ibid para 179.
[32] ibid para 189. Prior to this case, the Court had found tree violations of indirect discrimination without labelling them as such: *Zarb Adami* (n 10); *Aziz v Cyprus* ECHR 2004-V 201; *Thlimmenos v Greece* ECHR 2000-IV 263.
[33] *D.H.* (n 20) para 189.
[34] This concerns cases before the entry into force in 1998 of Protocol No 11 to the ECHR, restructuring the control machinery established thereby (European Treaty Series No 155). This Protocol transformed the ECtHR from its initial Commission-Court setup into a full-time court.
[35] Protocol No 14 to the ECHR, amending the control system of the Convention (Council of Europe Treaty Series no 194), introduced committees of three judges. Only seven of the violations analyzed were found by a committee.

of Article 14 ECHR or Article 1 of P12 before 2021 using the ECtHR's HUDOC database.[36] While the Court's case law also includes admissibility decisions issued by the different bodies, the search was narrowed to the Court's judgments in substance. No Advisory Opinion relating to Article 14 ECHR or Article 1 of P12 was issued during the time period considered for this study.[37] Nevertheless, the Court has since issued two Advisory Opinions in the context of cases with which it had previously dealt under Article 14 ECHR.[38]

Violations and non-violations of Articles 14 ECHR and 1 of P12 that were essentially based on the findings in a previous case were excluded. Where a Chamber judgment was followed by a GC judgment, only the GC judgment was considered. Finally, since the Court issues its judgments in English or French and not all judgments are translated,[39] those that had not been translated to English were analyzed using the French language version, while the remainder was analyzed using the English language version.

The methodology employed has several limitations. In particular, the present study does not consider cases relating to non-discrimination that were analyzed under Convention provisions other than Article 14 ECHR and Article 1 of P12. Like the exclusion of admissibility decisions, the study's limitation to Articles 14 ECHR and 1 of P12 was necessary to make the number of analyzed cases manageable and to secure comparability with the other jurisdictions analyzed in this book. The interplay of Article 14 ECHR with other provisions is particularly strong in the context of the right to life (Article 2 ECHR), the prohibition of ill-treatment (Article 3 ECHR), the right to a fair trial (Article 6 ECHR), and the right to respect for private and family life (Article 8 ECHR). Cases concerning equality and discrimination in these contexts may be analyzed under the respective provision only,

[36] <https://hudoc.echr.coe.int/eng> accessed 20 January 2025.

[37] Nevertheless, one Advisory Opinion dealing with a case of gestational surrogacy had touched upon matters deeply intertwined with equality and non-discrimination: *Advisory opinion concerning the recognition in domestic law of a legal parent–child relationship between a child born through a gestational surrogacy arrangement abroad and the intended mother* (requested by the French Court of Cassation, request no P16-2018-001, April 10, 2019). See Lydia Bracken, "The ECtHR's First Advisory Opinion: Implications for Cross-border Surrogacy Involving Male Intended Parenty" (2021) 21 Medical Law International 3, 15–18.

[38] *Advisory Opinion on the difference in treatment between landowners' associations "having a recognised existence on the date of the creation of an approved municipal hunters' association" and landowners' associations set up after that date* (requested by the French Conseil d'État, request no P16-2021-002, 13 July 2022) regarding *Chassagnou v France* [GC] ECHR 1999-III 21; *Advisory opinion on the applicability of statutes of limitation to prosecution, conviction and punishment in respect of an offence constituting, in substance, an act of torture* (requested by the Armenian Court of Cassation, request no P16-2021-001, April 26, 2022) regarding *Virabyan v Armenia* App no 40094/05 (ECtHR, October 2, 2012).

[39] Rule 76 of the Rules of Court (October 30, 2023) stipulates: "Unless the Court decides that a judgment shall be given in both official languages, all judgments shall be given either in English or in French," with the exception of GC judgments, which are given in both official languages, in which case "both language versions shall be equally authentic."

without the Court conducting a separate analysis under Articles 14 ECHR or 1 of P12. Assuming that the Court is not systematic in its case-by-case decisions on this matter,[40] this might lead to a certain bias.[41]

3.2 Results

Employing the filters described above to all judgments (not including admissibility decisions) concerning Articles 14 ECHR or 1 of P12 before 2021 using the ECtHR's HUDOC database resulted in 203 violations (42% of selected cases) and 280 non-violations (58% of selected cases). Only the violations were looked at more closely. This represents another limitation of the study. Nevertheless, the results of this closer analysis are presented in the following two subsections. Particular focus is placed on the grounds of distinction and the subject matter of the cases in which violations were found, as well as the types of reasoning employed by the Court and the margin of appreciation granted to respondent states in these cases.

3.2.1 Types of reasoning

The reasoning the Court performs under Articles 14 ECHR and 1 of P12 can be roughly grouped into five categories: equality, reasonableness, arbitrariness, procedural and indirect discrimination. All categories except indirect discrimination feature both suspect and non-suspect criteria. In the following, the categories will be presented first with respect to suspect criteria and then briefly with respect to non-suspect criteria.

Of the total of 203 violations, 87% concern suspect criteria of distinction. Twenty-three percent of the violations concerning suspect criteria were found employing more of an arbitrariness analysis than following the steps indicated above. This means that the Court found no objective and reasonable justification and concluded that there had been a violation of Articles 14 ECHR or 1 of P12 in a rather summary fashion. These 23% include cases in which the only attempt at a justification by the respondent government was essentially based on the prohibited ground.

[40] *Virabyan* (n 38) para 220, referring to *Nachova v Bulgaria* ECHR 2005-VII 1, para 161; *Bekos and Koutropoulos v Greece* ECHR 2005-XIII 1, para 70, among others.

[41] See eg Margarita S Ilieva, "J.I. v Croatia: Violence against Roma Women—Discrimination Not an Issue?" EJIL:Talk! (December 6, 2022) <https://www.ejiltalk.org/j-i-v-croatia-violence-against-roma-women-discrimination-not-an-issue/?utm_source=mailpoet&utm_medium=email&utm_campaign=ejil-talk-newsletter-post-title_2> accessed October 31, 2023; Eva Bredler, "Article 14 ECHR in the Closet: What the European Court of Human Rights Missed in Fedotova v Russia" Völkerrechtsblog (August 21, 2021) <https://voelkerrechtsblog.org/article-14-echr-in-the-closet/> accessed January 20, 2025.

One-fifth of the violations concerning suspect criteria concerns states' failure to take the necessary procedural steps to investigate racist,[42] political,[43] and religious[44] motives, mostly behind killings and ill-treatment.[45] At the center of the cases in this subset, we regularly find an analysis of whether the impugned treatment had been "motivated by a discriminatory attitude and stereotypes."[46] In these cases, the Court tests whether the respondent state met the procedural requirements under another article of the Convention.

In 21 (12%) of the violations concerning suspect criteria, the Court held that the distinction at issue had been unreasonable. Also part of this set are three violations in which the Court considered that the respondent state had "failed in its positive obligation to ensure equal opportunities for persons with disabilities [by ensuring] 'reasonable accommodation' that would help correct factual inequalities which are unjustified and therefore amount to discrimination."[47]

Finally, 25 violations were found in situations of indirect discrimination. This makes up to 12% of total violations and 14% of the violations concerning suspect criteria. Three quarters of these were found in or after 2010. In 15 of the cases concerning indirect discrimination, the Court did not explicitly refer to the concept.[48] Hence, in the majority of cases in which the Court found a violation of the ECHR's equality norms in situations of indirect discrimination, the Court avoided addressing the issue directly. This confirms the Court's hesitancy regarding indirect discrimination, in particular prior to *D.H. v Czech Republic*. Domestic violence has

[42] *Lingurar v Romania* App no 58886/15 (ECtHR, October 16, 2018); *Boacă v Romania* App no 40355/11 (ECtHR, January 12, 2016); *Škorjanec v Croatia* App no 25536/14 (ECtHR, March 28, 2007); *Grigoryan and Sergeyeva v Ukraine* App no 63409/11 (ECtHR, March 28, 2017); *Ciorcan v Romania* App nos 29414/09 and 44841/09 (ECtHR, January 17, 2017); *Antayev v Russia* App no 37966/07 (ECtHR, July 3, 2014); *Abdu v Bulgaria* App no 26827/08 (ECtHR, March 11, 2014); *Yotova v Bulgaria* App no 43606/04 (ECtHR, October 23, 2012); *Fedorchenko and Lozenko v Ukraine* App no 387/03 (September 20, 2012); *Makhashevy v Russia* App no 20546/07 (ECtHR, July 31, 2012); *B.S. v Spain* App no 47159/08 (ECtHR, July 24, 2012); *Turan Cakir v Belgium* App no 44256/06 (ECtHR, March 10, 2009); *Petropoulou-Tsakiris v Greece* App no 44803/04 (ECtHR, December 6, 2007); *Cobzaru v Romania* App no 48254/99 (ECtHR, July 26, 2007); *Angelova and Iliev v Bulgaria* App no 55523/00 (ECtHR, July 26, 2007); *Bekos and Koutropoulos* (n 40); *Nachova* (n 40).

[43] *Virabyan* (n 38).

[44] *Begheluri v Georgia* App no 28490/02 (ECtHR, October 7, 2014); *Milanović v Serbia* App no 44614/07 (ECtHR, December 14, 2010); *Members (97) of the Gldani Congregation of Jehovah's Witnesses v Georgia* App no 71156/01 (ECtHR, May 3, 2007).

[45] *Sampani v Greece* App no 59608/09 (ECtHR, December 11, 2012); *Sampanis v Greece* App no 32526/05 (ECtHR, June 5, 2008); *Lavida v Greece* App no 7973/10 (ECtHR, May 30, 2013); *D.H.* (n 20); *Oršuš v Croatia* [GC] ECHR 2010-II 247; *Horváth and Kiss v Hungary* App no 11146/11 (ECtHR, January 29, 2013).

[46] *Beizaras and Levickas v Lithuania* App no 41288/15 (ECtHR, January 14, 2020) para 124 (failure to properly investigate hateful comments based on sexual orientation, posted on the applicant's social network page, para 67).

[47] *G.L. v Italy* App no 59751/15 (ECtHR, September 10, 2020) paras 32 and 34; *Enver Şahin v Turkey* App no 23065/12 (ECtHR, January 30, 2018); *Guberina v Croatia* App no 23682/13 (ECtHR, March 22, 2016).

[48] The standard phrase first used by the Court in *Zarb Adami* (n 10) para 80 is "a policy or general measure [that] has disproportionately prejudicial effects on a group of people . . . even if it is not specifically aimed or directed at that group."

been treated both as indirect discrimination (five violations) and as a particular form of direct discrimination resulting from the state's failure to meet its due diligence obligations (five violations),[49] depending on the facts of the case.

Only 13% of all violations concerned non-suspect criteria of distinction. Nine (35%) of these violations concerned differentiations which the Court in essence found to be arbitrary.[50] The term "arbitrariness" was only mentioned in one of these reasonings.[51] More commonly, the Court stated, for instance, that it did not see any reason justifying the difference in treatment or that the respondent government had not advanced any justification to that end, and consequently found a violation.[52] In *Cassar*, the Court found that the decision to increase fixed rents of under 185 euros annually had been "solely based on a random choice of a numerical figure, with no real legitimate aim save that of creating an artificial distinction."[53]

In four cases concerning non-suspect criteria, the Court found a violation because it deemed the distinction in question to be unreasonable.[54] In contrast to the "arbitrariness violations," the Court considered the government's arguments in some depth before finding that the distinction had been unreasonable.

One violation concerning a non-suspect distinction concerned the failure to meet the procedural requirements of Article 11 ECHR (freedom of assembly and association) in a case concerning discrimination on the ground of union membership.[55] Finally, in the remaining half of the violations not involving a suspect criterion, the Court adhered to its standard equality formula. The identified grounds on which an unjustified distinction had been made were, for instance, the size of land owned or the ability to erect a costly, impenetrable fence,[56] whether one was renting from the state or from a private landlord,[57] being a pre-trial detainee rather than a convicted prisoner[58] or a former KGB officer.[59]

[49] *Eremia v the Republic of Moldova* App no 3564/11 (ECtHR, May 28, 2013) para 89.

[50] *Cassar v Malta* App no 50570/13 (ECtHR, January 30, 2018); *Topčić-Rosenberg v Croatia* App no 19391/11 (ECtHR, November 14, 2013); *M.C. v Italy* App no 5376/11 (ECtHR, September 3, 2013); *Gülay Çetin v Turkey* App no 44084/10 (ECtHR, March 5, 2013); *G.N. v Italy* App no 43134/05 (ECtHR, December 1, 2009); *Weller v Hungary* App no 44399/05 (ECtHR, March 31, 2009) (violation regarding the first applicant); *Driha v Romania* App no 29556/02 (ECtHR, February 21, 2008); *Beian v Romania (No 1)* App no 30658/05 (ECtHR, December 6, 2007); *Pine Valley Developments Ltd v Ireland* App no 12742/87 (ECtHR, November 29, 1991).

[51] *G.N.* (n 50) para 129.

[52] *Pine Valley Developments Ltd* (n 50) para 64; *Driha* (n 50) para 38; *Weller* (n 50) para 35; *Gülay Çetin* (n 50) para 132; *M.C.* (n 50) paras 100–102; *Cassar* (n 50) paras 79–80.

[53] *Cassar* (n 50) para 79.

[54] *Varnas v Lithuania* App no 42615/06 (ECtHR, July 9, 2013); *Hode and Abdi v UK* (n 26); *Bucheň v The Czech Republic* App no 36541/97 (ECtHR, November 26, 2002); *Grande Oriente d'Italia di Palazzo Giustiniani v Italy (No. 2)* App no 26740/02 (ECtHR, August 2, 2001).

[55] *Danilenkov v Russia* ECHR 2009-III 365.

[56] *Chassagnou* (n 38).

[57] *Larkos v Cyprus* [GC] ECHR 1999-I 557.

[58] *Chaldayev v Russia* App no 33172/16 (ECtHR, May 28, 2019); *Laduna v Slovakia* ECHR 2011-VI 127.

[59] *Sidabras and Džiautas v Lithuania* ECHR 2004-VIII 367.

3.2.2 Grounds of distinction, subject areas, and margin of appreciation

The most frequent suspect criteria concerned are race (46 violations), sex (32 violations), sexual orientation (24 violations), and religion (22 violations), followed by birth out of wedlock (14 violations). Within these categories, particular types of violations dominated: Three-quarters of all violations of the prohibition of racial discrimination were perpetrated against Roma, almost half of the violations of the prohibition of discrimination on the ground of religion concerned Jehova's Witnesses, one-third of violations on the ground of sex concerned domestic violence against women, and another third concerned disadvantages for men. The latter related to less favorable visiting rights in prison[60] and less prison leave,[61] lack of a statutory right to parental leave and parental allowance for servicemen,[62] lack of a tax allowance[63] and fewer social benefits[64] for widowers, a disproportionate requirement to perform jury service,[65] having to contribute to a child care benefits system[66] and pay a fire service levy,[67] not being able to use one's own name before the family name,[68] and not being eligible for family reunification.[69] In general, even where the Court mentions several factors, it does not address multiple and intersectional discrimination and, with the exception of *Wessels-Bergervoet*, performs its analysis limited to one criterion of distinction.[70]

The most frequent subject areas are criminal law (68 violations), family (42 violations), social benefits (23 violations), and education and public service (13 violations each), followed by immigration (10 violations). The Court's determination of the margin of appreciation enjoyed by the respondent state in a given case is based either on the criterion on which the alleged discrimination is based, or on the subject matter. Where the distinction concerns a member of a vulnerable group in the context of the society of the respondent state, the Court generally considers the margin of appreciation to be reduced. Criterion classes that, in the context of the Court's jurisprudence, indicate that the applicant was a member of a

[60] *Belyayev v Ukraine* App no 24620/02 (ECtHR, January 25, 2007).
[61] *Ēcis v Latvia* App no 12879/09 (ECtHR, January 10, 2019).
[62] *Konstantin Markin v Russia* App no 30078/06 (ECtHR, March 22, 2012).
[63] *Hobbs, Richard Walsh and Geen v UK* App nos 63684/00, 63475/00, 63484/00 and 63468/00 (ECtHR, November 14, 2006).
[64] *Zeman v Austria* App no 23960/02 (ECtHR, June 29, 2006); *Willis v UK* ECHR 2002-IV 311.
[65] *Zarb Adami* (n 10).
[66] *Van Raalte v the Netherlands* ECHR 1997-I.
[67] *Karlheinz Schmidt v Germany* (1994) Series A no 291B.
[68] *Burghartz v Switzerland* (1994) Series A no 280B.
[69] *Abdulaziz, Cabales and Balkandali v UK* (1985) Series A no 94, para 78.
[70] *Wessels-Bergervoet v The Netherlands* ECHR 2002-IV 239 (explicit: sex and marital status); *S.L. v Austria* ECHR 2003-I 71 (explicit: sexual orientation; implicit: sex); *Konstantin Markin* (n 62) (explicit: sex; implicit: profession); *B.S.* (n 42) (explicit: race, implicit: sex and profession); *Alković v Montenegro* App no 66895/10 (ECtHR, 5 Dec 2017) (explicit: ethnic origin; implicit: religion); *Carvalho Pinto de Sousa Morais* (n 12) (explicit: sex; implicit: age).

Table 4.1 Simplified margin of appreciation doctrine

Narrow	Wide if domestic balancing	Wide
birth out of wedlock	family life	armed forces
disability	freedom of assembly	consulting trade unions
nationality	freedom of expression	criminal policy
particularly vulnerable	press	education/curricula
race (ethnic origin)	private life	economic or social strategy
religion		electoral matters
sex		national security
sexual orientation		right to property

vulnerable group are sex,[71] sexual orientation,[72] ethnic origin,[73] disability,[74] mental faculties,[75] and positive HIV status.[76] The current margin of appreciation doctrine in the context of Article 14 ECHR[77] is summarized in a simplified manner in Table 4.1.

In the areas listed in the middle column of Table 4.1, the Court requires member states to apply certain minimum standards when dealing with an infringement of a Convention right. These standards may be defined in the Court's jurisprudence or by other CoE bodies.[78] As long as the domestic authorities duly considered these standards when balancing the various interests at stake, the Court grants the respondent state a wide margin of appreciation. Where the Court finds that the domestic authorities balanced these standards with the other interests in question in a comprehensible and proportionate manner, it will find that the applicant's rights were touched in a manner that did not violate the Convention.

In light of the most frequent criteria and subject areas and the margins applicable to them, it is obvious that the Court is frequently compelled to find a balance between different aspects advocating for either a wide or a narrow margin and to

[71] *Abdulaziz, Cabales and Balkandali* (n 69); *Burghartz* (n 68).

[72] *Schalk and Kopf v Austria* ECHR 2010-IV 409; *Smith and Grady v UK* ECHR 2000-VI 45.

[73] *D.H.* (n 20); *Timishev v Russia* App nos 55762/00 and 55974/00 (ECtHR, 13 Dec 2005).

[74] *Glor* (n 24).

[75] *Alajos Kiss v Hungary* App no 38832/06 (ECtHR, May 20, 2010); *Shtukaturov v Russia* App no 44009/05 (ECtHR, March 27, 2008).

[76] *Kiyutin* (n 17) para 63 (HIV-positive status).

[77] See also Steven Greer, *The Margin of Appreciation: Interpretation and Discretion under the European Convention on Human Rights* (CoE 2000). There, sex, religion, and nationality are described as "prima facie discriminatory" (11) and a wide margin is considered to apply with regards to the right to property (11 and 12).

[78] See eg *Cernea v Romania* App no 43609/10 (ECtHR, February 27, 2018) regarding the Venice Commission.

decide which one to apply to the particular case: The subject area may be one in which the Court highlights its subsidiary role, while the criterion of distinction calls for a narrow margin of appreciation.[79]

Lastly, a consensus among CoE member states on a particular issue is sometimes simply noted, for instance in the cases of sex-based discrimination[80] and discrimination of children born out of wedlock.[81] Other times it is assessed by way of a comparative study of the laws in the different CoE member states[82] or the Court cites "relevant international instruments and reports"[83] to indicate that states had agreed on a particular standard on the international level.[84] The "living instrument," too, is sometimes simply "observed," without elaborating on it or contextualizing it in the facts of the case.[85]

While European consensus is allegedly used to determine the stringency of the Court's proportionality assessment, a proportionality analysis was only performed in the minority of the violations in which the Court noted a European consensus (36% of violations concerning a suspect criterion, 42% of violations concerning a non-suspect criterion). A European consensus or standard concerning a particular issue seems instead to be used by the Court to justify the respondent state's reduced margin of appreciation:

In 47% of the violations in which the Court addressed the issue of a European consensus or standard, the respondent state's margin of appreciation was considered narrow. By contrast, in only 12% of violations in which the Court mentioned the same issue, the respondent state's margin of appreciation was considered wide. More generally, the Court tends to use the issue of a European consensus or standard in connection with state's margin of appreciation: It was addressed in 64% of violations found where the respondent state's margin of appreciation was considered narrow and in 46% of violations found where it was considered wide. By contrast, the Court only mentioned the issue of a European consensus or standard in 37.5% of times when it did not specify the respondent state's margin of appreciation.

[79] See eg immigration and sex-based discrimination in the case of *Abdulaziz, Cabales and Balkandali* (n 69); or social benefits ("economic or social strategy") and sex in *Stec* (n 21).

[80] See eg *Abdulaziz, Cabales and Balkandali* (n 69).

[81] See eg *Mazurek v France* ECHR 2000-II 1; *Pla and Puncernau v Andorra* App no 69498/01 (ECtHR, July 13, 2004); *Brauer v Germany* App no 3545/04 (ECtHR, May 28, 2009).

[82] See eg in *I.B.* (n 9), paras 82–83.

[83] *Kiyutin* (n 17) para 67.

[84] See eg in *Altinay v Turkey* App no 37222/04 (ECtHR, 9 July 2013) paras 43–44 (Committee of Ministers' Recommendation); *I.B.* (n 9) para 84 (United Nations Committee of Economic, Social and Cultural Rights and International Labour Organization Recommendation no 200 concerning HIV and AIDS and the World of Work); *Kiyutin* (n 17) paras 36–38, 65 (UNAIDS survey).

[85] See eg *E.B.* (n 18) para 92.

4. Conclusion

Overall, the ECtHR largely seems to follow the equality as non-discrimination model. While we did not measure success rates for different categories of distinction, the vast majority of successful cases concerns a suspect classification. In this context, it is interesting to note that the suspect criterion leading to most violations is race. This is noteworthy because race only plays a marginal role in most jurisdictions analyzed in this book outside the United States. While the number of successful cases not involving a suspect classification is not insignificant, most of these cases concern clearly arbitrary or at least unreasonable government conduct—a problem that is also addressed in many other jurisdictions following the equality as non-discrimination model.

This medium-level deference applied by the ECtHR is most likely to be due to its position as an international human rights court. The Court already faces quite significant resistance in some CoE member states where it is perceived as interfering with political affairs. This is most visible in the United Kingdom where a withdrawal from the ECHR has significant political support in the Conservative Party.[86] If the Court applied a non-deferential approach to the non-discrimination norms of the Convention and more frequently targeted distinctions not based on suspect classifications, it would risk even stronger involvement political clashes across Europe. Yet it is central to the Court's legitimacy that it corrects the gravest forms of discriminations, such as discriminations based on race, sex, sexual orientation, or religion. If it did not intervene in such cases, it would make itself irrelevant and also lose the support of more progressive members of the political spectrum in various member states.

[86] See Merris Amos, "The Future of Human Rights Law in the United Kingdom" (2019) 6 J International & Comparative Law 87, 96–99.

5
European Union

Niels Petersen

1. Introduction

The guarantee of equality and non-discrimination is one of the cornerstones of the EU legal order. In certain respects, however, the equality guarantees in the EU treaties differ significantly from equality norms in international human rights treaties and domestic constitutions. First, equality in the EU has historically been issue specific. Initially, the EU did not have a general equality or non-discrimination guarantee. Rather, it was concerned with specific kinds of discriminations that were obstacles to achieving a common market. This concerned, in particular, discrimination based on nationality, which is covered by Article 18 of the Treaty on the Functioning of the European Union (TFEU) and Article 21 (2) of the EU Charter of Fundamental Rights (EUChFR) as well as the freedom of movement provisions–guaranteeing the free movement of goods, workers, and services, and freedom of establishment. In the effort to establish a European single market, policing discriminations based on nationality is vital to prevent protectionist measures undermining the project.[1]

Moreover, the EU has a provision guaranteeing equal pay for men and women, which is guaranteed in Article 157 TFEU. Originally, this provision also had an instrumental character as it was aimed at easing competitive pressure from supposedly cheaper female labor.[2] However, the Court of Justice has quickly developed this guarantee into a general prohibition of sex discrimination in the area of employment-related benefits.[3] On the level of EU primary law, a broader non-discrimination clause focusing also on other suspect characteristics has only been introduced with the EUChFR, which was adopted in 2000 and gained direct legal force in 2009 with the Treaty of Lisbon.[4] Today, a general non-discrimination guarantee is contained in Article 21(1) EUChFR.

[1] See Mark Bell, "EU Anti-Discrimination Law: Navigating Sameness and Difference" in Paul Craig and Gráinne De Búrca (eds), *The Evolution of EU Law* (OUP 2021) 651.
[2] Olivier De Schutter, "Three Models of Equality and European Anti-Discrimination Law" (2006) 57 Northern Ireland Legal Quarterly 1, 5–6.
[3] Seminally Case 43/75 *Defrenne (No. 2)* [1976] ECR 456, para 10.
[4] See art 6(1) of the Treaty on European Union (TEU).

Niels Petersen, *European Union* In: *Equality's Guardians*. Edited by: Niels Petersen, Oxford University Press.
 DOI: 10.1093/9780198961109.003.0005

Next to these non-discrimination norms, the Court of Justice has also developed a general principle of equal treatment.[5] In its initial decisions, the Court merely stated the existence of a non-discrimination principle without justifying its origins.[6] Later, it derived the principle of equality from Article 40(2) TFEU, which prohibits a discrimination between producers and consumers in the area of agriculture. However, the Court argued that the specific provision in Article 40(2) TFEU was only an expression of a more general principle of equality.[7] Today, the principle of equal treatment is enshrined in Article 20 EUChFR. Finally, there are several anti-discrimination provisions of EU secondary law that focus on specific issues and complement the treaty guarantees. The most important of these legislative efforts is Council Directive 2000/78/EC on equal treatment in employment and occupation.[8]

A second important difference of equality in the European Union is its restriction to the field of application of EU law. While domestic constitutions and international human rights treaties usually cover the totality of state authority, the reach of EU equality provisions is limited. They only apply to member states if the latter act within the realm of EU law, for example by implementing an EU directive. This restriction also explains why the scope of EU anti-discrimination law was originally limited. Even today, Article 21(1) EUChFR does not establish an all-encompassing prohibition of discrimination. Therefore, certain kinds of discriminations, such as discriminations based on sex or nationality, are much more prominent in the EU case law than other suspect characteristics that are frequently addressed in domestic case law because the latter are often not covered by EU law.

The definition of the scope of application of EU law varies in different areas. For the EUChFR, Article 51(1) extends the obligations of the Charter to member states to the extent that these are "implementing Union law." The scope of application of the general prohibition of discrimination based on nationality in Article 18 TFEU is arguably slightly broader: According to the Court of Justice, the guarantee already applies when a Union citizen makes use of his or her freedom of movement in Article 21 TFEU and is lawfully present in another member state.[9] Finally, Article 157 TFEU is directly applicable to all situations coming within its scope; that is, any kinds of pay discriminations based on gender—regardless of whether they have been imposed by a member state or by a private employer.[10]

[5] Case 17/61 *Klöckner-Werke* [1962] ECR 326, 345; Case 19/61 *Mannesmann AG v High Authority of the ECSC* [1962] ECR 357, 375; Case 117/76 *Ruckdeschel* [1977] ECR 160, para 7.

[6] See *Klöckner-Werke* (n 5) 345; *Mannesmann* (n 5) 375.

[7] *Ruckdeschel* (n 5) para 7.

[8] Council Directive 2000/78/EC of 27 November 2000 establishing a general Framework for equal treatment in employment and occupation.

[9] Case C-85/96 *Martinez Sala* [1998] ECR I-2708, paras 61–64; Case C-274/96 *Bickel und Franz* [1998] ECR I-7650, para 15; Case C-184/99 *Grzelczyk* [2001] ECR I-6193, paras 32–36.

[10] *Defrenne (No. 2)* (n 3) para 39; Case 129/79 *Macarthys v Smith* [1980] ECR 1276.

The third characteristic that distinguishes the EU legal order from international human rights treaties and domestic constitutions is that it has two distinct set of addressees—the EU member states and the EU institutions themselves. This is primarily relevant for the scope of application for equality norms: While the scope with regards to member states is limited, the equality guarantees apply to all actions of EU institutions. But it might matter also in a more subtle way. It is often suspected that the Court of Justice applies more deference to EU institutions than to EU member states.[11]

The analysis of this chapter is limited in scope. On the one hand, we only focus on "pure" equality guarantees; therefore, the implicit equality guarantees contained in the freedom of movement provisions will not be analyzed in a systematic manner. Analyzing all freedom of movement cases would have been beyond the scope of this chapter because of the sheer number of cases. Furthermore, the mechanism should not work differently than in the context of Article 18 TFEU and Article 21(2) EUChFR. On the other hand, this chapter will focus—in line with the other chapters—only on constitutional guarantees, the equality norms enshrined in EU primary law. This means that there will be no systematic analysis of EU secondary law. Cases dealing with directives or regulations will only be included in the quantitative analysis if the Court of Justice sees these secondary equality norms as an expression of constitutional guarantees.

In the following, we will first look at the general doctrine that the Court of Justice has developed to implement the equality and non-discrimination guarantees of the EU treaty. In the next step, we will look at the results of the empirical analysis. Subsequently, we will explain the shape of the doctrine and the empirical findings. The final part concludes.

2. The equality doctrine of the Court of Justice of the European Union

2.1 Development of the equality doctrine

The general structure of the equality test is similar across the different equality provisions. The Court usually applies a two-step test. It first determines whether there is a difference in treatment of comparable situations. If it finds such a difference in treatment, it analyzes in a second step whether this difference is objectively

[11] See eg Christoph Herrmann, "Europarechtliche Fragen der deutschen Investitionskontrolle" (2019) 22 Zeitschrift für europarechtliche Studien 429, 465. See also Eckhard Pache, "Der Grundsatz der Verhältnismäßigkeit in der Rechtsprechung der Gerichte der Europäischen Gemeinschaften" [1999] Neue Zeitschrift für Verwaltungsrecht 1033, 1038–40; Martin Nettesheim, "Grundrechtliche Prüfdichte durch den EuGH" [1995] Europäische Zeitschrift für Wirtschaftsrecht 106, 107 (criticizing the deferential approach of the Court of Justice with regard to EU institutions).

justified. However, there are differences in the details so that we will have a closer, separate look at the interpretation of the different provisions.

The basic test for the principle of general principle of equality was first established in 1962 in *Mannesmann*.[12] It has been slightly reformulated in *Ruckdeschel* in 1977, where the Court argued that "[t]his principle requires that similar situations shall not be treated differently unless differentiation is objectively justified."[13] This test is still used today in similar form in the context of Article 20 EUChFR.[14] In many cases in which the Court of Justice applies the general principle of equality it finds that the two situations which are supposedly treated unequally are actually not comparable.[15] In these cases, it does not enter into the justification analysis. If it finds an unequal treatment, it regularly allows a broad margin of discretion to member states[16] and to EU institutions[17] in the justification analysis. In many judgments, there are explicit or implicit proportionality considerations[18] even if the Court of Justice does not systematically apply a proportionality test.[19]

With regards to non-discrimination norms, the Court of Justice also follows the two-step structure. In a first step, it asks whether there was a difference in treatment based on one of the concerned suspect characteristics, such as nationality in the context of Article 18 TFEU, sex for Article 157 TFEU, or one of the characteristics mentioned in Article 21 EUChFR.[20] Next to nationality and sex, age,[21]

[12] *Mannesmann* (n 5) 375.

[13] *Ruckdeschel* (n 5) para 7.

[14] See eg Case C-263/21, *Ametic* EU:C:2022:644, para 56.

[15] See eg Case C-149/96 *Portugal v Council* [1999] ECR I-8395, para 92; Case C-189/01 *Jippes* [2001] ECR I-5689, para 130; Case C-210/03, *Swedish Match I* [2004] ECR I-11893, para 71; Case C-250/11 *Lietuvos geležinkeliaim* EU:C:2012:496, para 46; Case C-477/14 *Pillbox 38* EU:C:2016:324, para 42; Case C-151/17 *Swedish Match II* EU:C:2018:938, para 29.

[16] See eg Case C-195/12 *IBV & Cie* EU:C:2013:598, para 80; Case C-143/16 *Abercombie & Fitch Italia* EU:C:2017:566, para 46.

[17] See eg Case C-267/88 *Wuidart* [1990] ECR I-435, para 18; *Jippes* (n 15) para 80; Case C-510/06 P *Archer Daniels Midland v Commission* [2009] ECR I-1843, para 82; Case C-59/11 *Association Kokopelli* EU:C:2012:447, para 39; Cases C-517/19 P and C-518/19 P *Alvarez y Bejarano and Others v Commission* EU:C:2021:240, para 53.

[18] See eg Case C-292/97 *Karlsson* [2000] ECR I-2737, para 45; Case C-535/03 *Unitymark and North Sea Fishermen's Organization* [2006] ECR I-2689, para 60; Case C-313/04 *Franz Egenberger* [2006] ECR I-6331, para 39; Case C-127/07 *Arcelor Atlantique et Lorraine* [2008] ECR I-9895, para 65; Case C-234/12 *Sky Italia* EU:C:2013:496, para 26.

[19] See Johanna Croon, "Comparative Institutional Analysis, the European Court of Justice and the General Principle of Non-Discrimination—or—Alternative Tales on Equality Reasoning" (2013) 19 ELJ 153, 154–58 (arguing that the Court of Justice implicitly applies three different standards of scrutiny).

[20] For art 157 TFEU, the Court additionally requires that the difference in treatment amounts to a difference in pay for the same work. However, the Court has interpreted the scope of the provision rather extensively, see Bell (n 1) 655. For a detailed discussion of the Court of Justice's case law regarding art 157 TFEU, see Evelyn Ellis and Philippa Watson, *EU Anti-Discrimination Law* (2nd edn, OUP 2012) 180–272.

[21] See Case C-144/04 *Mangold* [2005] ECR I-9981; Case C-540/03 *Parliament v Council* [2006] ECR I-5769; Case C-555/07 *Kücükdevici* [2010] ECR I-365; Case C-297/10 *Hennigs and Mai* [2011] ECR I-7965; Case C-476/11 *HK Danmark* EU:C:2013:590; Case C-432/14 *O* EU:C:2015:643; Case C-441/14 *DI* EU:C:2016:278; Case C-190/16 *Fries* EU:C:2017:513; *Abercombie & Fitch Italia* (n 16); Case C-49/18 *Escribano Vindel* EU:C:2019:106; Case C-24/17 *Österreichischer Gewerkschaftsbund* EU:C:2019:373; Case C-396/17 *Leitner* EU:C:2019:375; Case C-914/19 *Ministero della Giustizia*

disability,[22] and religion[23] are the most prevalent characteristics in the Court of Justice's case law. If the Court of Justice finds a distinction based on a suspect characteristic, it usually looks for a possible justification. The only situation where the Court apparently does not resort to a justification analysis are cases of direct sex discrimination.[24] By contrast, the Court has accepted a justification for direct distinctions based on nationality if the distinction is "based on objective considerations and . . . proportionate to the legitimate objective pursued."[25] Furthermore, the Court of Justice allows for justifications in indirect discrimination cases if the measure is "justified by objective factors unrelated" to the suspect characteristic in question.[26] In the justification analysis, it regularly uses the proportionality test to determine whether the measure follows a legitimate aim, is appropriate, and necessary.[27] While the Court does not always explicitly refer to proportionality *stricto sensu*, it often relies on balancing considerations.[28]

2.2 Indirect discrimination and positive measures

Very early in its case law, the Court of Justice recognized that the non-discrimination provisions of the EU treaties also protect against indirect discriminations. The Court of Justice argued in *Commission v Ireland* that Article 18 TFEU "forbid[s] not only overt discrimination by reason of nationality but also all covert forms of discrimination which, by the application of other criteria of differentiation, lead in fact to the same result."[29] In the concrete case, the Court argued

(Notaries) EU:C:2021:430; Case C-304/21 *Ministero dell'Interno (age limit for the recruitment of police officers)* EU:C:2022:897; Case C-569/21 *Ministero dell'Interno (age limit for the recruitment of police psychologists)* EU:C:2022:910.

[22] See Case C-13/05 *Chacón Navas* [2006] ECR I-6467; Case C-406/15 *Milkova* EU:C:2017:198; Case C-824/19 *Komisia za zashtita ot diskriminatsia* EU:C:2021:862.

[23] See Case C-68/17 *IR* EU:C:2018:696; Case C-193/17 *Cresco Investigation* EU:C:2019:43; Case C-243/19 *Veselibas Ministrija* EU:C:2020:872.

[24] In the few cases where direct sex discrimination cases have been unsuccessful, the Court already denied the comparability of the compared groups, see Case C-132/92 *Birds Eye Walls v Roberts* [1993] ECR I-868, paras 17–23; Case C-19/02 *Hlozek* [2004] ECR I-11491, paras 44–49.

[25] Case C-191/16 *Pisciotti* EU:C:2018:222, para 46.

[26] See eg Case C-167/97 *Seymour-Smith and Perez* [1999] ECR I-623, para 65.

[27] See eg Cases C-323/95 *Hayes and Hayes v Kronenberger* [1997] ECR I-1711, para 24; *Seymour-Smith* (n 26) para 77; Case C-285/98 *Kreil* [2000] ECR I-69, para 29; Case C-224/00 *Commission v Italy* [2002] ECR I-2965, para 25; Case C-319/03 *Briheche* [2004] ECR I-8807, para 31; *Mangold* (n 21) para 65; Case C-115/08 *CEZ* [2009] ECR I-10265, para 136; Case C-341/08 *Petersen* [2010] ECR I-47, para 71; *Kücükdevici* (n 21) para 41; Case C-628/11 *International Jet Management* EU:C:2014:171, para 74; Case C-528/13 *Léger* EU:C:2015:288, para 68; Case C-824/19 *Komisia za zashtita ot diskriminatsia* EU:C:2021:862, paras 53–64.

[28] See eg *Hayes and Hayes* (n 27) para 24; Case C-224/00 *Commission v Italy* [2002] ECR I-2965, para 25; *Briheche* (n 27) para 31.

[29] Case 61/77 *Commission v Ireland* [1978] ECR 417, para 78. The Court has consistently repeated this formula in later judgments, see Case C-29/95 *Pastoors and Trans-Cap* [1997] ECR I-285, para 16; *Commission v Italy* (n 28) para 15; Case C-28/04 *Tod's and Tod's France* [2005] ECR I-5781, para 19.

that Irish specifications for fishing vessels for permission to fish in Irish waters amounted to an indirect discrimination because the Irish fleet was better adapted to these waters than foreign vessels that had traditionally fished in Irish waters.[30]

Most prominently, the Court has applied the concept of indirect discrimination in the context of Article 157 TFEU.[31] A significant number of cases concern a difference in treatment between part-time and full-time workers in a work environment where most full-time workers were men while most part-time workers were women.[32] In *Jenkins v Kingsgate*, the Court had to deal with a situation where an employer had introduced a lower hourly rate for part-time workers than for full-time workers after he was prohibited from directly discriminating between men and women.[33] The Court suspected a discriminatory intention and argued that the scheme could not be justified if "it is in reality merely an indirect way of reducing the level of pay of part-time workers on the ground that that group of workers is composed exclusively or predominantly of women."[34]

While *Jenkins v Kingsgate* could still be interpreted as a prohibition of discriminatory intention,[35] the Court of Justice clarified later in *Bilka-Kaufhaus* that discriminatory intention was not a necessary requirement.[36] Instead, it argued that the differential pay practice had to be "explained by objectively justified factors unrelated to any discrimination on grounds of sex."[37] An objective justification required that the difference in pay between part-time and full-time workers "correspond[s] to a real need on the part of the undertaking, [is] appropriate with a view to achieving the objectives pursued and [is] necessary to that end."[38]

In principle, the Court of Justice applies non-discrimination provisions symmetrically. In particular, the Court has also applied Article 157 TFEU to situations in which men claimed to have been discriminated against.[39] Nevertheless, the Court of Justice has recognized that positive measures that aim at promoting women because of structural disadvantages can be justified.[40] Yet it has adopted a rather restrictive approach.[41] The Court requires that positive measures are proportionate to

[30] *Commission v Ireland* (n 29) para 79.

[31] *Defrenne (No. 2)* (n 3) para 18.

[32] See eg Case 96/80 *Jenkins v Kingsgate* [1981] ECR 911; Case 170/84 *Bilka-Kaufhaus* [1986] ECR 1607; Case C-360/90 *Arbeiterwohlfahrt der Stadt Berlin v Bötel* [1992] ECR I-3589; Case C-457/93 *Lewark* [1996] ECR I-243; Case C-4/02 *Schönheit und Becker* [2003] ECR I-12575; Case C-256/01 *Debra Allonby* [2004] ECR I-873; Case C-285/02 *Elsner-Lakeberg* [2004] ECR I-5861; Case C-300/06 *Voß* [2007] ECR I-10573; Case C-486/18 *Praxair MRC* EU:C:2019:379.

[33] *Jenkins v Kingsgate* (n 32).

[34] ibid para 15.

[35] De Schutter (n 2) 9.

[36] *Bilka-Kaufhaus* (n 32).

[37] ibid para 30.

[38] ibid para 36.

[39] See Case C-223/19 *YS (Occupational Pensions for Managerial Staff)* EU:C:2020:753.

[40] *Briheche* (n 27) paras 29–30.

[41] Uladzislau Belavusau and Kristin Henrard, "A Bird's Eye View on EU Anti-Discrimination Law: The Impact of the 2000 Equality Directive" (2019) 20 German Law Journal 614, 632–33; Bell (n 1) 658–60.

achieve the pursued aim.[42] Furthermore, the Court argued that hiring procedures could not give automatic preference to women.[43] Instead, they could only prefer women if the latter were indeed equally qualified as men[44] and the decision took into account the specific circumstances of the individual candidates.[45]

3. Empirical analysis of the equality case law

3.1 Generating and analyzing the sample

The sample for the empirical analysis consists of the equality case law of the Court of Justice until December 31, 2022. Three limitations were applied when constructing the sample. First, the analysis only includes decisions of the Court of Justice, not decisions of the General Court (formerly the Court of First Instance). Second, as already mentioned in the introduction, the analysis is only focused on equality provisions that are part of EU primary law: the EU treaties, the EU Charter of Fundamental Rights, or the general principles of EU law as developed by the Court of Justice. By contrast, it does not contain judgments dealing exclusively with equality provisions of EU directives or regulations, except if these judgments considered provisions of EU secondary law as expressions of more general principles of EU primary law.[46] Third, the sample does not contain judgments that dealt with discriminations based on nationality, but were resolved under the free movement provisions of the TFEU, such as Articles 34, 45, 49, 56, or 63 TFEU.

To construct the sample, we performed two search queries in two different EU law databases. The first query searched for the keywords "*equal*" or "*discrimin*" in the eur-lex database.[47] The second query performed a systematic search of certain subject matters in systematic classification scheme of the curia database.[48] The subject matters that were included in the search were "equality before the law" (1.04.03.20), "non-discrimination" (1.04.03.21), "principle of equality and non-discrimination" (A-01.02.02), "prohibition of discrimination on grounds of nationality" (1.09.01 and B-01.05), "equality for men and women" (4.14.01.02 and B-15.01), and "prohibition of discrimination" in the field of agriculture (B-03.03.03).

The first search generated more than 2,000 hits while the second led to roughly 600 hits. Both searches had to be filtered manually to exclude cases in which the

[42] *Briheche* (n 27) para 31.
[43] Case C-450/93 *Kalanke* [1995] ECR I-3051, para 22.
[44] Case C-407/98 *Abrahamsson and Anderson* [2000] ECR I-5539.
[45] Case C-409/95 *Marschall* [1997] ECR I-6363, para 33.
[46] See eg *Kücükdevici* (n 21).
[47] <https://eur-lex.europa.eu/advanced-search-form.html?action=update&qid=1694140088489> accessed January 20, 2025.
[48] <https://curia.europa.eu/juris/recherche.jsf?language=en> accessed January 20, 2025.

term equality was mentioned but the Court did not deal with a potential violation of equality in substantive terms, cases exclusively dealing with secondary law, and cases exclusively concerning equality within free movement provisions. Furthermore, the quantitative analysis does not include cases in which the Court did not make a clear pronouncement on whether an equality or non-discrimination provision was violated, but in which it deferred the questions to the domestic court having initiated a preliminary reference procedure. An exception was made where the Court of Justice technically deferred the decision but gave sufficiently clear guidance to the domestic court on how to decide the concrete case. The first filtering was usually done through an analysis of the operative part of the judgment and, if necessary, a cursory look at the reasoning. But some cases could only be filtered out through a closer analysis of the reasoning.

The final sample contains 343 judgments. The first judgment contained in the sample is Case 17/61, *Klöckner-Werke*, from July 13, 1962,[49] and the last case is Case C-569/21, *Ministero dell'Interno (age limit for the recruitment of police psychologists)*, from November 17, 2022.[50] However, it is reasonable to assume that the sample does not cover all equality cases of the Court of Justice. While the two search queries produced overlapping results, there was a significant number of cases which were only produced in one of the two queries. Consequently, it is likely that there are equality cases which were missed by both search queries. However, there is no indication that the cases that might have been missed are qualitatively different from the cases that are contained in the sample. Instead, the missed judgments are likely to be simply random misses. For this reason, it is reasonable to assume that the sample is representative of the Court of Justice's equality case law.

3.2 The results of the analysis

The results of the analysis show a clear difference in the success rates of cases involving suspect classifications and those that do not involve suspect classifications. The success rate for cases not involving a suspect classification is a mere 11.82% ($N = 203$). At the same time, the success rate for cases involving a suspect classification is 67.14% ($N = 140$). This suggests that the case law of the Court of Justice is in conformity with the non-discrimination model. If we look more closely at the cases involving a suspect classification, we see that the vast majority of cases concern distinctions based on sex or nationality—mirroring the specific discrimination prohibitions in Articles 18 and 157 TFEU (see Table 5.1). The success rate for sex discrimination cases is 71.74% ($N = 46$) and for cases involving discriminations based on nationality 66.20% ($N = 71$). The only other category

[49] *Klöckner-Werke* (n 5).
[50] *Ministero dell'Interno* (n 21).

Table 5.1 Success rate of cases involving suspect classifications

Suspect criterion	No of cases	Success rate
Sex	48	68.75%
Nationality	69	68.12%
Religion	3	66.67%
Residence	1	100%
Disability	3	66.67%
Age	15	60%
Sexual orientation	1	0%
Total	140	67.14%

with a significant amount of cases is discriminations based on age. These have a success rate of 60% ($N = 15$). This signals a significant difference to other jurisdictions where age discrimination cases usually have a comparatively low success rate.

We have seen that indirect discriminations play a significant role in the case law of the Court of Justice concerning discriminations based on sex and nationality. If we distinguish in these two categories between cases involving direct and indirect discrimination, we see that the success rate for direct discrimination cases is significantly higher. Cases involving direct sex discriminations have a success rate of 80.95% ($N = 21$), while indirect discrimination cases have a success rate of 59.26% ($N = 27$). Two of the cases in which the Court did not find a violation despite a direct difference in treatment based on sex concerned bridging pensions.[51] In these cases the women did not receive the bridging pensions because they already received old-age pensions because of their earlier retirement age. Consequently, the Court argued that men and women were not in a comparable situation. In two further cases, the Court argued that the adjustment of the retirement age for women to bring it in line with the retirement age for men did not constitute sex discrimination.[52]

The pattern is similar if we look at discriminations based on nationality. Here, direct discrimination cases have a success rate of 88.24% ($N = 34$), while indirect discrimination cases have a success rate of less than 50% (17 out of 35). Some of the unsuccessful direct discrimination cases concern cases against EU institutions.[53] In these cases, nationality is less of a suspect criterion. If member states use

[51] *Birds Eye Walls* (n 24); *Hlozek* (n 24).

[52] Case C-408/92 *Smith v Avdel Systems* [1994] ECR I-4435; Case C-28/93 *van den Akker v Stichting Shell Pensioenfonds* [1994] ECR I-4527.

[53] See Case 810/79 *Überschär* [1980] ECR 2747; Case 147/79 *Hochstrass* [1980] ECR 3005.

nationality as a criterion of distinction, there is always the danger of protectionism or favoritism of its own citizens. This danger is mostly absent when EU institutions act. There are only two cases in which the Court of Justice deemed a direct distinction based on nationality by a member state justified. One case concerned a Dutch rule which gave certain financial assistance only to Dutch students. The Court argued that this restriction was justified because it was expressly allowed by EU secondary legislation.[54] Another case concerned a constitutional privilege for German citizens, according to which the latter cannot be extradited to a third state for criminal proceedings. The Court argued that there was no obligation to extend this privilege also to citizens of other EU member states.[55]

Most of the cases not involving suspect classifications concern measures by EU institutions. The majority of these measures are secondary legislation in the areas of agriculture, fisheries, or economic regulation. A significant number of cases also concern decisions of the European Commission in antitrust cases. The Court usually applies a rationality review of the measures taken by the EU legislature. While the majority of these cases are unsuccessful, the Court has found a violation of the general principle of equality by an EU institution in roughly 10% of cases (17 out of 173).[56] This success rate does not differ significantly from the success rate of other courts applying the non-discrimination model.

Nevertheless, a comparison between the success rate of cases against EU institutions and cases brought against member states, *prima facie*, confirms the suspicion of the critics that the Court of Justice applies different standards to the EU and the member states. If we only look at cases not involving suspect classifications, these have a 9.83% success rate against the EU ($N = 173$) and a 20.69% success rate against member states ($N = 29$). This means that cases against member states are more than twice as likely to be successful.

However, we have to qualify this result in several respects. First, the number of cases brought against member states is quite small. This means that small variations in the successful cases can influence the results significantly. Second, we see a historical trend. Had we asked the question in 2000, the success rate for cases against EU institutions would have been at 15.9% ($N = 69$), while there was not a single successful case against a member states, albeit the overall number of cases

[54] Case C-233/14 *Commission v Netherlands* EU:C:2016:396, para 94.

[55] *Pisciotti* (n 25).

[56] Case 114/76 *Bela-Mühle v Grows Farm* [1977] ECR 1211; Case 116/76 *Granaria* [1977] ECR 1247; Case 119/76 *Ölmühle Hamburg* [1977] ECR 1269; *Ruckdeschel* (n 5); Case 124/76 *Moulins Pont-à-Mousson* [1977] ECR 1753; Case 103/77 *Royal Scholten-Honig* [1978] ECR 2037; Case 300/86 *Van Landschoot v Mera* [1988] ECR 3443; Case 265/87 *Schräder* [1989] ECR 2237; Case C-309/89 *Codorniu v Council* [1994] ECR I-1853; Case C-122/95 *Germany v Council* [1998] ECR I-973; Case C-364/95 *T. Port* [1998] ECR I-1023; Case C-182/03 *Belgium and Forum 187 v Commission* [2006] ECR I-5479; Franz Egenberger (n 18); Case C-221/09 *AJD Tuna* [2011] ECR I-1655; Case C-335/13, *Feakins* EU:C:2014:2343; Case C-580/12 P *Guardian Industries and Guardian Europe v Commission* EU:C:2014:2363; Case C-440/19 P *Pometon v Commission* EU:C:2021:214.

was very small (N = 6). Our observations might therefore be due to a learning effect. The EU institutions have internalized the expectations of the Court of Justice and adjusted their practice accordingly. The same cannot be observed with regards to member states. The overall number of equality cases not involving a suspect classification that concerns each member state is rather small. No member state was found to violate the general principle of equality more than once. Therefore, states will not have the same learning effect as EU institutions, in particular, if we consider that some of the member states that have violated the general principle of equality are new member states that acceded to the EU after 2000, such as Hungary[57] or Romania.[58] If we only look at cases against member states that acceded to the EU before 2000, then the success rate is 16.67% (*N* = 24).[59] This is still higher than the success rate for cases brought against EU institutions, however, these are hardly the kind of numbers that would suggest a significant bias of the Court of Justice against member states.

4. Explanation of the doctrine

It is ultimately not surprising that the Court of Justice follows a non-discrimination model. This is suggested by the norm structure. The founding treaties originally only contained very specific non-discrimination norms for discriminations based on nationality and for sex discrimination in the area of employment. The vast majority of cases involving a suspect classification, therefore, concern discriminations based on sex or nationality, while other factors are rarely relevant.[60] This is also due to the scope of application of the equality norms. As the Court of Justice can only apply Article 21 EUChFR to situations within the scope of EU law, it cannot address a significant number of discriminations that do occur because they are outside the scope of the Court of Justice's jurisdiction.

One of the principal innovations of the Court of Justice was the development of an extensive case law on indirect discrimination—first with regards to nationality and later also sex discrimination. Here, the Court was apparently inspired by the *Griggs v Duke Power* decision[61] of the US Supreme Court.[62] However, the Court of Justice did not follow the example of the US

[57] Case C-135/13 *Szatmári Malom* EU:C:2014:327.

[58] Case C-278/14 *Enterprise Focused Solutions* EU:C:2015:228.

[59] See Case C-442/00 *Rodríguez Caballero* [2002] ECR I-11915; Case C-309/06 *Marks & Spencer* [2008] ECR I-2283; Case C-226/09 *Commission v Ireland* [2010] ECR I-11807; Case C-100/20 *Hauptzollamt B (Optional Tax Reduction)* EU:C:2021:716.

[60] See Belavusau and Henrard (n 41) 615 (noting that there are very few cases regarding other characteristics even when we consider EU secondary law).

[61] *Griggs v Duke Power Co* 401 US 424 (1971).

[62] Jule Mulder, "Cultural Narratives and the Application of Non-Discrimination Law" in Barbara Havelková and Mathias Möschel (eds), *Anti-Discrimination Law in Civil Law Jurisdictions* (OUP 2019) 31.

Supreme Court any further. Instead of requiring a proof of discriminatory intention, as the Supreme Court has done in its more recent decisions,[63] the Court of Justice considers proof of disparate impact sufficient for a *prima facie* indirect discrimination claim.

The second pillar of the case law of the Court of Justice consists of the general principle of equality that the Court developed early in its case law—primarily as a means to review the rationality of EU legislation. The Court then later extended this principle to review the action of member states, predominantly when the latter acted to implement EU law. While the number of cases in which the general principle of equality was invoked by the applicant is high, the overall success rate is rather small. The general principle of equality is merely a residual control mechanism that only succeeds in exceptional cases. However, this approach is not exceptional but rather typical for courts that follow the non-discrimination model.

5. Conclusion

The equality guarantees in the EU legal order have a rather peculiar history. Initially, non-discrimination guarantees had an instrumental function to secure the establishment of a common market. They concentrated only on two characteristics—sex and nationality. However, the Court has extended these guarantees beyond their instrumental *telos* to full-scale non-discrimination provisions. It has developed a detailed case law, trying to reduce direct and indirect discriminations based on sex and nationality. While the EUChFR has introduced a general prohibition of non-discrimination with a more extensive list of suspect characteristics, the number of discrimination cases that do not involve distinctions based on sex or nationality is rather small. This is most likely due to the limited scope of the EUChFR, which only applies to situations covered by EU law.

Next to the non-discrimination guarantees, the Court of Justice has also developed a general principle of equality that does not require a distinction based on a suspect characteristic. This equality guarantee is usually applied to review the rationality of EU legislation, yet the success rate of general equality cases is rather small. Consequently, the EU case law is mostly in conformity with the non-discrimination model. Non-discrimination cases, in particular regarding sex and nationality, have a rather high success rate, while the general equality guarantee only targets residual cases of legislative or executive arbitrariness.

[63] See *Wash v Davis* 426 US 229 (1976); *McCleskey v Kemp* 481 US 279 (1987).

6
United Kingdom

Niels Petersen

1. Introduction

The United Kingdom has a plethora of different equality norms. Some of these are of domestic, others of international origin. Most domestic equality norms have been merged into the Equality Act 2010. Before this, there were different acts on different kinds of discriminations—the Equal Pay Act 1970, the Sex Discrimination Act 1975, the Race Relations Act 1976, the Disability Discrimination Act 1995, and the Equality Act (Sexual Orientation) Regulations 2007. The equality norms of international origin stem from EU law (while the UK was still member of the EU) and the European Convention on Human Rights (ECHR). With regards to EU law, this mostly concerns the prohibition of discrimination based on nationality in Article 18 of the Treaty on the Functioning of the European Union (TFEU), and the principle of equal pay for male and female workers in Article 157 TFEU. The ECHR has been made part of UK domestic law through the Human Rights Act 1998.[1] The discrimination norm of the ECHR applied by UK courts is Article 14 of the ECHR, the general prohibition of discrimination.

The empirical analysis of the case law for this chapter comprised all equality cases, including cases decided under the EU treaties, the ECHR, and the Equality Act 2010 and its predecessors. However, analysis of this chapter will predominantly focus on the constitutional equality guarantees to ensure comparability with the analyses of other jurisdictions. I do not want to enter deeply into the difficult debate regarding which norms form part of the UK Constitution.[2] However, it is probably safe to say that both the EU law norms and Article 14 ECHR via the Human Rights Act have constitutional character.[3] By contrast, I have mostly excluded the Equality Act 2010 and its predecessors from the core analysis because

[1] See s 6(1) Human Rights Act 1998.

[2] On this debate, see eg Noah Feldman, "Imposed Constitutionalism" (2005) 37 Connecticut LR 857; Mark Elliott, "The United Kingdom Constitution" in Roger Masterman and Robert Schütze (eds), *The Cambridge Companion to Comparative Constitutional Law* (CUP 2019) 69.

[3] See Elliott (n 2) 79–84.

Niels Petersen, *United Kingdom* In: *Equality's Guardians*. Edited by: Niels Petersen, Oxford University Press.
 DOI: 10.1093/9780198961109.003.0006

they do not seem to have constitutional character.[4] In particular, the Equality Act 2010 does not apply to the legislature itself.[5] Furthermore, all cases in our database challenging legislation were based either on EU law or on Article 14 ECHR. While this might not settle the debate about the extent of the UK Constitution, it seems a reasonable criterion to establish comparability with the other jurisdictions contained in this volume.

The remainder of this chapter is organized as follows. First, we will analyze the equality doctrine developed by the UK Supreme Court (and its predecessor, the House of Lords). Second, we will present the results of the empirical analysis. This will show that the UK Supreme Court mostly adheres to the equality as non-discrimination model even though it applies a somewhat deferential approach. Third, we will look at possible explanations for the Supreme Court's approach to the matter of equality. Here, in particular, the influence of the European Court of Human Rights (ECtHR) looms large. The final section of this chapter will conclude.

2. The equality doctrine of the UK Supreme Court

2.1 Development of the equality doctrine

Most of the "constitutional" equality cases before the UK Supreme Court were brought under Article 14 ECHR, which forms part of UK domestic law via the Human Rights Act 1998. When analyzing this norm, the UK Supreme Court largely follows the ECtHR and applies a four-step test. First, it analyzes whether the alleged discrimination falls into the ambit of another convention right; second, whether the differential treatment was based on a "status" in the sense of Article 14 ECHR; third, whether there was a differential treatment or impact; and finally, whether the differentiation can be justified.[6]

The requirement that the differentiation has to fall into the ambit of another convention right is a particularity of Article 14 ECHR, which is an accessory guarantee that only applies if another convention right is engaged. The ECtHR has

[4] See Brice Dickson, *Human Rights and the United Kingdom Supreme Court* (OUP 2013) 312–38 (arguing that the UK judges have mostly refrained from deriving a common law rights to equality from the parliamentary equality legislation).

[5] See sch 19 of the Equality Act 2010.

[6] See Rory O'Connell, "A Dialogue on Discrimination and Equality: The UK Supreme Court and Article 14 of the ECHR" in Brice Dickson and Conor McCormick (eds), *The Judicial Mind: A Festschrift for Lord Kerr of Tonaghmore* (Bloomsbury 2021) 279, 283–89. From the case law, see eg *R (Stott) v Secretary of State for Justice* [2018] UKSC 59, para 8 (per Lady Black); *R (DA) v Secretary of State for Work and Pensions* [2019] UKSC 21, para 136 (per Lady Hale); *A v Criminal Injuries Compensation Authority* [2021] UKSC 27, para 22 (per Lord Lloyd-Jones).

traditionally interpreted the concept of ambit broadly,[7] and this broad interpretation has also been adopted by the UK Supreme Court in its more recent jurisprudence.[8] The second condition requires a differentiation to be based on status. However, the list of suspect criteria in Article 14 ECHR is open-ended and also captures differentiations based on "other" status, yet the meaning of this concept was controversial in the Supreme Court's case law. In *Clift*, Lord *Bingham of Cornhill* argued:

> As Lord Walker of Gestingthorpe pointed out in *R(Carson) v Secretary of State for Work and Pensions* [2005] UKHL 37, [2006] 1 AC 173, para 52, "or other status" (in the French version "toute autre situation") is far from precise. But plainly the language is not intended to cover differential treatment on any ground whatever.[9]

Initially, some judges argued that other status necessarily had to refer to a personal characteristic.[10] In line with this strict interpretation, the House of Lords—and later the Supreme Court—occasionally rejected the existence of a sufficient status.[11] However, following the case law of the ECtHR and, in particular, the response of the ECtHR in the *Clift* case,[12] the Court has recently adopted a more "generous meaning to other status"[13] that also includes differentiations beyond personal characteristics and the traditional canon of suspect classifications.[14]

The third condition concerns a difference in treatment or a differential impact. Here, the Court discusses whether the complainant and the comparison group are indeed in a comparable situation.[15] However, in most cases, the judges do not deny an equality challenge because of the lack of comparability.[16] Instead, the

[7] See Niels Petersen, "The Principle of Non-Discrimination in the European Convention on Human Rights and in EU Fundamental Rights Law" in Yumiko Nakanishi (ed), *Contemporary Issues in Human Rights Law: Europe and Asia* (Springer 2018) 129, 131–32 (with further references).

[8] However, the Court used to be stricter in its early case law, see eg *Secretary of State for Work and Pensions v M* [2006] UKHL 11, paras 21–30 (per Lord Nicholls of Birkenhead) paras 62–88 (per Lord Walker of Gestingthorpe).

[9] *R (Clift) v Secretary of State for the Home Department* [2006] UKHL 54, para 27 (per Lord Bingham of Cornhill).

[10] See eg ibid para 42 (per Lord Hope of Craighead); *R (RJM) v Secretary of State for Work and Pensions* [2008] UKHL 63, para 36 (per Lord Neuberger of Abbotsbury).

[11] See *Clift* (n 9) para 28 (per Lord Bingham of Cornhill); *R (HC) v Secretary of State for Work and Pensions* [2017] UKSC 73, para 31.

[12] *Clift v UK* App. No. 7205/07 (ECtHR, 13 July 2010) paras 55–63. On the influence of the ECtHR case on the UK Supreme Court, see O'Connell (n 6) 284–85 and *Stott* (n 6) para 70 (per Lady Black).

[13] *RJM* (n 10) para 42 (per Lord Neuberger of Abbotsbury).

[14] See eg *DA* (n 6) paras 38–39 (per Lord Wilson); *Gilham v Ministry of Justice* [2019] UKSC 44, para 32 (per Lady Hale).

[15] This issue was discussed extensively in *Stott* (n 6) paras 82–156 (per Lady Black), where the majority of the Court concluded that the complainant was not in a comparable situation to other prisoners.

[16] O'Connell (n 6) 288.

main emphasis of the analysis lies on the justification analysis. Here, the Court applies a proportionality test, following the ECtHR.[17] The most important aspect in the proportionality analysis is the question of the intensity of review, where the Supreme Court differentiates between two different standards.[18]

On the one hand, it requires "very weighty reasons" to justify differentiations based on sex[19] and sexual orientation.[20] On the other hand, the Court applies a more deferential "manifestly without reasonable foundation" test.[21] This test is applied in questions relating to "social and economic policy, with major implications for public expenditure."[22] This "wide measure of appreciation"[23] even trumps the considerations for stricter scrutiny if differentiations are based on a suspect classification.[24] For example, the first benefits cap case concerned indirect sex discrimination as women were disproportionately negatively affected by the challenged cap on social benefits. Nevertheless, the majority of the Court applied the more deferential "manifestly without reasonable foundation" test because the measure was situated in the area of social policy.[25]

2.2 Indirect discrimination

The House of Lords and the UK Supreme Court have recognizedthat non-discrimination guarantees also extend to indirect discriminations[26] and that a discriminatory intent is not a necessary precondition for discrimination.[27] However, the Court had to grapple with the question of how to establish differential impact. In *Seymour-Smith*, the House of Lords clarified that not any difference in effect

[17] See eg *R (JS) v Secretary of State for Work and Pensions* [2015] UKSC 16, para 14 (per Lord Reed); *R (Steinfeld) v Secretary of State for International Development* [2018] UKSC 32, paras 41–53 (per Lord Kerr). See generally O'Connell (n 6) 289.

[18] See *R (SC) v Secretary of State for Work and Pensions* [2021] UKSC 26, para 118 (per Lord Reed).

[19] ibid.

[20] *Steinfeld* (n 17) para 20 (per Lord Kerr).

[21] On this test, see O'Connell (n 6) 290–93.

[22] *JS* (n 17) para 93 (per Lord Reed).

[23] *RJM* (n 10) para 54 (per Lord Neuberger of Abbotsbury).

[24] *Humphreys v Revenue and Customs Commissioners* [2012] UKSC 18, para 19 (per Lady Hale); *JS* (n 17) para 11 (per Lord Reed).

[25] ibid para 93 (per Lord Reed).

[26] See eg ibid para 61 (per Lord Reed). This is in line with the case law of the Cour of Justice of the European Union (CJEU) and the ECtHR. See Case 61/77 *Commission v Ireland* [1978] ECR 417, para 78 (regarding art 18 TFEU); Case 43/75 *Defrenne (No. 2)* [1976] ECR 456, para 18 (regarding art 157 TFEU); *D.H. v Czech Republic* [GC] ECHR 2007-IV 241. See also Chapter 4, section 4.2 and Chapter 5, section 2.2.

[27] See Sandra Fredman, *Discrimination Law* (3rd edn, OUP 2022) 262–71 (with extensive references).

automatically constitutes an indirect discrimination.[28] Instead, the difference had to be "considerable".[29] The case dealt with a waiting period before workers enjoyed certain procedural protection against unfair dismissal. The applicants argued that there was an indirect discrimination because more women than men were disqualified from the unfair dismissal protection because of the waiting period. However, the difference was not large: In 1985, roughly nine women qualified for every ten men while in 1993 the gap had narrowed to 19 women for every 20 men.[30] The House of Lords argued that the difference was not sufficiently "considerable" to constitute indirect discrimination.[31] However, it remained unclear where exactly to draw the line.[32] In its more recent case law, the UK Supreme Court also accepts the proof of a "particular disadvantage."[33] This approach adds more flexibility in cases where statistics are not available, contested or difficult to interpret.[34] But again, it is not always clear when to assume a "particular disadvantage."[35]

A further question that has been discussed by the Court is whether indirect discriminations are subject to a different standard of justification. This was suggested by Lady Hale in the first benefits cap case:

> However, it is important to understand that what is needed to justify indirect discrimination is different from what is needed to justify direct discrimination. In direct discrimination, it is necessary to justify treating women differently from men. In indirect discrimination, by definition, women and men are treated in the same way.... It is therefore the measure itself which has to be justified, rather than the fact that women are disproportionately affected by it.[36]

However, this does not mean that any legitimate aim *per se* justifies an indirect discrimination. To the contrary, in her dissenting opinion, Lady Hale argued that saving public money and incentivizing work, while in principle legitimate aims, could not justify the concrete benefits cap in question.[37] Instead, it seems that indirect discrimination cases lead to a lower burden of justification for the government.

[28] *R v Secretary of State for Employment ex p. Seymour-Smith (No. 2)* [2000] UKHL 12.
[29] ibid (per Lord Slynn of Hadley).
[30] ibid (per Lord Slynn of Hadley).
[31] ibid (per Lord Slynn of Hadley).
[32] See Fredman (n 27) 292–93 (calling the Supreme Court's approach "clumsy").
[33] See eg *Chief Constable of West Yorkshire Police v Homer* [2012] UKSC 15, paras 11–15 (per Lady Hale).
[34] See Fredman (n 27) 293–94.
[35] See ibid 294.
[36] *JS* (n 17) para 189 (per Lady Hale).
[37] ibid paras 194–210 (per Lady Hale).

3. Empirical analysis of the equality case law

3.1 Generating and analyzing the sample

The sample was generated through a search of the Thompson Reuters Westlaw UK database. We searched for all decisions of the UK Supreme Court and the House of Lords dealing with equality or non-discrimination, from 1998 to 2021. We chose 1998 as the start date because it coincides with the enactment of the Human Rights Act 1998. After collecting the cases, research assistants went through the sample and cleared it of cases that did not deal with a potential violation of equality or non-discrimination in substance. They also wrote a one-page synopsis for each of the cases remaining in the sample. Based on these synopses, I coded all the judgments based on the criteria discussed in the introductory chapter. For the analysis, we made a distinction between core and non-core cases to which I alluded in the introduction. The core cases deal either with the equality guarantees of the EU treaties or with Article 14 ECHR. The non-core cases comprise the statutory equality cases, which are based on the Equality Act 2010 or one of its predecessors. The statistical analysis will mostly focus on the core cases. The non-core cases are only used to check whether the statutory equality guarantees might have crowded out constitutional cases and thus skewed the picture of the core cases. The overall sample comprises 49 cases if we only consider the core cases and 77 cases if we also include the non-core cases. The first core case is *Barry v Midland Bank Plc* from July 22, 1999,[38] and the last core case *Elan-Cane* from December 15, 2021.[39]

3.2 The results of the analysis

If we concentrate on the core cases, the success rate of cases involving a suspect classification is 43.75% ($N = 32$). Table 6.1 shows that the success rate differs quite significantly, depending on the type of suspect classification. Most surprisingly, there has not been a single successful sex discrimination case. Instead, all six sex discrimination cases in our core sample have been unsuccessful.[40] All these cases were indirect discrimination cases. Two concerned men who argued that certain provisions indirectly discriminated against them.[41] *Barry* was a case about a severance payment scheme, which calculated the severance payment based on the final salary and the length of service.[42] This disadvantaged employees that had formerly

[38] *Barry v Midland Bank Plc* [1999] UKHL 38.
[39] *R (Elan-Cane) v Secretary of State for the Home Department* [2021] UKSC 56
[40] See *Barry* (n 38); *Seymour-Smith* (n 28); *Secretary of State and Industry v Rutherford* [2006] UKHL 19; *Humphreys* (n 24); *JS* (n 17); *SC* (n 18).
[41] *Rutherford* (n 40); *Humphreys* (n 24).
[42] *Barry* (n 38).

Table 6.1 Success rate depending on the type of suspect classification

Suspect criterion	No of cases	Success rate
Sex	6	0%
Race	2	50%
Nationality	8	37.5%
Religion	1	0%
Residence	2	0%
Extramarital birth	1	100%
Disability	2	100%
Sexual orientation	6	50%
Marital status	4	100%
Total	32	43.75%

worked full-time but were only employed part-time when their employment relationship ended. The applicant argued that this amounted to indirect discrimination. The Court rejected the claim and held that the calculation was justified because the payment was supposed to bridge the time between the end of employment and the beginning of another and was thus calculated based on the last salary.[43]

Seymour-Smith also concerned an indirect discrimination challenge regarding a qualification period for protection against unfair dismissal. However, the House of Lords denied the claim of indirect discrimination because it deemed the statistical difference between the affected men and women to be inconsiderable.[44] In *SC*, the applicant argued that the limit of a child tax credit to two children amounted to an indirect discrimination because the majority of parents were women.[45] The Court argued that the measure in question did not specifically discriminate against women, but that all reductions in childcare benefits accidentally will have a disproportionate effect on women.[46] Therefore, fiscal considerations were sufficient for justification.[47]

Probably, the most controversial case of the unsuccessful sex discrimination cases is the first benefits cap case.[48] In this case, the applicants challenged a rule that

[43] ibid (per Lord Slynn of Hadley).
[44] *Seymour-Smith* (n 28).
[45] *SC* (n 18).
[46] ibid paras 195–198 (per Lord Reed).
[47] ibid para 199 (per Lord Reed).
[48] *JS* (n 17).

imposed an absolute cap on the social benefits that households could receive if the head of the household did not work for at least 16 hours per week. This cap affected predominantly single parent households from London. As 92% of single parent households were headed by women, the applicants argued that the rule amounted to indirect sex discrimination. While the Court conceded that the rule had a disparate impact on women, the majority of the judges deemed the rule to be justified by budgetary considerations and the aim to incentivize work.[49] In reaching this conclusion, the Court took a very deferential approach, which was controversial even among the judges, as the narrow vote margin of three to two shows.[50]

As already noted, all the unsuccessful sex discrimination cases were indirect discrimination cases. The success rate of cases—across all suspect classifications—is 58.82% when we only look at the direct discrimination cases.[51] The majority of the unsuccessful cases have a migration context in which the applicants argued that they were discriminated against based on their nationality.[52] However, the Court argued that, "[i]n the context of immigration, nationality is not a particularly 'suspect' classification."[53] Another case concerned a rule disadvantaging British nationals living abroad. The Court again argued that residency status was not a "suspect" classification because it was a matter of choice.[54] The two remaining cases concerned differentiations based on sexual orientation and the choice of one's own sex. In *Secretary of State for Work and Pensions v M*, the majority of the Court argued that a difference between heterosexual and homosexual couples for the calculation of child support after a divorce did not violate Article 14 ECHR because the challenge did not fall into the ambit of Article 8 ECHR.[55] Finally, in *Elan-Cane*, the Court held that unavailability of a third sex designation in passports was justified for cost and security reasons.[56]

When we look at the cases not involving a suspect classification, the success rate is 5.88% ($N = 17$). The only successful case is *Gilham* where the Court had to deal with the challenge of a judge who did not enjoy whistleblower protection because

[49] ibid paras 67–77 (per Lord Reed).

[50] See ibid (Lady Hale and Lord Kerr dissenting).

[51] The (at least partially) successful cases are *A v Chief Constable of West Yorkshire Police* [2004] UKHL 21; *Ghaidan v Godin-Mendoza* [2004] UKHL 30; *A v Secretary of State for the Home Department* [2004] UKHL 56; *Clift* (n 9); *In re P* [2008] UKHL 38; *Principal Reporter v K* [2010] UKSC 56; *R (Johnson) v Secretary of State for the Home Department* [2016] UKSC 56; *In the Matter of an Application by Denise Brewster for Judicial Review* [2017] UKSC 8; *Steinfeld* (n 17); *Siobhan McLaughlin's Application for Judicial Review* [2018] UKSC 48.

[52] *R (Ali) v Secretary of State for the Home Department* [2015] UKSC 68; *Mirga v Secretary of State for Work and Pensions* [2016] UKSC 1; *R (Nouazli) v Secretary of State for the Home Department* [2016] UKSC 16; *HC* (n 11).

[53] *Ali* (n 52) para 57 (per Lady Hale).

[54] *R (Carson) v Secretary of State for Work and Pensions* [2005] UKHL 37, para 58 (per Lord Hoffman).

[55] *Secretary of State for Work and Pensions v M* [2006] UKHL 11, paras 21–30 (per Lord Nicholls of Birkenhead) paras 62–88 (per Lord Walker of Gestingthorpe).

[56] *Elan-Cane* (n 39) paras 36–67 (per Lord Reed).

she was not considered to be worker.[57] In its reasoning, the Supreme Court only briefly addressed the question of status.[58] The main emphasis of the argument was that there was no legitimate reason to exclude judges from whistleblower protection.[59] Therefore, it seems to be a case where the Court considered the differentiation to be clearly arbitrary so that the existence of a specific status or suspect classification was not deemed to be necessary.

The picture described above does not change significantly if we include the non-core cases so that our choice of core cases does not drive the result of the analysis.[60] Consequently, the UK equality case law predominantly fits the equality as non-discrimination model. There are almost no successful cases not involving a suspect classification. While the success rate for core cases involving a suspect classification might seem rather low, it is still higher than the comparable success rate in the Supreme Court of Canada.[61] Furthermore, if we only focus on direct discrimination cases, the success rate rises above 50%. Nevertheless, the first benefits cap case illustrates that the UK Supreme Court is rather on the deferential side compared to other courts applying the equality as non-discrimination model.

4. Explanation of the doctrine

The finding that the UK Supreme Court adheres to the equality as non-discrimination model is not particularly surprising. For a start, this is suggested by the structure of the norms that were the core focus of our analysis. Articles 18 and 157 TFEU and Article 14 ECHR are non-discrimination norms. Articles 18 and 157 TFEU each focus on one particular suspect classification—nationality and sex, respectively. It has to be acknowledged that Article 14 ECHR is more open-ended. Furthermore, the UK Supreme Court has accepted a broad interpretation of the criterion "other status" that goes beyond traditional understandings of suspect classifications in its more recent jurisprudence.[62] For example, in *Gilham*, Lady Hale argued that an "occupational classification" was a "recognizable status."[63] In the second benefits cap case, Lord Wilson held that being a lone parent and a child under a certain age also constituted a status in the sense of Article 14 ECHR.[64]

[57] *Gilham* (n 14).
[58] ibid para 32 (per Lady Hale).
[59] ibid paras 33–37 (per Lady Hale).
[60] For core and non-core cases combined, the success rate of cases not involving a suspect classification is not much different at 4.76%, ie there is no additional successful case. The success rate of cases involving a suspect classification is slightly lower at 39.29%.
[61] See Chapter 3, section 3.2.
[62] See n 14 and accompanying text.
[63] *Gilham* (n 14) para 32 (per Lady Hale).
[64] *R (DA) v Secretary of State for Work and Pensions* [2019] UKSC 21, paras 38–39 (per Lord Wilson).

Consequently, Article 14 ECHR would, in principle, have the potential to be interpreted as general equality norm.

Nevertheless, cases not involving a suspect classification are rarely successful. *Gilham* is the only example of a successful case not involving a suspect classification.[65] This may be due to two reasons. On the one hand, the influence of the ECtHR looms large. Section 2(1)(a) of the Human Rights Act 1998 obliges the UK Supreme Court to take into account the case law of the European Court. The discussion of the latter's case law is very prominent in the Supreme Court's reasoning.[66] The Court even departs from its own precedent if prompted by the Strasbourg Court.[67] Consequently, Nico Krisch argued that "the dominant position among the judges [of the House of Lords] is instead one of close attention and loyalty to Strasbourg judgments."[68] We have seen in the analysis of the case law of the ECtHR that the latter also adheres to an equality as non-discrimination model.[69] Given the influence of the latter on the UK Supreme Court, it seems obvious to observe a similar pattern in the UK Supreme Court.

On the other hand, the adoption of the equality as non-discrimination model is also facilitated by the deferential approach of the Supreme Court towards political authority. The Supreme Court is no traditional constitutional court vested with the power to review acts of the legislature. Instead, the fundamental British concept of parliamentary sovereignty is, in principle, hostile to judicial review of acts of parliament.[70] It was only through European integration[71] and the introduction of the Human Rights Act 1998 that the House of Lords and—later—the UK Supreme Court started to review parliamentary decisions.[72] Nevertheless, the Court is keenly aware of the delicacy to correct decisions of the democratically elected parliament and thus retains a rather deferential approach. Therefore, an equality as reasonableness review that is, for example, prevalent in the case law of the German Federal Constitutional Court,[73] would not have been characteristic for the UK Supreme Court. But it even shows in the deferential nature of the equality as non-discrimination review performed by the Court. This is particularly obvious in cases concerning social and economic policy where the Court applies a

[65] *Gilham* (n 14).
[66] On the "dialogue" between the two courts, see O'Connell (n 6).
[67] See Nico Krisch, "The Open Architecture of European Human Rights Law" (2008) 71 Modern LR 183, 203. From the equality case law, see eg *Stott* (n 6) para 70 (per Lady Black).
[68] Krisch (n 67) 203. See also Dickson (n 4) 333 (noting that the first time that the ECtHR corrected the House of Lords in the field of equality did not occur until 2013).
[69] See Chapter 4.
[70] Michael Gordon, *Parliamentary Sovereignty in the UK Constitution: Process, Politics and Democracy* (Bloomsbury 2015) 13–14; John McEldowney, "The UK Supreme Court and Parliament: Judicial and Political Dialogues" in Zoltán Szente and Fruszina Gárdos-Orosz (eds), *New Challenges to Constitutional Adjudication in Europe* (Routledge 2018) 214, 215.
[71] See *Factortame Ltd. v Secretary of State for Transport* [1989] 2 AC 85.
[72] See McEldowney (n 70) 217–24; Elliott (n 2) 77–84.
[73] See Chapter 7.

deferential "manifestly without reasonable foundation" test even if a suspect classification is involved.[74]

5. Conclusion

The UK Supreme Court largely follows an equality as non-discrimination approach. The success rate for cases involving a suspect classification is 43.75%. It rises slightly to 58.82% if we only consider direct discrimination cases. At the same time, there is only one successful equality case not involving a suspect classification, leading to a success rate of less than 10%. These numbers are largely in line with the success rates of other courts following the equality as non-discrimination approach. The success rate is lower than for the US Supreme Court,[75] but higher than for other common law courts, such as the Supreme Courts of Canada and New Zealand.[76] Overall, this result is not surprising. Apart from statutory non-discrimination guarantees, the equality guarantees applied by the UK Supreme Court have their origins in international and supranational treaties, such as the EU treaties and the ECHR. The approach of the UK Supreme Court is, therefore, heavily influenced by the CJEU and the ECtHR so that it is an obvious consequence that the jurisprudential patterns in the UK are similar to those observed in the corresponding European courts. Furthermore, a rather deferential approach of the Supreme Court is also in line with the concept of parliamentary sovereignty, which makes UK courts rather reluctant to review acts of parliament.

[74] See in particular *Humphreys* (n 24) para 19 (per Lady Hale); *JS* (n 17) para 11 (per Lord Reed). For a more detailed discussion, see nn 23–27 and accompanying text.

[75] See Chapter 2.

[76] See Chapters 3 and 16.

7
Germany

Niels Petersen

1. Introduction

The German Constitution contains various equality guarantees. The main equality guarantee is enshrined in Article 3 of the Constitution. Article 3(1) establishes a general equality guarantee, protecting equality before the law, while Article 3(3) features a non-discrimination guarantee, prohibiting discrimination based on an exclusive list of grounds, such as sex, race, language, religion, disability, or origin. Furthermore, the German Constitution includes several specific non-discrimination guarantees, such as the prohibition to discriminate against children born outside marriage in Article 6(5) or the prohibition to discriminate against married couples that is derived from Article 6(1). Finally, the Constitution encompasses a couple of area-specific equality guarantees, such as the guarantee of equality in relation to civic rights and duties and access to public positions (Article 33) and the guarantee of electoral equality (Article 38).

This chapter will predominantly focus on Article 3 of the Constitution—the general equality and non-discrimination guarantee—and on the prohibition to discriminate against extramarital children in Article 6(5) of the Constitution. Article 3 has an enormous importance for the German constitutional case law. Our research identified 1,592 cases that were decided in substance under this norm. Furthermore, the norm is responsible for a significant number of cases in which statutes were struck down because of their incompatibility with fundamental rights. Between 1951 and 2015, more than two-fifths of these cases were based on the violation of an equality norm.[1]

This chapter proceeds in three steps. First, I will discuss the development of the equality doctrine in Germany, which has gone through several different stages

[1] Niels Petersen, *Proportionality and Judicial Activism: Fundamental Rights Adjudication in Canada, Germany and South Africa* (CUP 2017) 84 has identified 250 cases in which the Court has struck down a statute because of a fundamental rights violation between 1951 and 2015 while excluding art 3 of the Constitution from his analysis (on the construction of the sample, see ibid 70). This study has identified 220 cases for the same period in which the Court has struck down a statute based on art 3 of the Constitution. Therefore, the share of art 3 cases is 46.81%. However, this includes some double counting because cases in which the Federal Constitutional Court relied on a fundamental liberty in combination with art 3 of the Constitution were included in the sample in both studies. Depending on how you classify these cases, the share of art 3 cases either slightly decreases or even slightly increases.

Niels Petersen, *Germany* In: *Equality's Guardians*. Edited by: Niels Petersen, Oxford University Press.
 DOI: 10.1093/9780198961109.003.0007

since the early inception in the *South-West State* decision that the Court issued in 1951.[2] Furthermore, the Court has also developed a number of specific doctrines that are applied in particular areas, such as political participation or taxation. Second, I will present the results of the empirical analysis. The empirical analysis will show that the German Federal Constitutional Court predominantly follows an equality as reasonableness approach. While the success rate for cases involving a suspect classification is higher than for cases without a suspect classification, the absolute number of successful cases not involving a suspect classification is far greater, suggesting that the latter are not mere exceptions. The third part of the chapter tries to explain the results. I will argue that the result can be explained by the strong institutional position of the Court and the prevailing belief in the rationality of legal decision-making in German legal thought.

2. The equality doctrine of the German Federal Constitutional Court

2.1 General equality guarantee

The equality doctrine of the Federal Constitutional Court operationalizing the general equality guarantee in Article 3(1) of the Basic Law found its earliest inception in the *South-West State* decision, where the Court developed an arbitrariness standard.[3] It argued that "[t]he principle of equality is infringed if a reasonable justification . . . cannot be found for the statutory classification . . ., in short if the provision has to be described as arbitrary."[4] However, the Court quickly deemed the arbitrariness standard to be too deferential and implicitly applied stricter standards.[5] This was acknowledged in 1980 when the Court explicitly modified its doctrinal approach and established the so-called *new formula (Neue Formel)*.[6] However, the Court continued to develop its equality doctrine.[7] The last step of

[2] BVerfGE 1, 14.
[3] ibid 52.
[4] ibid.
[5] Reiner Schmidt, *Die Bindung des Gesetzgebers an den Gleichheitssatz (Art. 3 Abs. 1 GG) in der Rechtsprechung des Bundesverfassungsgerichts* (Dissertation, University of Würzburg 1963) 110–11; Rudolf Wendt, "Der Gleichheitssatz" [1988] Neue Zeitschrift für Verwaltungsrecht 778, 778; Simon Kempny and Philipp Reimer, *Die Gleichheitssätze—Versuch einer übergreifenden dogmatischen Beschreibung ihres Tatbestands und ihrer Rechtsfolgen* (Mohr Siebeck 2012) 107. See also Alexander Somek, "The Deadweight of Formulae: What Might Have Been the Second Germanization of American Equal Protection Review" (1998) 1 University of Pennsylvania Journal of Constitutional Law 284, 300. See eg BVerfGE 4, 219, 247; 13, 331, 342–343; 18, 366, 375, and 379; 20, 374, 377.
[6] BVerfGE 55, 72.
[7] On the different stages of the doctrine, see Christoph Brüning, "Gleichheitsrechtliche Verhältnismäßigkeit" [2001] Juristenzeitung 669, 669; Kempny and Reimer (n 5) 105 et seq; Lerke Osterloh, "Der Gleichheitssatz zwischen Willkürverbot und Grundsatz der Verhältnismäßigkeit" in Claudio Franzius and others (eds), *Beharren. Bewegen: Festschrift für Michael Kloepfer zum 70. Geburtstag* (Duncker & Humblot 2013) 139, 141; Jost Pietzcker, "Der allgemeine Gleichheitssatz"

the doctrinal development was the establishment of the so-called *tierless formula* (*Stufenlosformel*) in 2011.[8] In its decision, the Court argued that the principle of equality encompassed a "continuous constitutional standard of review based on the principle of proportionality."[9] While it claims to avoid the delimitation of the different tiers of scrutiny, the Court mostly differentiates between a "more generous standard of review"[10] and a "stricter standard of review" in practice.[11] It usually applies a stricter standard if differentiations are based on personal characteristics or if they concern fundamental freedoms,[12] or if the concerned individuals cannot influence whether they meet the criterion of differentiation.[13]

2.2 Non-discrimination guarantee

The Federal Constitutional Court developed a distinct approach to the non-discrimination guarantee in Article 3 (3) of the Basic Law. It recognized early in its jurisprudence that the protection derived from the prohibition of sex discrimination had to be higher than the protection derived from the general equality guarantee.[14] Initially, the Court asked whether differentiations based on sex were justified by "objective biological or functional (concerning the division of labor) differences" between the sexes.[15] However, the Court changed its justification formula in the early 1990s and argued that a sex differentiation was only justified if it was "strictly necessary" to solve a problem that "according to its nature could

in Detlef Merten and Hans-Jürgen Papier (eds), *Handbuch der Grundrechte. Band V: Grundrechte in Deutschland: Einzelgrundrechte II* (C.F. Müller 2013) ch 125, paras 40 et seq; Gabriele Britz, "Der allgemeine Gleichheitssatz in der Rechtsprechung des BVerfG: Anforderungen an die Rechtfertigung von Ungleichbehandlungen durch Gesetz" [2014] Neue Juristische Wochenschrift 346; Gabriel Ducatti Lino Machado, *Verhältnismäßigkeitsprinzip vs. Willkürverbot: Der Streit um den allgemeinen Gleichheitssatz* (Duncker & Humblot 2015) 90 et seq; Joachim Englisch, "Art. 3 GG" in Klaus Stern and Florian Becker (eds), *Grundrechte-Kommentar* (3rd edn, Wolters Kluwer 2018) art 3, paras 11–12; Niels Petersen, "Gleichheitssatz und Einzelfallgerechtigkeit: Eine Rekonstruktion der Dogmatik von Art. 3 GG im Vergleich zur US-amerikanischen *equal protection* Doktrin" (2018) 57 Der Staat 327, 339–45; Thorsten Kingreen, "Artikel 3" in Wolfgang Kahl, Christian Waldhoff, and Christian Walter (eds), *Bonner Kommentar zum Grundgesetz* (202nd ed, C.F. Müller 2020) art 3, paras 321–328; Sigrid Boysen, "Art. 3 [Gleichheit vor dem Gesetz]" in Ingo von Münch and Philip Kunig (eds), *Grundgesetz-Kommentar* (7th ed, C.H. Beck 2021) art 3, paras 104–112.

[8] BVerfGE 129, 49.
[9] ibid 69.
[10] See eg ibid 69–70; BVerfGE 132, 372, 388.
[11] See eg BVerfGE 133, 59, 87; 138, 136, 184–85. See also BVerfGE 132, 179, 189–90 ("strict proportionality review").
[12] BVerfGE 129, 49, 69.
[13] ibid.
[14] BVerfGE 10, 59, 73–74. For a discussion of the issue of sex discrimination, see Susanne Baer, *Würde oder Gleichheit?* (Nomos 1995); Ute Sacksofsky, *Das Grundrecht auf Gleichberechtigung—Eine rechtsdogmatische Untersuchung zu Artikel 3 Absatz 2 des Grundgesetzes* (2nd edn, Nomos 1996).
[15] BVerfGE 10, 59, 74; 21, 329, 343; 31, 1, 4; 37, 217, 249; 48, 327, 337; 52, 369, 374; 57, 335, 343; 63, 181, 194; 68, 384, 390; 71, 224, 229; 84, 9, 18.

only occur in either men or women."[16] With regards to children born outside of marriage, differentiations can be justified if "equal treatment would not do justice to the different situation of the extramarital child," if it led to a "worsening of the situation of a subgroup of extramarital children,"[17] or if it "was strictly necessary to achieve the goal of equality... due to the different actual life situation."[18] In the case of differentiations based on disability, the Federal Constitutional Court requires the justification to be based on "compelling reasons."[19]

2.3 Differentiated specific doctrines

Next to the general equality doctrine and the specific formulae for differentiations based on the criteria in Article 3(3) or Article 6(5), the Federal Constitutional Court has also developed a number of area specific doctrines that it has derived from the general equality guarantee.[20] The most important of these specific doctrines are the principles of voting equality and of equal opportunities for political parties.[21] An important specification can also be found in the area of taxation.[22] The Court derived the principle of "tax justice" (*Steuergerechtigkeit*) from the equality guarantee in a 1957 decision.[23] It later developed this principle into the demand for an "equal tax burden" (*steuerliche Belastungsgleichheit*), according to which every individual had to be "taxed according to their economic ability."[24] Closely related to the principle of an equal tax burden is the consistency requirement

[16] BVerfGE 85, 191, 207; 92, 91, 109; 114, 357, 364; 132, 72, 97–98. See also Somek (n 5) 293 (arguing that this new test was reminiscent of the "compelling interest" test of the US Supreme Court in the context of strict scrutiny).

[17] BVerfGE 84, 168, 185.

[18] BVerfGE 118, 45, 62.

[19] BVerfGE 151, 1, 25.

[20] See Petersen (n 7) 341–43.

[21] On these principles, see Klaus Kröger, "Schematische Parteiengleichheit als Grundbedingung der Demokratie" in Friedrich J Kroneck and Thomas Oppermann (eds), *Im Dienste Deutschlands und des Rechts. Festschrift für Wilhelm G. Grewe zum 70. Geburtstag* (Nomos 1981) 507; Heinz-Werner Kleffmann, "Chancengleichheit im Wahlkampf" [1983] Neue Zeitschrift für Verwaltungsrecht 532; Hans Herbert von Arnim, "Der strenge und der formale Gleichheitssatz" [1984] Die öffentliche Verwaltung 85; Uwe Volkmann, *Politische Parteien und öffentliche Leistungen* (Duncker & Humblot 1993) 189 et seq; Martin Morlok, "Parteienrecht als Wettbewerbsrecht" in Peter Häberle, Martin Morlok, and Vassilios Skouris (eds), *Festschrift für Dimitris Th. Tsatsos* (Nomos 2003) 408; Niels Petersen, "Verfassungsgerichte als Wettbewerbshüter des politischen Prozesses" in Dominik Elser and others (eds), *Das letzte Wort—Rechtsetzung und Rechtskontrolle in der Demokratie* (Nomos 2014) 59, 67–69.

[22] See Uwe Kischel, "Art. 3 [Gleichheit vor dem Gesetz]" in Volker Epping and Christian Hillgruber (eds), *Grundgesetz* (54th edn, C.H. Beck 2023) art 3, para 141.

[23] BVerfGE 6, 55, 70. See also BVerfGE 9, 237, 244.

[24] BVerfGE 43, 108, 120. The Court has later extended this principle also to other public charges beyond taxes, see BVerfGE 132, 334, 349.

(*Folgerichtigkeit*).[25] This principle is predominantly applied in cases relating to tax legislation, even though it is sometimes also employed in other areas. According to this requirement, the legislature has to implement a legislative conception in a consistent way.[26] Exceptions to the consistency requirement are allowed if they are reasonably justified.[27]

Furthermore, the Federal Constitutional Court has retained its arbitrariness standard for the review of decisions of ordinary courts. It quashes these decisions if they lack an objective justification.[28] The Court has applied this principle in all subject matters, ranging from criminal law over private law to tax or administrative law. One situation where the Court has resorted particularly often to the arbitrariness review is the decision about financial aid for court proceedings (*Prozesskostenhilfe*).[29] The Court sees financial aid as an instrument to guarantee that all individuals have access to court, regardless of their financial means.[30] For the review of civil procedure questions in court proceedings, the Federal Constitutional Court has finally developed the principle of procedural equality of arms,[31] which means that both parties have to have equal opportunities to be heard and that their procedural costs are reimbursed according to the same standards.

[25] The consistency requirement can be traced back to BVerfGE 1, 208 and BVerfGE 17, 122. For a more detailed discussion of this requirement see eg Lothar Michael, "Folgerichtigkeit als Wettbewerbsgleichheit—Zur Verwerfung von Rauchverboten in Gaststätten durch das BVerfG" [2008] Juristenzeitung 875; Gerd Morgenthaler, "Gleichheit und Rechtssystem—Widerspruchsfreiheit, Folgerichtigkeit" in Rudolf Mellinghoff and Ulrich Palm (eds), *Gleichheit im Verfassungsstaat: Symposium aus Anlass des 65. Geburtstages von Paul Kirchhof* (C.F. Müller 2008) 51; Oliver Lepsius, "Anmerkung" [2009] Juristenzeitung 260; Christian Bumke, "Die Pflicht zur konsistenten Gesetzgebung" (2010) 49 Der Staat 77; Joachim Englisch, "Folgerichtiges Steuerrecht als Verfassungsgebot" in Klaus Tipke and others (eds), *Gestaltung der Steuerrechtsordnung: Festschrift für Joachim Lang zum 70. Geburtstag* (Verlag Dr. Otto Schmidt 2010) 167; Philipp Dann, "Verfassungsgerichtliche Kontrolle gesetzgeberischer Rationalität" (2010) 49 Der Staat 630; Mehrdad Payandeh, "Das Gebot der Folgerichtigkeit: Rationalitätsgewinn oder Irrweg der Grundrechtsdogmatik?" (2011) 136 Archiv des öffentlichen Rechts 578; Lerke Osterloh, "Folgerichtigkeit: Verfassungsgerichtliche Rationalitätsanforderungen in der Demokratie" in Michael Bäuerle, Philipp Dann, and Astrid Wallrabenstein (eds), *Demokratie-Perspektiven: Festschrift für Brun-Otto Bryde zum 70. Geburtstag* (Mohr Siebeck 2013) 429; Niels Petersen, "Gesetzgeberische Inkonsistenz als Beweiszeichen: Eine rechtsvergleichende Analyse der Funktion von Konsistenzargumenten in der Rechtsprechung" (2013) 138 Archiv des öffentlichen Rechts 108; Henning Tappe, "Festlegende Gleichheit—folgerichtige Gesetzgebung als Verfassungsgebot?" [2016] Juristenzeitung 27; Laurence O'Hara, *Konsistenz und Konsens: Die Anforderungen des Grundgesetzes and die Folgerichtigkeit des Gesetzes* (Mohr Siebeck 2018).

[26] BVerfGE 17, 122, 132.

[27] BVerfGE 122, 210, 231.

[28] See eg BVerfGE 40, 1, 4.

[29] See BVerfGE 78, 104, 117–18.

[30] ibid.

[31] BVerfGE 74, 78, 92.

2.4 Indirect discrimination and positive measures

The Federal Constitutional Court was rather late to acknowledge the concept of indirect discrimination. The first decision, in which the Court explicitly mentioned the concept was a decision from November 1997, in which the Court dealt with a rule that denied certain old-age pension benefits for public servants to part-time employees.[32] Explicitly influenced by the jurisprudence of the European Court of Justice (CJEU),[33] it argued that a distinction is "based on gender even if the regulation is formulated in a gender-neutral manner, but primarily affects women."[34] Indirect discriminations may be justified if the legislature aims at protecting competing constitutional values.[35]

While the concept of indirect discrimination has recently gained traction, the concept of positive measures to support vulnerable or underprivileged groups has only played a marginal role in the German case law. Even though the German Constitution contains an obligation actively to promote the equality of men and women and thus empowers the legislature to implement measures that positively support women,[36] the Federal Constitutional Court rarely had the opportunity to rule on this issue. Cases challenging positive measures to support women were probably crowded out by the CJEU with its differentiated case law on the issue.[37]

In a recent decision from December 2021, the Federal Constitutional Court required the legislature to establish a positive, protective measure for vulnerable individuals.[38] The concrete case concerned the distribution of limited medical resources in the context of the COVID-19 pandemic. The Court argued that the prohibition of discrimination against disabled individuals contained a positive obligation of the legislature to protect disabled people, in particular against attacks to their dignity, against risks for important fundamental rights, such as the right to life, or against structural discrimination.[39] For this reason, it asked the legislature to establish measures to protect disabled individuals in situations where doctors are unable to give all patients the same level of care.[40]

[32] BVerfGE 97, 35, 43–44.

[33] Case 170/84 *Bilka-Kaufhaus* [1986] ECR 1607.

[34] BVerfGE 97, 35, 43.

[35] BVerfGE 121, 241, 257.

[36] See Susanne Baer and Nora Markard, "Art. 3 Abs. 2 und 3 GG" in Peter Michael Huber and Andreas Voßkuhle (eds), *Grundgesetz. Band 1: Präambel, Artikel 1–19* (C.H. Beck 2018), art 3, paras 366–375.

[37] See Case C-450/93 *Kalanke* [1995] ECR I-3051; Case C-409/95 *Marschall* [1997] ECR I-6363; Case C-158/97 *Badeck* [2000] ECR I-1902; Case C-407/98 *Abrahamsson* [2000] ECR I-5562. See also Chapter 5, section 2.2.

[38] BVerfG 1 BvR 1541/20 (December 16, 2021) [2022] NJW 380.

[39] ibid para 97.

[40] ibid paras 126–128.

3. Empirical analysis of the equality case law

3.1 Generating and analyzing the sample

The empirical analysis of the German equality case law is based on an examination of all published cases of the Federal Constitutional Court that were decided under Articles 3 and 6(5) of the Constitution from 1951, when the Court issued its first decision, until the end of 2021. To construct the sample, we used the database JURIS, which is the most comprehensive database for German case law. We searched for the norms Article 3 and Article 6(5) and included all cases that matched these criteria in the preliminary sample. This sample was subsequently cleaned manually in order to discard cases that did not contain a substantive discussion of equality, either under Article 3 or under Article 6(5). This concerned, in particular, cases where the Court deemed the case to be inadmissible. However, not all non-acceptability decisions were removed from the sample as the Court sometimes includes substantive considerations in such decisions. The latter decisions were retained in the sample. Overall, the sample contained 1,608 cases. Roughly half of the analyzed decisions (52.99%) were decided by a full senate of eight judges, and half of the decisions by a three-judge panel (47.01%). The first analyzed case was the already mentioned *South-West State* case from October 23,1951,[41] the last analyzed case was a decision taken by a three-judge panel of the second senate that dealt with the rejection of an application for a referendum in Bavaria due to a lack of a sufficient number of signatures.[42]

After the construction of the sample, all cases contained therein were analyzed. The first analysis was done by research assistants who wrote a one-page summary of the cases and identified some of the crucial factors for the analysis, such as whether the distinction concerned a suspect classification or whether the equality challenge was successful. Then I coded the cases according to the coding scheme introduced in the introductory chapter.[43] It has to be noted that the construction of the sample is likely to lead to biased results when calculating the success rates of equality challenges. As has already been noted in the introductory chapter, the German Federal Constitutional Court only publishes a small fraction—about 1–2%—of the cases that it decides.[44] Furthermore, we can assume that the Court is more likely to publish successful cases than unsuccessful ones. Therefore, any calculation of the success rate will most likely overestimate the real success rate of equality challenges.

[41] BVerfGE 1, 14.
[42] BVerfG 2 BvR 1844/20 (21 Dec 2021) [2022] NVwZ 1286.
[43] See Chapter 1, section 4.2.
[44] See Chapter 1, section 4.3.

3.2 The results of the analysis

If we analyze the whole sample of cases, the success rate for cases involving a suspect criterion is 62.02% and the success rate for cases not involving a suspect criterion is 36.39%. Many of the successful cases not involving a suspect criterion concern the review of court decisions. As we saw in the explanation of the doctrine, the Federal Constitutional Court has derived a general arbitrariness test from the equality guarantee in Article 3(1) and uses this test frequently to review decisions of lower courts, which range from local courts (*Amtsgerichte*) to the federal courts, in particular the Federal Supreme Court in civil and criminal matters (*Bundesgerichtshof*) as well as the Federal Tax Court (*Bundesfinanzhof*). Many of these cases concern financial aid for court procedures (*Prozesskostenhilfe*)—our sample contains a total of 150 of such decisions.

However, we can assume that this overall sample is highly biased. Unsuccessful challenges of lower court decisions based on the arbitrariness standard are unlikely to be published because these are routine decisions that rarely contain interesting pieces of information. For example, in our sample, more than 80% of all challenges to financial aid decisions are successful, which is highly implausible. Instead, it seems more likely that unsuccessful challenges of financial aid decisions are so uninteresting that they are regularly not published. For this reason, I have selected a sub-sample of all cases for a more detailed analysis. This sub-sample comprises all cases in which the Federal Constitutional Court analyzed the constitutionality of a statute because of equality concerns. Therefore, all cases that predominantly analyzed the compatibility of a court decision or an executive act (including executive or municipal regulations) with the constitutional equality guarantees were excluded from the sub-sample. The assumption underlying this selection is that an unsuccessful challenge of a statute is more likely to be published than the unsuccessful challenge of a court decision. This will not totally exclude bias. While all successful challenges of legislation are always published because they have to be taken by the full senate (section 93c(1) sentence 2 of the Constitutional Court Act), it cannot be excluded that some unsuccessful challenges to legislation remain unpublished. Nevertheless, challenges to legislation are more likely to be published because they usually involve more complex legal questions than the mere arbitrariness review of courts decisions so that we can expect to get less biased results when restricting the analysis to the sub-sample.

This sub-sample contained 893 cases. When analyzing these cases, we find that the success rate for cases not involving a suspect classification decreases to 25.07%. This success rate is also remarkably consistent across the different iterations of the equal protection formulae of the Federal Constitutional Court. It ranges from 23.97% from the time of the arbitrariness formula to 27.6% after the introduction of the tierless formula, a difference that is probably just due to statistical noise. This suggests that the changes in doctrinal formula did not have much of an effect in practice.

Table 7.1 Success rate for direct discriminations.

Suspect criterion	No of cases	Success rate
Sex	31	61.29%
Nationality	11	36.36%
Residence	13	15.38%
Extramarital birth	13	46.15%
Disability	3	66.67%
Age	5	20%
Sexual orientation	1	0%
Marital status	15	40%
Total	92	43.47%

3.2.1 Suspect classifications

For a closer analysis of cases involving a suspect classification, we start looking exclusively at cases involving a direct discrimination (Table 7.1). We see that the category with the most cases and the highest chances of success is sex discrimination. The success rate for these cases is 61.29%. Most of the unsuccessful cases concern early decisions of the Constitutional Court that were predominantly driven by the judges' assumptions about the typical social role of men and women that were prevalent at the time.[45] This concerns, in particular, challenges of rules that assumed that the man was the main breadwinner of the family for social security purposes.[46] The first of these cases came to the Court in 1963. In the concerned cases, the applicants had, for example, applied for a widower's pension, but their application was rejected because their deceased wife had not been the main breadwinner of the family. The applicants challenged these rules and argued that they constituted sex discrimination because women received a widow's pension without having to show that their husband had been the main breadwinner of the family. However, the Court rejected the sex discrimination claims. It argued that the legislature was allowed to generalize because the husband was the main breadwinner in the vast majority of cases.[47] The Federal Constitutional Court revisited

[45] See BVerfGE 5, 9; 17, 1; 17, 62; 17, 99; 17, 168; 39, 169; 39, 196. The other unsuccessful early cases concern the criminalization of male homosexuality in contrast to female homosexuality, see BVerfGE 6, 389; 36, 41.

[46] BVerfGE 17, 1; 17, 62; 39, 169; 39, 196. The other cases concerned eg the wife's obligation to assume the name of her husband after marriage (BVerfGE 17, 168). Here the Court argued that the norm did not lead to a sex discrimination because it concerned both partners "in the same way."

[47] BVerfGE 17, 1, 23–26.

the question in two decisions in 1975.[48] Here, the Court acknowledged that the understanding of the role of women as housewives was changing but that the new distribution of roles had not yet been generally accepted[49] so that it still deemed the legislative generalization to be justified.[50] These cases show that the corrective role of courts is limited by the social understandings that judges have in particular times. Nevertheless, overall, the Federal Constitutional Court has used the prohibition of sex discrimination as a tool to strike down legislation disadvantaging women or trying to entrench existing stereotypes. After 1975, the success rate for sex discrimination cases rises to 76.92%. The unsuccessful cases all concerned challenges to statutes that disadvantaged men.[51]

Furthermore, it is interesting to note that we see a significant shift from direct to indirect sex discrimination cases after the year 2000. For this century, our sample only contains two cases regarding direct sex discrimination—both successful—while there has been a sharp increase in indirect discrimination cases. In the same period, the Court has decided seven indirect discrimination cases with a success rate of 71.43%. This pattern is not surprising. Influenced by the Court's increasingly strict stance on direct sex discrimination, legislation directly disadvantaging women has become increasingly rare, therefore the focus of litigation has shifted rather to the issue of indirect discrimination. We observed a similar pattern in the jurisprudence of the US Supreme Court on racial discrimination, where cases involving direct racial discrimination have equally become rare, while there is an increasing focus on indirect discrimination.

If we look at the other suspect categories, we find that distinctions based on disability have a success rate of 66.67% even though the underlying number of cases that fit this category is very small. The one unsuccessful case concerned a technicality in the social security law, according to which a disability pension could be taken into account in order to reduce an old-age pension, while some other social benefits did not have a negative effect on the calculation of the old-age pension.[52] The Court deemed this distinction to be justified and referred to the different purposes of the compared social benefits. Distinctions based on the marital status of the parents at birth have a success rate of 46.15%. Most of the unsuccessful cases were brought by children born in wedlock challenging positive measures supporting those born without.[53] The other unsuccessful cases concerned transitional arrangements,[54] a procedural distinction that did not impose any disadvantages

[48] BVerfGE 39, 169; 39, 196.
[49] ibid 187–88.
[50] ibid 194–95.
[51] BVerfGE 56, 363; 74, 163; 87, 1.
[52] BVerfGE 77, 370.
[53] BVerfGE 17, 280; 26, 44; 58, 377.
[54] BVerfG 1 BvR 2257/03 (November 20, 2003) [2004] FamRZ 433; BVerfG 1 BvR 2436/11 (March 18, 2013) [2013] NJW 2103.

Table 7.2 Success rate for indirect discriminations

Suspect criterion	No of cases	Success rate
Sex	11	72.72%
Nationality	5	0%
Religion	3	0%
Extramarital birth	6	0%
Disability	6	33.33%
Sexual orientation	10	30%
Poverty	1	0%
Total	42	30.95%

on extramarital children according to the Court,[55] and a situation in which the Constitutional Court did not strike down legislation because it deemed that an interpretation in conformity with the Constitution was possible.[56]

If we look at indirect discriminations, we see that for the vast majority of suspect criteria, indirect discrimination claims are unsuccessful. The only suspect criterion where indirect discrimination claims are more likely than not to be successful is sex (see Table 7.2). There were eleven cases in our sample, in which the Federal Constitutional Court dealt with indirect gender discrimination, and the success rate was 72.72%.[57] For example, in a case from 2010, the Court had to deal with the privatization of a public hospital in Hamburg.[58] While most of the direct employees of the hospital were legally entitled to return to the public service despite the privatization, such an entitlement was missing for the cleaning personnel that had been outsourced to a separate private entity. The Court argued that this arrangement amounted to an indirect discrimination based on sex because most of the affected employees were women.[59] The cases which were not successful failed for different reasons. In one case, the Court refused to grant a positive measure that would have favored women over men.[60] In another case, the Court found that a

[55] BVerfG 1 BvR 718/88 (April 27, 1989).
[56] BVerfGE 8, 210.
[57] See BVerfGE 40,65; 67, 348; 68, 143; 109, 64; 126, 29; 132, 72; 149, 86. In the early case law, the Federal Constitutional Court did not explicitly mention the concept of indirect discrimination but struck down regulations that typically had a negative effect on women. For example, in BVerfGE 68, 143 it found a violation of the principle of equality because single parents could not deduct childcare expenses as work-related expenses from their taxable income. While the majority of single parents are typically women, the Court did not mention this fact in its legal reasoning.
[58] BVerfGE 126, 29.
[59] ibid 53–54.
[60] BVerfG 1 BvR 1171/88 (July 6, 1989).

factual disadvantaging of women was caused by traditional gender roles in families and that the role of the challenged law as a whole was to counteract such traditional gender roles.[61] The final case concerned school closures during the COVID-19 pandemic, where the Court denied an indirect discrimination of women even though they were arguably more strongly affected than men.[62]

Another area in which indirect discriminations played a significant role is distinctions based on sexual orientation. The early cases that were decided by the Court typically concerned monetary public benefits or privileged access to these benefits for married couples, while individuals living in a same-sex partnership were not eligible for comparable benefits.[63] While these rules formally distinguished between the type of partnership that a couple had entered into, they constituted an indirect discrimination because they had a disparate impact on same-sex couples, who could not get married at the time.[64] The Court usually did not find a discrimination.[65] It argued that there was a difference between same-sex partnerships and marriage because married partners—unlike same-sex partners—had legal mutual maintenance obligations and because Article 6 of the Constitution had conferred special constitutional protection to the institution of marriage.[66]

In more recent cases, the Court has been increasingly accommodating towards correcting discriminations of same-sex couples. In a decision from 2010, the Court argued that exemptions from inheritance taxes that were granted to married spouses, but not to same-sex partners violated the equality guarantee.[67] Three years later, the Court held that the same-sex partner had to have the right to adopt a child that had already been adopted by the other partner if this privilege was also granted to married couples.[68] Finally and most significantly, the Court held that the tax privilege of a joint assessment of taxes that married couples enjoyed also had to be extended to same-sex partners.[69] This shift came after the *Maruko*

[61] BVerfG 1 BvR 2712/09 (June 6, 2011) [2011] NJW 2869.

[62] BVerfGE 159, 355.

[63] The same-sex partnership was a form of legal partnership that existed between 2001 and 2017, when the German legislature introduced same-sex marriage.

[64] See BVerfG 2 BvR 855/06 (September 20, 2007) [2008] NJW 209, para 21.

[65] BVerfG 1 BvR 726/98 (May 21, 1999) [1999] NZA 878; BVerfG 1 BvR 155/05 (February 28, 2005) [2005] NJW 1709; BVerfG 2 BvR 855/06 (September 20, 2007) [2008] NJW 209; BVerfG 2 BvR 1830/06 (May 6, 2008) [2008] NJW 2325. The other decisions denying an indirect discrimination based on sexual orientation concerned the non-inclusion of the same-sex partner on the birth certificate of a child born by the other partner (BVerfG 1 BvR 666/10 (July 2, 2010) [2011] NJW 988), the denial of an automatic residence permit for a same-sex partner under the same conditions as for married spouses (BVerfG 2 BvL 16/09 (December 16, 2010) BVerfGK 18, 308), and a reference procedure concerning the constitutionality of a norm where the Constitutional Court argued that the referring court could have achieved the result of treating same-sex couples equally through an interpretation of the challenged norm in conformity with the Constitution (BVerfG 1 BvR 2853/10 (June 8, 2012) BVerfGK 19, 436).

[66] See BVerfG 2 BvR 855/06 (September 20, 2007) [2008] NJW 209, paras 22–23.

[67] BVerfGE 126, 400.

[68] BVerfGE 133, 59.

[69] ibid 377.

decision of the CJEU, in which the Court argued that the denial of a survivor's pension which was granted to married partners of deceased employees but not to partners in a same-sex partnership constituted discrimination based on sexual orientation.[70]

3.2.2 Non-suspect distinctions

Outside the field of sex discrimination, the defining feature of the German equality case law is the high number of successful cases that do not involve a suspect classification. The success rate of 25.07% is higher than in most other jurisdictions. However, what is truly striking is the absolute number of successful cases. There were 189 successful cases not involving a suspect classification, compared to 53 successful cases involving a suspect classification. While the German Federal Constitutional Court has played an important role particularly in combating sex discrimination, the analysis nevertheless suggests that the Court follows an equality as reasonableness approach, where the success of a case does not necessarily depend on the presence of a suspect criterion of distinction.

This characterization is supported by a more detailed analysis of the substance of these cases (see Table 7.3). A significant number of cases deal with political participation: 48 cases are political participation cases, which have a success rate of 45.83%. In these cases, the court examined the rules of political competition, such as minimum quora for the representation in Parliament or rules on campaign financing. Even in the absence of a suspect classification, constitutional courts have an important role to play in this field. They act as arbiters of the political competition in order to prevent that incumbent parties bend the rules to their political advantage.[71]

Outside the field of political participation, a significant number of successful equality claims correct statutes in the area of taxation, public charges, social benefits, or public employment. The success rate in these areas ranges between 24% and 31%. Here, the Federal Constitutional Court predominantly exercises a reasonableness review of the legislature. One recent example is its 2018 decision concerning the reform of the public broadcasting tax. According to the challenged legislation, households had to pay a broadcasting tax, regardless of whether they were actually in possession of a TV or radio.[72] While the Court generally upheld the new tax, it argued that it violated the principle of equality to the extent that individuals having two apartments were taxed twice.[73] If the same individual had two apartments, she could nevertheless only make use of the public broadcasting offer once so that it was inappropriate to demand the tax twice for the same service.[74]

[70] Case C-267/06 *Maruko* [2008] ECR I-757. See also Case C-147/08 *Römer* [2011] ECR I-3591.

[71] Seminally, Samuel Issacharoff and Richard H Pildes, "Politics As Markets: Partisan Lockups of the Democratic Process" (1998) 50 Stanford Law Review 643. For Germany, see Petersen (n 21).

[72] BVerfGE 149, 222.

[73] ibid 272–74.

[74] ibid 272.

Table 7.3 Success rate of equality claims by subject area

Subject area	No of cases	Success rate
Tax and public charges	156	30.12%
Social benefits	180	24.44%
Family	11	9.09%
Profession	79	21.52%
Criminal law	40	7.5%
Migration	2	50%
Political participation	48	45.83%
Public employment	79	30.38%
Civil procedure	24	20.83%
Property/inheritance	31	6.45%
University	29	48.28%
Other	75	12%
Total	754	25.07%

Another example is the already mentioned commuter tax allowance case, in which the Court struck down a reform because it had not been implemented in a consistent manner.[75]

These illustrations show that the German Federal Constitutional Court predominantly operationalizes the equality guarantee as a review of the legislature's reasonablness. Considering the sheer number of successful cases not involving a suspect classification, this reasonableness review cannot be qualified as a mere exception. Furthermore, as the two examples demonstrate, it is not only used as a residual instrument to correct cases of obvious arbitrariness. Rather, the Court applies a rather low degree of deference. Finally, outside distinctions based on sex, extramarital birth, and—more recently—sexual orientation, differentiations based on suspect criteria only play a marginal role in the case law of the Federal Constitutional Court.[76] This suggests that the German case law can best be characterized as an expression of our equality as reasonableness model: It goes beyond the mere policing of discriminations based on suspect criteria and often affords little deference toward the legislature.

[75] BVerfGE 122, 210, 235–36. On this case, see nn 44–48 and accompanying text.
[76] See Baer and Markard (n 36) para 410.

4. Explanation of the doctrine

If we look superficially at factors influencing the equality case law of the Federal Constitutional Court, the example of equal protection doctrine of the US Supreme Court looms large. The arbitrariness test that the Court initially used in order to operationalize equality seems to be modeled after the rational basis test of its US counterpart.[77] This impression is supported by the fact that one of the judges in the Senate deciding the case, Gerhard Leibholz, had referred to the concept of arbitrariness in his earlier academic writing[78] and was explicitly influenced by the US experience.[79] Furthermore, the tiered scrutiny that was introduced through the new and the newest formulae are also reminiscent of the US practice.[80]

Yet, despite the formal resemblances of the doctrines, the approaches of the US Supreme Court and the Federal Constitutional Court lead to very different results.[81] While the equal protection doctrine of the US Supreme Court mostly fits our non-discrimination model, the case law of the Federal Constitutional Court can instead be characterized as forming part of the equality as reasonableness model. Doctrinally, there are several reasons for this.[82] First, the German arbitrariness test is less deferential than the rational basis test of the US Supreme Court. Second, the German Federal Constitutional Court applies the heightened level of scrutiny to a broader range of situations than its US counterpart. Finally, the Federal Constitutional Court has developed several specific doctrines for specific situations, such as the voting equality principle or the principle of an equal tax burden, that do not have equivalents in the US doctrine.

One possible explanation for this observation focuses on the historical context.[83] Post-war Germany did not have social problems comparable to the racial segregation prevalent in the United States in the 1950s and 1960s when the US Supreme Court started to develop its system of tiered scrutiny.[84] Therefore,

[77] Somek (n 5) 296. See also Konrad Hesse, "Der Gleichheitssatz in der neueren deutschen Verfassungsentwicklung" (1984) 109 Archiv des öffentlichen Rechts 174, 186; Machado (n 7) 49.

[78] Hesse (n 77) 178, referring to Gerhard Leibholz, *Die Gleichheit vor dem Gesetz: Eine Studie auf rechtsvergleichender und rechtsphilosophischer Grundlage* (Liebmann 1925).

[79] See Somek (n 5) 296 (with further references).

[80] Konrad Hesse, "Der allgemeine Gleichheitssatz in der neueren Rechtsprechung des Bundesverfassungsgerichts zur Rechtsetzungsgleichheit" in Peter Badura and Rupert Scholz (eds), *Wege und Verfahren des Verfassungslebens: Festschrift für Peter Lerche zum 65. Geburtstag* (C.H. Beck 1993) 121, 127; Michael Sachs, "Die Maßstäbe des allgemeinen Gleichheitssatzes—Willkürverbot und sogenannte neue Formel" [1997] Juristische Schulung 124, 127; Lerke Osterloh, "Der verfassungsrechtliche Gleichheitssatz—Entwicklungslinien der Rechtsprechung des Bundesverfassungsgerichts" (2002) 29 Europäische Grundrechte Zeitschrift 309, 311; Jost Pietzcker, "Rechtsvergleichende Aspekte des allgemeinen Gleichheitssatzes" in Reinhard Hendler, Martin Ibler, and José Martínez Soria (eds), *"Für Sicherheit, für Europa": Festschrift für Volkmar Götz zum 70. Geburtstag* (Vandenhoeck & Ruprecht 2005) 301, 314.

[81] See also Petersen (n 7) 352–53.

[82] ibid 352.

[83] See ibid 354.

[84] See Chapter 2, section 2.1.

discrimination based on suspect criteria of distinction were less salient.[85] Certainly, gender equality was an important issue that received a prominent role in the jurisprudence of the Federal Constitutional Court, but this was not specific to Germany. However the historical context might be a plausible explanation in the simple comparison between Germany and the United States, it cannot explain differences when we compare the German doctrine to other jurisdictions that have also applied an equality as non-discrimination approach. For example, the Supreme Court of Canada is in many respects comparable to the German Federal Constitutional Court.[86] Similarly to its German counterpart, the Supreme Court uses proportionality as its central doctrinal tool for fundamental rights review,[87] and racial discrimination does not play a significantly more prominent role in the Canadian equality jurisprudence than in Germany.[88] Nevertheless, the Supreme Court of Canada adheres to an equality as non-discrimination model, which suggests that the historical context is probably not the predominant explanatory factor of the German equality doctrine.

Instead, the belief in legal rationality is part of the traditional understanding of the German judge as an apolitical legal expert that merely applies the law.[89] In contrast to the United States, the demystification of legal doctrine through legal realism and critical legal studies has never really caught on in Germany.[90] Consequently, the political ideology of judges is a much less salient factor in German constitutional law scholarship and also in the public perception than in the United States.[91] Furthermore, the Federal Constitutional Court can be considered as a strong court with a high level of public legitimacy.[92] The Court is regularly among the most

[85] This does not suggest that racial discrimination is not present in German society; to the contrary: See eg the study of Michael Grünberger and others, *Diversität in Rechtswissenschaft und Rechtspraxis* (Nomos 2021) 26–46 on structural discrimination in the German legal profession. It is just less salient than in other societies with a higher share of racial diversity.

[86] See András Jakab, Arthur Dyevre, and Giulio Itzcovich, "Conclusion" in András Jakab, Arthur Dyevre, and Giulio Itzcovich (eds), *Comparative Constitutional Reasoning* (CUP 2017) 761, 778.

[87] *R v Oakes* [1986] 1 SCR 103. On the so-called *Oakes* doctrine, see Sujit Choudhry, "So What is the Real Legacy of *Oakes*? Two Decades of Proportionality Analysis under the Canadian *Charter*'s Section 1" (2006) 34 Supreme Court LR 501.

[88] See Chapter 3, section 3.2.

[89] See the excellent account of Michaela Hailbronner, *Traditions and Transformations: The Rise of German Constitutionalism* (OUP 2015) 69–95.

[90] See Kristoffel Grechenig and Martin Gelter, "The Transatlantic Divergence in Legal Thought: American Law and Economics vs. German Doctrinalism" (2008) 31 Hastings International and Comparative Law Review 295.

[91] There are few empirical studies on the role of ideology in constitutional court decision-making. However, the few studies that exist suggest that the influence of ideology is less prevalent than in the United States, see Susumu Shikano and Verena Mack, "Judges' Behaviour and Relationship with Political Parties in a Non-Common-Law Country: The Case of the German Federal Constitutional Court" (University of Konstanz Working Paper, 2014); Benjamin G Engst and others, "Zum Einfluss der Parteinähe auf das Abstimmungsverhalten der Bundesverfassungsrichter—eine quantitative Untersuchung" (2017) 72 Juristenzeitung 816.

[92] On the relationship between institutional strength and public legitimacy, see Georg Vanberg, *The Politics of Constitutional Review in Germany* (CUP 2005) 19–57.

popular and trusted German institutions.[93] This allows German judges to offer less deference to the legislature. The less deferential approach may even contribute to the legitimacy of the Court as individual groups of citizens usually benefit from court decisions correcting tax legislation, while the costs for the taxpayer in general are not sufficiently significant and salient to dent the Court's popularity.[94]

Finally, we can also observe a certain influence of the jurisprudence of the CJEU on the later non-discrimination case law.[95] This concerns, in particular, the Federal Constitutional Court's jurisprudence regarding indirect discrimination, which was heavily influenced by the CJEU's case law.[96] Furthermore, the more accommodating approach of the Federal Constitutional Court in the case of discrimination based on sexual orientation came after the *Maruko* decision of the CJEU.[97] Therefore, it is likely that the German Constitutional Court was influenced by the EU case law even though the CJEU was not cited in the former's jurisprudence.[98] Finally, it seems plausible that the reason why the Federal Constitutional Court never had to take a position on the admissibility of positive measures favoring women over men was the early activity of the CJEU in this field.[99]

5. Conclusion

The German Federal Constitutional Court has developed quite a complex doctrine to implement the constitutional equality guarantee. The general doctrine has seen several developmental steps, evolving from a mere arbitrariness review to the current "tierless" formula, according to which the Court differentiates its level of scrutiny depending on different factors. But the Court has also developed distinct doctrinal formulae for several suspect criteria that are explicitly mentioned in the non-discrimination guarantee of Article 3(3) of the Constitution. Finally, it has established specific doctrines for particular subject areas, such as tax law, political competition, or civil procedure.

[93] Hailbronner (n 89) 151–52 (with further references).

[94] See James L Gibson, Gregory A Caldeira, and Vanessa A Baird, "On the Legitimacy of National High Courts" (1998) 92 APSR 343 (arguing that constitutional courts build coalitions of support by deciding cases in favor of groups of individuals).

[95] Generally on the relationship between the Court of Justice and the German Federal Constitutional Court, see Niels Petersen, "Germany" in Fulvio Maria Palombino (ed), *Duelling for Supremacy: International Law vs. National Fundamental Principles: A Comparative Law Perspective* (CUP 2019) 89.

[96] Baer and Markard (n 36) paras 429–430.

[97] *Maruko* (n 70).

[98] Laura Adamietz, *Geschlecht als Erwartung* (Nomos 2011) 203–06; Jule Mulder, "Cultural Narratives and the Application of Non-Discrimination Law" in Barbara Havelková and Mathias Möschel (eds), *Anti-Discrimination Law in Civil Law Jurisdictions* (OUP 2019) 31, 50; Kingreen (n 7) paras 613–614; Boysen (n 7) para 176. On the complicated relationship between the German and EU case law in the field of same sex partnerships see Jule Mulder, *EU Non-Discrimination Law in the Courts: Approaches to Sex and Sexualities Discrimination in EU Law* (Hart 2017) 238–42.

[99] See section 2.4 earlier in this chapter.

If we analyze the results of our empirical analysis, we observe that the equality understanding of the Court best fits the equality as reasonableness model. While the success rate for cases involving a suspect classification is higher than for cases not involving a suspect classification, the latter is still significant. Furthermore, in absolute terms, the number of cases in which the Court declared a statute to be unconstitutional even though no suspect classification was involved is far higher than the number of cases in which the Court struck down a law making a distinction based on a suspect classification. This suggests that the Court not only uses the equality guarantee outside of suspect classifications as a residual instrument to correct obviously arbitrary state action but also to correct the rationality of legislation, often leaving little deference to the legislature. The model can best be explained as a consequence of the Court's strong institutional position and a widely held belief in the rationality of legal argumentation in German legal thought.

8
France

Joanna Mrozińska

1. Introduction

Since 1789, equality is unquestionably of fundamental value in France. Under the motto "liberté, égalité, fraternité," the French Revolution brought a breakthrough by implementing the ideal of equality into the modern legal orders, transforming a moral and political concept of equality into a constitutional value.[1] The Declaration of the Rights of Men and Citizens[2] (Declaration) proclaimed in Article 1 that men are "born and remain free and equal in rights." The republican understanding of equality assumed "a universalist application of legal rules, triggered by the ideal of the abstract man/citizen."[3] This approach centered on an unspecified, general notion of a legal subject, staunching the recognition of differences between individuals. Tied to a formal understanding of equality, it presupposed an equal application of legal rules for those who were in the same situation.[4]

Unsurprisingly, equality has remained a centerpiece of the contemporary French legal order, being a part of its constitutional identity.[5] Equal protection is multilayered, ensured by several norms of a constitutional value, composing "le bloc de constitutionnalité." These norms are enshrined not only in the current 1958 Constitution[6] but also in the former 1946 Constitution[7] and the Declaration.[8]

[1] Ferdinand Melin-Soucramanien, "Le principe d'égalité dans la jurisprudence du Conseil constitutionnel. Quelles perspectives pour la question prioritaire de constitutionnalité?" (2010) 29 Les Nouveaux Cahiers du Conseil Constitutionnel (Dossier: La question prioritaire de constitutionnalité) 89, 89.

[2] The programmatic document of the French Revolution, approved by the National Assembly of France on August 26, 1789.

[3] Stéphanie Hennette-Vauchez and Elsa Fondimare, "Incompatibility between the 'French Republican Model' and Anti-Discrimination Law? Deconstructing a Familiar Trope of Narratives of French Law" in Barbara Havelková and Mathias Möschel (eds), *Anti-Discrimination Law in Civil Law Jurisdictions* (OUP 2019) 56, 57.

[4] Hennette-Vauchez and Fondimare (n 3) 58, 66–67.

[5] Melin-Soucramanien (n 1) 89.

[6] Constitution of the V French Republic (4 Oct 1958).

[7] The former Constitution, of the IV French Republic, ensured equality through its Preamble and reaffirmation of the Declaration. It referred abundantly to various aspects of equality in its Preamble.

[8] The complementary nature of these texts follows from Decision no 71-44 DC (July 16, 1971); for applying it for the first time in the context of equality, see Decision no 73-51 DC (December 27, 1973).

Joanna Mrozińska, *France* In: *Equality's Guardians*. Edited by: Niels Petersen, Oxford University Press.
 DOI: 10.1093/9780198961109.003.0008

While these texts include altogether more than a dozen of equality references, the following provisions are the most crucial.

When it comes to the sources of the principle of equality, the Declaration, besides Article 1, stipulates in Article 6 that "[the Law] must be the same for all, whether it protects or punishes. All citizens, being equal in its eyes, shall be equally eligible to all high offices, public positions and employments, according to their ability, and without other distinction than that of their virtues and talents." The 1958 Constitution provides for equality in Article 1, stating that France "shall ensure the equality of all citizens before the law, without distinction of origin, race or religion. It shall respect all beliefs."[9]

In addition, the constitutional codes emphasize equality of genders. The preamble to the 1946 Constitution underlines equality of sexes by providing "[t]he law guarantees women equal rights to those of men in all spheres." The second sentence of Article 1 of the 1958 Constitution opens the door for the legislature to adopt gender quotas, stipulating that "Statutes shall promote equal access by women and men to elective offices and posts as well as to professional and social positions."

Concerning other more specific provisions on equality, Article 3 of the 1958 Constitution ensures equality in elections by providing that "[s]uffrage . . . shall always be universal, equal and secret." Article 6 of the Declaration ensures equality in access to public offices. Finally, Article 13 of the Declaration establishes the principle of equality in public charges, stipulating that "a general tax . . . must be equally distributed among all citizens, in proportion to their ability to pay."

2. Methodology

If these norms are important for defining the framework of equal protection, it is not uncommon for judges of the French Constitutional Council (*Conseil constitutionnel*, in the following, the Council) to refer simply to "the principle of equality," without referencing a concrete equality norm.[10] Against this backdrop, the present chapter is the result of a systematic analysis of the equality jurisprudence of the Council based on a filter "equality" (*égalité*). The results were obtained by using the official database. The search spans from October 4, 1958[11] to December 31, 2020.

[9] Before constitutional amendments, it was Art. 2. The current 1958 Constitution has been modified several times. For a historical overview see <https://www.legifrance.gouv.fr/loda/id/JORFTEXT000000571356> accessed January 20, 2025.

[10] See on this account Guy Braibant, "Le principe d'égalité dans la jurisprudence du Conseil constitutionnel et du Conseil d'État" in Xavier Browaeys and others (eds), *La Déclaration des droits de l'homme et du citoyen et la jurisprudence: Colloque des 25 et 26 mai 1989 au Conseil constitutionnel* (Presses Universitaires de France 1989) 97, 99–101; Marie-Claire Ponthoreau, *Les principes d'égalité et de non-discrimination, une perspective de droit comparé: France* (Parlement européen 2021) 15.

[11] Marking the adoption of the 1958 Constitution and the official establishment of the Council.

The dataset includes rulings (*décisions*) on substantive constitutional problems of equality under the applied filter. However, it is probable that not all decisions concerning equality were captured by the search filter applied. Nevertheless, such omissions are unlikely to be systematic. Therefore, we can assume that our sample is representative of the French case law. For our qualitative analysis of the doctrine, we have added three important equality problems that have escaped the formal filter,[12] but we have not included these decisions in our quantitative analysis, in order to avoid bias.

The results were further narrowed down by excluding decisions where the Council acts as an electoral judge.[13] Consequently, our quantitative data consists solely of applications for an *a priori* review of constitutionality of statutes (DC cases) and applications for priority preliminary rulings on the issues of constitutionality (QPC decisions).

The list of suspect criteria for the purpose of our study has been refined to reflect universal approaches to protection against discrimination and resonate with approaches regarding other jurisdictions analyzed in this book. Hence, our list comprises gender, race/ethnicity, nationality, religion, residency status,[14] birth out of wedlock, disability, age, sexual orientation, marital status, and language.

3. The equality doctrine of the French Constitutional Council

3.1 The principle of equality and its specific aspects

The equality doctrine has developed significantly since the famous tax case of 1973.[15] The law differentiated taxpayers based on their taxation basis regarding evidence rules for obtaining a discharge from tax liability, established in an *ex officio* tax decision. Invalidating this rule, the Council concisely considered that the law discriminated between citizens and impaired the principle of equality before the law under the Declaration and the Preamble to the Constitution. Subsequently, the Council endeavored to clarify the meaning of the principle of equality[16] and

[12] This includes the gender quota in Decision no 98-407 DC (January 14, 1999); the opening of marriage to persons of the same sex in Decision no 2013-669 DC (May 17, 2013) and racial and ethnic statistics indirectly assessed under equality in Decision no 2007-557 DC (November 15, 2007).

[13] Disputes regarding various elections ("AN," "SEN," "ELEC," and "PDR") and referenda ("REF"). These cases feature mild scrutiny, and finding violations of equality is unlikely. No violations were detected for over 60 sourced decisions. In addition, we omitted observations of the Council regarding elections. Other types of cases did not raise equality issues pertinent for the study.

[14] Note that in France, the principle of equality is applicable to territorial communities. Because of the specificity of the territorial structure of the Republic, rules involving differentiations based on geographical criteria were not automatically considered as suspect cases based on residence.

[15] Decision no 73-51 DC (27 Dec 1973). See also Melin-Soucramanien (n 1) 89.

[16] For varied formulations, see Decision no 78-101 DC (January 17, 1979), Decision no 79-112 DC (January 9, 1980).

developed its operationalization, by tying equality justifications to differences of situations and reasons of general interest.[17] Building upon these premises, a fully-fledged equality formula appears in 1988 and reads: "[t]he principle of equality does not preclude the legislature from regulating different situations in different ways, nor from derogating from equality for reasons of general interest, provided that, in either case, the resulting difference in treatment is related to the purpose of the law establishing it."[18] Later, judges clarified that the relation to the purpose of the law must be direct.[19]

Differences in situations justify a differentiated treatment if they reflect different categories of individuals. The considerations have been initially limited to formally pointing out a difference in situations without engaging in explaining the motives,[20] but have incorporated over time the relation to the aim of the law.[21] Reasons of general interests raise the threshold of justification, rendering differentiated treatment within categories less acceptable by default. Defining these motives case by case, the Council has accepted, for instance, recovery of companies with difficulties,[22] protection of natural sites and environments,[23] prevention of tax evasion,[24] or good administration of justice.[25] Moreover, the correlations between aims and means are relevant, as the well-known carbon emission tax case shows.[26] The Council confirmed that the creation of such an additional tax in view of combatting the CO_2 emissions reflected the aim of general interest. However, the regulations would have led to exempting 93% of all industrial emissions from tax, which contradicted the aim of fighting against climate change.[27]

[17] See an important Decision no 81-132 DC (January 16, 1982) regarding the nationalization of banks. In this regard, the Council followed the footsteps of the Council of State (*Conseil d'État*). Compare the latter's early conceptualization of equality in *Denoyez et Chorques*, no 88032, 88148 (May 10, 1974); the two courts subsequently align in defining the principle of equality, see *Barroux*, no 200903 (Council of State, May 15, 2000). For details see Braibant (n 10). cf also Cécile Barrois de Sarigny, "Le principe d'égalité dans la jurisprudence du Conseil constitutionnel et du Conseil d'État" (2020) 4 Titre VII: Les Cahiers du Conseil constitutionnel (Le principe d'égalité) 18.

[18] Decision no 87-232 DC (January 7, 1988).

[19] Decision no 96-375 DC (April 9, 1996); Decision no 97-388 DC (March 20, 1997); Decision no 98-401 DC (June 10, 1998).

[20] See eg Decision no 81-132 DC (n 17) concerning the first group of banks.

[21] See Decision no 2018-716 QPC (June 29, 2018); Decision no 2016-551 QPC (July 6, 2016). In addition, considerations of general interest might occasionally occur, see Decision no 89-254 DC (July 4, 1989).

[22] Decision no 84-183 DC (January 18, 1985).

[23] Decision no 85-189 DC (July 17, 1985).

[24] Denoted as "objective of a constitutional value" in Decision no 2011-638 DC (July 28, 2011).

[25] Denoted as "objective of a constitutional value" in Decision no 2019-778 DC (March 21, 2019).

[26] Decision no 2009-599 DC (29 Dec 2009). cf Decision no 2010-8 QPC (June 18, 2010) for a positive assessment of the aim-means link.

[27] Besides, the judicial practice is richer regarding the application of equality in particular cases. For proportionality considerations, see eg Decision no 87-232 DC (January 7, 1988) or Decision no 2004-496 DC (June 10, 2004); in turn, for a more restrained review see Decision no 94-343/344 DC (July 27, 1994) concerning the bioethics law.

In addition, the Council has developed specific equality doctrines as extensions of the principle of equality in several legal areas, particularly in tax matters.[28] While the approaches to equality in tax cases are abundant, main traits can be identified.[29] First, the legislature must base its assessment on "objective and rational criteria"[30] directly related to the aim of the law.[31] Second, only serious breaches of the principle of equality before public charges are prohibited,[32] assuming corrections of manifest errors of assessment. Such a breach would occur if the legislature placed excessive burdens on citizens regarding their "contribution capacities"[33] or of a confiscatory nature.[34] For instance, the Council struck down a rebate of the generalized social contribution on the in-work income. The legislature did not consider all the taxpayer's contributory capacities, that is, neither their income other than deriving from work or the income of other household members, nor dependent persons in the household. The solution resulted in a manifest disparity between taxpayers, in breach of Article 13 of the Declaration.[35] Finally, we find reflections regarding the admissibility of preferential tax treatment for reasons of general interest.[36]

3.2 Direct, indirect, and positive discrimination

The notion of discrimination has been interpreted broadly, as denoting unjustified unequal treatment.[37] However, the Council has also developed a narrower meaning of discrimination, targeting morally invidious grounds.[38] In this regard, Article 1 of the 1958 Constitution expressly precludes distinctions based on origin, race, and religion.[39] Such a prohibition of discrimination renders certain

[28] Discussing each would merit a separate contribution. Besides taxes, specific approaches appear in the areas of justice, see Decision no 75-56 DC (July 23, 1975) and Decision no 80-127 DC (January 20, 1981); elections, see Decision no 86-208 DC (July 2, 1986) and Decision no 2008-573 DC (January 8, 2009); and public service, see Decision no 85-204 DC (January 16, 1986) and Decision no 87-229 DC (July 22, 1987).

[29] The principle of equality in tax matters formally encompasses the principle of equality before tax law and the principle of equality before public charges. See Olivier Fouquet, "Le Conseil constitutionnel et le principe d'égalité devant l'impôt" (2011) 33 Les Nouveaux Cahiers du Conseil Constitutionnel (Dossier: Le Conseil Constitutionnel et l'impôt) 7.

[30] We find the first reference to them in Decision no 83-164 DC (December 29, 1983) regarding the large fortune tax.

[31] Decision no 2000-436 DC (December 7, 2000).

[32] Decision no 85-200 DC (January 16, 1986).

[33] Decision no 83-164 DC (December 29, 1983).

[34] See Decision no 2000-437 DC (December 19, 2000); Decision no 2005-530 DC (December 29, 2005).

[35] Decision no 2000-437 DC (19 Dec 2000).

[36] See Decision no 84-184 DC (29 Dec 1984) or Decision no 2000-442 DC (28 Dec 2000).

[37] See Decision no 91-302 DC (December 30, 1991), or a recent Decision no 2019-778 DC (March 21, 2019).

[38] See Decision no 2019-805 QPC (September 27, 2019), where the measures did not "discriminate based on ethnic origin."

[39] The list is not exhaustive, see Melin-Soucramanien (n 1) 92–93.

legislative distinctions per se inadmissible, at least in some cases. For example, the Council automatically annulled gender quotas[40] or a measure regarding the special treatment of the population of French Polynesia referring to criteria reflecting ethnicity, involving one's nationality, their place of birth or those of their parents.[41]

The Council has not established a specific doctrine regarding indirect discriminations. While judges acknowledge that the law might be problematic in its effects, this applies to any legal distinctions.[42] Interestingly, the Council recognizes a weaker factual position of certain groups of individuals when the legislature adopts measures aiming to compensate for it.[43] In 1986, the Council sanctioned measures that aimed to foster employment of young people, considering that "no principle or rule of constitutional value prevent[ed] the legislature from taking measures aiming to help disadvantaged categories of people."[44] However, positive measures in the form of sex-based quotas fell under separate standards. The Council's restrictive stance regarding gender quotas contributed to enshrining the parity principle (*principe de parité*) in the Constitution.[45]

4. The empirical findings

4.1 General overview: an evolution towards less self-restraint

Equality is one of the most frequently applied norms of reference in the French constitutional review.[46] In total, we have sourced 697 judgments with 1,265 equality

[40] Decision no 82-146 DC (November 18, 1982); Decision no 2001-445 DC (June 19, 2001). cf Decision no 2003-483 DC (August 14, 2003).

[41] See Decision no 2004-490 DC (February 12, 2004) on the regime of property transfers *inter vivos*, aiming to preserve them within the hands of the population and the official commentary to this decision. See also Decision no 2007-557 DC (November 15, 2007) striking down provisions on processing of personal data pertaining to race and ethnicity.

[42] cf Decision no 2002-463 DC (December 12, 2002) concerning the reimbursement of expenses for medicines, acknowledging that while the law in question did not directly create differences between insured persons, the law could ultimately produce such effects. For a case involving a suspect criterion, see Decision no 2016-539 QPC (May 10, 2016).

[43] Generally, the principle of equality allows for, but does not require, different treatment of different situations, see Decision no 85-200 DC (January 16, 1986); Decision no 2003-489 DC (December 29, 2003).

[44] Decision no 86-207 DC (June 26, 1986). Similarly, see Decision no 2005-521 DC (July 22, 2005). For other illustrative examples, see Decision no 2003-483 DC (14 Aug 2003) concerning social benefits for women, Decision no 2003-471 DC (April 24, 2003) on priority for scholarship students or Decision no 2004-490 DC (February 12, 2004) on measures fostering employment of population in French Polynesia.

[45] The Council invalidated, in the name of equality of citizens, a quota first in Decision no 82-146 DC (November 18, 1982), and reiterated its position in Decision no 98-407 DC (January 14, 1999). The fifth sentence of art 3, inserted in 1999 to the Constitution, provided that "Statutes shall promote equal access by women and men to electoral offices and posts." As a result, the Council accepted quotas only for electoral offices and posts, see Decision no 2000-429 DC (May 30, 2000); Decision no 2001-445 DC (June 19, 2001) and Decision no 2006-533 DC (March 16, 2006). Another constitutional reform of 2008 extended the parity principle to "professional and social positions" and recodified it in art 1.

[46] cf Melin-Soucramanien (n 1); Ponthoreau (n 10).

Table 8.1 Cases and success rates in a timespan

Types of cases	1963–2009	2010–2020
All cases	584 | 13 %	681 | 18%
Non-suspect distinction cases	494 | 13%	580 | 16%
Suspect distinction cases	90 | 13%	101 | 27%

problems. The overwhelming share of 84.9% concerned non-suspect cases (1,074 cases). Cases involving suspect classifications constituted the remaining 15.1% (191 cases). Challenges to norms falling under both categories resulted in finding breaches of equality in 198 cases, constituting 15.7% of all cases. However, looking at the success rates from a temporal perspective, we see that this rate has evolved. In Table 8.1, we divided the data according to two periods, marking a breaking development concerning the introduction of the priority preliminary rulings procedure. Before the reform introduced this mechanism, the core competency of the Council consisted of an *a priori* review of constitutionality of legal provisions before their promulgation. Through the *a posteriori* procedure, potentially all litigants can contest—via the competent courts who may refer the matter to the Council—the consistency of a legal provision in force with their rights and freedoms enshrined in the Constitution.

The results demonstrate that the success rates increased in the post-2009 period, notably, by 5 percentage points; that is, 3 percentage points for non-suspect cases and 14 percentage points in suspect cases.[47] Considering the low baseline, the increase is notable. It reflects a move towards a less deferential review. This change should be mostly associated with the constitutional *a posteriori* review.

Our conclusion regarding a move towards less deferential review is further supported by an observation regarding the recurring use of interpretative judgments, developed over time in both types of cases. Making reservations of interpretation (formula *sous réserve*), the Council formally does not encroach upon the legislative discretion but circumscribes the meaning of the problematic rule.[48] In turn, when we categorize cases according to legal areas, we see their numbers, as well as chances of success, are subject to variations depending on the category (see

[47] The results show a significantly higher increase in suspect cases. However, this high increase is likely to be caused by recurrent violations in tax cases involving residency criteria, often pertaining to the localization of economic entities. For an example, see Decision no 2013-679 DC (December 4, 2013). Without residence, the success rate for all remaining suspect distinctions amounts only to 17%.

[48] For a good illustration see Decision no 2002-463 DC (December 12, 2002) or Decision no 2015-517 QPC (January 22, 2016).

Table 8.2 Classifications according to subject areas and their success rates

Subject area	Non-suspect cases		Overall results	
Tax/social and other public charges	367	16%	409	18%
Social benefits	86	10%	109	17%
Family	5	0%	19	11%
Profession	118	10%	137	10%
Press/media	32	22%	32	22%
Criminal law	84	25%	89	26%
Immigration/citizenship	20	10%	64	5%
Election/political parties	71	20%	85	20%
Public service	76	14%	80	16%
Other	215	12%	241	12%
Total	1074	14.8%	1265	15.7%

Table 8.2). The overall rates range in principle from 10% for profession to 26% in criminal law, oscillating between moderately low and average success rates.

Immigration matters are an outlier. Overall, it is the category with the lowest success rate. These results demonstrate the Council's reluctance to interfere with legislative policies in this area.[49] For example, the Council readily accepted legislative decisions regarding deprivation of nationality in view of combatting terrorism[50] and increasingly stricter policies fighting against irregular migration.[51] But the bulk of the jurisprudence consists of non-suspect distinction cases in tax matters. Overall, approximately one-third of non-suspect cases fall under this category. This abundance, in our view, can be associated partly with the existence of extensive legislation in this area and the fact that the Council reviews annual finance laws. Non-suspect cases considered alone reach a moderate success rate of 16%. While this rate assumes that the Council remains predominantly deferential, the judicial review generally goes beyond corrections of mere manifest errors. To the contrary, the jurisprudence has become an important factor for shaping the contents of tax legislation.[52]

[49] On this account see Louis Imbert, "Endorsing migration policies in constitutional terms: the case of the French Constitutional Council" (2022) 14 European Journal of Legal Studies 63.

[50] Decision no 2014-439 QPC (January 23, 2015); Decision no 96-377 DC (July 16, 1996). See also regarding the fight against terrorism Decision no 2016-606/607 QPC (January 24 2017).

[51] See eg Decision no 97-389 DC (April 22, 1997); Decision no 2003-467 DC (March 13, 2003); Decision no 2011-631 DC (June 9, 2011). See also Decision no 2017-674 QPC (December 1, 2017).

[52] Fouquet (n 29) 13.

Table 8.3 Suspect classification cases and success rates

Type of suspect classification	Number of cases	Success rates
Gender	20	25%
Race/ethnicity/origin	31	13%
Nationality	26	38%
Religion	3	33%
Residence	59	25%
Disability	6	33%
Age	20	0
Sexual orientation	7	0
Marital status	14	14%
Language	5	0

4.2 Suspect cases

Suspect classification cases reached a success rate of 20.4%. However, we see certain variations between different types of suspect characteristics when we take a closer look (see Table 8.3). Distinctions based on, for example, gender, nationality, residency status reached relatively high success rates, approaching or surpassing 30%.[53] In contrast, challenges to rules involving legal distinctions of race, and marital status have less chances of success, with success rates of 13% and 14%, respectively. No positive results are noted for age, sexual orientation, and language.[54]

The most successful category concerns cases involving nationality distinctions, with a success rate of 38%. This high rate can be at least partly associated with several social benefits cases effectively precluding limitations on access to benefits. For example, in the first priority preliminary ruling case, the Council found a nationality distinction for the revaluation of civil and military pensions for war veterans of former French colonies to be in breach of the principle of equality. As a consequence, the same conclusion pertained to an exclusion of Algerian nationals from the scope of holders of veterans' disability pensions and retirement pensions, challenged in the same case.[55]

[53] Disability and religion cases note high results over 30% but such cases remain scarce against the backdrop of other distinctions.

[54] There were no cases concerning birth out of wedlock.

[55] Decision no 2010-1 QPC (May 28, 2010). See also, similarly Decision no 89-269 DC (22 Jan 1990); Decision no 2010-18 QPC (July 23, 2010); Decision no 2010-93 QPC (February 4, 2011) or Decision no 2017-690 QPC (February 8, 2018).

Turning to the least successful cases, the category of sexual orientation merits attention. In this area, the Council took a deferential position, readily accepting the legislative choices. This applies both to restrictive and progressive measures. For instance, in 1980, the Council upheld a differentiation of criminal liability for sexual acts against minors depending on whether the act in question concerned two persons of the same or different sex.[56] In 2011, the Council accepted the constitutionality of provisions prohibiting same-sex marriage because of the different situation of homosexual and heterosexual couples.[57] However, two years later, the Council did not oppose the extension of marriage to same-sex couples. Judges argued that they could not encroach upon the evolving position of the legislature, which considered that differences between the two types of couples no longer justified an exclusive access to the marriage for different-sex couples.[58]

The categories analyzed above can overall be considered as reliable indicators of the Council's position towards discrimination issues. However, the case law also tends to focus on equality in the formal sense and results in suppressing differences. This is most prominent regarding the sex quota cases where gender status was seen as inadmissible ground for differentiation until the constitutional amendments were enacted. Concerning race, the Council struck down the provision of special rights to certain minorities or recognizing differentiations based on ethnic criteria, even in the name of recognition of minorities. For example, the Council overturned a provision of special regulations for Corsica which emphasized the "Corsican people" as a component of the French people.[59] Similarly, provisions of the European Charter for Regional or Minority Languages conferred specific rights on "groups" of speakers of regional or minority languages within "territories" in which these languages were used. The Council found them to be in breach, *inter alia*, of equality before the law and the unity of the French people.[60]

In a similar vein, examples of non-violation cases perpetuating indirect discriminations are frequent. Assessing the controversial issue of a total concealment of faces in public, the Council argued that the legislature was allowed considered that full-face veils placed women in "a situation of exclusion and inferiority," manifestly incompatible with the principle of freedom and equality and confirmed a legislative ban on wearing such veils in public.[61] Nevertheless, the Council ignored

[56] Decision no 80-125 DC (December 19, 1980).

[57] Decision no 2010-92 QPC (January 28, 2011).

[58] Decision no 2013-669 DC (May 17, 2013). Note that while this decision contains many equality problems included in our study, the rule on opening the marriage to persons of the same sex is not among the collected empirical data since it did not appear under the filter "equality."

[59] Decision no 91-290 DC (May 9, 1991).

[60] Decision no 99-412 DC (June 15, 1999).

[61] Decision no 2010-613 DC (October 7, 2010). See also Decision no 2003-467 DC (March 13, 2003) regarding housing of travelling communities, such as Roma people. cf also Decision no 2019-805 QPC (September 27, 2019); Decision no 2010-13 QPC (July 9, 2010); Decision no 2012-279 QPC (October 5, 2012).

the issue of disproportionate impact of the criminalization on religious beliefs.[62] More recently, the Council assessed regulations establishing reductions in social contributions for additional work hours of employees and public servants. The applicants claimed that there was a difference in treatment because mostly full-time workers and men would benefit from these reductions to the detriment of part-time employees and women. The Council considered that the reductions applied equally to full- and part-time workers as well as to male and female employees.[63]

5. Concluding remarks

In trying to understand the overall deference of the Council and the predominant focus on non-suspect distinctions, the nature and the history of the institution are important factors. The Council has been conceived by the 1958 Constitution in view of protecting the executive powers, and its designation as a "Council" allegedly shows reluctance to considering it as a typical judge-composed court.[64] The Council's members include ordinary members, composed often of former politicians, and appointed by elected politicians, as well as the former presidents of the Republic. Politics and the wish to avoid an open conflict with it are more ingrained in the nature of the institution than in typical constitutional counterparts on the Continent.

The legitimacy of this institution in the French legal culture is solidified by respecting the principle of separation of powers and the exercise of self-restraint.[65] If not, the Council faces the criticism of judicial activism.[66] In addition, the initial prerogative of the Council centered on the limited review of legal acts before their promulgation.[67] Assessing what effects the law, not yet in force, would

[62] In this vein, later, the ECtHR accepted the regulations prohibiting full face veils but recognized that the law could indirectly discriminate based on religious grounds. Yet, this impact was justified. However, the UN HRCttee took the position that a general ban criminalizing wearing such veils in public disproportionately affected women's freedom of religion. See decisions *S.A.S v France* [GC] ECtHR 2014-III 341; *Yaker v France* CCPR/C/123/D/2747/2016 (HRCttee, July 17, 2018); and *Hebbadj v France* CCPR/C/123/D/2807/2016 (HRCttee, July 17, 2018).

[63] Decision no 2018-776 DC (December 21, 2018). Another example involves the exclusion from the temporary residence permit to foreigners "living in polygamy" as detrimental to women who often did not have a choice or knowledge regarding it, see Decision no 97-389 DC (April 22, 1997). For indirect male discrimination see Decision no 2019-826 QPC (February 7, 2020).

[64] Imbert (n 49) 70. In addition, we speak about decisions of the Council ("décisions") rather than judgments ("arrêts"). The highest administrative jurisdiction is also named similarly, ie the Council of State (*Conseil d'État*). However, the administrative jurisdiction powers grew as secondary to the initial primary task of the Council of State consisting of advising the Government.

[65] Natașa Danelciuc-Colodrovschi, "The Principle of Equality in the French Constitutional Council's Case Law: What Changes After Ten Years of Ex Post Review Implementation?" (2020) 150 Problems of Legality 292, 298–99.

[66] cf Bernard Rullier, "Les Décisions du Conseil Constitutionnel qui ont fait l'actualité" (Fondation Jean Jaurès 2023) <https://www.jean-jaures.org/publication/les-decisions-du-conseil-constitutionnel-qui-ont-fait-lactualite/> accessed January 20, 2025.

[67] The review of constitutionality of norms has been practically impossible afterwards.

produce is difficult,[68] and further explains the Council's initial more reserved attitude. However, the prerogatives of the Council have grown since 2010 with the introduction of the priority preliminary rulings procedure, opening the door for an *a posteriori* review. This "indirect constitutional complaint"[69] assimilates the institution to a guardian of rights, ruling on legal provisions as related to concrete situations, and moves the French constitutional review closer towards a wider European context.[70]

Certainly, the case law has not been immune to various foreign impacts.[71] However, overall, the impact does not seem to take precedence over the specificity of the French legal order and tradition. While the constitutional judges have developed a more stringent attitude towards certain suspect classification cases, less deference does not always equal better anti-discrimination protection. Instead, in finding violations the Council at times proves to be a proponent of the commitment to formal equality, while being skeptical of substantive equality acknowledging differences among groups.

The importance of the principle of equality in the French legal order is immeasurable, as is the depth of the Council's jurisprudence. When making an overall assessment, we argue that the Council's case law fits the model of equality as reasonableness. While the overall success rate is lower than in other jurisdictions following this model, the total number of successful cases is equally high. In addition, cases involving suspect criteria only constitute a small part of the jurisprudence and their overall success rate is not considerably higher than for cases not involving suspect classifications. Finally, numerous decisions reveal that the French case law does not always stand for a progressive approach protecting vulnerable groups.

[68] Danelciuc-Colodrovschi (n 65) 299–300.

[69] Otto Pfersmann, "Concrete Review as Indirect Constitutional Complaint in French Constitutional Law: A Comparative Perspective" (2010) 6 EuConst 223, 223.

[70] Xavier Philippe, "Constitutional Review in France: The Extended Role of the Conseil Constitutionnel Through the New Priority Preliminary Rulings Procedure (QPC)" (2012) 53 Annales U Sci Budapestinensis Rolando Eotvos Nominatae 65.

[71] For instance, the inclusion of the proportionality standards appears to be borrowed from the German Federal Constitutional Court and the CJEU. Valérie Goesel-Le Bihan, "Le contrôle de proportionnalité exercé par le Conseil constitutionnel" (2007) 22 Les Nouveaux Cahiers du Conseil constitutionnel (Dossier: Le réalisme en droit constitutionnel) 208.

9
Poland

Joanna Mrozińska

1. Introduction

The discussion on the equality jurisprudence of the Polish Constitutional Tribunal (PCT) has to be analyzed in the context of the trajectories of contemporary constitutional adjudication in Poland. The idea of constitutional review had been germinating in opposition to the arbitrariness of monopolistic state power since the 1980s. The PCT emerged in this context as the "unwanted child"[1] of the Communist regime in 1985, albeit with severely constrained powers and limited authority.[2]

The first period of the meaningful constitutional adjudication of the PCT began with the democratic transformation in 1989 and ends in late 1997 with the adoption of the new Constitution of Poland.[3] In this period, the PCT's powers increased yet remained weak. However, the PCT found its place in an unstable constitutional environment. It assumed an active role in establishing important limits to the lawmaking process.[4] The PCT not only facilitated the transition to a new legal and political order but also fostered modern democratic standards based on the rule of law.[5] One of the most important legal standards that the PCT applied to provide legal guardrails for the transition was equal protection.[6]

[1] Janina Zakrzewska, "Prezentacja Trybunału Konstytucyjnego" in *Prawa człowieka w orzecznictwie sądów konstytucyjnych: polsko-holenderskie kolokwium* (1991) 4, 14; as cited in Mark F Brzeziński and Leszek Garlicki, "Judicial Review in Post-Communist Poland: The Emergence of a Rechtsstaat" (1995) 31 Stanford Journal of International Law 13, 58.

[2] For a detailed account see for example Brzeziński and Garlicki (n 1) 21 et seq.

[3] The Constitution of the Republic of Poland (April 2, 1997), published in Dziennik Ustaw No 78, item 483. It entered into force on October 17, 1997.

[4] Lech Garlicki, "Constitutional Court and Politics: The Polish Crisis" in Christine Landfried (ed), *Judicial Power: How Constitutional Courts Affect Political Transformations* (CUP 2019) 141, 142–43.

[5] Aleksandra Kustra-Rogatka, "The Polish Constitutional Court and Political "Refolution" After 1989: Between The Continuity and Discontinuity of The Constitutional Narrative" (2016) 6 Wroclaw Review of Law, Administration & Economics 62, 66–69; Tomasz Warczok and Hanna Dębska, "Sacred Law and Profane Politics: The Symbolic Construction of the Constitutional Tribunal" (2014) 188 Polish Sociological Review 461, 465.

[6] See Mark Brzeziński, "Constitutional 'Refolution' in the Ex-Communist World: The Rule of Law" (1997) 12 American University International LR 45, 90–94.

Joanna Mrozińska, *Poland* In: *Equality's Guardians*. Edited by: Niels Petersen, Oxford University Press.
 DOI: 10.1093/9780198961109.003.0009

Between 1997 and 2015, the constitutional adjudication developed under the 1997 Constitution. In principle, the PCT preserved the continuity of its case law by upholding earlier interpretations,[7] including the concept of equality.[8] The jurisprudence flourished particularly in the area of fundamental rights.[9] Favorable conditions for jurisprudential developments were created by granting the PCT fully-fledged powers of a modern constitutional court. According to the 1997 Constitution, the PCT largely reviews the constitutionality of sub-constitutional acts after they come into force. The control is triggered by the applications for retrospective constitutionality review of certain institutions, by courts' referrrals regarding the constitutionality of norms, and by constitutional complaints.[10] The latter mechanism has a limited nature since it targets the legal basis of the decision which allegedly infringes constitutional rights or freedoms of an individual. In addition, there is a preliminary review of the constitutionality of bills upon the application of the President of the Republic.[11] Within these modes of review, the PCT examines the respect of equality in enacted statutory and sub-statutory acts, in other words, equality *in* the law.[12]

The jurisprudential activity of the PCT has declined and became questionable in recent years due to the infamous constitutional crisis that started in late 2015. At first, the Law and Justice party conducted abrupt and hasty reforms aiming at paralyzing the PCT's functioning. The beginning of 2017 marks a transition from an enfeebled but still independent court into a politically dependent actor. No further attacks were needed at the time. The Law and Justice had gradually "packed" the institution with new members, including the President of the Court.[13] In mid-2021, the last "old-regime" judge left the PCT.[14]

2. Equality doctrine under the 1997 Constitution

The Polish Constitution of 1997 guarantees individuals equality before the law and the right to equal treatment by public authorities in Article 32(1). Article 32(2) prohibits discrimination for any reason in political, social, and economic life. Article 33 underlines equal rights of men and women. In addition, the Constitution

[7] Garlicki (n 4) 144.

[8] See in particular Judgment of December 16, 1997, case K 8/97.

[9] Garlicki (n 4) 144.

[10] See in particular arts 79, 188, 190–191, 193 of the 1997 Constitution.

[11] Art 122(3)–(6) of the 1997 Constitution.

[12] The PCT also distinguishes another dimension of equality, namely equality before the law. It concerns the law application, which falls beyond the constitutional review.

[13] Wojciech Sadurski, "Polish Constitutional Tribunal under PiS: From an Activist Court, to a Paralysed Tribunal, to a Governmental Enabler" (2019) 11 Hague Journal on the Rule of Law 63, 73.

[14] Leon Kieres' term of office ended in July 2021.

contains special provisions concretizing equality in specific spheres of life,[15] to which Article 32 is *lex generalis*.[16]

2.1 The principle of equality and its operationalization

The principle of equality enshrined in Article 32(1)—even if not strictly speaking accessory in nature—is seen primarily as requiring equality in the context of constitutional rights or freedoms.[17] In all circumstances, equality must be tied to another constitutional right or freedom for a constitutional complaint to be reviewed. It is because the right to equality is a "second-degree" right or a "meta right" that requires another constitutional reference to determine the constitutional status of an individual.[18]

The principle of equality requires that "all subjects characterized to an equal degree by a relevant feature shall be treated equally, according to the same measure, without any differentiations, whether discriminatory or favourable."[19] The formula implies that equal and similar persons should be treated similarly and assumes different treatment of different persons.[20] To specify the equal treatment requirement, judges have elaborated a tripartite analysis.[21] The first step aims to find a common relevant—factual or legal—feature characterizing similar subjects.[22]

[15] They include art 25(1) on equal rights of churches and other religious organizations; art 64(2) on protection of property on an equal basis for all; art 60 on access to public service based on the principle of equality. For the full list, see Judgment of April 2, 2003, case K 13/02. This chapter focuses on art 32 as the most prevalent provision.

[16] Jerzy Oniszczuk, *Konstytucja Rzeczypospolitej Polskiej w orzecznictwie Trybunału Konstytucyjnego* (Zakamycze 2000) 269.

[17] The provision might be applied independently, also for problems beyond the sphere of constitutional rights and freedoms; see eg Judgment of December 16, 2009, case K 49/07; Judgment of July 26, 2012, case P 8/11.

[18] See Decision of October 24, 2001, SK 10/01, OTK ZU 2001, nr 7, poz. 225. See also Michał Ziółkowski, "Zasada równości w prawie" (2015) 5 Państwo i Prawo 94, 102–05; Cezary Paluchniak, "Dopuszczalność oceny zgodności z Konstytucją przepisów postępowania cywilnego kształtujących tzw. przedsąd w postępowaniu zainicjowanym skargą konstytucyjną" (2017) 7–8 Palestra 139, 144 et seq; Jadwiga Potrzeszcz, "Zasada równości w orzecznictwie polskiego Trybunału Konstytucyjnego dotyczącym skargi konstytucyjnej" in Sławomira Wronkowska (ed), *Polska kultura prawna a proces integracji europejskiej* (Zakamycze 2005) 293.

[19] Judgment of November 5, 1997, case K 22/97, following Decision of December 12, 1994, case K 3/94.

[20] Occasionally, the PCT requires different treatment of different persons, see Judgment of October 26, 2004, case SK 7/04; Judgment of February 7, 2005, case SK 49/03; cf also Judgment of March 5, 2003, case K 7/01.

[21] Note that the equality test is distinctive from the proportionality test under the limitation clause in art 31(3), which is default for assessing limitations of constitutional rights and freedoms. See Anna Śledzińska-Simon, *Analiza proporcjonalności ograniczeń konstytucyjnych praw i wolności: Teoria i praktyka* (E-Wydawnictwo, Prawnicza i Ekonomiczna Biblioteka Cyfrowa. Wydział Prawa, Administracji i Ekonomii Uniwersytetu Wrocławskiego 2019). On the non-application of the proportionality test to the right to equality see Witold Borysiak and Leszek Bosek, "Komentarz do artykułu 32 Konstytucji RP" in Marek Safjan and Leszek Bosek (ed), *Konstytucja RP. Tom I. Komentarz do Art. 1–86* (Legalis C.H. Beck 2016) 818. To varying degrees, the proportionality test applies to specific equality norms, including arts 64(2) and 60; see Judgment of June 2, 1999, case K 34/98 or Judgment of November 23, 2009, case P 61/08.

[22] It is identified by examining the aim and the content of regulations in which the reviewed norm is included; see Judgment of May 12, 1998, case U 17/97 or by the legal area in question.

Next, the PCT examines whether a differentiation of similar persons takes place. The principle of equality is violated unless sufficiently convincing arguments justify the differentiation. These arguments must be relevant, proportionate, and related to other constitutional values, principles, or norms.[23]

An important case illustrating this test is case K 9/12 regarding the indexation of pension benefits related to disability and old age.[24] For one year, the legislature departed from a standard percentage-based increase, substituting it with an adjustment involving a specific quota. The legislature foresaw an identical increase for all beneficiaries. This solution treated pensioners with higher pensions less favorably than those with lower pensions. According to the PCT, the measure was reasonably related to the aim and the content of the regulation in question. The regulation was an element of a broader program of balancing the public finances, aimed at halting the increase in public debt and decreasing the budget deficit. At the same time, the increase of the lowest value pension benefits was above the rate of inflation, in accordance with the principle of social solidarity. Next, the constitutional interests at stake were adequately balanced. The adjustment was temporary and the least burdensome for pensioners who received higher pensions since their pensions lost the lowest possible value. Furthermore, the solution would result in a slight slowing down in the economic stratification of society, desirable for the value of the common good. Finally, the measure aligned with the constitutional values, principles and norms. The budgetary balance and social solidarity, as well as other values stemming from the principle of social justice, justified the quota-based adjustment.[25]

While the PCT, in principle, accepts differentiation among various groups of people, the constitutional equality review may shift to a more general level, targeting the choice of the relevant feature criterion, and its legitimacy. An example can be found in case K 6/09[26] on lowering the retirement pensions of former Communist secret service agents. In particular, the legislature significantly lowered the old-age pensions of the officers of the Military Council of National Salvation (MCNS). This was a non-constitutional and junta-like authority that governed Poland during the period of martial law between 1981 and 1983. The PCT decided that decreasing pensions of the officers for each year of their service in the Polish Army, before MCNS was set up, was arbitrary and unreasonable. Until December 11, 1981, their members were no different from other professional soldiers of the People's Republic of Poland.[27]

[23] Judgment of December 16, 1997, case K 8/97; Judgment of May 12, 1998, case U 17/97. See also these judgments for definition of these conditions.

[24] Judgment of December 19, 2012, case K 9/12.

[25] Less meticulous considerations are also frequent; see eg Judgment of October 24, 2001, case SK 22/01 or Judgment of November 28, 2001, case K 36/01.

[26] Judgment of February 24, 2010, case K 6/09.

[27] Depending on the case and the allegation, the assessment can also involve other prongs of testing, including the consistency with constitutional axiology and the principle of social justice, see Judgment of March 12, 2002, case P 9/01, or Judgment of November 20, 2002, case K 41/02. See also Judgments of June 10, 2003, case K 16/02 and of October 20, 2009, case SK 15/08 for testing similar to considering unequal treatment.

2.2 The prohibition of discrimination in Article 32(2) and indirect discrimination

The prohibition of discrimination under Article 32(2) is first a corollary of the principle of equality. Defining more precisely the limits of admissible differentiations of subjects of law, the provision determines that no criterion can lead to unjust solutions that discriminate against these subjects.[28] A more recent conceptualization denotes the prohibition of discrimination as a qualified form of unequal treatment.[29] It prohibits the adoption of differentiations motivated only by the personal characteristics of addressees, such as sex, age, or social origin.[30] However, this approach has rarely been applied by the PCT in practice.

The PCT has not developed the concept of indirect discrimination under Article 32.[31] However, elements of protection against indirect discrimination can be found in judicial considerations regarding the effects of norms and factual situations. Take the judgment in case SK 11/98.[32] A professional soldier wanted to terminate his service relationship prematurely for belief-related reasons. To effectively leave the military service, he first had to repay the equivalent costs related to his military training in full without having the option to pay in several installments. The PCT observed that the solution did not only unreasonably differentiate based on termination reasons[33] but also based on one's financial status. In effect, persons without adequate means to repay immediately were treated worse than those who were financially better off because they were effectively barred from leaving the military service prematurely.

2.3 Positive measures

The PCT has recognized the admissibility of positive measures in the gender area. "Compensatory privileges" are legal privileges aimed to diminish inequalities between men and women in social life[34] that are admissible if justified by social or biological differences between sexes.[35] Accepting them is tied to the constitutional

[28] Judgment of October 23, 2001, case K 22/01; Judgment of April 14, 2003, case K 34/02. See also Judgment of December 16, 1997, case K 8/97; Judgment of May 12, 1998, case U 17/97, and our example in note 26 where the review involved art 32.

[29] Judgment July 5, 2011, case P 14/10; Judgment of July 12, 2016, case K 28/15; Judgment of June 20, 2017, case K 16/15.

[30] Judgment July 5, 2011, case P 14/10. The exemplification aligns with art 233(2), prohibiting to limit the freedoms and rights of persons and citizens on several grounds in a period of state emergency or martial law.

[31] Judgment of July 5, 2011, case P 14/10, is the only decision where the PCT briefly discussed indirect discrimination under art 32(2). However, the case does not offer guidance on this concept's implementation. cf mentions of the concept in Judgment of July 15, 2010, case K 63/07 and Judgment of February 6, 2007, case P 25/06.

[32] Judgment of February 16, 1999, case SK 11/98. See also Judgment of September 7, 2004, case P 4/04.

[33] Persons who misbehaved were dismissed without any on-the-spot repayment obligation.

[34] Judgment of June 13, 2000, case K 15/99 or Judgment of December 5, 2000, case K 35/99, referring to older cases.

[35] See eg Judgment of December 5, 2000, case K 35/99; Judgment of July 15, 2010, case K 63/07.

postulate of equality between the sexes, enshrined in Article 33, and the principle of social justice.[36] An example of sanctioning a compensatory privilege can be found in the landmark judgment K 63/07, which approved the mechanism foreseeing an earlier female retirement age within the general pension system.[37] Beyond the criterion of gender, some preferential treatment of vulnerable groups is permitted through the back door of the principle of social justice, used as a corrective to current inequalities.[38]

3. The results of the empirical study of the case law

3.1 Methodology

The study analyzed the judgments issued from late 1997 to 2020. The starting date was chosen according to the first decision made by the PCT relating to the current, post-communist Constitution. The analysis selected the equality cases from the PCT's official database, using the search term "equality." The results were further narrowed down to judgments declaring norms to be "consistent with the Constitution" (*zgodny z Konstytucją*) or "not consistent with the Constitution" (*niezgodny z Konstytucją*), while judgments ruling that a norm "is not inconsistent with the Constitution" (*nie jest niezgodny z Konstytucją*) have been excluded.[39] Subsequently, judgments were cleaned manually to include only those addressing the question of equality on substance, excluding repetitive or fairly similar issues. The sample contains 464 judgments but 548 cases denoting units of review that were examined; one judgment could contain several units of review. In the study, suspect criteria include gender, nationality, residency status, age, religion, race (ethnicity), sexual orientation, birth out of wedlock, language, and economic status.[40]

[36] Judgment of December 5, 2000, case K 35/99; Judgment of July 15, 2010, case K 63/07; cf also Judgment of May 7, 2014, case K 43/12.

[37] Judgment of July 15, 2010, case K 63/07.

[38] See n 24 and accompanying text. Similarly, see Judgment of October 30, 2007, case P 36/06. Beyond gender cases, the concept of compensatory privileges appears once in the Judgment of March 12, 2002, case P 9/01, regarding favoring parties not represented by a professional lawyer in court proceedings.

[39] Despite incoherencies in early cases, the PCT clarified over time that the latter formula marks inadequate constitutional benchmarks of review. It means that the review cannot solve the constitutionality question, see especially Judgment of May 11, 2007, case K 2/07.

[40] Note that our sample includes cases that did not explicitly discuss the criterion as suspect or even rejected it as such.

Table 9.1 Subject areas and success rates

Subject area	Total	Success rate
Tax	34	38%
Social benefits	125	38%
Public service	70	39%
Profession	55	31%
Civil law	33	33%
Criminal law	16	25%
Administrative law	33	42%
Proceedings	67	48%
Housing	73	51%
Elections/political	12	8%
Other	30	37%
Total	548	39%

3.2 Results

3.2.1 The predominance of non-suspect cases over suspect cases

Out of a total of 548 cases, the Court found 214 violations, leading to a success rate of 39%. The rate suggests that the PCT is rather non-deferential in its approach. Cases concerning social benefits, housing, and public service are the most numerous (see Table 9.1). In general, many constitutional problems in these areas resulted from the transformation of the political system. Adapting state structures and creating new administrative apparatus, making socio-economic arrangements,[41] and shifting towards the free-market economy required intensive regulation and adjustments. As such, these cases predominantly involve non-suspect distinctions.

The housing category includes 73 cases and has the highest success rate with 51%. This result is not unexpected given the enhanced protection that the 1997 Constitution gave to private property.[42] For instance, this category includes

[41] For example, in 1998 there was a major reform of the pension system. It was motivated by unfavorable demographic conditions and the need to ensure an effective and stable social security system. New solutions were recurrently reviewed by the PCT. See, in particular, Judgment of September 12, 2000, case K 1/00; Judgment of April 24, 2006, case P 9/05; Judgment of December 11, 2006, case SK 15/06.

[42] See eg Judgment of June 13, 2011, case SK 41/09. In particular, differentiation of protection of property rights by regulations giving the state and public subjects a more favorable position compared to persons of private law is prohibited under art 64(2); see in this respect judgment of January 31, 2001, case P 4/99; Judgment of January 9, 2007, case P 5/05; Judgment of March 17, 2008, case K 32/05. National

numerous cases regarding the return of formerly expropriated properties where the PCT boldly rectified legislative activity. In case SK 22/01, judges corrected an underinclusive norm enabling the return of expropriated properties that did not include a case comparable to the ones for which a return was possible.[43] Another illustration can be found in judgment SK 41/09.[44] The PCT remedied unjustified restrictions on the types of real estate in Warsaw for which it was possible to claim compensation for expropriation conducted after the war, aimed at rebuilding the capital. Moreover, the housing category contains cases regarding various regulations related to an ongoing adaptation of housing relationships in the new post-socialist reality. For instance, we note frequent issues regarding tenancy or transformations of ownership and property structures with regards to complex regulations on housing cooperatives.[45]

The high number of cases in the area of public service, 70 cases and a success rate of 39%, must be seen in the context of administrative changes that took place because of political transformation. Equality norms, for example, were recurrently relied on to examine many issues of public service formations. Moreover, equality review served as a check for lustration regulations, aiming to protect the new democracy against the threats of the totalitarian past by revealing the involvement of public servants in the repression apparatus.[46] For example, judges did not accept a collective publication of data on individual involvement without distinguishing more precisely the form of involvement. Uniform disclosure was detrimental to those whose involvement was less significant than others. It violated the requirement of equal protection of affected persons with regards to protection of their reputation under the right to privacy.[47]

The relatively high success rate in the category of social benefits group[48] (38%) is surprising, given that the PCT often highlights a large degree of discretion of the

property was seen as requiring less diligent protection than private property, and legislative discretion concerning differentiation in this sphere is broader; see Judgment of October 20, 2009, case SK 15/08.

[43] Judgment of October 24, 2001, case SK 22/01.

[44] Judgment of June 13, 2011, case SK 41/09.

[45] With regards to tenancy, see eg Judgment of June 2, 1999, case K 34/98; Judgment of July 14, 2003, case K 35/01; Judgment of May 17, 2006, case K 33/05; with regards to housing cooperatives, see eg Judgment of April 20, 2005, case K 42/02; Judgment of December 21, 2005, case SK 10/05; Judgment of September 5, 2006, case K 51/05; Judgment of December 17, 2008, case P 16/08; Judgment of July 15, 2009, case K 64/07.

[46] In general, in lustration proceedings, persons performing public functions under lustration obligation had to file an affidavit revealing their work or service in the totalitarian state security organs or collaborating with them between 1944 and 1990. The sanction for a lustration lie was a ban on holding certain public functions, later on also extended to cases of a non-submission of an affidavit. For such cases, see eg Judgment of October 21, 1998, case K 24/98; Judgment of June 19, 2002, case K 11/02; Judgment of March 5, 2003, case K 7/01; Judgment of May 28, 2003, case K 44/02; Judgment of May 11, 2007, case K 2/07.

[47] Judgment of March 5, 2003, case K 7/01.

[48] This abundance also stems from the fact that cases regarding benefits related to old age and incapacity to work in public service are in principle assigned to the social benefits category.

legislature in this area. Yet, the PCT willingly corrects certain social inequalities. For example, the PCT did not accept distinctions based on the source of income with regards to access to certain social benefits. In case K 12/01,[49] the challenged statutes provided an income assessment formula based on real income. However, for the self-employed, the norms took into account the declared income, which could not be below 60% of the average monthly remuneration. The PCT considered that the solutions discriminated against the self-employed and could in extreme cases deprive poor persons of due help.

The non-deferential approach is further confirmed by the low share of cases involving suspect classifications. Only 53 out of 548 cases concerned suspect classifications (approximately 10%). The success rate of 49% for suspect classification cases is slightly higher than the general 39% success rate. Challenges to affirmative action measures were successful in 60% of cases while indirect discrimination cases had a success rate of 50%. When analyzing the suspect criteria cases more closely, the analysis unveils significant differences (see Table 9.2). There are suspect criteria with a high success rate (residency status, nationality, gender), moderately successful categories (economic status, disability, age), and those that are entirely unsuccessful (religion).[50] There were no cases concerning race, sexual orientation, and birth out of wedlock.

The success rate for cases involving differentiation based on gender must be qualified. Most cases concerning the allegedly more beneficial retirement age rules for women eventually burdened them because they did not possess a choice regarding the use of this "privilege" and were thus qualified as a violation of equality.[51] Had these solutions not been mandatory, they would have been less likely to fail constitutional review.[52] Without the cases regarding the lower retirement age (4 violations and 1 non-violation),[53] the success rate for gender would have been 67% (4 out of 6 cases). This also includes four cases concerning the disadvantaging of men—a non-violation case which implemented a sturdy pro-constitutional interpretation[54] and three violations protecting men against discrimination.[55] Finally,

[49] Judgment of October 15, 2001, case K 12/01; see also Judgment of January 18, 2000, case K 17/99; Judgment of October 3, 2006, case K 30/05.

[50] The one language result is not representative. Another language distinction in the same judgment was classified by us as a nationality distinction. If it was not so, the success rate of the two cases with a criterion of language would be 50%.

[51] It was like this for appointed teachers: Judgment of March 28, 2000, case K 27/99; directors of pharmacies: Judgment of June 13, 2000, case K 15/99; appointed state or local self-government employees: Judgment of December 5, 2000, case K 35/99; and appointed employees of the Supreme Audit Office: Judgment of December 11, 2008, case K 33/07.

[52] As we can infer from Judgment of July 15, 2010, case K 63/07 sanctioning the lower retirement age for women as a general construct in the retirement system. See also Judgment of December 11, 2008, case K 33/07.

[53] The non-violation case was Judgment of July 15, 2010, case K 63/07.

[54] Judgment of June 29, 2006, case P 30/05.

[55] Judgment of July 6, 1999, case P 8/98; Judgment of October 23, 2007, case P 10/07; Judgment of May 7, 2014, case K 43/12.

Table 9.2 Suspect criteria and success rates

Criterion	Total	Success rate
Gender	11	73%
Nationality	4	75%
Residence	7	86%
Language	1	0
Age	9	22%
Economic status	8	50%
Disability	7	43%
Religion	6	0

the violations regarding the mandatory female retirement age also explain the high success rate for affirmative action cases. If we removed them, we would obtain a much lower success rate of 33% for affirmative action (2 violations out of 6 cases).

These numbers already suggest that the PCT's gender case law is not unequivocally progressive. In addition, a major case of 2010 sanctioning the basic lower retirement age in the general pension system emphasized the traditional role of women.[56] All three female judges on the bench dissented.[57] In their opinions, the solution entrenched existing inequalities, put pressure on women to use this option, and perpetuated women's lower pensions. After this ruling, the PCT upheld the introduction of the same retirement age for both sexes as constitutional in 2014, considering societal changes. In this context, the judges also confirmed the temporary nature of compensatory privileges.[58]

Finally, cases concerning religion not only reflect the unwillingness of the PCT to tackle socially sensitive issues but also show a tendency to cater to the interests of the majority religion.[59] The PCT often appears very supportive of the Catholic Church, while applying hardly credible reasoning. For example, in case U 10/07 of December 2, 2009, the PCT legitimized the inclusion of grades from religion in the student's average, even though students not adhering to the Catholic faith had

[56] See case K 63/07 (n 37).

[57] Judges Łętowska, Liszcz, and Wronkowska-Jaśkiewicz.

[58] Judgment of May 7, 2014, case K 43/12. However, the female lower retirement age was reinstated in 2017. Note that the PCT's position on whether the Polish legislature is obliged or merely mandated to undertake measures leading to factual equality between sexes is unclear, see Michał Ziółkowski, "Uprzywilejowanie wyrównawcze" (2016) 4 Państwo i Prawo 98, 100–01.

[59] cf Anna Śledzińska-Simon, "Proportionality Analysis by the Polish Constitutional Tribunal" in Mordechai Kremnitzer, Tayla Steiner, and Andrej Lang (eds), *Proportionality in Action: Comparative and Empirical Perspectives on the Judicial Practice* (CUP 2020) 385, 389–90; Brzeziński and Garlicki (n 1) regarding pre-1997 case law.

almost no alternative in practice. Since it was commonly known that religion was not a demanding subject to study, the students not participating in a class on religious education risked a lower average. Concerning the principle of equal rights of churches and religious organizations and state neutrality in Articles 25(1) and (2),[60] the applicant's allegations were quickly discarded. In particular, the PCT found that the applicant had not sufficiently proven that the inclusion of grades from religion or ethics would have led to an increase of the average grade.[61]

3.2.2 Equality jurisprudence throughout the years: focus on recent political changes

An analysis of the case law of the PCT cannot close its eyes before the profound political changes that occurred after 2015 with the Law and Justice party coming to power.[62] As already signaled at the outset of this chapter, the capture of the Court started in late 2015 but the paralysis ignited in 2016 and transformed into political dependence in 2017.[63] When examining all equality cases, the success rate has changed over the years, ranging from 25% (1997, 1998) to 67% (2007). The year 2016 presents an outlier because the PCT did not find any violation of equality. Against this backdrop, the success rate of the jurisprudence of the "New Constitutional Court"[64] after the reforms of the judiciary in 2017 equals 49%. This is higher than for the previous case law, but well within the general range.

When examining the period 2017–2020 more closely,[65] the general doctrinal approach to equality (in its varying nuances) does not seem to have changed. This does not contest the political change that certainly took place and the negative impact that the reforms of the judiciary have had on the judicial system. For example, in case Kp 1/17 of March 16, 2017, the PCT upheld, in a rather incomprehensible and unstructured reasoning, a privileged position of assemblies with regular meeting cycles.[66] The legislative changes were proposed shortly after the Independence Day celebrations, that in recent years had become more violent and

[60] Similarly, an evasive approach concerns allegations in light of art 32(1), analyzed subsequently in the judgment.

[61] For a critique of the PCT's position, see Kazimierz Bem, "Glosa do wyroku TK z dnia 2 grudnia 2009 r., U 10/07" (2010) LEX/el. Subsequently, Poland was found to be in breach of the ECHR regarding these issues, see *Grzelak v Poland* App no 7710/02 (ECtHR, June 15, 2010).

[62] For a more detailed account of these changes, see eg Ewa Łętowska and Aneta Wiewiórowska-Domagalska, "A 'Good' Change in the Polish Constitutional Tribunal?" (2016) 62 Osteuropa-Recht 79; Wojciech Sadurski, "How Democracy Dies (in Poland): A Case Study of Anti-Constitutional Populist Backsliding" Sydney Law School Legal Studies Research Paper no 18/01 (2018); Sadurski (n 13).

[63] On this account, see Sadurski (n 13). See also Piotr Czarny and Monika Florczak-Wątor, "Precedents and Case-based Reasoning in the Case Law of the Constitutional Tribunal of the Republic of Poland" in Monika Florczak-Wątor (ed), *Constitutional Law and Precedent: International Perspectives on Case-Based Reasoning* (Routledge 2022) 162, 162–63.

[64] Lech Garlicki defines by this term the PCT as of 2017, see Garlicki (n 4) 153.

[65] Note that, for empirical coherency, we did not exclude any judgments from this period, even those issued in the contested court compositions.

[66] For a criticism of the case see Monika Florczak-Wątor, "Zgromadzenia cykliczne. Glosa do wyroku TK z dnia 16 marca 2017 r., Kp 1/17" (2017) LEX/el.

that received support from the Law and Justice party.[67] The new type of public assemblies was also said to facilitate monthly commemorations of the airplane crash in Smoleńsk.[68] Furthermore, the judgment K 5/17 of June 20, 2017 accepted desired changes to the law on the National Council of the Judiciary.[69] While the reasoning is roughly in conformity with the existing equality framework, the justification analysis does not really engage in substantive discussion.

However, the impact of the changes in the judiciary appears to pertain to specific cases of heightened political importance rather than to equality jurisprudence in general. A closer look at cases according to review types further supports this position. Between 2017 and 2020, the "New Constitutional Court" reviewed six cases initiated as applications for constitutionality control in abstract, retrospective review. If we omit the problematic case K 5/17, we obtain five decisions. Three of these five were violations, equal to a success rate of 60%. All five cases were initiated by the Ombudsmen appointed before the electoral victory of the Law and Justice party in autumn 2015. Likewise, many constitutional complaints are unlikely to be politically motivated. Their success rate increased from 27% between 1997 and 2016 to 47% between 2017 and 2020. The success rate for referrals by courts for constitutional review decreased marginally, from 49% to 45%.

In addition, our sample shows that judges not appointed by the Law and Justice party still served as judge rapporteurs in many cases and rarely issued dissenting opinions on substance.[70] Thus, we contend that—at least until 2020—the equality doctrine continued to be applied normally in routine cases. What has changed significantly though is the number of cases decided. As Table 9.3 shows, the average number of cases before the judicial reform amounted to almost 27 per year, whereas it has oscillated around 9 since the reform. As the PCT does not have formal control of its docket, this decrease in cases is likely to reflect the damage that the legal reforms did to the legitimacy of the PCT, lowering the influx of cases and diminishing the jurisprudential output.[71]

[67] Helsińska Fundacja Praw Człowieka, *Uwagi Helsińskiej Fundacji Praw Człowieka do poselskiego projektu ustawy o zmianie ustawy - Prawo o zgromadzeniach (druk sejmowy nr 1044)* 2180/2016/MPL/BGM (29 Nov 2016).

[68] Sadurski (n 62) 50.

[69] Unsuprisingly, Leon Kieres, the "old-regime" judge was removed from the court composition, see Ryszard Balicki, "Nie-glosa do nie-wyroku, czyli kilka uwag na marginesie sprawy K 5/17" (2017) 2 Kwartalnik Stowarzyszenia Sędziów Polskich "IUSTITIA" 91. For a detailed criticism of the judgment, see Sadurski (n 13) 78.

[70] A significant exception includes Judgment of March 16, 2017, case Kp 1/17.

[71] For such findings for the period of 2014–2017 see Fundacja Im. Stefana Batorego, Raport Zespołu Ekspertów Prawnych Fundacji im. Stefana Batorego, *Funkcjonowanie Trybunału Konstytucyjnego w latach 2014–2017* (2018).

Table 9.3 Evolution of cases before and after the political subjugation

	1997–2015	2016–2020	2017–2020	2016	2017	2018	2019	2020
Cases	26,6	8,6	8,8	8	14	7	8	6
Success rate	39%	39,5%	48,6%	0%	50%	43%	63%	33%

N.B. In the first part of the table focusing on periods, calculations refer to an average of cases within a given period.

4. Context

Lech Garlicki wrote in 1999 that "the principle of equality has reached a stage of development where it can be regarded as one of the most important reference points in adjudicating the constitutionality of specific legal provisions."[72] The results of this study show that this finding has remained valid. The extent of the analyzed sample is considerable—it shows that Article 32 is one of the most frequently invoked constitutional benchmarks and it confirms the broad scope of review targeting any legislative actions. Comparatively, the success rate of 39% remains very high, in particular, considering that the vast majority of cases did not involve a suspect classification.

The development of the equal protection doctrine started with the PCT's first rulings in 1986[73] based on a re-interpretation of existing—and formerly merely ornamental—equality provisions of the 1952 Constitution. The core provision was the non-discrimination norm of Article 67(2). Despite a closed list of criteria, the provision was interpreted broadly, targeting the fairness and reasonableness of a wide array of legal distinctions.[74] With subsequent judgments, the PCT discussed the content and consequences of its sprouting doctrine more broadly.[75] Once the 1997 Constitution entered into force, the doctrine was carried over to Article 32,[76] while being further discussed and developed.

In developing the equal protection doctrine, the PCT had recourse to Article 2 of the International Covenant on Civil and Political Rights and Article 14 of the European Convention on Human Rights.[77] Following the European Court of Human Rights, the meaning of equality was tied to justice and read as requiring equal treatment of persons within a group defined based on a relevant feature and

[72] Leszek Lech Garlicki, "The Principle of Equality and The Prohibition of Discrimination in the Jurisprudence of the Constitutional Tribunal of Poland" (1999) Saint Louis-Warsaw Transatlantic LJ 1, 3.

[73] Decision of May 28, 1986, case U 1/86, OTK ZU 1986, poz. 2; Decision of November 5, 1986, case U 5/86 OTK ZU 1986, poz. 1. See also Leszek Garlicki, "Constitutional Developments in Poland" (1988) 32 Saint Louis University LJ 713, 732 et seq.

[74] Decision of May 28, 1991, case K 1/91, OTK ZU 1991, poz. 4; Brzeziński and Garlicki (n 1) 45.

[75] For an excellent account see Garlicki (n 72).

[76] See, most importantly, Judgment of February 24, 1999, case SK 4/98, but also Judgment of December 16, 1997, case K 8/97.

[77] Garlicki (n 72) 4.

allowing different treatment of different persons.[78] Moreover, the equality review addressing both distinctions within groups of individuals and delineating those groups resembles the approach of the French Constitutional Council.[79]

However, the impact of the German case law was probably most significant.[80] The reasonableness review of the PCT is closely related to a balancing assessment.[81] Furthermore, the depth of inquiry differs for establishing distinctions in law and distinctions treating group members unequally.[82] For the latter, judges impose a heavier burden of a sufficiently convincing justification, requiring the criteria of relevance, proportionality, and relation to constitutional values, principles, or norms. In addition, in targeting predominantly non-suspect cases, the Polish review reflects the pattern of rationality guiding the German Court.[83]

Still, the Polish context has significantly influenced the shape of the equality review. As underlined at the beginning of this chapter, the legitimization of the PCT was related to the wish to circumscribe the arbitrariness of the socialist reality. Hence, the focus on targeting any legislative classifications fits well within this mission of the PCT.[84] When it comes to suspect cases, we might think of a variety of influences. At least certain categories of suspect cases trigger stricter scrutiny, just as in suspect cases decided under the German Constitution.[85] Yet, in some nationality and residence cases, the PCT makes direct references to EU or international law standards and often includes considerations on the consistency of norms in question with supranational norms.[86] The same pertains to gender cases, where the PCT referred to the Convention on the Elimination of All Forms of Discrimination against Women and EU law.[87]

[78] Decision of October 23, 1995, case K 4/95, OTK ZU 1995, poz. 31; Decision of May 13, 1997, case K 20/96, OTK ZU 1997, nr 2, poz. 18; see also Piotr Czarny and Florczak-Wątor (n 63) 177; Garlicki (n 72) 4–9. In addition, perceiving equality in the context of other substantive constitutional rights or freedoms and limiting the right to equality to this scope resembles the doctrine under of art 14 of the ECHR.

[79] According to the formula of the French Constitutional Council expressed in an early Decision no. 89-254 DC (July 4, 1989): "the principle of equality does not preclude the legislature from regulating different situations in different ways, nor from derogating from equality for reasons of general interest, provided that, in either case, the resulting difference in treatment is related to the purpose of the law establishing it."

[80] See Chapter 7. As Lech Garlicki pointed out, many judges received education in Germany and were impacted by the German legal thought; online seminar "Judicial Law-Making in European Constitutional Courts" (January 28, 2021), organized by the Centre for Interdisciplinary Constitutional Studies Jagiellonian University in Kraków.

[81] See Chapter 7; Alexander Somek, "The Deadweight of Formulae: What Might Have Been the Second Germanisation of the American Equal Protection Clause" (1998) 1 University of Pennsylvania Journal of Constitutional Law 284, 300–01.

[82] cf Donald P Kommers and Russell A Miller, *The Constitutional Jurisprudence of the Federal Republic of Germany* (Duke University Press 2012) 421–23.

[83] See Chapter 7.

[84] For an interesting account on the contextual analysis of the legitimization of the PCT see Hanna Dębska and Tomasz Warczok, "Sakralizacja i profanacja. Trybunał Konstytucyjny jako struktura mityczna" (2018) 5 Państwo i Prawo 63, 65–70.

[85] cf Kommers and Miller (n 82).

[86] See Judgment of March 28, 2007, case K 40/04; Judgment of July 5, 2010, case P 31/09; Judgment of June 25, 2013, case P 11/12; Judgment of October 30, 2019, case P 1/18.

[87] Judgment of March 28, 2000, case K 27/99; Judgment of December 5, 2000, case K 35/99; Judgment of July 15, 2010, case K 63/07.

Finally, in post-socialist jurisdictions, there is a prevalent opinion that the notion of equality does not ensure social equality.[88] Instead, substantive equality is to be achieved through social rights. In Poland, they have been broadly codified in the 1997 Constitution. Some of them explicitly privilege certain vulnerable groups, including disabled persons.[89] In case K 37/13,[90] questioning regulations that do not take account of vehicles adjusted to a disabled persons' needs in driving license exams, the PCT rejected a breach of Article 32(1). Nevertheless, it found a violation of Articles 69 and 20 of the UN Convention on the Rights of Persons with Disabilities because there were no effective support mechanisms.[91]

5. Conclusion

The present analysis has been a holistic but brief attempt to classify and explain the PCT's approach to equality protection, which still leaves some issues unresolved. Nevertheless, we can conclude that the equality jurisprudence of the Polish Constitutional Tribunal most closely fits the equality as reasonableness model. Throughout recent years, equality guarantees served for reviewing a wide range of regulations, including those related to the political transformation of the country and its new socio-economic reality. The predominant logic of rationality certainly does not exclude a specific protection of vulnerable groups against discrimination. However, the latter remains limited, considering the number of suspect cases and the restrictive approach to substantive equality. Currently, equal protection before the subjugated PCT has almost vanished. If we look beyond our sample analysis, we see that the number of equality cases has decreased even further in the last two years. Based on our search method, as of writing this chapter, we could find a mere total of three cases for 2021 and 2022. However, these changes are probably not specific to equality but rather reflect the fundamental changes to the judicial system in Poland that we have witnessed after the Law and Justice party came to power in 2015. Whether this trend will be reversed after the victory of the democratic opposition in the 2023 elections remains to be seen.

[88] See, with regards to judicial interpretation, Goran Selanec, *A Betrayed Ideal: The Problem of Enforcement of EU Sex Equality Guarantees in the CEE Post-socialist Legal Systems* (SJD Dissertation, University of Michigan 2012). See also in this respect Barbara Havelková, *Gender Equality in Law: Uncovering the Legacies of Czech State Socialism* (Hart 2017) 273–75 (and *passim*).

[89] Borysiak and Bosek list the following social rights provisions as exceptions to the formal principle of equality: art 69 providing for state aid for disabled persons in certain spheres of life; art 71(1) sentence 2 guaranteeing state help for families in difficult material and social circumstances; art 71(2) providing that mothers shall have the right to special assistance from public authorities before and after giving birth; art 68(3) providing for special healthcare protection for children, pregnant women, disabled and elderly persons, see Borysiak and Bosek (n 21).

[90] Judgment of June 8, 2016, case K 37/13.

[91] Interestingly, in Judgment of February 6, 2007, case P 25/06, the PCT recognized protection against indirect discrimination under art 69.

10

Inter-American Court of Human Rights

Tainá Garcia Maia

1. Introduction

In 1994, the Inter-American Commission on Human Rights (IACommHR) took the case *El Amparo v Venezuela* to the Inter-American Court of Human Rights (IACtHR). The case concerned the murder of 14 fishermen committed by the Venezuelan Military and police forces under the presumption that the victims had been members of the *guerrilla*. For the first time since its creation, the Court had been asked to decide an equality claim in a contentious case.

The judgment was published in 1995 but it did not include a decision of the merits because Venezuela recognized its international responsibility, leading to the ceasing of the dispute. It was only in 2005, in *YATAMA v Nicaragua*, that the Court found, for the first time, a violation of the right to equality and non-discrimination in a contentious case in which the respondent had not recognized its international responsibility.[1] The case concerned the exclusion of the candidates presented by the indigenous regional political party "YATAMA" from the municipal elections of autonomous regions of Nicaragua.

Before the Court's first finding of discrimination, advisory opinions constituted the main vehicle through which the IACtHR developed the content and scope of the two equality provisions of the American Convention on Human Rights (ACHR), Articles 1(1) and 24.[2] In 1984, in the Advisory Opinion concerning

[1] From 1995 to 2004, the Court decided four cases in which it discussed the principle of equality and non-discrimination. In one of them, no equality claim had been made, but equality was used for the interpretation of another provision of the ACHR, namely the right of children to protective measures. See Judgment (Merits), *"Street Children" (Villagran-Morales et al.) v Guatemala* (November 19, 1999). The remaining three cases included equality, yet two of these cases did not involve a suspect classification, and they did not lead to a finding of violation either. See Judgment (Merits, reparations, and costs), *Genie Lacayo v Nicaragua* (January 29, 1997); and Judgment (Merits, reparations, and costs), *La Cruz Flores v Perú* (November 18, 2004). In the remaining case, the Court merely accepted the state's recognition of international responsibility for the violation of a series of rights, including the right to equality before the law. See Judgment (Merits), *Masacre Plan de Sánchez v Guatemala* (April 29, 2004).

[2] Previous to the 2005 judgment in the *YATAMA* case, the Court had already published five advisory opinions discussing equality and non-discrimination: Advisory Opinion, *Proposed Amendments to the Naturalization Provision of the Constitution of Costa Rica*, OC-4/84 (January 19, 1984); Advisory Opinion, *The Right to Information on Consular Assistance in the Framework of the Guarantees of the Due Process of Law*, OC-16/99 (October 1, 1999); Advisory Opinion, *Juridical Condition and Human*

Tainá Garcia Maia, *Inter-American Court of Human Rights* In: *Equality's Guardians*. Edited by: Niels Petersen, Oxford University Press. © Tainá Garcia Maia 2025. DOI: 10.1093/9780198961109.003.0010

Proposed Amendments to the Naturalization Provision of the Constitution of Costa Rica (OC-4/84), the Court identified an indissociable link between equality and human dignity and drafted a three-step analysis for finding discrimination.[3] In 1990, the Court made explicit that positive obligations emanate from Article 1(1) of the ACHR.[4] In 2003, in the Advisory Opinion on the *Juridical Condition and Rights of Undocumented Migrants* (OC-18/03), it recognized the principle of equality and non-discrimination as a basic principle of international law,[5] an obligation *erga omnes*,[6] and a peremptory norm with *jus cogens* character.[7] It emphasized the "inseparable connection" between the principle of equality and non-discrimination and the obligation to respect and guarantee human rights[8]—thus negative and positive obligations—and stated that its interpretation must bear in mind the "continuing development of international law."[9] Additionally, the Court found that the principle of equality and non-discrimination can create obligations for individuals and generate responsibilities for companies,[10] and it imposes upon states an obligation "to take affirmative action to reverse or change discriminatory situations."[11]

From 2004 onwards, there has been a notable expansion of equality cases in the IACtHR, particularly cases involving a suspect classification.[12] This expansion coincides with the proliferation of Inter-American instruments addressing the right to equality since the mid-1990s. In 1994, the Inter-American Convention on the Prevention, Punishment and Eradication of Violence against Women (Convention of Belém do Pará) was adopted, addressing violence against women and its connections to discrimination. In 1999, the Inter-American Convention on the Elimination of All Forms of Discrimination Against Persons with Disabilities was adopted. Finally, the Inter-American Convention against Racism, Racial Discrimination and Related Forms of Intolerance and the Inter-American Convention Against All Forms of Discrimination and Intolerance entered into force in 2017 and 2020, respectively.

Rights of the Child, OC-17/2002 (August 28, 2002); and Advisory Opinion, *Juridical Condition and Rights of Undocumented Migrants*, OC-18/2003 (September 17, 2003).

3 OC-4/84 (n 2).

4 Advisory Opinion, *Exceptions to the Exhaustion of Domestic Remedies (Arts 46(1), 46(2)(a) and 46(2)(b) American Convention on Human Rights)*, OC-11/90 (August 10, 1990). Nine years later, in OC-16/99, the Court discussed the positive obligation emanating from the right to equality in the context of the due process of law.

5 OC-18/2003 (n 2) para 86.

6 ibid para 109.

7 ibid para 110.

8 ibid para 85.

9 ibid para 120.

10 See Judgment (Preliminary objections, merits, reparations, and costs), *Olivera Fuentes v Peru* (February 4, 2023) para 103.

11 OC-18/2003 (n 2) paras 104 and 110.

12 Cases with a suspect classification constitute approximately 73.6% of the equality cases decided by the IACtHR between 2004 and 2020.

Despite this expansion of Inter-American instruments protecting the right to equality and non-discrimination, the enlargement of the content and scope of Articles 1 and 24 of the ACHR has generally not taken place through the adoption of new conventions and protocols. Instead, the work of the IACtHR itself has been pivotal to the evolution of the principle of equality and non-discrimination in Inter-American Human Rights Law.

An instance of the Court's expansion of the content and scope of equality and non-discrimination is its enlargement of the protected categories of Article 1 (1). For example, in the 2017 Advisory Opinion on *Gender identity, and equality and non-discrimination of same-sex couples* (OC-24/17), the Court concluded that Article 1(1) covered sexual orientation, gender identity, and gender expression as prohibited categories of discrimination.[13] This conclusion was reached by relying on the *pro persona* principle (formerly called the *pro homine* principle) and documents adopted outside of the Inter-American System of Human Rights, including soft law instruments. Grounded on the right to equality and non-discrimination of LGBTI persons, the Court recognized the right of same-sex couples to marriage and the right of individuals to change their names and rectify public documents in accordance with their gender identity and without being required to undertake medical treatment or surgery. Throughout its case law, the IACtHR has also recognized the categories of age,[14] persons with disabilities,[15] persons with HIV,[16] migratory status,[17] refugee status,[18] displaced persons,[19] and poverty, which are not mentioned in Article 1(1), as protected groups against discrimination. Poverty has been understood as being susceptible to inclusion in the categories "economic status," "social origin," or "other social condition" of Article 1(1).[20]

[13] Advisory Opinion, *Gender Identity, and Equality and Non-Discrimination of Same-Sex Couples—State Obligations Concerning Change of Name, Gender Identity, and Rights Derived from a Relationship Between Same-Sex Couples*, OC-24/17 (November 24, 2017) para 78. See also Judgment (Merits, reparations, and costs), *Atala Riffo and Daughters v Chile* (February 24, 2012); Judgment (Preliminary objections, merits, reparations, and costs), *Duque v Colombia* (February 26, 2016); Judgment (Preliminary objections, merits, reparations, and costs), *Flor Freire v Ecuador* (August 31, 2016); Judgment (Merits, reparations, and costs), *Ramírez Escobar and others v Guatemala* (March 9, 2018).

[14] For example, OC-17/2002 (n 2); OC-18/2003 (n 2) para 101; *"Street Children" (Villagran-Morales et al.) v Guatemala* (n 1).

[15] Judgment (Preliminary objections, merits, reparations, and costs), *Furlan and family v Argentina* (August 31, 2012); Judgment (Preliminary objections, merits, reparations, and costs), *Artavia Murillo et al. ("In Vitro Fertilization") v Costa Rica* (November 28, 2012).

[16] Judgment (Preliminary objections, merits, reparations, and costs), *Gonzales Lluy and others v Ecuador* (September 1, 2015); Judgment (Preliminary objections, merits, reparations, and costs), *Cuscul Pivaraland others v Guatemala* (August 26, 2018).

[17] Judgment, *Girls Yean and Bosico v República Dominicana* (September 8, 2005).

[18] Judgment (Preliminary objections, merits, reparations, and costs), *I.V. v Bolivia* (November 30, 2018) para 142.

[19] Judgment (Preliminary objections, merits, reparations, and costs), *Afro-descendant Communities displaced from the Cacarica River Basin (Operation Genesis) v Colombia* (November 20, 2013).

[20] Judgment (Preliminary objections, merits, reparations, and costs), *Workers of the Fireworks Factory in Santo Antônio de Jesus and their Families v Brazil* (July 15, 2020) para 185.

This chapter aims to understand the nature and evolution of the IACtHR's equality doctrine and its application in practice. Section 2 of this chapter will introduce the protection granted to equality and non-discrimination in the ACHR and the Court's equality test. Subsequently, Section 3 will engage in an empirical investigation of the Court's equality case law. Lastly, Section 4 discusses key influences that could explain the Court's equality jurisprudence and the patterns identified in Section 3.

2. Equality doctrine of the IACtHR

2.1 Equality and non-discrimination in the ACHR

Article 1(1) establishes the obligation of states to respect and guarantee the rights safeguarded in the ACHR without any discrimination. In other words, it safeguards the right against discrimination in the implementation of each and every provision of the ACHR.[21] In turn, Article 24 safeguards the right of individuals against *de jure* or *de facto* discrimination both in the implementation of the ACHR's provisions and under the state parties' domestic laws.[22]

There are two notable differences in the wording of the two provisions. First, Article 24 refers both to equality before the law and non-discrimination, while Article 1(1) does not contain the word "equality" but only refers to discrimination based on certain grounds. However, this difference does not have practical effects in the IACtHR's case law as the Court argues that it is difficult to separate equality from non-discrimination.[23] Rather, equality must be guaranteed without discrimination.[24] Together, these two concepts constitute "an outstanding element of the human rights protection system" that permeates the whole juridical system and serves as the foundation upon which the "juridical framework of national and international public order rests."[25]

Secondly, while Article 1(1) contains a list of prohibited grounds of discrimination, Article 24 is a general equality clause with no reference to protected groups.[26] However, the Court has argued that the analysis of suspect classifications applies to both provisions.[27] Furthermore, it has repeatedly recognized the

[21] Organization of American States (OAS), *American Convention on Human Rights, "Pact of San Jose" (ACHR)*, Costa Rica (November 22, 1969) art 1.1.

[22] cf *Operation Genesis v Colombia* (n 19) para 333. The words of the provision are: "All persons are equal before the law."

[23] OC-18/2003 (n 2) para 83.

[24] ibid.

[25] Judgment (Preliminary objections, merits, reparations, and costs), *YATAMA v Nicaragua* (June 23, 2005) para 184.

[26] ACHR (n 21) art 1.1.

[27] See *Flor Freire v Ecuador* (n 13) paras 114–124.

non-exhaustive nature of this list.[28] It found that the inclusion of the term "any other social condition" in Article 1(1) covered groups that simultaneously (i) face a relative disadvantage in society, that is, "are traditionally marginalized, excluded or subordinated";[29] (ii) share personal traits linked to their identity; and (iii) suffer a negative treatment based on irrelevant criteria for the equitable distribution of rights, freedoms, or social benefits.[30] While the analysis of suspect classifications applies to Articles 1(1) and 24, the presence of a suspect classification is not necessary for the Court to find a violation of equality. Whether a case concerns a suspect classification will determine the level of scrutiny applied by the Court.[31]

Since 2017, the duties to respect, protect, and fulfil the right to equality and non-discrimination derived from the ACHR apply not only in relation to civil and political rights but also social and economic rights. This shift was first expressed in the 2017 case of *Lagos del Campo v Peru*, where the IACtHR recognized that Article 26 of the ACHR (on the progressive development of economic, social, cultural, and environmental rights) was justiciable. Through this move, the Court expanded its competence *ratione materiae* and the justiciable obligations assumed by states under the ACHR, all of which must be guaranteed without discrimination. This expansion reverberated in the Court's equality jurisprudence, making equality and non-discrimination no longer an exclusive matter of civil and political rights.[32]

The 2020 *Fireworks Factory* case is perhaps the best example of the expansion of the content and scope of the right to equality and non-discrimination as a direct consequence of the *Lagos del Campo* jurisprudential turn. The case concerns an explosion that took place in 1998 in a fireworks factory in Brazil, killing 64 persons, including pregnant women and children. The IACtHR noted that 60% of the women working in the factory were Afro-descendants, and most of the workers of the factory came from neighborhoods characterized by poverty, lack of access to formal education, lack of infrastructure, and low income. The victims had continued to work at the factory despite its dangerous conditions and exploitation because of their poverty and the absence of any other economic alternative. The IACtHR found that the case was inserted in a context of social exclusion and poverty, and, amidst that context, Brazil had been omissive. It concluded that Brazil had failed to adopt positive measures to the benefit of a historically marginalized

[28] OC-24/17 (n 13) para 66; *Atala Riffo and Daughters v Chile* (n 13) para 85.
[29] *I.V. v Bolivia* (n 18) para 240.
[30] ibid; OC-24/17 (n 13).
[31] See section 2.2 of this chapter.
[32] The first case in which the Court found that the state had violated its obligation to guarantee economic, social, cultural, and environment rights in accordance with the right to equality was adopted in 2018, in the case of *San Miguel Sosa and others v Venezuela*. The case concerns the dismissal of three employees from the Venezuelan National Border Council based on their political opinion. See Judgment (Preliminary objections, merits, reparations, and costs), *San Miguel Sosa and others v Venezuela* (February 8, 2018); see also *Cuscul Pivaral and others v Guatemala* (n 16); *Workers of the Fireworks Factory* (n 20).

group that found itself in a situation of structural poverty. By failing to address or effectively reverse this situation of structural poverty and marginalization, Brazil violated the right to equality and non-discrimination under Article 24 of the ACHR.[33]

2.2 The equality test

The Court's methodology for finding inequality and discrimination has evolved in the last four decades. In the 1984 Advisory Opinion on *Proposed Amendments to the Naturalization Provision of the Constitution of Costa* Rica, the IACtHR defined a permitted measure of differentiation as one that is based on substantial factual differences, has a legitimate purpose, and is proportionate.[34] In 2002, in the Advisory Opinion on the *Juridical Condition and Human Rights of the Child* (OC-17/02), it simplified its description by referring merely to the need for "an objective and reasonable justification."[35] This simplified description became a *dictum* in the Court's equality jurisprudence.[36]

In the 2010s, the Court discussed the legal effects that a differentiation based on a suspect classification has on the equality test, making explicit what was until then an implicit element of its assessment.[37] If a differentiation is based on a suspect classification, this has two main consequences. First, there is a presumption of discriminatory treatment.[38] The burden of proof is inverted in favor of the alleged victim, meaning that it is up to the state to prove that "their decision did not have a discriminatory purpose or effect."[39] Second, the Court applies an enhanced level of scrutiny.[40] In practice, this is a high burden of justification. Until now, no case has arrived at the Court in which it has concluded that the enhanced thresholds of

[33] *Workers of the Fireworks Factory* (n 20).

[34] OC-4/84 (n 3) para 57.

[35] OC-17/2002 (n 2) para 55; OC-18/2003 (n 2) para 84; *YATAMA v Nicaragua* (n 25) para 185. cf Judgment (Merits, reparations, and costs), *Norín Catrimán y otros (Dirigentes, Miembros y Activista del Pueblo Indígena Mapuche) v Chile* (May 29, 2014) para 200; OC-24/17 (n 13) para 66.

[36] See *YATAMA v Nicaragua* (n 25) para 185; *Norín Catrimán and others v Chile* (n 35); *Duque v Colombia* (n 13) para 124; *Flor Freire v Ecuador* (n 13) para 125; Judgment (Merits, reparations, and costs), *López Soto and others v Venezuela* (September 26, 2018), para 231; Judgment (Preliminary objections, merits, reparations, and costs), *Jenkins v Argentina* (November 26, 2019) para 91; Judgment (Merits, reparations, and costs), *Almeida v Argentina* (November 17, 2020) para 185. In *Norín Catrimán and others v Chile*, the Court explained that the lack of objective and reasonable justification refers to the lack of a legitimate purpose and a reasonable relationship of proportionality.

[37] *Atala Riffo and Daughters v Chile* (n 13); *Gonzales Lluy and others v Ecuador* (n 16); Judgment (Preliminary objections, merits, reparations, and costs), *Granier and others (Radio Caracas Televisión) v Venezuela* (June 22, 2016) para 228.

[38] *I.V. v Bolivia* (n 18) para 240.

[39] *Granier and others v Venezuela* (n 37) para 228.

[40] *I.V. v Bolivia* (n 18) para 241; *Atala Riffo and daughters v Chile* (n 13) para 124. The enhanced level of scrutiny means that the impugned measure must (i) pursue an imperative social need; (ii) respond to real and proven risks; (iii) be proportionate.

justification were met. In the few cases concerning suspect classifications in which the applicant's claim of discrimination did not succeed, failure usually resulted from insufficient proof of detrimental treatment based on a suspect classification.

In contrast, distinctions based on non-suspect classifications are subject to a more flexible assessment. What is required from states is to refrain from arbitrary distinctions; that is, to justify their measures on rational and objective reasons.[41] Furthermore, there is no inversion of the burden of proof.

A discriminatory intent is not an element of the Court's equality test. For the Court to find indirect discrimination, it relies on the demonstration of a negative and disproportionate impact on a vulnerable group that cannot be justified by the respondent state. For example, in *Artavia Murillo et al. ("In Vitro Fertilization") v Costa Rica*, the Court found that the prohibition of *in vitro* fertilization (IVF) had a disproportionate impact on women, persons with disability, and infertile couples who did not have the necessary financial resources to undergo IVF treatment abroad. The finding of indirect discrimination was based on balancing the interests of those groups and the importance of protecting the embryo.[42]

3. Empirical analysis

3.1 Methodology

This study's empirical analysis examined decisions, judgments, and advisory opinions published by the IACtHR from 1979, the year in which the Court was established, to December 2020. This analysis aims to better understand the jurisprudential patterns of the court's case law. It is centered on Articles 1(1) and 24.

I used the IACtHR's "jurisprudence finder" and the *Digesto* as databases to construct the sample. The search words used in the "jurisprudence finder" were "*igualdad*" and "*discriminación*." The *Digesto* was searched for Articles 1 and 24 of the ACHR. Additional cases were found based on cross-references in the Court's

[41] In *Jenkins v Argentina* (November 26, 2019), a case in which the Court assessed whether Argentina had violated the right to equality by preventing revision of the penalty of detention applied to persons convicted for the crime of narcotraffic and illicit association, the Court explained that "difference in treatment is discriminatory when it does not have an objective and reasonable justification, that is, when it does not pursue a legitimate aim, and there is no reasonable relation of proportionality between the means and the pursued aim." It found that the automatic exclusion based only on the type of crime attributed to the Mr. Jenkins did not explain the specific aim of this difference in treatment, its suitability, necessity, proportionality and, finally, the personal circumstances involved. See *Jenkins v Argentina* (n 36) paras 91–94. The same considerations were made in Judgment (Preliminary objections, merits, reparations, and costs), *Montesinos Mejía v Ecuador* (January 27, 2020). Yet, the reference to necessity in these two cases is rather brief and insufficient to lead to the conclusion that the Court in fact applied a test of necessity to find inequality based on non-suspect classification. Furthermore, such a broad reference to proportionality is not present in the Court's subsequent case concerning non-suspect classifications: see *Almeida v Argentina* (n 36).

[42] *IVF v Costa Rica* (n 15).

judgments and advisory opinions. A final check was conducted through the IACtHR's online catalogue and its database "*Thesaurus*."

By applying this method, 71 relevant cases and 9 advisory opinions were found. Yet in 18 of the 71 cases, the Court did not reach a decision of merits on the equality claim.[43] For this reason, these cases were excluded from the quantitative analysis. Nonetheless, they were still included in the qualitative analysis regarding the development of the Court's doctrine to the extent that they were relevant.

3.2 Identified patterns

If we analyze the decisions of the Court empirically, we observe that it found a violation of the guarantees of equality and non-discrimination in 73.6% of the cases.[44] The success rate of cases without a suspect classification is remarkably lower (28.6%), compared to 89.7% of the cases with a suspect classification (see Table 10.1).[45]

Of all the cases, 41.5% discuss omissions of the state to comply with its positive obligations to protect and fulfil the right to equality and non-discrimination. In other words, in almost half of the Court's judgments, equality transcends its negative dimension and incorporates a positive dimension in the Court's jurisprudence. In cases concerning positive obligations, the most preponderant suspect classifications are gender/sex (13 cases), followed by race/ethnic origin, age, and economic condition (4 cases each). In these cases, the element of context plays a crucial role.

Context refers to a series of historical, social, and political events that allows the Court to demarcate the facts surrounding the dispute "within the scope of the specific circumstances in which they occurred."[46] The Court has explained that the identification of a context has "allowed for the characterization of the facts as part of a systematic pattern of human rights violations, as a practice that is applied or tolerated by the state or as part of massive and systematic or generalized attacks against a certain sector of its population."[47] While context does not constitute a

[43] In seven cases, the Court decided not to pronounce itself on the equality claim. In three cases, it was omissive. In the remaining eight cases, the principle of equality and non-discrimination was only used as a tool for the interpretation of other provisions of the ACHR or for the determination of the reparations.

[44] Out of the 53 cases in which the Court made a ruling on an alleged violation to equality and non-discrimination, 38 led to a finding a violation, 13 did not, and the remaining 2 cases had 2 claims each, half of which led to a finding of violation. Accordingly, the success rate of the equality cases before the IACtHR is 38 + 2 (½ a case)/53 cases.

[45] Out of the 39 cases with a suspect classification, 34 led to a finding of violation, 3 did not, and the remaining 2 cases (1 on race and the other on sexual orientation) had 2 claims each, half of which led to a finding of violation. Accordingly, the success rate of cases with a suspect classification is 34 + 2 (½ a case)/39 cases.

[46] Judgment (Preliminary objections, merits, reparations, and costs), *Velásquez Paiz and others v Guatemala* (November 19, 2015) para 43. Translation by the author.

[47] *Velásquez Paiz and others v Guatemala* (n 46) para 43 (translation by the author).

Table 10.1 Success rate disaggregated by criterion of distinction

Criterion	Violation	No violation	Total	Success rate
Not suspect	4	10	14	28.6
Gender/sex	16	0	16	100
Race/ethnic origin	12	1	13	92.3
Economic status	8	0	8	100
Sexual orientation/gender expr.	5	1	6	83.3
Age	4	0	4	100
Migratory status	4	0	4	100
Language	3	0	3	100
Disability	2	0	2	100
National origin	2	1	3	66.7
HIV and other medical condition	2	0	2	100
Political opinion	2	2	4	50
Refugee status	1	0	1	100
Total number of cases	39	14	53	

Note: The aggregated sum of each column exceeds the total number of cases due to cases of intersectionality or multiple discrimination, in which the equality claim referred to two or more suspect classifications.

component of the equality test *per se*, it produces legal consequences on the Court's equality assessment. Context is a relevant element in the Court's determination of the scope of the positive obligation to act with due diligence, the analysis of evidence, and the determination of reparations.[48] If the state is or should have been aware at the time of the facts of a situation of particular vulnerability to a group, it is bound by an enhanced or stricter duty of due diligence.[49]

Context has had a particularly preeminent position in cases of gender-based violence. One example is the 2014 case of *Véliz Franco v Guatemala*, concerning the investigation carried out by Guatemala on the disappearance and murder of 15-year-old Isabel Véliz Franco. The Court explained that the facts and the context of the case would determine the degree to which the state was required to be aware of a situation of risk and act on it. In the concrete case, it found a context

[48] cf ibid para 43.

[49] Judgment (Preliminary objections, merits, reparations, and costs), *Gutiérrez Hernández and others v Guatemala* (August 24, 2017) para 139. cf Judgment (Preliminary objections, merits, reparations, and costs), *Véliz Franco v Guatemala* (May 19, 2014); *Workers of the Fireworks Factory* (n 20). To see the legal consequences of the absence of a context in the Court's assessment, see *Gutiérrez Hernández* (n 49) para 139.

of increased lethal violence against women in Guatemala at the time of the facts. It also found that female children were particularly vulnerable to violence. This translated into an obligation for the state to act with "greater and more rigorous diligence to protect and ensure the exercise and enjoyment of rights of girl children in response to the fact or the mere possibility of their vulnerability in the presence of acts that actually or potentially involve gender-based violence or could result in this type of violence."[50] Because Guatemala had failed to adopt a gender perspective in the investigation, among other failures to act in due diligence, it violated its obligation to ensure the free and full exercise of fundamental rights without discrimination.

The analysis of the Court's jurisprudence also reveals that only four successful judgments of its equality case law did not involve a suspect classification. These four cases can largely be classified as cases of arbitrary state action. They are generally cases in which the Court identified that the state unjustifiably differentiated between equal situations. In addition, they mostly concern structural challenges in the region, such as the fight against drugs and transitional justice. In *Almeida v Argentina*, the Court found a violation of equality when Argentina granted a reparation to Mr. Almeida for his detention at the time of the military dictatorship but not for the period in which he was under surveillance under a regime that was similar to a *de facto* parole system.[51] *Jenkins v Argentina* and *Montesinos Mejía v Ecuador* concerned arbitrary detentions for the crimes of narcotrafficking and the unjustified denial of a revision of the detentions and the need to maintain them.[52] Finally, *Barbani Duarte and others v Uruguay* concerned the proceedings provided by Uruguay to safeguard the rights of a group of 539 depositors whose funds were improperly transferred by the private *Banco de Montevideo* to the Trade & Commerce Bank in the Cayman Islands without the depositors' consultation or consent, and alleged differentiations applied by the state to the cases of different depositors.[53]

4. Factors explaining the Court's jurisprudence

The IACtHR has often relied on the work of UN treaty bodies and the jurisprudence of the European Court of Human Rights (ECtHR) when developing the meaning of equality, notably when resorting to an evolutive interpretation of the Convention. External referencing notably takes place when it supports the Court's interpretation in accordance with the *pro persona* principle. For example, in *Atala*

[50] *Véliz Franco v Guatemala* (n 49) para 134.
[51] *Almeida v Argentina* (n 36).
[52] ibid; *Montesinos Mejía v Ecuador* (n 41).
[53] Judgment (Merits, reparations, and costs), *Barbani Duarte and others v Uruguay* (October 13, 2011).

Riffo and Daughters v Chile and OC-24/17, the Court recalled that sexual orientation had already been recognized as a suspect category of discrimination by the ECtHR, the UN Human Rights Committee (HRCttee), and the Committee on Economic, Social, and Cultural Rights.[54]

The analysis of the IACtHR's case law also reveals a practice of referencing the ECtHR with regard to the recognition of indirect discrimination as a category that does not require discriminatory intent.[55] In addition, the jurisprudence of the ECtHR appears to have been a relevant factor in the early developments of the IACtHR's methodology for finding discrimination. In OC-17/02, the IACtHR defined discriminatory measures as those lacking "an objective and reasonable justification and that do not have as their only objective, ultimately, exercise of the rights set forth in the Convention."[56] This definition, widely repeated in the IACtHR's equality jurisprudence, may have found its origins in the ECtHR's case law. Nine paragraphs before presenting the abovementioned definition of discrimination in OC-17/02, the IACtHR referred to the jurisprudence of the Strasbourg court. More specifically, it explained that not every difference in treatment offends human dignity and noted that the ECtHR, "based on 'the principles that can be inferred from the juridical practice of a large number of democratic States,' warned that a distinction is only discriminatory when it 'lacks objective and reasonable justification.'"[57] The practice of the ECtHR linking discrimination to the absence of an objective and reasonable distinction had already been observed by the IACtHR in its first advisory opinion tackling equality, OC-4/84.[58]

In any case, the Court has a practice of referring to the work of human rights bodies and international instruments. A context of bilateral meetings and exchanges between the IACtHR and other human rights bodies arguably boosts this practice. In a pronouncement from 2018, the then President of the IACtHR, Judge Eduardo Ferrer Mac-Gregor Poisot, explained that the IACtHR has maintained a close relationship and dialogue with the other regional human rights courts, in addition to carrying out exchanges of staff from the Secretariat/Registry by exchanging lawyers from the working team of one court to the others.[59] According to the Judge, these practices have allowed for exchanges on critical subjects, such as current developments in case law, the impact of the work of the three regional

[54] *Atala Riffo and Daughters v Chile* (n 13) paras 87–89; OC-24/17 (n 13) paras 68, 203–205.

[55] *IVF v Costa Rica* (n 15) para 286; Advisory Opinion, *Right to Freedom of Association, Right to Collective Bargaining and Right to Strike, and Their Relation to Other Rights, with a Gender Perspective*, OC-27/21 (May 5, 2021) para 171.

[56] OC-17/02 (n 2) para 55.

[57] ibid para 46. cf OC-18/03 (n 2) paras 89–90.

[58] OC-4/84 (n 2) para 56.

[59] Eduardo Ferrer Mac-Gregor Poisot, "Dialogue between Regional Human Rights Courts" in Inter-American Court of Human Rights (ed), *Dialogue Between Regional Human Rights Courts* (I/A Court HR 2010) 35, 37–38.

human rights courts, existing and potential challenges, and relationships with domestic courts.[60]

While the jurisprudential dialogue with the African Human Rights System is more incipient, a factor explained by Judge Ferrer as deriving from the still recent installation of the African Court on Human and Peoples' Rights, the Judge explains that "[c]urrently, no decision is adopted by the Inter-American Court until it has previously studied the relevant Strasbourg precedents."[61] The practice of the IACtHR shows that in non-repetitive cases, Judge Ferrer's statement is not an exaggeration. This dialogue is expected to increase in connection with the signing of the 2018 Declaration of San José, in which the Presidents of the three regional human rights courts agreed to establish a permanent forum between the three courts for regular institutional dialogue.[62] Finally, in addition to exchanges with the other regional human rights courts, the IACtHR also conducts bilateral meetings with UN treaty bodies.[63]

However, reference to external sources is insufficient to explain the Court's jurisprudence and its contributions to promote changes in the state parties. In particular, the development of positive obligations in the context of equality is a genuine innovation of the IACtHR. While other international treaty bodies have also resorted to positive obligations derived from equality, particularly in the context of violence against women, this development seems to have started in the Inter-American system,[64] and the IACtHR has extended the reach of positive obligations to many more areas than the UN HRCttee or the ECtHR did.

One explanation for this strong emphasis on positive state obligations derived from equality is the influence of individual judges that have shaped the Court's jurisprudence. This is particularly the case for the late Antônio Augusto Cançado Trindade, President of the IACtHR from 1999 to 2003.[65] Justice Cançado Trindade was an advocate of the theory of the humanization of international law, which sees the protection of humankind as the fundamental basis of international law.[66] Under this theory, legal responses to patterns in state behaviour should not result in a substantial increase in the vulnerability of the human person. Instead, legal

[60] ibid 38.

[61] ibid 39.

[62] Joint Declaration of the Presidents of the African Court on Human and Peoples' Rights, the European Court of Human Rights and the Inter-American Court of Human Rights on the occasion of the 40th Anniversary of the entry into force of the American Convention on Human Rights and the creation of the Inter-American Court of Human Rights (July 18, 2018).

[63] For example, OHCHR, "Bilateral Meeting between the Interamerican Court of Human Rights and the Chairs of the United Nations Human Rights Treaty Bodies" (February 24, 2023).

[64] See *Maria da Penha Maia Fernandes v Brazil* Report No. 54/01, Case 12.051 (IACommHR, April 16, 2001).

[65] Trindade was a Judge at the IACtHR from 1995 to 2006, and the Court's Vice-President from 1998 to 1998.

[66] cf Antônio Augusto Cançado Trindade, *International Law for Humankind: Towards a New Jus Gentium* (Martinus Nijhoff Publishers 2006) 216.

analysis should be conducted considering the ultimate purpose of protecting humankind. Trindade was also a strong defender of the *pro persona* principle and the interactive interpretation of human rights instruments. He was opposed to state voluntarism in international human rights law and was highly critical to the doctrine of margin appreciation, a concept that remains, to a great extent, foreign to the Inter-American System of Human Rights.

Other influential judges to the Court's equality jurisprudence include Judges Eduardo Ferrer Mac-Gregor Poisot, Margarette May Macaulay, and Cecilia Medina Quiroga. Judge Ferrer, President of the Court from 2018 to 2019, advocated for the justiciability of Article 26 of the ACHR since his first case sitting on the Court as a Judge in 2013. Judge Macaulay has also argued for the justiciability of Article 26 in her Concurring Opinion in the 2012 Furlan case. She was one of the few female Black judges to sit at the Court and has also served as the Rapporteur on the Rights of Women of the Organization of the American States (OAS) (2016–2019) and, concomitantly, as the OAS Rapporteur on the Rights of Persons of African Descent and against Racial Discrimination (2016–2019). Finally, Judge Quiroga, the Court's first female President (2008–2009), was a member of the HRCttee for eight years (1995–2002) and authored General Comment 28 ("The Equality of Rights Between Men and Women"), published on March 29, 2000. In the *Cotton Fields* case, a leading case on gender-based violence, she published a concurrent opinion stressing that states have an obligation to adopt positive measures if they have knowledge of a pattern of violence or a real and imminent risk to women.

Lastly, one factor explaining the Court's general position as a non-deferential tribunal may be found in the historical context of the Inter-American human rights system. At the time of the creation of the IACtHR, multiple states in the South Cone were ruled by military dictatorships. After the fall of most of the dictatorships in the region, the Court played an active role in adjudicating disputes concerning violations committed during the dictatorial period. The tribunal became a relevant actor in the promotion of transitional justice, deciding the merits of cases even when states themselves had already acknowledged their international responsibility for the facts. This historical background may explain the Court's self-understanding as an institution at the forefront of the promotion of human rights in the region, a promotion that often takes place through a top-down approach.

Our identification of the abovementioned position of the IACtHR as an institution that perceives itself as being at the forefront of the promotion of human rights and responsive to structural challenges in the region is consistent with what Armin von Bogdandy and René Urueña call "the IACtHR's transformative mandate."[67] The latter refers to a specific approach of interpreting and applying the ACHR as

[67] Armin von Bogdandy and René Urueña, "International Transformative Constitutionalism in Latin America" (2020) 114 AJIL 403, 408.

a response to Latin America's structural problems and with the aim of promoting deep social change. In the words of the authors, this approach to legal interpretation is guided, among other aims, by the interpretive objective of "transforming realities in the region—in particular to address structures of violence, exclusion, and weak institutions."[68]

While this transformative—or, to critics of the Court's approach, activist—practice may lead to lower rates of compliance with the Court's decisions, von Bogdandy argues that compliance is not the decisive criterion for evaluating the work of an international court, notably when the latter perceives its mandate as contributing to transformative constitutionalism.[69] In his words, "[i]n transformative constitutionalism, compliance should give way to the wider concern of impact, which also accounts for the process (and not just the result) of compliance, and the numerous actors involved in that process."[70] The aim of the Court's activities and arguably the standard of evaluation of its work and effectiveness would then shift from full compliance to the broader notion of (transformative and structural) impact. This shift away from a primary focus on full compliance is arguably not an unconscious byproduct of the Court's practice but a deliberate choice of a model of constitutionalism (transformative constitutionalism), which manifests itself in the Court's interpretation of the substantive provisions of the ACHR and its victim-centered model of reparations.[71] In the understanding of von Bogdandy, "[i]f the Court was looking for full compliance, it would have to give up on its [transformative] mandate."[72]

5. Conclusion

The IACtHR has been active in finding discrimination in cases with a suspect classification. When a differentiation is based on a suspect classification, a presumption of discrimination emerges, the burden of proof is inverted, and the Court applies a stricter level of scrutiny in the justification step. As a result of this practice, 89.7% of the cases with a suspect classification led to a finding of violation.

68 ibid 407.

69 Armin von Bogdandy, "The Mandate of the Inter-American System: Transformative Constitutionalism by a Common Law of Human Rights" in Inter-American Court of Human Rights (ed) (n 59) 61. Note that transformative constitutionalism is understood as the interpretation of constitutional law (including international constitutionalism) as a result-oriented body of norms, responsive to the historical and structural challenges in the region and a direct instrument for the promotion of change. See von Bogdandy and Urueña (n 67).

70 von Bogdandy (n 69) 72.

71 On the work of the IACtHR and the tension between a focus on full compliance and the focus on impact in the determination of judicial remedies, see Tom M Antkowiak, "An Emerging Mandate for International Courts: Victim-Centered Remedies and Restorative Justice" (2011) 47 Stanford Journal of International Law 279, 288–92, and 304–06.

72 von Bogdandy (n 69) 72.

Furthermore, cases have not been restricted to an analysis of whether the actions of the state interfered with the right to equality and non-discrimination of individuals. Almost half of them also concerned omissions of the state to adopt measures to reverse structural disadvantages, stereotypes, and other oppressions. In other words, the right to equality and non-discrimination has been understood by the IACtHR as generating a legal obligation to confront and respond to vulnerabilities that affect marginalized groups. This positive obligation emanates from the Court's interpretation and application of Article 1(1) of the ACHR, that explicitly determines that the states parties to the Convention are under the obligation to respect and ensure rights, and Article 2 of the same instrument, which determines that the state parties are under the obligation to give domestic legal effects to the rights and freedoms protected in the Convention. The Court has interpreted the latter provision as encompassing a positive obligation to adopt the necessary legislative measures to guarantee the exercise of the rights enshrined in the Convention.[73]

This obligation to act is enhanced when the facts of the case are inserted in a context of particular vulnerability, discrimination, or marginalization against a protected group. This development shows that the Court's jurisprudence fits in the positive equality model. This is similar to the findings regarding the Brazilian Federal Supreme Court and the Colombian Constitutional Court. That this is a common feature in the studied Latin American jurisdictions might be an indication of the influence of transformative constitutionalism in the region and its application in the field of equality and non-discrimination law.

[73] cf *Atala Riffo and Daughters v Chile* (n 13) para 279; *Furlan and family v Argentina* (n 15) para 300; *IVF v Costa Rica* (n 15) para 335.

11
Colombia

Tainá Garcia Maia

1. Introduction

Scholars have described the Colombian Constitutional Court as a tribunal engaged in transformative constitutionalism[1] and even as an activist court.[2] Yet the implementation of a "transformative mandate" at the Constitutional Court does not seem to be a singularity of the tribunal. Instead, it is a concept guiding Colombian constitutional law since 1991, the year of the promulgation of the Constitution currently in force in the state.

The 1991 Constitution was created amidst a context of doubt in the capacity of the former constitutional framework to respond to the great challenges faced at the time by Colombian society, which included extreme partisan violence, the rise of insurgent groups, militia, and drug cartels. Against this background, the 1991 Constitution was conceived as an instrument with a transformative role, which should overcome legal formalism and revise the role of law itself.

The understanding of law as purpose-oriented to the promotion of substantive justice manifests itself in the constitutional protection granted to equality and non-discrimination. The 1991 Constitution protects equality in three dimensions: equality before the law; equality in the laws; and equality as a positive concept to be actively promoted by the State through the adoption of positive measures in favor of vulnerable groups. Accordingly, from its very conception in the 1991 constitutional text, equality transcends its negative dimension[3] to include the positive dimension as an intrinsic and indispensable part of the right.

This chapter conducts an empirical study of the equality case law of the Colombian Constitutional Court. Section 2 introduces the Court's equality doctrine by explaining how equality and non-discrimination are protected under the 1991 Constitution and providing an overview of the Court's equality analysis. Section 3 presents and discusses the main findings of the empirical investigation. Lastly, Section 4 analyses possible explanations for the identified patterns.

[1] See Armin von Bogdandy and René Urueña, "International Transformative Constitutionalism in Latin America" (2020) 114 AJIL 403, 407.

[2] See Paulo Maycon Costa da Silva, "Jurisdição constitucional na Colômbia e o poder político do cidadão diante da Corte Constitucional" (2014) 51 Revista de Informação Legislativa 185.

[3] That is, the duty to refrain from interfering with the right to equality.

Tainá Garcia Maia, *Colombia* In: *Equality's Guardians*. Edited by: Niels Petersen, Oxford University Press.
 DOI: 10.1093/9780198961109.003.0011

2. The equality doctrine of the Colombian Constitutional Court

2.1 Equality in the Colombian Constitution

Article 13 of the Colombian Constitution recalls that all persons are born free and equal before the law, and authorities shall provide everyone with the same protection and treatment. Subsequently, the provision prohibits discrimination based on sex, race, national or family origin, religion, and political or philosophical opinion. Lastly, it recalls that the state is under the obligation to guarantee real and effective equality. It brings forth an obligation for the state to promote positive measures in favor of discriminated or marginalized groups and to protect "especially persons who, due to their economic, physical or mental condition, find themselves in a situation of manifest vulnerability."[4]

These three dimensions of equality were discussed in detail in C-507/2004, when the Court was analyzing the constitutionality of a norm of the Colombian Civil Code that prescribed different marriage minimum ages for men and for women.[5] The first dimension is equality before the law, which guarantees equal application of the law to all persons. It regulates only the *application* of the law. The second dimension is equal treatment, which establishes an obligation for the *legislature* to refrain from creating unreasonable differences in treatment. The third dimension is equal protection, which aims to guarantee that all persons enjoy the same rights, freedoms, and opportunities. Equal protection encompasses a positive and a substantive subdimension. It is substantive because it considers the situation in which each social group finds itself to determine whether the type and degree of protection conferred to them are unequal in relation to the rest of society. In turn, it is positive because, in cases of unjustified inequality in the enjoyment of rights, it imposes the adoption of positive measures by the state to guarantee equal protection.

The substantive dimension of equality is related to Article 1 of the Constitution, which recognizes Colombia as a social state under the rule of law.[6] The positive dimension is related to Article 2 of the Constitution, which recognizes the promotion of general prosperity and the effectiveness of principles, rights, and duties as one of the essential objectives of the state.[7]

While the Constitution does not refer to the term "affirmative action," the concept is present in the Constitutional Court's jurisprudence. The Court defined affirmative measures as "policies or measures aimed at favouring certain persons or groups, either to eliminate or to reduce social, cultural or economic inequalities

[4] Political Constitution of the Republic of Colombia (October 27, 1991) art 13 (translation by the author).
[5] C-507/04 (May 25, 2004) 61–66.
[6] C-108/94 (March 10, 1994) 11.
[7] C-507/04 (n 5).

that affect them, or to ensure that members of an underrepresented group, usually a group that has been discriminated against, have a greater representation."[8] Examples of these measures include scholarships to students with scarce economic resources and any "positive or inverse discrimination."[9] Positive or inverse discrimination is distinct from the other types of affirmative action because it takes into consideration suspect classifications in contexts in which there is a special scarcity of the desired goods (such as accession to university or a work position). Hence, favoring certain groups through this type of affirmative action leads to an adverse impact on other groups.[10] However, the Court recognizes affirmative action, including positive discrimination, as a means of realizing equality to the extent that it aims at attaining a society that is less inequitable and more aligned with the objective of pursuing a just order.[11]

2.2 Equality test

The equality test applied by the Constitutional Court has changed over the decades, specifically with regard to the justification analysis. From 1992 to 2001, the Court's analysis was centered around the concepts of rationality and reasonability; that is, on an analysis of whether the impugned measure pursued a legitimate aim and the extent to which there was a link of rationality and proportionality between the impugned treatment and the aim pursued.

From 2001 on,[12] the focus has changed. The Court continues to carry out the proportionality test but it incorporates different levels of scrutiny into its analysis. The lower the level of scrutiny, the higher the margin of discretion afforded to the legislature. The levels of scrutiny depend on the regulation's subject, the constitutional principles that are affected by it, and the groups that benefit or are harmed by the difference in treatment.[13]

The Court generally applies a low level of scrutiny and a presumption of constitutionality of the legislative norm.[14] This deferential approach is generally applicable to cases concerning economic issues, tax law, international politics, topics that the Constitution has specifically assigned to the competence of a constitutional organ, pre-constitutional norms that have been derogated but still produce effects, and cases in which there is no *prima facie* threat to a right.[15]

8 C-371/00 (March 29, 2000) 47.
9 ibid.
10 ibid 47–48.
11 ibid 50.
12 See C-093/01 (January 31, 2001); C-673/01 (June 28, 2001).
13 C-748/09 (October 20, 2009).
14 C-345/19 (July 31, 2019).
15 ibid; C-227/04 (March 8, 2004); C-028/09 (January 30, 2019); C-128/2019 (March 28, 2019).

The intermediate level of scrutiny applies to cases that might affect the enjoyment of a constitutional but not fundamental right.[16] It also applies to affirmative action cases and cases in which there is an indication of arbitrariness reflected in a serious impact on free competition in an economic context.[17]

Finally, the strict level of scrutiny applies to cases with a suspect classification and cases that involve groups that are marginalized, discriminated against, or which find themselves in manifest vulnerability. It also applies to cases in which there is a *prima facie* grave impact on a fundamental constitutional right and to disputes involving the creation of privileges.[18] However, the Court has not explained what it understands as a privilege for the purposes of triggering strict scrutiny.

Article 13 provides a non-exhaustive[19] list of suspect classifications. Beyond the specifically mentioned criteria, a classification is considered "suspect" if it refers to motives or criteria that should be irrelevant as a factor leading to differences in treatment. In the words of the Court, this classification covers categories that "(i) are based on permanent traits of individuals, which one cannot abandon by his or her own will or without running the risk of losing his or her identity; (ii) categories that have been historically subject to belittlement under patterns of cultural valuation; and (iii) that do not constitute, *per se*, criteria based on which a rational and equitable distribution or division of goods, rights, or social contributions can take place."[20] In summary, this definition refers to criteria historically associated with practices placing certain groups in a situation of disadvantage.[21] On this basis, the Constitutional Court has recognized additional categories of suspect classifications, including disabilities,[22] economic situation,[23] and sexual orientation.[24] The categorization of age is less straightforward. The Court explained that minimal age requirements do not, in principle, constitute a suspect classification.[25] On the other hand, age limits are a "problematic" or, in other words, a "semi-suspect" classification.[26]

[16] C-015/14 (January 23, 2014); C-227/04 (n 15); C-028/19 (n 15); C-345/19 (n 14). Not every right protected in the Constitution is included in the Constitution's list of fundamental rights under Chapter 1 of the constitutional text. Despite this difference, the Court itself has recognized that the distinction between fundamental and constitutional rights is unclear and does not reside in the mere location of a right under a certain chapter of the Constitution. The Court has also explained that the definition of "fundamental rights" is the object of debate among scholars and judges. See T-760/08 (July 31, 2008).

[17] C-345/19 (n 14).

[18] ibid.

[19] C-371/00 (n 8) 48.

[20] ibid 49; C-519/2019 (November 5, 2019) 74.

[21] C-371/00 (n 8) 48.

[22] cf Carlos Bernal Pulido, "El juicio de la igualdad en la jurisprudencia de la Corte Constitucional Colombiana" in Juan Vega Gómez and Edgar Corzo Sosa (eds), *Instrumentos de tutela y justicia constitucional Memoria del VII Congreso Iberoamericano de Derecho Constitucional* (UNAM 2002) 63.

[23] C-663/09 (September 22, 2009); C-385/14 (June 25, 2014); C-028/19 (n 15).

[24] C-075/07 (February 7, 2007).

[25] C-227/04 (n 15); C-131/14 (March 11, 2014).

[26] ibid.

There is a presumption of unconstitutionality in disputes involving a suspect classification.[27] For example, in case C-075/2007, the Court discussed the omission of the law regulating *de facto* marital unions to cover same-sex couples. It recognized that same-sex couples have historically been subject to discrimination. Accordingly, differentiations based on sexual orientation are presumed to be unconstitutional, and strict scrutiny applies. In the concrete case, the Court found that there was no reasonable justification to differentiate between heterosexual couples and same-sex couples with regard to the recognition of *de facto* marital unions.[28]

In addition, the Court has inverted the burden of proof in cases with suspect classifications.[29] In judgment T-691/2012, a case concerning declarations made by a professor who used analogies with a racial connotation to explain a technical concept, the Court recalled that acts of discrimination are difficult to prove. Hence, the burden of proof must shift and fall on the authority who creates or applies a norm, particularly when the act affects groups falling under a suspect classification or "a situation of subordination and defencelessness."[30]

3. Empirical analysis

3.1 Methodology

The database used in the research was the Constitutional Court's jurisprudence finder.[31] Using the Court's tool of search by topics,[32] I looked for cases with the search word "*igualdad*." Since the Court was created after the promulgation of the 1991 Constitution, the results were from 1992 onwards.

The Court issues different types of judgments. Constitutionality judgments (in Spanish, "*sentencias de constitucionalidad*," C-judgments) are judgments in which the constitutionality of a legal norm is the subject of the dispute through a concentrated constitutional review. The Court also issues unification decisions (in Spanish, "*sentencias de unificación*," SU-judgments), judgments in which it establishes a unified judicial interpretation on a relevant topic in which there is legal disagreement.[33] Finally, it decides "*acciones de tutela*" (T-judgments), in which it

[27] See C-507/04 (n 5) 81; C-075/2007 (n 24) 45.
[28] ibid.
[29] T-691/12 (28 Aug 2012) 27; C-174/04 (March 2, 2004) 20; T-335/19 (July 29, 2019) 23.
[30] T-691/12 (n 29); Cf. C-174/04 (n 29). The latter judgment concerns the protected group of persons with disabilities.
[31] Colombian Constitutional Court, "Relatoría," <https://www.corteconstitucional.gov.co/relatoria/> accessed January 20, 2025.
[32] Using the words of the database, "Tema de la sentencia."
[33] Three types of legal disagreements can be grounds for an SU judgment: (i) disagreement between the Chambers of the Constitutional Court when deciding cases of *tutela*; (ii) disagreements between lower courts in cases of *tutela*; and (iii) juridical insecurity that leads to disagreements in the legislatures, members of the Executive, or even third parties interpret and apply the decisions of the

reviews a decision issued by a lower tribunal concerning a fundamental constitutional right jeopardized or threatened by the action or omission of a public authority or, in some cases, private parties. Due to the large number of T-judgments, they were not included in the initial sample of cases integrating this study. As the study aims to characterize the equality doctrine of the Court beyond the most prominent cases, including T-judgments without a filter would not be viable.

However, even after narrowing the results of the search to C-sentences and SU-sentences, the sample still included over 2,000 cases. Two criteria were thus adopted to narrow the number of cases further while ensuring the sample's representativeness. First, a subsample was created restricted to cases of concentrated constitutional review; that is, C-judgments. Next, we made a random selection of different years to study. First, I randomly selected a starting year from 1992 (the year the Court held its first session) to 1996. Then, I proceed in five-year steps. The first year randomly chosen in the study was 1994. Accordingly, the empirical study covers all C-judgments on equality decided by the Court in the following years: 1994, 1999, 2004, 2009, 2014, and 2019. The cases concerning equality falling in these two criteria were the object of quantitative analysis.

For the purposes of a qualitative analysis only, I considered the SU-judgments decided in the abovementioned five years and the Court's leading cases on equality and non-discrimination. To ensure consistency in the definition of a leading case, I used the classification provided by the Constitutional Court itself. Entering the English version of the Court's website, I accessed the decisions classified by the Court as "main decisions." Using the search words "equality" and, subsequently, "discrimination," I found a number of C-sentences, SU-sentences, and T-sentences. Complementarily, I added to the qualitative analysis of leading cases the judgments included in the chapter "Equality" of the book *Colombian Constitutional Law: Leading Cases* by Manuel José Cepeda Espinosa, former Justice of the Colombian Constitutional Court, and David Landau.

In total, I analyzed 255 judgments. Out of those, 15 were leading cases, 6 were SU-sentences and 53 were disputes in which the Court either found the equality claim to be inadmissible or did not discuss equality in substance. Accordingly, those 74 cases were not integrated into the quantitative analysis and were considered for qualitative purposes only. Relevant to the quantitative study were 181 judgments because they included a decision of merits on equality and/or non-discrimination. Those 181 cases are the object of the analysis presented in the section that follows.

Constitutional Court—an example of a unification judgment based on the latter type of disagreement is SU-214/16, in which the Court ordered the legalization of same-sex marriage throughout Colombia after legal uncertainty had arisen in the application of its decision in C-577/11.

3.2 Jurisprudential patterns

Among the 181 analysed cases, 68 led to a finding of violation of equality. In 102 cases, the Court did not find a violation, and 11 cases were multiple-claim cases that resulted both in a finding of violation and a finding of no violation. If we attribute half a violation to these multiple-claim cases, then 73.5 cases out of the total sample led to a finding of violation. Therefore, the total success rate of equality cases the Colombian Constitutional Court decided in the period under analysis was approximately 40.6%.

A more detailed analysis shows that the success rate of cases involving suspect classifications is significantly higher than the average success rate of equality claims in this jurisdiction. 70.19% of the cases with a suspect classification resulted in a finding of violation. By contrast, 28.7% of the cases not involving a suspect classification were successful (see Table 11.1).

Table 11.1 Success rate disaggregated by criterion of distinction

Criterion	Violation	No violation	Total	Success rate
Not suspect	37	92	129	28.7
Gender/sex	9	1	10	90
Race/ethnic origin	2	1	3	66.7
National origin	1.5	4.5	6	25
Residence	2	1	3	66.7
Birth out of wedlock	2.5	1.5	4	62.5
Disability	5	3	8	62.5
Sexual orientation	2	0	2	100
Marriage	7.5	2.5	10	75
Economic status/social class	6	2	8	75
Religion	4.5	1.5	6	75
Family origin	2	0	2	100
Age (age limits only)	3	0	3	100
Total number of cases	73.5	107.5	181	

Note: The aggregated sum of each column exceeds the total number of equality cases due to cases of intersectionality or multiple discrimination, in which the equality claim referred to two or more suspect classifications. Additionally, observe that the columns "violation" and "non-violation" encompass deciles. This is explained by cases involving multiple claims, in which only some claims led to a finding of violation.

The success rate of cases with a suspect classification is even higher if we remove from the sample those cases in which the Court found a non-violation because it upheld the constitutionality of a positive measure. Notably, two of the three findings of non-violation in cases concerning persons with disabilities, and the only finding of non-violation concerning ethnic origin were decisions in which the Court upheld the constitutionality of a positive measure in favor of a vulnerable group.[34]

We find that the success rate is positively correlated to the level of scrutiny.[35] Among the 15 cases in which the Constitutional Court applied a low level of scrutiny, 3 resulted in a finding of violation (success rate of 20%). Among the eight cases in which it applied an intermediary level of scrutiny, four resulted in a finding of violation (success rate of 50%). Finally, 15 out of 17 cases in which the Court applied strict scrutiny led to a finding of violation (success rate of 88.2%). This result confirms that the Court grants a greater margin of discretion to the legislature in cases in which it applies a lower level of scrutiny.

The study also shows that the Court has generally upheld the constitutionality of positive measures. Out of the 14 cases concerning positive measures, it reduced the scope of a measure in only 1 case. In an additional case, it denied a request to expand the scope of the measure. By contrast, it either expanded or reaffirmed a positive measure and the obligation to implement it in 9 cases. The 3 remaining disputes involved positive measures instituted to the benefit of women. The Court expanded the scope of these measures to cover men in certain vulnerable situations, such as men who were the primary carers of their minor sons.[36]

It is interesting to note that the Court's findings of violation have not always led to the unconstitutionality of the impugned norm. In 38.6% of the cases in which the Court found a violation of equality, it made the constitutionality of the norm conditional upon the adoption of a specific legal interpretation—which often expanded the scope of the norm to include an excluded group—or, more rarely, determined that Congress had to legislate on the matter to fill a legal gap. The Court's equality jurisprudence thus covers both acts and omissions of the state, and it refers to equality in its negative and positive dimensions. Finally, the Court has also found indirect discrimination in a significant number of cases. Indirect discrimination was the subject of analysis in 14 cases. 64.3% of these cases led to a finding of violation.

[34] See 058/94 (February 17, 1994); C-174/04 (n 29); C-640/19 (December 16, 2019).

[35] This analysis of success rate only included cases in which the Court expressly stated the level of scrutiny it was applying.

[36] cf C-044/04 (January 27, 2004).

4. Explaining the identified patterns in the Court's equality jurisprudence

4.1 Transformative constitutionalism

The constitutional history of Colombia is entangled with the country's social and political history. While, on a certain level, this holds true for every state, this connection is particularly important in the case of Colombia. At the end of the 20th century, Colombia was the stage of different forms of violence, including political violence and conflicts involving drug cartels, militia, and guerrilla movements.[37] In the words of Manuel J. Cepeda Espinosa, "at the end of the 1980s there were six active guerrilla groups and half of Colombians believed, according to the polls, that the only way to make a change in Colombia was through violent revolution."[38] In this context, the discussions around the need for constitutional reform were increasing, and, in August 1990, the recently elected President César Gaviria issued the Siege Decree No 1926, stressing the importance of a Constituent Assembly and setting a framework for its creation.[39] The 1991 Constitution thus emerged as an answer to the search for transformation and an alternative to revolution. It would be for the law, thus, to promote change.

Manuel José Cepeda Espinosa, Justice at the Colombian Constitutional Court from 2001 to 2009, refers to the concept of responsive law to explain the conveying of the Constituent Assembly. This conceptualization of the law, developed by Philip Selznick and Philip Nonet, departs from a formalistic view of the law and its perception as essentially autonomous from politics. Instead, responsive law integrates legal and political aspirations to promote substantive justice. It is a particular conceptualization of the law as result-oriented; that is, as a system that responds to institutional problems and promotes transformation.[40]

Espinosa shares that he suggested to President Gaviria that the new Constitution represented "an opportunity to overcome legal formalism and move in the direction of a type of law that was more in tune with the evolution of Colombian society and the challenges that the country had to face at the time," a suggestion that was met with enthusiasm.[41] In his speech defending the creation of a Constitutional Court and its access through *tutela*, President Gaviria recalled the need for a result-oriented law; in other words, a law with open eyes, and not law as "a blind

[37] Lydia Brashear Tiede, *Judicial Vetoes: Decision-making on Mixed Selection Constitutional Courts* (CUP 2022) 101–12.

[38] Manuel J Cepeda Espinosa, "Responsive Constitutionalism" (2019) 15 Annual Review of Law and Social Science 21, 26.

[39] Decree 1926 (August 25,1990).

[40] Espinosa (n 38); Philippe Nonet and Philip Selznick, *Law & Society in Transition: Toward Responsive Law* (2nd edn, Routledge 2017).

[41] ibid 27.

and obstinate tyrant."[42] In a later speech, the President affirmed that, "[w]ith the Constitution of 1991 [,] a new conception of law was born."[43]

The concept of responsive law has been a guiding idea in the conception of the 1991 Constitution. This influence is particularly noticeable in the Constitution's formulation of the right to equality. Article 13 of the Colombian Constitution not only protects formal equality and prohibits discrimination but also puts forth an obligation for the state to adopt positive measures responding to the challenges of structural and historical discrimination and marginalization in Colombian society. One example of the recognition of this duty in the case law of the Constitutional Court is the well-known judgment T-025/04 concerning the rights of internally displaced persons. In this case, the Constitutional Court recalled that the state is obliged to adopt and implement policies, program, or positive measures promoting substantive equality, correcting social inequalities, and facilitating the inclusion and participation of marginalized and vulnerable populations in the social and economic life of the nation.[44] The Court recognized a "state of unconstitutional affairs"[45] in relation to the conditions of life of the internally displaced population and ordered a number of individual and structural orders to protect this vulnerable group.[46]

In summary, transformative constitutionalism and the historical context leading to its emergence are primary factors explaining the Court's general practice in relation to positive measures. A self-understanding of the role of the law and the Constitutional Court as the promoter of change and guardian of rights is a relevant factor explaining the Court's practice of upholding the constitutionality of positive measures and recognizing a direct obligation of the State to actively adopt measures promoting equality.

4.2 Foreign influences

The Colombian Constitutional Court itself identified two major influences in foreign law to its equality doctrine. First, Europe's reasonability or proportionality test (two terms often used interchangeably by the Colombian Constitutional

[42] César Gaviria Trujillo, "Palabras del Señor Presidente de la República" (17 April 1991), <https://ridum.umanizales.edu.co/xmlui/handle/20.500.12746/4557?show=full> accessed January 20, 2025.

[43] César Gaviria Trujillo, "La necesidad de un nuevo derecho," cited after Espinosa (n 38) 27.

[44] T-025/04 (January 22, 2004).

[45] Since 1997, the Colombian Constitutional Court has recognized on a few occasions a state of unconstitutional affairs. The latter relates to a condition of repetitive and constant violation of fundamental rights affecting multiple individuals and requiring structural intervention by various organs. On the basis of this declaration, the Court issues structural orders and remedies to the benefit not only of the petitioners but also of other individuals in the same situation who were not parties to the *tutela* action. See T-025/04 (n 44) 70–74; Manuel José Cepeda Espinosa and David Landau, *Colombian Constitutional Law: Leading Cases* (OUP 2017) 382–86.

[46] T-025/04 (n 44).

Court), and, secondly, the doctrine of tiered scrutiny of the United States.[47] The first method finds its inspiration in the European Court of Human Rights, the German Federal Constitutional Court, and the Spanish Constitutional Court.[48] In 1996, the Colombian Constitutional Court explained the so-called reasonability test as an attempt to answer the question of whether the justification provided for a difference in treatment was sufficient to qualify the latter as reasonable. Quoting the jurisprudence of the German Federal Constitutional Court, it found that this analysis could only be conducted in a satisfactory manner if connected to a more specific principle: the principle of proportionality.[49] From 2001 on, as the Court's equality test shifted away from the focus on reasonability, the European influence remained present, manifesting itself in the assessment of the proportionality of the impugned measure.

A second method to find a violation of the constitutional right to equality is the application of distinct levels of scrutiny, which was mainly developed by the US Supreme Court. This method recognizes three levels of scrutiny: weak, intermediary, and strict scrutiny.

Having recalled these two methods, Justice Ortiz Delgado, acting as the author of the majority opinion in decision C-345/19, explained that the constitutional jurisprudence of Colombia merged the abovementioned methods, since they are compatible with one another and complementary.[50] The merger resulted in Colombia's "integrated equality assessment." The integrated equality assessment applies the steps of the proportionality test to equality cases but qualifies these steps based on levels of scrutiny.

The US influence is also identified in the background of one influential Justice of the Colombian Constitutional Court, Cepeda Espinosa. He was the Presidential Advisor for the Constituent Assembly that drafted the 1991 Constitution and, a decade later, became a Justice at the Colombian Constitutional Court and, subsequently, the Court's President. Espinosa studied in the United States—at Georgetown University and Harvard—and was strongly influenced by the work of two Berkeley professors, Selznick and Nonet, on responsive law.[51]

Another foreign influence that is relevant to the equality jurisprudence of the Colombian Constitutional Court is the Inter-American System of Human Rights. While the Inter-American System does not appear to have impacted the formal steps of the equality test adopted by the Colombian Court, it is an important source for the Colombian Constitutional Court's interpretation of the content and scope of equality. Instruments from the Inter-American System of Human Rights, as well

[47] C-345/19 (n 14); cf Pulido (n 22).

[48] C-345/19 (n 14); C-022/1996 (January 23, 1996).

[49] C-022/1996 (n 48).

[50] The Justice explained that, differently from the US test, the integrated assessment benefits from the analytical advantages of the reasonability test, C-022/1996 (n 48).

[51] Espinosa (n 38) 25

as decisions and pronouncements from the Inter-American Commission and the Inter-American Court of Human Rights, have been cited by the Constitutional Court in its reasoning in cases involving suspect classifications, notably cases concerning sexual orientation, race, persons with disabilities, and violence against women.[52] The Constitutional Court has recalled that since Colombia is a party to the American Convention on Human Rights, it could take into consideration the equality doctrine of the Inter-American Court, including the latter's recognition of equality as a *jus cogens* norm.[53]

5. Conclusion

Three main conclusions emerge from this empirical investigation. First, the study shows that the Colombian Constitutional Court has been active in tackling omissions of the state as violations of the obligation to realize equality. The Court has also been active in upholding and, at times, expanding positive measures. This practice is consistent with the concept of transformative constitutionalism and responsive law, which have been fundamental in the drafting of the 1991 Constitution.

Second, equality claims with a suspect classification have had a higher success rate in the Court. Of the cases involving suspect classifications, 70.19% have resulted in a finding of inequality, whereas only 28.7% of the cases not involving a suspect classification were recognized by the Court as involving a violation of the right to equality.

However, a 28.7% success rate for cases not involving suspect classifications is nonetheless high when compared to other jurisdictions analyzed in this book. In addition, in absolute terms, cases not involving suspect classifications constitute almost half of the violations found by the Constitutional Court. While these are indications of the application of the equality as reasonableness model, the Court's strong focus on the positive dimension of the right to equality tilts the balance in favor of the positive equality approach.

The Constitutional Court has addressed state action that interfered with the right to equality, as well as inaction to protect and promote equality. In addition, the Court has not only recognized but also expanded the scope of positive measures in some disputes. Finally, although cases on positive measures are not as prominent in the Colombian jurisdiction as in the Brazilian Federal Supreme Court and the Inter-American Court of Human Rights, the Colombian Constitutional Court's conceptualization of equality is strongly focused on substantive equality

[52] cf T-1090/05 (October 26, 2005); T-248/12 (March 26, 2012); T-012/16 (January 22, 2016); C-329/19 (July 24, 2019).
[53] cf T-248/12 (n 52).

and influenced by transformative constitutionalism. Even in disputes that do not concern positive measures, the Colombian Constitutional Court often highlights the constitutionality and relevance of positive measures *in abstract*. It stresses that equality is a right not only to be respected by the state but also promoted through concrete measures. Equality thus transcends its negative dimension, an understanding that is central to the Court's very conceptualization of the principle. Explaining factors for this conceptualization of equality can be found in the impact of transformative constitutionalism in the drafting of the 1991 Constitution (which recognizes Colombia as a social state already in the first Article of the Constitution and guarantees substantive and positive equality in Article 13), the educational background of the Justices and their *habitus*,[54] and the self-understanding of the Court as a promoter of change.

[54] As the term is defined in Bourdieu's relational sociology. See Pierre Bourdieu, *Practical Reason: On the Theory of Action* (Stanford University Press 1998).

12
Brazil

Tainá Garcia Maia

1. Introduction

In early 1964, a *coup d'état* ushered in a military dictatorship in Brazil that lasted for over two decades. It was only in 1985 that the Electoral College, formed by the then state and federal members of congress, senators, and governors, indirectly elected a civilian government. Before the elections, the streets of Brazil had been taken over by the *Diretas Já* (which translates to "Direct elections now"), one of the biggest social movements to have happened in the country in the 20th century. Despite the popular clamor, the National Congress in power during the final years of the military dictatorship rejected a constitutional amendment that would have paved the way for the first direct presidential elections after the 1964 *coup d'état*. Instead, the transition to democracy reflected the promise made by the Military President Ernesto Geisel in the 1970s, ensuring the conservative sectors of society that the return to democracy would be "slow, gradual and safe."[1]

While the 1985 indirect presidential election was highly criticized for the lack of civil society participation, the drafting of the first democratic Constitution following the dictatorship was to take a different path. In 1986, a new National Congress was designated through direct elections with universal suffrage—the first in 104 years to extend the right to vote of illiterate people.[2] The elected members of Congress would simultaneously be members of the Constituent Assembly, which was required to conduct public hearings and take into consideration suggestions from civil society presented through popular amendments.[3]

[1] cf Rodrigo Pereira Chagas, "Florestan e a 'Transição Transada' da Reforma Partidária ao Colégio Eleitoral" (2013) 23 Textos & Debates 69.

[2] Tribunal Superior Eleitoral, "Emenda Constitucional de 1985 garantiu o direito ao voto aos eleitores analfabetos" (TSE, 2016) <https://www.tse.jus.br/imprensa/noticias-tse/2016/Novembro/constituicao-de-1985-garantiu-o-direito-ao-voto-aos-eleitores-analfabetos> accessed January 20, 2025; Câmara dos Deputados, "Década de 80: as Diretas-Já" (Agência Câmara de Notícias, August 5, 2010) <https://www.camara.leg.br/noticias/90151-decada-de-80-as-diretas-ja> accessed January 20, 2025.

[3] Flávia Danielle Santiago Lima, "Revisitando os Pressupostos da Juristocracia à Brasileira: Mobilização Judicial na Assembleia Constituinte e o fortalecimento do Supremo Tribunal Federal" (2018) 63 Revista da Faculdade de Direito UFPR 145, 157.

Tainá Garcia Maia, *Brazil* In: *Equality's Guardians*. Edited by: Niels Petersen, Oxford University Press.
 DOI: 10.1093/9780198961109.003.0012

Despite tensions that often accompany a Constituent Assembly in situations of democratic transition, the Assembly found consensus about the need for fundamental rights. Flávia Danielle Santiago Lima explains that this consensus emerged "from the need to overcome the former political regime and from the Constituents' commitment to meet this expectation."[4] Similarly, Justice Cármen Lúcia argues that the 1988 Constitution of the Federative Republic of Brazil (CF/88) embodied the understanding that law would be the means used to attain social democracy and social justice.[5]

According to Justice Cármen Lúcia, the Constitution was born out of the profound crisis that deeply shook the Brazilian society, in which the social, economic, and regional inequalities that entangled Brazilian politics played a crucial role.[6] Consequently, it is unsurprising that the drafters of the CF/88 safeguarded equality as a supreme value of a democratic society, a fundamental objective and principle of the Republic, and a subjective right, covering both the negative and the positive dimensions of equality. More specifically, the CF/88 protects the principle of equality and non-discrimination in its formal and substantive dimensions. It also imposes a positive obligation on the state to adopt measures promoting the equality of historically marginalized groups. Affirmative action is explicitly required from the state in the constitutional text. Furthermore, racism is criminalized.

Beyond the formalities of the legal text, the content and scope of the right to equality have gradually expanded in the jurisprudence of the Brazilian Federal Supreme Court (STF) since 1988. The STF has, for example, found that discrimination against vulnerable groups, including homophobia and transphobia, was criminalized under the CF/88—in addition to racism.[7] It also recognized, *inter alia*, the right of same-sex couples to form a civil partnership.[8]

This chapter will analyze the equality jurisprudence of the STF and identify patterns in the judicial practice of the Court when addressing equality or non-discrimination claims. For this purpose, collegiate decisions of the STF that were published from October 1988 to October 2020 were analyzed. The analysis starts

[4] ibid 156 (translation by the author).

[5] Cármen Lúcia Antunes Rocha, "Ação afirmativa: O Conteúdo Democrático do Princípio da Igualdade Jurídica" (1996) 33 Revista de Informação Legislativa 283, 288. The focus on fundamental rights and social justice is clear from the Preamble of the CF/88: "We, representatives of the Brazilian people, gathered in a National Constituent Assembly to establish a Democratic State, destined to ensure the exercise of social and individual rights, freedom, security, well-being, development, equality and justice as the supreme values of a fraternal, pluralistic and unprejudiced society, founded on social harmony and committed, in the internal and international order, to the peaceful solution of controversies, enact, under the protection of God, the following CONSTITUTION OF THE FEDERATIVE REPUBLIC OF BRAZIL." See Constitution of the Federative Republic of Brazil of 1988 (October 5, 1988) (translation by the author).

[6] Antunes Rocha (n 5) 288.

[7] *ADO 26/DF* (June 13, 2019, Justice rapporteur: Celso de Mello); *MI 4.733/DF* (June 13, 2019, Justice rapporteur: Edson Fachin).

[8] *ADI 4.277/DF* (May 5, 2011, Justice rapporteur: Ayres Britto); *ADPF 132/RJ* (May 5, 2011, Justice rapporteur: Ayres Britto); *AgR 477.554/MG RE* (August 16, 2011, Justice rapporteur: Celso de Mello).

in October 1988 because the date marks the promulgation of the democratic Constitution that is currently in force. Section 2 of this chapter will introduce the STF's equality doctrine by describing the constitutional provisions protecting equality in the CF/88 and briefly discussing the equality test applied at the STF. Section 3 will present the results of our empirical study and identify patterns in the Court's practice in deciding equality claims. Finally, Section 4 will discuss possible explanations for the identified patterns in the STF's equality jurisprudence.

2. The equality doctrine of the STF

2.1 Equality and non-discrimination in the 1988 Constitution

The first four Articles of the CF/88 list the fundamental principles that shall guide the Republic and its organization. The guarantee of equality is read into several of these principles. Article 1.III recognizes the dignity of the human person as a pillar of the Republic. The STF has read this as an early indication of the right to equality in the Constitution.[9] Article 3.III establishes as a fundamental objective of the Republic "to eradicate poverty and marginalization and to reduce social and regional inequalities."[10] This is followed by Article 3.IV, which safeguards another fundamental principle, the promotion of the well-being of all "without prejudice based on *origin, race, sex, colour, age or any other forms of discrimination*."[11]

The operational general equality clause is contained in Article 5, according to which "*everyone is equal before the law, without distinction of any nature*, so as to guarantee to Brazilians and foreigners residing in the country the inviolability of the right to life, to freedom, *equality*, safety and property."[12] The drafting history of Article 5 shows that this provision was first conceived as a non-discrimination clause, prohibiting discrimination based on "race, sex, colour, civil status, age, rural or urban work, religious belief, sexual orientation, political or philosophical conviction, mental or physical disabilities, or social condition."[13] This proposal was later changed to omit the reference to sexual orientation as a protected group, and, eventually, it changed from a non-discrimination clause with explicit reference to protected grounds to a general equality clause.

Article 5 prescribes that "*everyone is equal before the law, without distinction of any nature* (…), *in the following terms*."[14] The expression "the following terms" refers to the 78 items that comprised this provision (Article 5.I—5.LXXVIII), most

[9] *RE 646.721/RS* (May 10, 2017, Justice rapporteur: Roberto Barroso), vote of the *rapporteur* 16–17.
[10] CF/88 (n 5) art 3, III (translation by the author, emphasis added).
[11] ibid art 3, IV (translation by the author, emphasis added).
[12] ibid art 5 (translation by the author, emphasis added).
[13] ibid 27, "FASE A—Anteprojeto do Relator."
[14] ibid.

of which protect civil and political rights. A separate chapter of the Constitution protects social rights (Chapter II, on "Social Rights," composed of Articles 6 to 11). Despite this formal division, it is common practice of the STF to refer to the general equality clause in cases concerning the right to equality in the enjoyment of social and economic rights.[15]

The general equality clause is complemented by a series of constitutional articles that can be classified as specific equality provisions.[16] They are built into Article 5 and specify it in relation to a negative or positive obligation of the State and, generally, with reference to a specific protected group. The specific equality provisions of the CF/88 can be divided into three groups: (i) clauses that prohibit discrimination in the enjoyment of one specific right and, as a general rule, with reference to one specific protected group; (ii) clauses prescribing positive measures for protected groups; and, finally, (iii) clauses reiterating that the principle of equality is to be applied by the state when carrying out its functions (eg in healthcare, education, and tax law). One example is Article 37.VIII, which provides a state obligation to institute quotas for persons with disabilities in admission to public employment.[17] Affirmative action based on disabilities is the only strong distributive positive measure that is constitutionally protected. In contrast, quota systems based on race and economic condition have been prescribed by infra-constitutional law.

While Article 5 embodies a general equality clause, it has been read by the STF as a multidimensional concept that goes beyond formal equality.[18] One illustrative case in this regard is *ADC 41* (2017), concerning the constitutionality of racial quotas for admission to a public university in Brazil. The Justice rapporteur, Luís Roberto Barroso, explained that the 1988 Constitution safeguards three dimensions of equality:[19] formal equality; substantive equality; and equality as recognition. The first dimension is an expression of formal equality and protects against the creation of privileges and discriminatory treatment.[20] The second dimension refers to "redistribution of power, wealth and social well-being."[21] Finally, equality as recognition means "respect for minorities, their identity and their differences, be them racial, religious, sexual or any other."[22]

[15] See eg *ADPF 186/DF* (April 26, 2012, Justice rapporteur: Ricardo Lewandowski); *ADC 41/DF* (June 8, 2017, Justice rapporteur: Roberto Barroso).

[16] Arts 5–7; 37; 39; 40, III and § 4th; 150–152; 201, § 1st; 205; 206; 227; 244.

[17] Art 37, VIII, reads: "the law will reserve a percentage of the positions and public employments to persons with disabilities, and it will define the criteria for their admission" (translation by the author).

[18] See *ADI 2.144/DF* (June 2, 2016, Justice rapporteur: Teori Zavascki).

[19] This description of the dimensions of equality by Justice Barroso coincides with what has been described by legal scholars as the multiple dimensions of equality; Sandra Fredman, "The Potential and Limits of an Equal Rights Paradigm in Addressing Poverty" (2011) 22 Stellenbosch LR 566; cf Shreya Atrey, "The Intersectional Case of Poverty in Discrimination Law" (2018) 18 Human Rights LR 411.

[20] See art 5 *caput* CF/88.

[21] See art 3, I and III CF/88.

[22] *ADC 41/DF* (n 15), para 21. See art 3.IV and 5.XLII CF/88.

This conceptualization of equality is not merely a doctrinal construction of Justice Barroso. Quite to the contrary, the STF has a *jurisprudence constante* of referring to substantive equality as a central concept in equality cases, which calls for positive measures, structural transformation, and the promotion of recognition.[23] In other words, the Court adopts a conceptualization of equality as substantive equality with manifestations in multiple dimensions.

2.2 The STF's equality test

As a general equality clause, Article 5 CF/88 does not include a list of protected groups or suspect classifications. In addition, the expression "suspect classification" is generally not present in the Court's jurisprudence.[24] However, despite the absence of suspect classifications in Article 5 and the rare presence of the term in the STF's equality jurisprudence, the concept has a certain significance in the Court's case law. Justices have upheld that, as a general rule, grounds related to historical marginalization (eg race, gender, sexual orientation) may not be used as factors of differentiation justifying the application of a targeted norm against oppressed groups.[25] Furthermore, the Court has consistently recognized specific collectives as being subject to historical and pervasive discrimination and, as such, constituting protected groups. As a direct consequence, it has called for equality not only in a negative but also in a positive dimension to the benefit of these groups.[26]

In determining whether an impugned measure, action, or inaction violates equality and non-discrimination as safeguarded in the CF/88, the STF applies an equality assessment that is formally tierless. However, the empirical analysis will show that, in practice, the Court appears to apply two standards of scrutiny, depending on whether the case refers to a suspect classification or not.

[23] For illustrative purposes, see *ADPF 186/DF* (n 15); *ADI 5.617/DF* (March 15, 2018, Justice rapporteur: Edson Fachin); *RE 1.058.333/PR* (November 21, 2018, Justice rapporteur: Luiz Fux); *RE 494.601/RS* (August 9, 2019, Justice rapporteur: Edson Fachin); *ADI 5.543/DF* (May 11, 2020, Justice rapporteur: Edson Fachin).

[24] A rare exception is *ADPF 291/DF* (October 28, 2015, Justice rapporteur: Roberto Barroso) paras 52–53.

[25] See eg *ADI 3.330* (May 3, 2012), in which the Justice rapporteur, Ayres Britto, relied on art 3.IV of the CF/88 to identify grounds that may not be used as factors of differentiation for determining one's social values (paras 37–39). The Justice applied the same understanding to historic-cultural factors of differentiation, such as socio-economic status. Similarly, in *RE 898.450* (August 17, 2016), the rapporteur, Justice Luiz Fux, recalled that factors that are intrinsic to a person, such as sex, residency status, age, race, among others, cannot justify the application of a targeted norm against these groups, unless the *raison d'être* of the differentiation directly relates to said characteristics. Similarly, in *RE 898.450*, the rapporteur, Justice Luiz Fux, recalled that factors that are intrinsic to a person, such as sex, residency status, age, race, among others, cannot justify the application of a targeted norm against these groups, unless the *raison d'être* of the differentiation directly relates to said characteristics.

[26] See eg *Pet. 3.388/RR* (March 19, 2009, Justice rapporteur: Ayres Britto); *ADI 4.424/DF* (February 9, 2012, Justice rapporteur: Marco Aurélio).

Another important element of the Court's equality doctrine is its assessment of affirmative action. In cases of affirmative action, the assessment of proportionality, notably the requirement of necessity, is particularly relevant. Affirmative action is only legitimate to the extent needed to achieve its aims. When the intended results are achieved in a sustainable manner, the means adopted—that is, preferential treatment—must be phased out. The proportionality test in affirmative action cases, thus, also embodies a temporal dimension.

3. Empirical analysis of the equality case law

Having described how equality is protected in theory, this section will focus on the application of this right in practice at the STF. Section 3.1 will present the methods used in this empirical study. Next, Section 3.2 will introduce the results of the empirical analysis focusing on the success rate of equality claims decided by the Court and the levels of scrutiny applied by the tribunal. Finally, Section 3.3. will identify patterns in the decisions of the STF concerning positive measures.

3.1 Methodology

Our empirical study aimed to map all collegiate decisions in which the STF made a ruling addressing equality and non-discrimination. It used the STF's jurisprudence database to find the relevant judicial decisions.[27] The word "equality"[28] was searched in connection to Articles 5–7; 37; 39; 40, III and §4th; 150–152; 201, §1st; 205; 206; 227; and 244 of the 1988 Constitution. To count for possible mistakes in the categorization of cases in the database, I also searched for the words "equality AND discrimination," unconnected to any provision of the Constitution. Lastly, I included additional cases cited as precedents in the analyzed decisions.

The analysis is restricted to collegiate decisions. This choice was made for the following reasons: monocratic decisions are taken in matters already defined in the prevailing jurisprudence of the Court. Furthermore, while they represent most

[27] Search tool "pesquisa no banco de jurisprudência" <https://jurisprudencia.stf.jus.br/pages/search> accessed January 20, 2025. Decisions that are identical in their content and scope and, in addition, are highly similar in their formalities—for example, they were decided by the same group (plenary or full bench), among other characteristics—are not shown in the results provided by the database. The STF's department working with the database is responsible for downloading the cases in the platform, together with relevant technical information, such as a list of the doctrine and jurisprudence cited by the Justices. This information comes in a digital document called "mirror of the judgment," available in the database for each of the search results. The "mirror" brings forth all the technical information of the judgment, including a list of the cases that are considered by the Department to be repetitive. These highly repetitive cases, which the Court refers as "compiled cases," are thus masked from the results of the search. To avoid a bias result, the study did not include those "hidden" cases.

[28] "Igualdade" and "Igualdade e discriminação."

of the precautionary decisions adopted by the Court, the collegiate can revise these decisions. Therefore, the analysis of collegiate decisions arguably remains representative of the Court's jurisprudence and reflects judicial patterns.

The sample covered legal actions for abstract and concrete review, conducted through concentrated judicial review (abstract control of constitutionality)[29] and diffuse judicial review (extraordinary appeals, ordinary appeals, extradition actions, *habeas corpus*, injunction, writ of *mandamus*, among others). It is largely composed of final judgments, but also includes appeals against interlocutory decisions and injunctions that discussed equality and non-discrimination in the merits.

Approximately 730 cases were identified through the database search.[30] Out of those, 267 decisions were relevant for further analysis in light of the substantive criteria described above. In seven of these cases, the STF found that it lacked the competence to make a ruling on the merits. This means that the Supreme Court made a ruling addressing the principle of equality and non-discrimination in substance in a total of 259 cases, which formed part of the content analysis and coding.

In each case, a rapporteur is randomly assigned by the Court. The rapporteur is the Justice assigned by the STF to prepare the syllabus of the judgment and write the tribunal's decision, called "*acórdão*." The latter is composed of a few paragraphs (in some cases, it has even been composed of a single paragraph) that summarize whether or not there was a finding of unconstitutionality/a decision in favor of the applicant. Hence, the *acórdão* offers little help in determining the reasons for the majority decision. Therefore, the analysis was largely based on the vote of the rapporteur. This choice is justified by the fact that, in the overwhelming majority of the cases included in the sample, the *acórdão* stated that the decision of the majority was made "under the terms of the *rapporteur*" or, alternatively, the syllabus that opens the judgment generally repeated the words and the main arguments of the rapporteur (88.5% of the cases). In the exceptions in which this did not take place, I examined the votes of all the Justices that constituted the majority opinion and identified the common grounds among them to determine whether the Justices had expressed the wish to follow the vote of the rapporteur. By using this method, the research aimed to present results that are representative not only of the reasons for the vote of the rapporteur but also of the decision reached jointly by the Court.[31]

[29] ADI, ADC, ADO, and ADPF.

[30] Because the STF department responsible for the database constantly updates the latter and, at times, changes the qualification of a case as a repetitive one to be merely included in the "mirror" of the document, a new search done now covering the same period might lead to a different total number of cases. A difference in the total number of cases might also occur due to the delay of the tribunal in publishing a judgment.

[31] Reliance on the vote of the rapporteur as representative of the majority decision has been the method chosen by the Supreme Court's Department of Higher Studies. See Supremo Tribunal Federal, *Convenção Americana sobre Direitos Humanos: Anotada com a jurisprudência do Supremo Tribunal Federal e da Corte Interamericana de Direitos Humanos* (2nd edn, STF, Secretaria de Altos Estudos, Pesquisas e Gestão da Informação 2022) 8. See also Danilo dos Santos Almeida and André Martins

3.2 Identified patterns

The analysis covers 259 cases published from October 1988 to the end of October 2020. In 126 cases, the STF found a violation of equality and non-discrimination, while it did not find a violation in 130 cases. The remaining three cases involved multiple equality claims, half of which led to findings of violation. If we add these cases to the quantitative analysis, we find that the Court declared a violation in 127.5 cases and no violation in 131.5 cases, amounting to a success rate of 49.2%.[32] The success rate of cases involving a suspect classification is only slightly higher, at 52.7%.

However, this does not mean that the involvement of a suspect classification barely makes a difference. Table 12.1 introduces the success rate of equality and non-discrimination claims disaggregated by the criterion of differentiation. The suspect classification that has been most often present in the findings of violation is sexual orientation, which has a perfect success rate of 100%. In terms of the absolute number of successful cases, it is followed by sex/gender, age, disability, and residency.

And yet the success rates for these latter categories differ significantly. The high number of non-violations of distinctions based on sex should not be interpreted as an indicator of a lenient behaviour of the STF towards restrictive measures on women's rights. Quite the contrary, one factor that explains this rate is the Court's *jurisprudence constante* of upholding the constitutionality of positive measures to the benefit of women. Eight of the 22 cases of non-violation concerned decisions in which the Court upheld the constitutionality of positive measures in favor of women. Furthermore, many of the remaining findings of non-violation refer to the dispute of whether a widower of a female public servant has the right to a survivor's pension.[33] In the many cases brought to the STF, the Court generally recognized

Bogossian, "'Nos Termos do Voto do Relator': considerações acerca da fundamentação coletiva nos acórdãos so STF" (2016) 2 Revista Estudos Institucionais 263.

[32] That is, there were 127.5 cases of violation (ie 126 cases + 3 (½ a case)), and 131.5 cases of non-violation (130 + 3 (½ a case)). Another way of quantifying this data is disaggregating the number of cases by suspect classification and non-suspect classification. One of the 259 cases involved two claims, one of which referred to a suspect classification and the other one did not. This means that the STF decided 91 cases involving a suspect classification, with a success rate of 52.7% (47 cases led a finding of violation, and two cases were multiple claims, half of which led to a finding of violation. Thus, violations = 47 cases + 2 × 0.5 claims = 48). It also decided 169 cases involving a non-suspect classification, 80 of which led to a finding of violation and one involved multiple claims, half of which led to a finding of violation (violations = 80 cases + 0.5 claim = 80.5).

[33] *RE 204.193-9* (May 30, 2001, Justice rapporteur: Carlos Velloso); *RE 205.896-3* (May 30, 2001, Justice rapporteur: Ellen Gracie); *RE 204.735-0* (May 30, 2001, Justice rapporteur: Carlos Velloso); *RE 247.080-5* (October 9, 2001, Justice rapporteur: Néri da Silveira); *RE 203.250-6* (October 16, 2001, Justice rapporteur: Moreira Alves); *RE 224.837-1 AgR* (May 28, 2002, Justice rapporteur: Ellen Gracie); *RE 205.787-8 AgR* (June 25, 2002, Justice rapporteur: Carlos Velloso); *RE 203.069-4 AgR* (June 28, 2002, Justice rapporteur: Ilmar Galvão); *RE 354.368-7* (October 8, 2002, Justice rapporteur: Moreira Alves); *RE 406.710-2 ED* (February 3, 2004, Justice rapporteur: Carlos Velloso); *RE 429.931-3 Ag* (November 9, 2004, Justice rapporteur: Carlos Velloso).

Table 12.1 Success rate disaggregated by criterion of distinction

Criterion	Violation	No violation	Total	Success rate
Not suspect	81	89	170	47.6
Sexual orientation	9	0	9	100
Gender/sex	8	22	30	26.7
Race/ethnic origin	0	5	5	0
Economic status	5	5	10	50
Disability	8	5	13	61.5
Age	8	3	11	72.7
Residency	7	2	9	77.8
National origin	4	4	8	50
Gender identity	3	0	3	100
Marriage	2	0	2	100
Religion	0	2	2	0
Total number of cases	127.5	131.5	259	

Note: The aggregated sum of each column exceeds the total number of cases due to cases of intersectionality or multiple discrimination, in which the equality claim referred to two or more suspect classifications.

ongoing changes in society's social and economic dynamics that would eventually lead to the impossibility of granting survivor's pensions exclusively to female widows. However, the Court repeatedly refused to expand this right by itself, arguing that a specific law on the topic was needed. Only in October 2020 did it declare regulations establishing different criteria for widowers and widows of male and female public servants to access pension benefits unconstitutional.[34] It can be expected that the prevalence of this suspect classification in non-violation findings will be reduced significantly in the future.

Another category that has been prevalent in the findings of non-violation is race. Once again, this is due to the upholding of positive measures. This is equally the case with regard to the classifications "economic status" and "disability." In fact, the STF has only decided cases related to disability or race that concern positive measures.[35] Similarly, three of the five findings of non-violation regarding economic

[34] cf *RE 659.424* (October 13, 2020, Justice rapporteur: Celso de Mello). As this judgment was published in November 2020, it did not integrate the quantitative analysis.

[35] All the cases with the suspect classifications race and disability decided by the STF concerned an allegation that the state failed to fulfil its duty to implement a positive measure, a claim that the measure was underinclusive, or an impugnation of the consonance of positive measures with the principle of equality.

status were decisions recognizing the constitutionality of positive measures applied to the benefit of vulnerable groups. Additionally, one of the remaining two cases of non-violation regarding economic status is a decision in which the Court upholds the constitutionality of a measure prohibiting privileges in accessing public health services based on economic status.[36]

More generally, without challenges to positive measures, the success rate of cases involving suspect classifications increases to 57.8%. If it disregards the findings of non-violation concerning a widower's right to survivor's pension following the death of a female public servant, the success rate of cases involving suspect classification increases even further to 73.8%.

The analysis also revealed that the STF has been active in finding violations in indirect discrimination cases. The Court found a violation in 7 of 9 cases (success rate of 77.8%).[37] Four of these concerned the criterion of economic status, two gender, and one each religion and sexual orientation.

Lastly, while the STF does not make an explicit distinction between different levels of scrutiny,[38] the analysis revealed differences in the application of the equality test to cases involving a suspect classification. For example, the number of cases involving a discrimination with a suspect classification that failed the strict proportionality test and the test of legitimate aim is more than double the cases not involving a suspect classification (44.9% against 18.5%, and 22.4% to 6.2%, respectively).

3.3 Positive measures

The STF has decided 40 cases concerning positive measures. In 29 cases, it took a decision that either reaffirmed or expanded the impugned measure. In addition, in five cases, it challenged an omission of the State to adopt a positive measure in favor of a vulnerable group and established an obligation to act in the protection and realization of equality. One example is *ADO 26 (2019)*, where the Court found that the omission of the state to criminalize homophobia and transphobia constituted an obstacle to fulfilling the obligation to punish discrimination and to protect this group as a victim of persecution, intolerance, hostilities, and aggression. The Court decided that crimes of homophobia and transphobia should be covered

[36] See *RE 581.488/RS* (December 3, 2015, Justice rapporteur: Dias Toffoli).

[37] The cases in which the Court did not find indirect discrimination were *ADI 4.439* (2017) and *ADPF 541* (2018). The former concerned teaching of religion in public schools, and the latter concerned the claim that the cancellation of electoral cards due to failure to conduct a biometric registration disproportionately affected poor people and people residing in remote locations. In both cases, the STF found that the measures were in consonance with constitutionally protected interests and with the criterion of legitimate aim.

[38] An exception is *ADPF 291* (n 24).

by the law that criminalizes racism until Congress approved a specific law on the matter.[39]

In only three cases did the Court strike down a positive measure or found that the content of the measure had to be reduced for it to be proportional.[40] In one case, it rejected a claim according to which the positive measure was underinclusive.[41] The remaining two cases involved multiple grounds, some of which were reaffirmed by the Court, and others struck down.[42] This means that in 87.5%[43] of the cases concerning positive measures, the measure was reaffirmed or expanded.

The STF expanded a positive measure in eight cases. One example is *ADI 5.617 (2018)*, concerning the constitutionality of a provision that reserved 5 to 15% of the public funds granted to political parties for the political campaign of women candidates. The STF noted that, even if the maximum percentage established by the regulation were applied, this would still mean that 85% of the funding would be allocated to the campaign of male candidates. Such a result lacked reasonable and rational justification. The STF thus concluded that the minimum percentage for allocation of public funds to women's political campaigns should match the quota established by law for minimum female representation in politics (30%). If more than 30% of the candidates were women, the financial resources should be allocated to them in the same proportion. Finally, the Court declared the unconstitutionality of the deadline established for the expiration of the positive measure—the measure applied only to the following three elections according to the text of the legal provision. The tribunal found that the measure should stay in force for as long as the gender quota for candidacies was justified.

4. Explaining the identified patterns

The analysis reveals the influence of the Inter-American System of Human Rights in the STF's interpretation of equality, manifested through references to Inter-American instruments, reports of the Inter-American Commission on Human Rights, and decisions and advisory opinions of the Inter-American Court of Human Rights. While references to the work of the Inter-American Court are less frequent than references to United Nations documents, it appears that the former has been particularly relevant in the STF's landmark decisions on LGBTI rights.

[39] *ADO 26* (n 7).

[40] *MS 26.310-5/DF* (September 20, 2007, Justice rapporteur: Marco Aurélio); *MC 6.039 ADI* (March 13, 2019, Justice rapporteur: Edson Fachin); *ADI 5.139/AL* (October 11, 2019, Justice rapporteur: Cármen Lúcia).

[41] *AgR 6.984 MI* (September 28, 2018, Justice rapporteur: Roberto Barroso).

[42] *ADI 4.923/DF* (November 8, 2017, Justice rapporteur: Luiz Fux); and *ADI 4.868/DF* (March 27, 2020, Justice rapporteur: Gilmar Mendes). In the latter decision, by striking down the grounds of residence as incompatible with the right to equality, the STF expanded the scope of the positive measure.

[43] (34 cases + 2 × 0.5 claims)/40 cases.

However, the influence of the IACtHR on the STF's jurisprudence is insufficient to explain the patterns identified in Section 3 earlier.

A relevant factor for understanding the Court's low deference and its active position in relation to positive measures can be found in the concept of transformative constitutionalism.[44] A transformative role of Brazilian constitutional law appears to derive from the drafting of the 1988 Constitution and the context in which it was enacted. As Santiago Lima explains, the Constitution emerged from the determination to overcome the regime of military dictatorship that preceded it and from the commitment of the Constituents to meet such expectation.[45] Similarly, Justice Cármen Lúcia claims that the understanding that law is an instrument for promoting social justice and social democracy was embodied in the CR/88.[46] In her understanding, Article 3 of the CF/88, which lists the fundamental principles of the Republic (including the promotion of equality and the eradication of poverty), brings forth the conceptualization of law as an instrument for the concretization of democracy.[47] Accordingly, Article 3 of the CF/88 sets an obligation for the state to adopt "an active conduct" towards implementing the fundamental principles listed in that provision.[48]

The transformative role of the CF/88 was also the object of consideration by Justice Marco Aurélio in the context of the right to equality and affirmative action. In *ADPF 186 (2012)*, on the institution of a racial quota system in the public university UnB, Justice Aurélio affirmed that throughout Brazilian constitutional history, equality had been safeguarded in a formal rather than transformative manner. A fundamental change took place with the promulgation of the CF/88. The latter protected equality no longer in a merely negative or static manner. Instead, it safeguarded effective and dynamic equality by explicitly establishing in Article 3 an obligation for the state to act for social transformation.[49] Noting this background, the Justice considered that, over the years, state neutrality had proven to be "a huge failure" for the promotion of equality of rights in Brazil. Positive action was therefore necessary.[50]

[44] The concept goes back to Karl E Klare, "Legal Culture and Transformative Constitutionalism" (1998) 14 South African Journal on Human Rights 146. For the Latin American context, see Armin von Bogdandy and René Uruena, "Constitucionalismo transformador internacional na América Latina" (2021) 11 Brazilian J of Public Policy 28.

[45] Lima (n 3) 157.

[46] Antunes Rocha (n 5) 288. The focus on fundamental rights and social justice is clear from the Preamble of the CF/88: "We, representatives of the Brazilian people, gathered in a National Constituent Assembly to establish a Democratic State, destined to ensure the exercise of social and individual rights, freedom, security, well-being, development, equality and justice as the supreme values of a fraternal, pluralistic and unprejudiced society, founded on social harmony and committed, in the internal and international order, to the peaceful solution of controversies, enact, under the protection of God, the following CONSTITUTION OF THE FEDERATIVE REPUBLIC OF BRAZIL." See Constitution of the Federative Republic of Brazil of 1988 (translation by the author).

[47] Antunes Rocha (n 5) 289; *ADC 41/DF* (n 15) 171–73.

[48] *ADC 41/DF* (n 15) 171–73.

[49] *ADPF 186/DF* (n 15) 210–13.

[50] ibid 215.

Justice Fachin upheld a similar understanding in an interview conducted for this research. The Justice explained that the CF/88 is committed to "overcoming the past, to the end of the dictatorship, and to the restoration of democracy with public spaces open to popular participation, via representation or direct action."[51] On the other hand, it rests on "the commitment to the future, with the transformation of a social, economic and cultural scenario marked by injustice, inequality and discrimination."[52] This "dual-memory" of the CF/88, which looks at the past and aims at the future for the promotion of a transformation of patterns of injustices and inequalities, has "the nature of a binding norm," according to the Justice.[53]

These reflections from the Justices indicate that the transformative role of the CF/88 derives from its origins and is not a recent phenomenon derived from any particular factor of political instability in Brazil in the 21st century. While the tendency of reading a transformative role into the 1988 Constitution may have been reinforced by recent political crises in the state, including the massive *Mensalão* and *Lavo Jato* corruption scandals, the 2016 presidential impeachment, and the rise of the extreme right in the country, its roots are found in the history of Brazilian constitutionalism and in the context of the drafting and promulgation of the 1988 Constitution.

An additional explaining factor for the Court's low level of deference and its adoption of a conceptualization of equality as positive equality may be found in its independence and strong position in the Brazilian legal and political system. The STF is often portrayed as the supreme guardian of democracy and fundamental rights in the country. Furthermore, the 2021 report from FGV/SP on the Confidence in Brazilian Justice Index (*ICJBrasil*) indicates that the level of confidence in the judiciary and in the STF specifically (40% and 42% respectively) is higher than the level of confidence in the President of the Republic (29%), the National Congress (12%), political parties (6%), as well as social media (19%) and TV channels (34%).[54] It is, however, considerably lower than public confidence in the Armed Forces (63%), the Catholic Church (53%), and large companies (49%).[55]

A similar finding was identified by *Datafolha*, showing that the level of confidence in the political parties, the National Congress, and the Presidency of the Republic declined significantly from 2012 to 2018, facing a brief increase in 2019 and then declining again from 2019 to 2021.[56] In contrast, the level of confidence

[51] Interview with Justice Edson Fachin, question 8, 5 (translation by the author).
[52] ibid.
[53] ibid.
[54] <IBT<FGV Direito SP, *Relatório ICJBrasil* (2021) 11 and 16.
[55] ibid. Similar findings are discussed by Leonardo Avritzer in Leonardo Avritzer, "A Cara da Democracia no Brasil e na Argentina" *Instituto da Deocracia e da Democratização da Comunicação* <https://www.institutodademocracia.org/single-post/2019/04/23/a-cara-da-democracia-no-brasil-e-na-argentina> accessed January 20, 2025.
[56] Datafolha, *Grau de confiança nas instituições* (2019) <http://media.folha.uol.com.br/datafolha/2019/07/10/9b9d682bfe0f1c6f228717d59ce49fdfci.pdf> accessed August 30, 2023;

in the judiciary, including the STF specifically, has remained relatively stable, with a very slight decline from 2012 to 2021 in the case of the STF.[57] This small decrease in confidence in the STF in recent years should be read in context. In the last few years, explicit threats have been made both to the institution[58] and to the physical integrity of the Justices, and the Court has been in the social and political spotlight.[59] A concrete attack against the Court took place on January 8, 2023, when the STF, the presidential palace, and the National Congress were invaded and vandalized following Jair Bolsonaro's defeat in the 2022 presidential elections.[60] Future research may evaluate possible impact (if any) of these attacks and threats on the work of the Court in topics that raise political controversies, such as the dynamic interpretation of the right to equality.

5. Conclusion

The analysis of the equality jurisprudence of the STF leads to three main conclusions. First, the Court has been active in finding direct and indirect discrimination in cases with suspect classification. While an uncontextualized analysis of the success rate of the equality claims could indicate a medium success rate independent of whether the case involves a suspect classification or not, this chapter reveals that such a conclusion is misleading. Half of the cases with a suspect classification in which the STF did not find a violation refer to cases in which the constitutionality of positive measures was questioned. In addition, 11 of the 22 cases in which the Court did not find a violation of equality in cases concerning sex/gender refer to the Court's now-changed jurisprudence on the right of female public servants to offer a survivor's pension to their spouses in case of death.

"Datafolha: Cai confiança da população nas instituições e nos três Poderes" *Folha de SPaulo* (September 24, 2021) <https://www1.folha.uol.com.br/poder/2021/09/datafolha-cai-confianca-da-populacao-nas-instituicoes-e-nos-tres-poderes.shtml> accessed August 30, 2023.

[57] ibid.

[58] The January 8, 2023 invasion and attacks on the premises of the STF, the National Congress, and the presidential palace like to be the most significant episode.

[59] See eg in 2021, the Congressman Daniel Silveira published a video on YouTube making threats against Justices Fachin, Barroso, Mendes, Aurélio, Toffoli, and Moraes. Justice Moraes ordered the arrest *in flagrante delicto* of the Congressman. Other examples include personal attacks and threats made to Justice Cármen Lúcia and Justice Alexandre de Moraes, respectively, prior to and in the aftermath of the 2022 presidential elections.

[60] Priscila Camazano, "Entenda os ataques golpistas de 8 de janeiro e seus desdobramentos" (February 7, 2023) *Folha de São Paulo* <https://www1.folha.uol.com.br/poder/2023/02/entenda-os-ataques-golpistas-de-8-de-janeiro-e-seus-desdobramentos.shtml> accessed January 20, 2025; Chris Cameron, "The Attack on Brazil's Seat of Government Resembles the Storming of the U.S. Capitol on Jan. 6, 2021" (New York, January 8, 2023) *The New York Times* <https://www.nytimes.com/2023/01/08/world/americas/brazil-jan-6-riots.html> accessed January 20, 2025.

Secondly, the success rate of cases not involving a suspect classification is high in the STF jurisprudence compared to the other jurisdictions analyzed in this book. Furthermore, the vast majority of decisions in which the Court found a violation concerned cases not involving a suspect classification. The low deference granted to the legislator in equality cases, regardless of whether the dispute involves suspect classifications, could, at first sight, point to the application of the equality as reasonableness approach in the STF. However, our study shows that such a conclusion would be incomplete.

The STF has been particularly active in upholding the constitutionality of positive measures and even extending these. The Court has not only discussed the admissibility of positive measures but has also applied equality in its positive dimension, creating a positive obligation for the state to protect and promote the right to equality of vulnerable groups. The centrality of the positive dimension of equality in the STF's doctrine suggests that the positive equality model is the best fit. The Court applies this model combined with features of the equality as reasonableness approach, which is expressed by the high number of successful cases not involving a suspect classification. The resulting combination leads to an approach that grants little deference to the legislature and the executive in equality cases.

13
India

Shubhangi Roy

1. Introduction

The Indian Constitution includes within it both the equal protection clause as well as non-discrimination clauses. Article 14 of the Constitution is the general equal protection clause which guarantees individuals equality before law and equal protection of law.[1] Articles 15 and 16 refer to the protection against discrimination on specific criteria under the Constitution.[2] While class legislations are constitutionally prohibited, the Supreme Court has derived a constitutional test that does permit reasonable classification.[3]

The Constitution also explicitly protects the right of the government to make special provisions with respect to education for "advancement of any socially and educationally backward classes of citizens or for the Scheduled Castes and Scheduled Tribes."[4] In addition, special reservations with respect to public employment in favor of "any backward classes of people which, in the opinion of the government, are underrepresented in the services" is also permitted by the Constitution.[5]

Over the past seven decades, the Indian Supreme Court has had to interpret these constitutional provisions in order to define the ambit of the equal protection clause as well as the contours of affirmative action within the Constitution. What does equal protection of the law entail? Does it forbid classification or only unreasonable classification? How is reasonable classification defined? Is affirmative action an exception to or an extension of the equality doctrine? How should "backward classes" be defined? And, most importantly, what level of judicial scrutiny and involvement is permissible in shaping answers to these questions?

The courts have, over time and through multiple judgments, sought to answer each of these questions. There is considerable literature discussing the landmark

[1] Art 14 Constitution of India.
[2] Arts 15 and 16 Constitution of India.
[3] Gautam Bhatia, *The Transformative Constitution: A Radical Biography in Nine Acts* (HarperCollins India 2019).
[4] Art 15 Constitution of India.
[5] Art 16(4) Constitution of India.

Shubhangi Roy, *India* In: *Equality's Guardians*. Edited by: Niels Petersen, Oxford University Press.
 DOI: 10.1093/9780198961109.003.0013

cases that shaped the equality doctrine in India.[6] Section 2 of this chapter briefly discusses the test as laid out by the court. There is, however, no systematic review of how the court applies this test to the cases that come before it. The chapter aims to address this gap in research by analyzing all judgments of the Indian Supreme Court, with a bench strength of five and more, which dealt with Articles 14, 15, and 16. Subsection 3.1 provides the methodology of case selection as well as the data collection process. In Section 3.2, the chapter describes and analyses the empirical data that was obtained through this exercise. In Section 4 the chapter maps the empirical findings on the test laid out by the court.

This chapter contributes to the larger discourse of the book in two ways. First, it maps the equality doctrine in the Indian jurisdiction in comparison to other jurisdictions. It helps us to understand how the court and the society shaped each other's perception about constitutionally protected equality. Second, it empirically tests whether the Supreme Court applies the tests, as laid out by itself, to the cases that come before it. Undertaking this exercise reveals how the court, while applying the same judicial test to all cases, has still managed to frame and analyze the issues surrounding prohibited classification, especially caste-related issues, differently and in light of the social context of India. However, as the chapter concludes, there is an urgent need to expand the judicial test to include these considerations explicitly within the judicial analysis. The findings also provide some data to try to understand the complex role of judiciary, often considered as an activist court, within the Indian polity.

2. Judicial tests that apply to the equal protection clause of the Indian Constitution

This section summarizes how the Indian Supreme Court interprets the equal protection clause (2.1), the anti-discrimination clause (2.2), and the scope of affirmative action within the Indian Constitution (2.3).

2.1 Reasonableness standard of review

The Indian courts are relatively deferential to the legislative and executive branches of the government. The Court proceeds with a presumption of constitutionality in

[6] See Tarunabh Khaitan, "Equality: Legislative Review Under Article 14" in Sujit Choudhry, Madhav Khosla, and Pratap Bhanu Mehta (eds), *The Oxford Handbook of Indian Constitutional Law* (OUP 2016) 699; Vinay Sitapathi, "Reservations" in ibid 720; Munmun Roy, "Backward Classes, The Social Order and The Constitutional Arrangement: The Indian Perspective" (2013) 74 The Indian Journal of Political Science 533.

any judicial review, including review on the basis of Articles 14, 15, or 16.[7] The burden to disprove this presumption is on the one challenging the regulation.[8] This also extends to the classifications made by the executive or the legislature.[9] To test whether there is a violation of the equal protection clause, the court applies two tests: the classification test and the arbitrariness test.[10] These two tests together constitute the reasonableness standard of review.

The classification test requires the petitioner first to prove that there is unequal treatment between similarly circumstanced individuals[11] or equal treatment of unequally placed individuals.[12] Then the court investigates the object of legislation and tries to see if there is a reasonable nexus between a legitimate state interest and the unequal treatment. The analysis of legitimate state interest is considered deferential because there is no need for the stated "interest" to cross an "importance" threshold.[13] Interests such as *administrative convenience*[14] and *protection of agricultural livestock*[15] were considered as legitimate state interests for unequal treatment. There is no need to prove that the state interest was an important one or that this classification was the only/most effective route to achieve the stated interest.

The arbitrariness test is the less developed of the two tests. One of the few cases where the arbitrariness doctrine was developed by the majority bench was the *E.P. Royappa* case.[16] For an enactment to be considered arbitrary, there is no need to prove unequal treatment. What exactly constitutes as arbitrary is less clear. Arbitrariness is most frequently used with respect to executive decisions.[17] However, the test is not well defined.[18] In the case of *Shayaro Bano* decided in 2017 by a constitutional bench, the court described arbitrariness as follows:

[7] *Ram Krishna Dalmia v Justice S.R. Tendolkar and Ors* AIR 1958 SC 538 (The Court summarized the judicial test for equality in this judgment).

[8] See eg *Chiranjit Lal Chaudhary v Union of India and others* 1951 AIR 41; *Kathi Raning Rawat v State of Saurashtra*; *Syed Qasim Razvi v The State of Hyderabad and Ors*; *V.M. Syed Mohammad and Company v The State of Andhra*; *Budhan Choudhry and Ors v The State of Bihar*; *Ram Krishna Dalmia v Justice S.R. Tendolkar and Ors*; *Sri Venkata Seetaramanjaneya Rice and Oil Mills and Ors v State of Andhra Pradesh and Ors*

[9] *Madhubhai Amathalal Gandhi v The Union of India (UOI).*

[10] Tarunabh Khaitan, "Beyond Reasonableness—A Rigorous Standard of Review for Article 15 Infringement" (2008) 50(2) Journal of the Indian Law Institute 177, 188.

[11] *Probhudas Morarjee Rajkotia and Ors v Union of India (UOI) and Ors*; *St. Stephen's College and Ors v The University of Delhi and Ors.*

[12] *Bennett Coleman & Co. and Ors v Union of India (UOI) and Ors* (The legislation treated national dailies and local newspapers equally without considering their different readership etc).

[13] Khaitan (n 10).

[14] *Supt. & Remembrancer of Legal Affairs v State of West Bengal* AIR 1975 SC 1030.

[15] *Mohd. Hanif Quareshi and Ors v The State of Bihar.*

[16] *E P Royappa v State of Tamil Nadu* AIR 1974 SC 555, para 85 (per Bhagwati J) (emphasis added).

[17] See eg *Jyoti Pershad v The Administrator for The Union Territory of Delhi*; *Raghubar Dayal Jai Prakash v The Union of India (UOI) and Ors*; *D.R. Nim v Union of India*; *Maneklal Chhotalal and Ors v M.G. Makwana and Ors*; *State of Maharashtra and Ors v Lok Shikshan Sansatha and Ors.*

[18] Khaitan (n 10); T R Andhyarujina, *Judicial Activism and Constitutional Democracy in India* (Tripathi 1992) 30–31; H M Seervai, *Constitutional Law of India* (4th edn, Tripathi 1991) 436–42.

> Manifest arbitrariness, therefore, must be something done by the legislature capriciously, irrationally and/or without adequate determining principle. Also, when something is done which is excessive and disproportionate, such legislation would be manifestly arbitrary.[19]

To an extent, this takes the discussion back to the interest analysis contained within the classification test.[20] However, what constitutes as excessive or disproportionate is unclear. It is also unclear how much discretion the judiciary can and should employ in deciding whether a legislation is manifestly arbitrary considering the strong presumption of constitutionality.[21] In most cases, therefore, any claim arguing violation of the equality provision discusses both the classification and stated interest of legislation. To this extent, in practice, the two tests are not as clearly differentiated, and decisions contain a general enquiry into the purpose of legislation and factors surrounding the case in question.[22]

2.2 Antidiscrimination clause in the Indian Constitution and its judicial interpretation

Article 15 is the general antidiscrimination clause in the Constitution which prohibits discrimination on grounds only of religion, race, caste, sex, place of birth, or any of them. Article 16 prohibits non-discrimination in public employment on prohibited grounds mentioned therein. Articles 15(4) and 16(4) protect measures of positive discrimination taken by the government for the advancement of a historically underprivileged community from being considered as a violation of the equality or antidiscrimination doctrine. The reasonableness standard as well as the presumption of constitutionality also apply to Articles 15 and 16.[23]

Some recent cases of the Supreme Court, though not constitutional bench cases, have tried to apply a stricter review, a proportionality test, with respect to Article 15.[24] A two-judge bench in *Anuj Kumar* applied the strict scrutiny analysis to

[19] *Shayara Bano v Union Of India* (2017) 9 SCC 1.

[20] Shankar Narayanan, "Rethinking Non-Arbitrariness" (2017) 4 NLUD Law Journal 133.

[21] See Eklavya Dwivedi, "The Doctrine Of 'Manifest Arbitrariness'—A Critique" (India Law Journal Blog) <https://www.indialawjournal.org/the-doctrine-of-manifest-arbitrariness.php> accessed January 20, 2025.

[22] Aparna Chandra, "Limitation Analysis by the Indian Supreme Court" in Mordechai Kremnitzer, Talya Steiner and Andrej Lang (eds), *Proportionality in Action: Comparative and Empirical Perspectives on the Judicial Practice* (CUP 2020) 458.

[23] Art 15(4) reads: "(4) Nothing in this article or in clause (2) of Article 29 shall prevent the State from making any special provision for the advancement of any socially and educationally backward classes of citizens or for the Scheduled Castes and the Scheduled Tribes." Art 16(4) reads: "(4) Nothing in this article shall prevent the State from making any provision for the reservation of appointments or posts in favor of any backward class of citizens which, in the opinion of the State, is not adequately represented in the services under the State."

[24] See *Om Kumar v Union of India* (2001) 2 SCC 386; *Anuj Garg and Others v Hotel Association of India and Others* AIR 2008 SC 663, (2008) 3 SCC 1.

strike down an old legislation which prevented employment of any women on any premise where intoxicating substances and liquor was consumed by public.[25] The court, in these cases and others,[26] did so by reasoning that the reasonability review has always contained an element of proportionality. As Khaitan noted, this claim is respectfully incorrect.[27] In fact, a 2003 judgment by the constitutional bench of the Indian Supreme Court explicitly dealt with the issue and concluded as follows:

> The strict scrutiny test or the intermediate scrutiny test applicable in the United States of America as argued by Shri Salve cannot be applied in this case. Such a test is not applied in Indian Courts.[28]

Perhaps the confusion can be better understood by reading in the same judgment further. The court goes on to say that "in any event, such a test may be applied in a case where legislation ex facie is found to be unreasonable."[29] However, it concludes the discussion by reiterating that courts must extend a strong presumption of constitutionality to all legislations. Therefore, the law of the land as it exists today rejects the proportionality approach or, if applied, its application is more a semantic choice than a real change in law.

2.3 Affirmative action in the Indian Constitution

Within the Indian Constitutional scheme, governments are allowed to make provisions for the advancement of socially and educationally backward groups of citizens (SEBCs).[30] These groups may vary across states with the same group being disadvantaged in one area but not another. The power to classify groups as disadvantaged rests with the central and state governments. With the presumption of constitutionality in place, the court has spent considerable time and effort in defining the nature of groups and the type of affirmative action permissible under the Constitution. At the onset, the Supreme Court has clarified that affirmative action is an extension of, rather than an exception to, the equal protection clause.[31]

The Court, however, tries to balance affirmative action with what it considers as the general interests of society. In the 1950s, the Supreme Court laid down one of the first guidelines on affirmative action when it restricted the number of seats

[25] *Anuj Garg and Others v Hotel Association of India and Others* AIR 2008 SC 663, (2008) 3 SCC 1.
[26] *Subhash Chandra v Delhi -Subordinate Services Selection Board* (2009) 11 SCALE 278; *Om Kumar v Union of India*, (2001) 2 SCC 386.
[27] Khaitan (n 10).
[28] *Saurabh Chaudri and Ors v Union of India (UOI) and Ors* (2003) 11 SCC 146. (However, they too add to the confusion as the court continues to say that the strict scrutiny could be applied in very limited situations where there is manifest discrimination).
[29] ibid.
[30] Arts 15(4), 16(4), and 29(2) Constitution of India (1950).
[31] Bhatia (n 3).

reserved for backward classes to 50%.[32] It also provided considerations for the governments to keep in mind while determining which groups qualify for affirmative action. Apart from the Scheduled Castes and Tribes,[33] the court has created a "caste-plus" test that the executive has to consider when considering a group for inclusion into SEBCs.[34] For example, the judiciary excluded the "creamy layer," the affluent members of the SEBCs, from benefiting from affirmative action.[35] Furthermore, a constitutional bench judgment of the Supreme Court led to the establishment of the National and State level Backward Class Commissions with the aim of providing greater transparency to the process through which different groups were made eligible for affirmative action.[36] Through these interpretations of Article 15, the court has shaped the affirmative action envisaged under the Constitution.

3. Empirical analysis of the equality case law

3.1 Data collection and coding

The empirical analysis of the Indian jurisdiction is based on an examination of all Supreme Court cases with a bench strength of five or more (constitutional benches) where matters concerning Articles 14 and 15 were dealt with by the court substantially. Constitution bench is the name given to the bench comprising five or more judges constituted to decide any case "involving a substantial question of law as to the interpretation" under Article 145 or a matter referred to the court by the President of India under Article 143 of the Constitution.[37] The Chief Justice of India has the discretion to decide which cases will be heard by the constitutional bench and the strength and composition of these benches.[38] Precedents of the constitutional bench cannot be overturned except by future benches of the same strength or greater. High courts as well as smaller Supreme Court benches regularly deal with and answer constitutional questions, and the "constitutional bench" does not have exclusive jurisdiction to deal with such cases. However, in case of conflicting judicial precedents, the judgment of the constitutional bench will be considered conclusive and binding on all other judicial forums.

The cases were selected for the dataset by accessing all Supreme Court judgments available within the *Manupatra* (manupatra.in) database for bench

[32] *M.R. Balaji v State of Mysore* 1963 AIR 649.
[33] Sitapathi (n 6).
[34] *Indira Sawhney etc. v Union of India and others* AIR 1993 SC 477; *Ashok Thakur v Union of India* 2008 6 SCC 1.
[35] *Indira Sawhney etc. v Union of India and others* AIR 1993 SC 477.
[36] The National Commission for Backward Classes Act (1993).
[37] Art 145(3) Constitution of India (1949).
[38] ibid.

strengths of five or higher where the phrase "Article 14" and/or "Article 15" were mentioned. *Manupatra*, while a private database, is well recognized in legal practice in India and its citations have been previously accepted by courts, including the Supreme Court, as part of legal proceedings before them. The search filters available which allowed us to search on bench strength and familiarity with the database for the primary researcher made it an appropriate choice. The time period considered is from 1950 to 2020. Articles 14 and 15 are the general equality and antidiscrimination clauses. Therefore, the search was restricted to these two clauses. The other two articles that can be relevant for the discussion are Article 16 (discrimination in public employment) and Article 29 (discrimination in public education). However, most cases in which there is an infringement of these clauses also discuss the general discrimination clause and will be covered in the discussion through Article 15.

The preliminary search results in 354 cases with the phrase "Article 14" and 75 cases with the phrase "Article 15" was mentioned in cases heard by a bench comprising five or more judges. Bigger benches of five or more judges are referred to as "constitutional benches" which are constituted when there is a substantial question of law with respect to the interpretation of the constitution that needs to be answered.[39] These cases were manually cleaned to select the ones where the judgment substantially addresses any of the two provisions. Finally, 238 judgments were hand-coded and recorded according to the template provided in the introductory chapter.[40] The analysis in the subsequent sections is derived from these judgments.

3.2 Data findings

Prior to moving into substantive discussions on the findings, it is important to explain the range of judgments across the various decades. Even if all Supreme Court judgments delivered by a bench of five or more judges were recorded for all years, the decades prior to 2000 seem overrepresented when we consider the absolute number of judgments for different time periods. The court delivered 218 of the total of 238 judgments prior to the year 2000. This decline in the number of judgments post 2000 is in consonance with the findings of Robinson, Agarwal, and others who found that the number of cases heard and disposed by five-judge bench or higher fell from 15.5% in the 1950s to 0.12% in the 2000s.[41] In addition, in their five-year analysis, from 2010 to 2015, of Indian Supreme Court judgments,

[39] Art 145 Constitution of India (1950).

[40] See Chapter 1, section 4.2.

[41] Nick Robinson and others, "Interpreting the Constitution: Supreme Court Constitution Benches since Independence" (2011) 46(9) Economic & Political Weekly 27.

Table 13.1 Success rate of different types of cases

Cases with equality claims	Total Number of Cases	Violations
Cases w/o prohibited criterion of classification	188	32 (17.02%)
Cases with prohibited criterion for classification	50	22 (44%)
Cases involving affirmative action measures	32	14 (43.75%)
Total cases	238	54 (22.6%)

Chandra, Hubbard, and Kilantry found that only around 5.3% of all cases disposed of by the court concern constitutional matters.[42] Given that the present research is restricted to constitutional benches (five or more judges) and regard a constitutional subject matter, the reduced number of judgments over the decades is consistent with the data found in other empirical studies on the Indian Supreme Court. The courts were much more likely to constitute constitutional benches prior to 2000, and cases concerning constitutional matters, in general, do not constitute a large part of the judicial load.

Having addressed the range of the data points, we can now consider what this data can potentially reveal about the equality doctrine in India. When considered as a whole, in 22.6% of cases, that is, 54 cases out of 238, the court held there had been a violation of the equality principle (see Table 13.1). This is reasonably deferential to the legislation and can be considered in consonance with the principle laid down by the court. However, slicing the data further reveals certain discrepancies in the types of cases where the court is likely to be less/more deferential. In matters involving a prohibited criterion for classification, the court held a violation of the equality doctrine in 44% cases, while in matters not involving them the percentage of cases in which violation was observed is 17%. Therefore, empirically speaking, the court is more likely to rule in favor of the government when the classification is not on criteria specifically prohibited under the Constitution. This is the case even when the judicial test applied in India does not involve different judicial tests for the equality and antidiscrimination clauses.

Interestingly, the rate remains similar when we consider the cases where an affirmative action measure was challenged in the court. In 43.75% of the cases where an affirmative action was challenged, the court held these measures to be in violation of the equality and antidiscrimination principle enshrined in the constitution.

[42] Aparna Chandra, William H J Hubbard, and Sital Kalantry, "The Supreme Court of India: A People's Court?" (2017) 1(2) Indian LR 145.

Table 13.2 Success rate for different prohibited criteria

Prohibited classification	Total Number of Cases	Violation	Affirmative Action cases	Violation
Caste	22	10 (45.5%)	20	9 (45%)
Religion	8	4 (50%)	5	3 (60%)
Sex	3	2 (66%)	1	0 (0%)
Residence	7	1 (14%)	3	0 (0%)
Nationality	2	1 (50%)	0	0 (0%)
Descent	2	2 (100%)	2	2 (100%)
Place of birth	4	1 (25%)	2	0 (0%)
Age	3	2 (66%)	1	0 (0%)
Sexual orientation	1	1 (100%)	0	0 (0%)

Of 32 cases dealing with affirmative action, the court held the measures to be in violation 14 times. Twenty-two cases involved the question of caste. Out of these, 20 cases involved affirmative action on the basis of caste. The Court held these affirmative action measures to be in violation of the equality provision in 45% of cases. Eight cases involved classification on the basis of religion, and five of these were in reference to affirmative action on the basis of religion. The Court held these measures to be in violation in 60% of the cases. Cases under the different prohibited criteria are shown in Table 13.2. Two different cases involved two prohibited criteria and hence were counted twice in this table.

This raises an interesting question on how much deference the courts give to the legislature and the executive. On paper, the presumption of constitutionality is uniformly applied to all types of legislative and executive decisions.[43] In the view of the Indian Supreme Court, the legislature "understands and correctly appreciates the needs of its people."[44] The Court has also on multiple occasions specified that this presumption of constitutionality also extends to any classifications made by a legislative or executive decision, including classification for purposes of affirmative action.[45] In fact, there has been increasing demand by constitutional scholars as well as interest by smaller benches of Supreme Court and High Court

[43] See eg *Chiranjit Lal Singh v Union of India and others; State of Bombay and others v F.N. Balsara; Budhan Choudhry and Ors v The State of Bihar; Ram Krishna Dalmia v Justice S.R. Tendolkar and Ors; Sri Venkata Seetaramanjaneya Rice and Oil Mills and Ors v State of Andhra Pradesh and Ors; R.K. Garg v Union of India (UOI) and Ors.*

[44] *State of Bombay and Others v F.N. Balsara* AIR 1951 SC 318.

[45] *Madhubhai Amathalal Gandhi v The Union of India (UOI)* AIR 1961 SC 21.

to introduce a stricter scrutiny in cases where historically disadvantaged groups are involved since currently the two types of cases are—formally—treated equally.[46] The present data, however, indicates that the Court is clearly not as uniformly deferential to the government in practice. The Court is almost three times as likely to find a violation of the equality doctrine in matters where the government had proposed caste-based affirmative action measure than in general equality cases. In Section 4, the chapter discusses likely explanations for why the court is considerably less deferential to the executive and legislative when it comes to matters of affirmative action.

4. Explanation of the findings

The equality doctrine developed by the Indian Supreme Court is, in principle, a deferential one. It does not, on paper, require much analysis of the nature of interest that the legislation or classification serves as long as the government can show that there is a legitimate state interest. State interests such as *maintaining the way of life of military professionals* when permitting alcohol sale to military officers in a state where otherwise alcohol is banned,[47] and *protection of agricultural livestock*[48] to allow a ban on the slaughter of cows of certain age have been considered as legitimate state interest. Additionally, the judicial test does not involve any further investigation on whether the discrimination envisaged is the most effective route to achieve the state interest. To this extent, the judicial test provided in landmark cases is applied uniformly to general matters alleging a violation of the equality doctrine.

When, however, we look at all equality judgments of the constitutional bench, there seems to be an implicit analysis of interest, especially when the classification is based on prohibited criteria. This can be most easily witnessed when affirmative action policies are challenged. The Court considers matters of affirmative action as a trade-off between the interests of the society at large and the groups benefitting from these policies. In the *Balaji* case, one of the first landmark judgment on the subject, the Court considered the issue as an *adjustment of competing claims* between the interests of the minority groups and the community at large.[49] The facts of the case involved a challenge against the national reservation policies through which 68% of the seats in government universities would have been reserved for different classes of citizens. Similarly, in a more recent case, the court observed that *the very concept of reservation implies mediocrity* and rejects the reservations

[46] Khaitan (n 10).
[47] *State of Bombay and Others v F.N. Balsara* AIR 1951 SC 318.
[48] *Mohd. Hanif Quareshi and Ors v The State of Bihar* 1961 AIR 448.
[49] *M.R. Balaji v State of Mysore* 1963 AIR 649.

in specialty and super-specialty medical courses.[50] When discussing the case, the court goes into the analysis of how to achieve the advancement of backward classes in medical professions and state that reservations at levels of primary education, admission to medical colleges and the like could be a more effective mechanism. The case and this formulation of the policy trade-off that the court highlights clarifies three things. First, the court undertook an analysis of the legitimacy of the state interest. Second, it considered whether the proposed policy was the most effective route to attain the stated state interest. Thirdly, in the opinion of the court, there is a trade-off between the welfare of the whole of society and that of specific communities. Similarly, the doctrine of the court on matters of positive discrimination in public employment, as provided by the 11-bench judgment in *Indra Sawhney v Union of India*, is that all forms of measures including but not limited to reservation of seats are constitutional *as long as it is consistent with the maintenance of efficiency of administration.*[51] The court, therefore, again aims to balance interests and take a more proportional approach. It also, again, presumes that there is a fall in the quality of candidates when affirmative action is employed. This additional layer of scrutiny, though not cemented explicitly to the judicial test, could explain why the success rate of cases involving prohibited criterion for classification is overall higher than in all other cases. Clearly, the court classifies these cases differently from the rest of the docket.

The first explanation for this additional level of scrutiny is the different institutional incentives that different branches of government—the executive, legislative, and judiciary—have within the Indian constitutional scheme. Within the Indian constitutional design, the executive has the authority to determine which communities need to be included within the list of backward classes and what kind of protections they should receive.[52] This can and does create perverse political incentives within a democratic system like India's where many voters vote based on their caste and religious identities.[53] Political parties already use multiple tactics to influence voters and their caste identities through methods like selecting local candidates based on their group identity and political campaigns based around this.[54] Reservations can, therefore, be easily politicized since they already exist largely

[50] *Faculty Association of AIIMS v Union of India (UOI) and Ors.*

[51] *Indira Sawhney etc. v Union of India and others* AIR 1993 SC 477.

[52] *Ram Singh and Others v Union of India* (2015) 4 SCC 697; *Indira Sawhney etc. v Union of India and others* AIR 1993 SC 477.

[53] Christoph Jafferelot, "The Caste Based Mosaic of Indian Politics" (Sciences Po) <https://spire.sciencespo.fr/hdl:/2441/53r60a8s3kup1vc9k749hag43/resources/the-caste-based-mosaic-of-indian-politics.pdf> accessed January 20, 2025; Susanne Hoeber Rudolph and Lloyd Rudolph, "Caste Associations To Identity Politics: From Self-Help And Democratic Representation To Goonda Raj And Beyond" (2012) 85 Pacific Affairs 371.

[54] Sangeeta and Priyanka Goel, "Power Structure in India: Institutional and Social (Caste, Dalit-Bahujan, Class, Patriarchy)" in Pravin Kumar Jha (ed), *Indian Politics in Comparative Perspective* (Pearson 2012) 99; Christophe Jaffrelot, "Class and Caste in the 2019 Indian Election–Why Have So Many Poor Started Voting for Modi?" (2019) 7(2) Studies in Indian Politics 149.

around group identities. In the recent past, in states like Haryana, Gujarat, and Maharashtra, affluent and dominant castes have held lengthy protests to obtain reserved places in state universities and government jobs.[55] Many interest groups, such as the Marathas in Maharashtra and Jatts in many northern states, were able to secure certain reservations as well and the Supreme Court had to step in to invalidate the reservations on grounds that these violated the equality doctrine.[56] The basis of their claim was not rooted in historical oppression or social justice but a demand for numerical equity in outcomes. The commissions on backward classes (statutory bodies) rejected many of such claims but the governments, sensitive to political outcomes, classified these castes as backward and eligible for reservations anyway.

The court is cognizant of this potential of misuse and, therefore, tries to limit the power of state governments from adding to and expanding the list of groups that can benefit from affirmative action. In fact, in *Indira Sawhney v Union of India*, in its 500-page 11-judge bench judgment, the Supreme Court established a permanent executive body (that later came to be known as National Commission of Backward Classes) to reduce the potential perverse political incentives.[57] The government would have had to respond in writing their reasons for rejecting any proposals made by these bodies. The aim was clearly to make the process less susceptible to political manipulation. The politicization, however, did not necessarily stop. In *State of Maharashtra v Milind and Others*,[58] decided in 2000, the court observed that preventing state governments from unilaterally changing presidential orders which list the protected groups in a particular state removes "the pressure or burden of tinkering with the Presidential Orders either to gain popularity or secure votes."[59] Similarly, while rejecting reservations for Jatts in parts of North India in 2014, the court recognized that powerful political mobilization and one or two parameters reflecting relative backwardness should not be grounds for obtaining reservation.[60]

In fact, in August 2021, the Parliament amended the Constitution through the 127th Constitutional Amendment Bill to emphasize that the states should have the power to determine which groups should be included in the SEBCs eligible

[55] Ashwini Deshpande and Rajesh Ramchandran, "Dominant or Backward?: Political Economy of Demand for Quotas by Jats, Patels, and Marathas" (2017) 52(19) Economic & Political Weekly 81; Vipul Mudgal, "The Absurdity of Jat Reservation" (The Wire, February 22, 2016) <https://thewire.in/politics/the-absurdity-of-jat-reservation> accessed January 20, 2025; Sohnee Harshey, "Jats, Marathas and Patels Want Quotas, But Do They Need Them?" (2017) Economic & Political Weekly of India—Engage, <https://www.epw.in/engage/article/jats-patels-and-marathas-want-quotas-but-do-they-deserve-them> accessed January 20, 2025.

[56] *Ram Singh and Others v Union of India* (2015) 4 SCC 697.

[57] *Indira Sawhney etc. v Union of India and others* AIR 1993 SC 477.

[58] AIR 2001 SC 393.

[59] *State of Maharashtra v Milind and Others* AIR 2001 SC 393.

[60] *Ram Singh and Others v Union of India* (2015).

for reservations.[61] This amendment was a direct response to the earlier Supreme Court judgment made in May 2021 where the Supreme Court had interpreted previous amendments to restrict the powers of states to determine their lists of castes.[62] This back and forth between the judiciary and the other branches of the government is not new to the discussion on reservation. It highlights, however, the different incentives that different branches of the government are motivated by on the issue. The governments, at the state and central level, would not want to take measures that disturb politically mobilized caste groups that support them. State governments are most sensitive to these groups since caste mobilization is geographically sensitive. The judiciary, meanwhile, seeing the risk, wants to minimize scope for excessive rent-seeking by these groups by introducing statutory bodies, taking the power away from state governments, limiting the number of seats which can be reserved etc. Rajagopalan, in her analysis of constitutional amendments surrounding the issue of reservations, highlights how, through multiple interpretations of Articles 14 and 15, the Court has created restrictions around affirmative action policies. The *de facto* rule is that any changes now need to be ratified by the judiciary.[63] This could explain why over the years, fewer and fewer inclusions have been made to the central and state lists of backward classes, despite many demands made by interest groups.[64]

However, this explanation fails to take into account an additional problem that may be responsible, at least in part, for how the court views and frames the issue. Up until 1980, there were no judges in the Supreme Court from the Scheduled Caste and Tribes or Other Backward Classes.[65] Since then, generally, a maximum of one or two of all judges serving simultaneously belong to these communities.[66] Therefore, a second explanation for additional scrutiny in matters involving affirmative action can be found in the lack of diversity and representation within the judicial institution itself. The framing of the issue as a trade-off between representation and quality of candidates implies that in the opinion of the court, candidates selected through affirmative action are sub-par to those who are not—an assertion not rooted in any empirical evidence. Focusing on the alleged mediocrity that reservations create and recommending that the Parliament consider how to phase out caste-based reservations rather than focusing on how institutions should

[61] The Constitution (One Hundred and Twenty-seventh Amendment) Bill (2021), <https://prsindia.org/files/bills_acts/bills_parliament/2021/Constitution%20(One%20Hundred%20and%20Twenty-seventh%20Amendment)%20Bill,%202021.pdf> accessed January 20, 2025.

[62] *Ram Singh and Others v Union of India* (2015).

[63] Shruti Rajagopalan, "Constitutional Change: A Public Choice Analysis" in Choudhry, Khosla and Bhanu Mehta (eds) (n 6) 127.

[64] Deshpande and Ramchandra (n 55).

[65] Namit Saxena, "Disproportionate Representation at the Supreme Court: A Perspective Based on Caste and Religion of Judges" (Bar and Bench, May 23, 2021) <https://www.barandbench.com/columns/disproportionate-representation-supreme-court-caste-and-religion-of-judges> accessed January 20, 2025.

[66] ibid.

address caste-based discrimination rampant in the Indian society has led scholars like Kailash Jeengar and Rashmi Venkatesan to argue that the Indian Supreme Court has a flawed understanding of caste-based issues in India.[67] This may be exacerbated by the lack of representation within the Indian judiciary.

5. Conclusion

The Indian Constitution makers were aware of and aimed to address the persistent inequality of the Indian society when drafting Article 14 and Article 15. It aspired to an individualistic view of equality but recognized that there were multiple communities discriminated against based on their group identity.[68] The Supreme Court, similarly, has interpreted equality through the individualistic lens as well as the collective one. It also had to balance the politics around the subject when discussing the issue, while the judicial test captures little of this nuance.

Some constitutional scholars, like Khaitan, have been arguing for the equality doctrine to be revisited and brought more into consonance with the tiered approach of the proportionality review.[69] The few Supreme Court cases with smaller benches, where the Court applied a tiered approach, highlight that the Court too recognizes the need for change. This empirical analysis gives support to this argument in favor of a reform in the judicial approach to equality. For all practical purposes, the Court has applied a stronger test in equality matters involving prohibited criteria for classifications. Similarly, it has investigated the legitimacy of interest and balance competing interests in these matters. The Supreme Court has also recognized the perverse political incentives that exist within the existing jurisprudence. Adopting the proportionality standard of review will enable the Supreme Court as well as lower courts to undertake the same exercise but with greater legitimacy and certainty. The reframing of the judicial test will also create scope for more transparency in its handling of cases involving affirmative action and help reveal any implicit biases it may have on the issue due to the social backgrounds of its judges.

[67] See Kailash Jeenger, "When It Comes To Reservations, the Supreme Court Needs To Change Its Approach" (The Wire, 1 April 2021) <https://thewire.in/law/supreme-court-caste-reservation-approach-change-social-justice> accessed January 20, 2025; Rashmi Venkatesan, "Creamy Layer Judgment Ignores the Reality of Workplace Caste Discrimination" (The Wire, October 8, 2018) <https://thewire.in/rights/supreme-courts-application-of-creamy-layer-to-sc-st-employees-hides-caste-and-class-bias> accessed January 20, 2025.

[68] Nicole Lillibridge, "The Promise of Equality: A Comparative Analysis of the Constitutional Guarantees of Equality in India and the United States" (2005) 13 William & Mary Bill of Rights Journal 1301; Rochana Bajpai, "Constituent Assembly Debates and Minority Rights" (2000) 35 Economic & Political Weekly 1837; Ishita Banerjee-Dube, *A History of Modern India* (CUP 2015) 436–65.

[69] Khaitan (n 10).

14
Singapore

Niels Petersen

1. Introduction

The Singaporean Constitution contains an equality guarantee in Article 12.[1] The provision contains both an equal protection clause as well as a non-discrimination guarantee. According to paragraph 1 of the article, all persons are "equal before the law and entitled to the equal protection of the law." The non-discrimination guarantee in paragraph 2 contains several specifics. First, it is subject to limitations that are contained in other provisions of the Constitution ("Except as expressly authorized by this Constitution"). Second, it has only a very limited number of prohibited grounds of discrimination, which consist of religion, race, descent, and place of birth. Most notably, sex discrimination is missing from this list. This limited number of prohibited grounds is all the more striking because the grounds listed in Article 12(2) are exhaustive. In its jurisprudence, the Court of Appeal has explicitly refused to expand the prohibited grounds beyond the ones explicitly listed in the provision.[2] It is, therefore, not surprising that Article 12(2) has only limited importance in the judicial practice compared to the general equal protection clause in Article 12(1).

The Singapore Court of Appeal has developed two tests in order to make the equal protection clause in Article 12(1) of the Constitution operational. The so-called reasonable classification test is applied for the review of legislation, while a different test has been developed for the review of administrative and prosecutorial practice. The following section will describe these tests in more detail (2). If we look at the pattern that emerges from studying the case law of the Singapore Court of Appeal and the Singapore High Court, it is notable that the courts take a very deferential approach. In our analysis, we did not find a single case in which the courts found a violation of the equality guarantee either by the legislature or the executive (3). Section 4 of this chapter will try to explain this pattern. Singaporean courts generally seem to have a rather deferential approach to the review of state

[1] Constitution of the Republic of Singapore (August 9, 1965, last revised on December 1, 2021) <https://sso.agc.gov.sg/Act/CONS1963> accessed January 20, 2025.

[2] *Lim Meng Suang and another v Attorney-General and another appeal and another matter* [2014] SGCA 53, para 92.

Niels Petersen, *Singapore* In: *Equality's Guardians*. Edited by: Niels Petersen, Oxford University Press.
 DOI: 10.1093/9780198961109.003.0014

action. In particular, they have developed several doctrines that express that the power for politically controversial decisions lies with the executive and the legislature rather than with the courts (Section 4). The final part of the chapter concludes (5).

2. The equality doctrine of the Singapore Supreme Court

2.1 Development of the doctrine

The Singapore Supreme Court has always understood the equal protection guarantee in Article 12 of the Constitution as a general equality guarantee that does not focus on specific suspect classifications. While Article 12(2) of the Constitution contains a non-discrimination guarantee, this provision has had very limited relevance in the judicial practice. The general approach to the equal protection clause was first established by Lord Diplock in the Privy Council decision of *Ong Ah Chuan*.[3] The Court adopted a formal approach to equality, according to which "like should be compared with like."[4] Consequently, differentiations between different classes of individuals are possible if there is "some difference in the circumstances."[5] In *Eng Foong Ho*, the Court of Appeal specified this approach and argued that "there [has to be] a reasonable nexus between the state action and the objective to be achieved by the law."[6] Such a reasonable connection was missing if an executive act amounts to "intentional *and* arbitrary discrimination," that is, if it acted in bad faith.[7]

This approach has, for a long time, been very deferential. As the Court of Appeal held in *Ramalingam Ravinthran*, there is a presumption of constitutionality regarding the actions of public authorities.[8] Accordingly, an applicant complaining of a violation of Article 12 of the Constitution by the executive has to make a *prima facie* case of discriminatory intention.[9] The mere fact that individuals in comparable situations have been treated differently is not sufficient for such a *prima facie* case:

> Given that there are many legitimate reasons for the Prosecution to differentiate between the charges brought against different offenders involved in the same

[3] Privy Council, October 15, 1980, *Ong Ah Chuan v Public Prosecutor* [1980–1981] SLR 48, 64 [35].
[4] ibid.
[5] ibid.
[6] *Eng Foong Ho v Attorney-General* [2009] SGCA 1, para 25.
[7] ibid para 30 (emphasis added).
[8] *Ramalingam Ravinthram v Attorney-General* [2012] SGCA 2, paras 44–48. For a critical discussion of the principle, see Jack Tsen-Ta Lee, "Rethinking the Presumption of Constitutionality" in Jaclyn L Neo (ed), *Constitutional Interpretation in Singapore: Theory and Practice* (Routledge 2016) 139.
[9] *Ramalingam Ravinthram* (n 8) para 70.

> criminal enterprise, such differentiation per se does not necessarily mean that the Prosecution has not given unbiased consideration to the offender or offenders in question, or that the Prosecution has taken into account irrelevant considerations. Put another way, such differentiation, without more, does not raise an inference of breach of Art 12(1). Rather, in the absence of prima facie evidence to the contrary, the inference would be that the Prosecution has based its differentiation on relevant considerations.[10]

It is only once the applicant has made such a *prima face* case that the public authorities are asked to justify their decision and the court analyzes whether the differentiation could indeed by justified. The Court seems to have slightly relaxed this standard in *Ridzuan*, where it argued that the applicant did not have to produce evidence directly impugning the decision-making process of the Public Prosecutor.[11] Instead, a *prima facie* case could be made by showing that the applicant was in a "practically identical" situation as another individual who had been treated more leniently by the authorities.[12] Yet, in the concrete case, the Court did not consider these conditions to be fulfilled.[13]

In the recent decision of *Syed Suhail*, there are signs for a less deferential approach.[14] The Court of Appeal adopted a more searching standard for cases "affect[ing] the appellant's life and liberty to the gravest degree."[15] In the specific case, the Court found that the Attorney-General's decision in the concrete case was not consistent with the general guidelines that the Attorney-General supposedly pursued in scheduling death sentences, thus establishing a *prima facie* case for commencing judicial review.[16] Whether the decision indeed violated the equal protection guarantee was left open for a later stage of the proceeding.[17]

The Supreme Court's approach for reviewing legislation differed slightly from the approach applied vis-à-vis the review of executive action. When reviewing legislation on its conformity with Article 12 of the Constitution, the Court applies the so-called reasonable classification test.[18] This test was first developed in *Taw*

[10] ibid para 71.
[11] *Muhammad Ridzuan bin Mohd Ali v Attorney-General* [2015] SGCA 53, para 43.
[12] ibid para 51.
[13] ibid paras 53–66.
[14] *Syed Suhail bin Syed Zin v Attorney-General* [2020] SGCA 122. See Kenny Chng, "A Reconsideration of Equal Protection and Executive Action in Singapore" (2021) 21 Oxford University Commonwealth LJ 295 for a detailed discussion of this development. See also Alec Stone Sweet, "Intimations of Proportionality? Rights Protection and the Singapore Constitution" (2021) 2021 Singapore Journal of Legal Studies 231 (highlighting judicial developments outside the equality framework as further signs for a less deferential approach of Singaporean courts).
[15] *Syed Suhail bin Syed Zin* (n 14) para 63.
[16] ibid para 77.
[17] ibid paras 77–79.
[18] For a discussion of the reasonable classification test, see Jaclyn L Neo, "Equal Protection and the Rational Classification Test in Singapore: After Lim Meng Suang v. Attorney-General" (2016) 2016 Singapore Journal of Legal Studies 95.

Cheng Kong in 1998[19] and later specified in *Lim Meng Suang*.[20] It consists of two steps.[21] First, the Court inquires whether the classification of a statute prescribing a differentiating matter is founded on an intelligible differentia. Second, it analyzes whether there is a rational relation between the challenged classification and the purpose that is sought by the statute. The Court emphasizes that the first limb establishes a very low threshold.[22] The Court only requires that it is possible to identify who falls within the classification and who is excluded by the classification.[23] The test will only fail if the classification is "so unreasonable as to be illogical and/or incoherent."[24] In particular, the Court does not second-guess the legitimacy of the legislative purpose:[25]

> To permit the court the power—over and above its power of scrutinising legislation pursuant to the "reasonable classification" test—to declare a statute inconsistent with Art 12(1) (and, therefore, unconstitutional under Art 4) because the object of that statute is illegitimate would precisely be to confer on the court a licence to usurp the legislative function in the course of becoming (or at least acting like) a "mini-legislature."

The second limb requires a rational relationship between the measure and its purpose. However, the Court does not require a perfect fit or a complete coincidence.[26] Originally, this was a very deferential standard.[27] However, the Court has recently alluded to the possibility that it could apply the more stringent approach developed in *Syed Suhail* to the review of legislation. In the recent case of *Tan Seng Kee*, the Court of Appeal contrasted the *Lim Meng Suang* approach to the one adopted in *Syed Suhail*, but explicitly left open whether the latter could also be applied in the context of the review of legislation because it found that the applicant lacked standing in the concrete case.[28]

2.2 Indirect discrimination and positive measures

Most of the equality cases before the Singapore Supreme Court concern the arbitrary exercise of discretion by public authorities or the constitutionality of

19 *Public Prosecutor v Taw Cheng Kong* [1998] SGCA 37.
20 *Lim Meng Suang v Attorney-General* (n 2). For an extensive discussion, see also *Tan Seng Kee v Attorney-General* [2022] SGCA 16, paras 305–328.
21 *Lim Meng Suang* (n 2) para 60; *Tan Seng Kee* (n 20) para 305.
22 *Lim Meng Suang* (n 2) para 65.
23 ibid para 110.
24 ibid para 67.
25 ibid para 82.
26 ibid para 68.
27 ibid para 66.
28 *Tan Seng Kee* (n 20) para 329.

statutes because of over- or under-inclusiveness. Indirect discrimination cases or cases concerning positive measures are rare so it is difficult to discern a particular doctrinal approach. But there are a couple of cases where these issues came up. The High Court had to deal with the issue of indirect discrimination in its 2021 *Syed Suhail and others* decision.[29] The applicants in the case had been convicted for drug trafficking or drug importation and sentenced to death. They were all of Malay ethnic origin and argued that their death sentence was discriminatory because Malays were vastly overrepresented among individuals sentenced to death for drug offences. While Malays only make up 13.5% of the resident population in Singapore, 77% of residents sentenced to death between 2010 and 2021 were of Malay ethnic origin.[30] They alleged that this amounted to indirect racial discrimination. The Court rejected this argument. It held that the mere statistical discrepancy was not sufficient to prove a *prima face* case of discrimination.[31] Instead, the Court required evidence that the investigatory practices of the public authorities were targeted specifically against Malays.[32] It held that the "plaintiffs' statistical evidence provided no basis for the court to infer such a causal link between the AG's decisions to prosecute Malay suspects and their ethnicity."[33] Instead, the Court argued that the statistical disparity might have been due to a multitude of other factors so the applicants had not established a *prima facie* case requiring the Attorney-General to justify the disparity.[34] The approach of the High Court towards indirect discrimination is thus similar to the approach of the US Supreme Court and implicitly also requires the proof of discriminatory intent.[35]

There is even less jurisprudential evidence regarding positive actions. But an *obiter dictum* in the High Court's decision in *Ravi s/o Madasamy* suggests that the Court would be rather accommodating regarding legislative schemes designed to support minority groups in society.[36] The decision concerned the constitutional requirements for standing in the presidential elections. According to Article 19B of the Constitution, the election for the office of the President is reserved for members from ethnic communities whose members have not held the office of the President for the five most recent terms of office. The Court held that this provision did not amount to racial discrimination.[37] It argued that "the purpose of reserved elections is to *ensure* that the office of President will be representative of our multiracial society and to *foster* multiracialism."[38]

[29] *Syed Suhail bin Syed Zin and others v Attorney-General* [2021] SGHC 274.
[30] ibid para 26.
[31] ibid para 39.
[32] ibid para 47.
[33] ibid para 63.
[34] ibid paras 71–72.
[35] See ibid para 63.
[36] *Ravi s/o Madasamy v Attorney-General* [2017] SGHC 163.
[37] ibid para 91.
[38] ibid (emphasis in the original).

3. Empirical analysis of the equality case law

3.1 Generating and analyzing the sample

The empirical analysis of the Singaporean equality case law comprises the case law both of the Court of Appeal and the High Court, which together form the Singapore Supreme Court. While the Court of Appeal is nominally the highest court in Singapore's legal hierarchy, there are certain cases, in particular those concerning administrative action, where the High Court is the court of last instance. Furthermore, the inclusion of the High Court also permitted me to broaden the volume of cases that could be analyzed. The sample consists of all cases dealing with Article 12 of the Singaporean Constitution that were decided by the High Court or the Court of Appeal between 1 January 2000 and 28 February 2022. It comprises a total of 46 cases, of which 19 stem from the Court of Appeal and 27 from the High Court. The first analyzed case was the Court of Appeal decision in *Thiruselvam s/o Nagaratnam* from March 2, 2001,[39] while the last case was *Teo Ghim Heng* from February 23, 2022.[40] The cases were identified by executing a search for the term "12" within the vicinity of 5 words from the term "constitution" in the public database of the Singaporean courts that contains all Supreme Court cases from the year 2000.[41] This sample was subsequently cleaned manually because not all hits actually concerned equality cases. Furthermore, if a case was dealt with by both the High Court and the Court of Appeal, I included only the Court of Appeal case in the sample. A case was only considered to be an equality case if the Court engaged in a substantive discussion of a potential violation of Article 12 of the Singapore Constitution and decided that this provision was either violated or not violated. If the Court mentioned Article 12 of the Constitution without making a substantive pronouncement on a potential violation of the norm, or if the Court held that the analysis of Article 12 of the Constitution was precluded, such cases were not included in the sample. After the construction of the sample, all cases contained therein were analyzed. The variables were coded according to the coding scheme introduced in the introductory chapter.[42]

3.2 The results of the analysis

The results of the empirical analysis are straightforward. There is not a single case in our sample in which either the Court of Appeal or the High Court found that the

[39] *Thiruselvam s/o Nagaratnam v Public Prosecutor* [2001] SGCA 13.

[40] *Teo Ghim Heng v Public Prosecutor* [2022] SGCA 10.

[41] <https://www.judiciary.gov.sg/judgments/judgments-case-summaries> accessed January 20, 2025.

[42] See Chapter 1, section 4.2.

executive or the legislature had violated Article 12 of the Constitution. The analysis thus confirms the impression of the doctrinal analysis that the Supreme Court's approach is highly deferential. Certainly, the results as such do not necessarily indicate a high level of deference. Instead, it could also be due to the kind of cases that come to the courts. Therefore, the following section aims to give slightly more detail regarding the kinds of cases that were decided by the High Court and the Court of Appeal in the time frame covered by the sample.

Most of the cases coming to the Courts concerned the exercise of executive discretion. There were many cases in which the applicants challenged decisions of the public prosecutor to bring specific charges for more severe crimes or to issue certificates of cooperation that would have excluded the imposition of a mandatory death penalty in drug trafficking cases.[43] The Court of Appeal has been highly deferential in these cases, usually not even requiring the public prosecutor to justify its decisions. In *Thiruselvam s/o Nagaratnam*, the Court argued that "[t]he prosecution has a wide discretion to determine what charge or charges should be preferred against any particular offender, and to proceed on charges of different severity as between different participants of the same criminal acts."[44] Similarly, the Court held in *Ridzuan* that

> [i]t is for this reason (the need to avoid jeopardising the operational capability of CNB) that we accept . . . that the Judge is not the appropriate person to determine the question of whether a convicted drug trafficker has rendered substantive assistance. Section 33B expressly confers upon the [Public Prosecutor] the discretion to make the decision on substantive assistance.[45]

The courts have applied a similar deference to administrative decisions outside the field of criminal law.[46] For example, the case of *Eng Foong Ho* concerned an urban planning decision regarding the expropriation of temple property for redevelopment after the construction of a nearby Mass Rapid Transit station.[47] The applicants had argued that the expropriation violated the equal protection clause because it only concerned the Buddhist temple, while an adjacent mission and Christian church were not expropriated. The Court held that an executive act only violated Article 12 of the Constitution "if it amounts to intentional and arbitrary

[43] See *Thiruselvam s/o Nagaratnam* (n 39); *Ramalingam Ravinthram* (n 8); *Chan Heng Kong v Public Prosecutor* [2012] SGCA 18; *Yong Vui Kong v Public Prosecutor* [2012] SGCA 23; *Quek Hock Lye v Public Prosecutor* [2012] SGCA 25; *Muhammad Ridzuan bin Mohd Ali* (n 11).

[44] *Thiruselvam s/o Nagaratnam* (n 39).

[45] *Muhammad Ridzuan bin Mohd Ali* (n 11) para 66.

[46] See *Eng Foong Ho* (n 6). See also *Borissik Svetlana v Urban Redevelopment Authority* [2009] SGHC 154; *Yap Keng Ho and others v Public Prosecutor* [2011] SGHC 39; *Chee Soon Juan and Others v Public Prosecutor* [2011] SGHC 40; *Yap Keng Ho and others v Public Prosecutor* [2011] SGHC 41; *Vijaya Kumar s/o Rajendran and others v Attorney-General* [2015] SGHC 244; *Tan Liang Joo John v Attorney-General* [2019] SGHC 263.

[47] *Eng Foong Ho v Attorney-General* (n 6).

discrimination."[48] In the concrete case, the Court came to the conclusion that the acquisition of temple property was "based solely on planning considerations"[49] and was "proceeded with in good faith."[50]

A substantive amount of deference can also be observed in cases concerning the review of legislation.[51] These decisions often concerned the over- and under-inclusiveness of legislation. For example, the Court had to decide several cases concerning the mandatory death sentence that the Penal Code imposed if the accused had been in possession of a certain minimum amount of specific drugs. The Court of Appeal rejected the argument that the provision was over-inclusive. It held that the amount of drugs in possession of the accused was broadly proportionate to the harm that these drugs caused to society.[52] While it conceded that one might reasonably disagree about the correct criterion for differentiation, it argued that this was a policy question for the legislature to decide.[53]

The vast majority of the cases decided by the Court of Appeal and the High Court did not concern suspect classifications so that many other apex courts would also have applied a rather deferential standard of review in these cases. There are only very few cases which arguably involve a suspect classification. In the 2015 *Yong Vui Kong* case, the applicant complained about caning as punishment for drug offenses.[54] He argued that the punishment discriminated based on sex because it was only applied to men, not to women. The Court of Appeal rejected the argument and held that the "obvious physiological differences between males and females" justified the differentiation.[55] For the same reason, the Court also held that there was no age discrimination even though the punishment of caning was only applied to men under the age of 50.[56] The Court also denied age discrimination in a case concerning the criminal liability of children.[57] The defendant had argued that a strict minimum age for criminal liability was discriminatory because it did not take into account that maturity did not always correspond to biological age. The Court conceded that the delimitation criterion was not perfect, but argued that it was sufficient that age was a meaningful proxy for maturity.[58]

[48] ibid para 30.
[49] ibid para 35.
[50] ibid para 31.
[51] *Nguyen Tuong Van v Public Prosecutor* [2004] SGCA 47; *Kok Chong Weng and Others v Wiener Robert Lorenz and Others (Ankerite Pte Ltd, intervener)* [2009] SGCA 7; *Yong Vui Kong v Public Prosecutor and another matter* [2010] SGCA 20; *Quek Hock Lye v Public Prosecutor* [2015] SGCA 7; *Jabing Kho v Public Prosecutor* [2016] SGCA 21; *Kho Jabing v Attorney-General* [2016] SGCA 37; *Saravanan Chandaram v Public Prosecutor* [2020] SGCA 43; *Yuen Ye Ming v Public Prosecutor* [2020] SGCA 80; *Teo Ghim Heng v Public Prosecutor* [2022] SGCA 10. See also decisions listed below in nn 54–67.
[52] *Yong Vui Kong* (n 51) para 112.
[53] ibid para 113.
[54] *Yong Vui Kong v Public Prosecutor* [2015] SGCA 11.
[55] ibid para 110.
[56] ibid para 116.
[57] *Public Prosecutor v ASR* [2019] SGCA 16.</IBT<
[58] ibid para 88.

Two High Court cases concerned potential racial discrimination.[59] However, both cases were unsuccessful. In *Ravi s/o Madasamy*, the High Court held that a constitutional provision aiming at increasing the chances of members of racial minorities to attain the office of the President did not violate the Article 12(2) of the Constitution because it served the purpose of ensuring the representativeness of the office in a multiracial society.[60] In *Syed Suhail and others*, the applicants had argued that their sentencing to death penalties for drug offenses had been discriminatory because individuals of Malay ethnicity were vastly overrepresented among the individuals that were convicted for drug charges.[61] The Court rejected the claim. It held that the mere statistical correlation was not sufficient to prove a *prima facie* case of discrimination and that the applicants had failed to produce evidence on discriminatory intent by the prosecution.[62]

The most controversial cases decided by the Supreme Court concern a series of decisions relating to discrimination based on sexual orientation.[63] These concerned section 377A of the Singapore Penal Code, which criminalized sexual activity between homosexual males. In *Lim Meng Suang*, the Court of Appeal applied a deferential standard, arguing that it did not have the power to second-guess the aims that the legislature pursued with its differentiation because the latter would amount to judicial activism.[64] Furthermore, the Court also argued that sexual orientation was no suspect classification in the sense of Article 12(2) of the Constitution because the list of prohibited grounds in that provision was exhaustive and did not contain a reference to sexual orientation.[65] In the eyes of the Court, it was up to the legislature and not the courts "to ensure that the Singapore Constitution reflects the prevailing social mores as well as aspirations of Singapore society."[66]

The Court of Appeal took a more sophisticated and balanced approach in its latest decision in the issue in *Tan Seng Kee*.[67] After a lengthy discussion of the equality issue in the case, the Court left open whether section 377A of the Penal Code indeed violated Article 12 of the Constitution.[68] Instead, it argued that the provision was unenforceable in its entirety so that the applicants lacked standing.[69]

59 *Ravi s/o Madasamy* (n 36); *Syed Suhail bin Syed Zin* (n 29). These cases are discussed in more detail in Section 2.2 of this chapter.

60 *Ravi s/o Madasamy* (n 36) paras 91–92.

61 *Syed Suhail bin Syed Zin* (n 29).

62 ibid para 63.

63 See *Lim Meng Suang* (n 2); *Tan Seng Kee* (n 20). See also *Lim Meng Suang and another v Attorney-General* [2013] SGHC 73; *Tan Eng Hong v Attorney-General* [2013] SGHC 199; *Ong Ming Johnson v Attorney-General and other matters* [2020] SGHC 63. For a normative defence of the position of the Singaporean courts in these cases, see Li-Ann Thio, *A Treatise on Singapore Constitutional Law* (Academy Publishing 2012) paras 13.041–13.054.

64 *Lim Meng Suang* (n 2) para 82.

65 ibid para 102.

66 ibid para 92 (emphasis in the original).

67 *Tan Seng Kee* (n 20).

68 ibid para 329.

69 ibid para 149.

The Court of Appeal based its reasoning on a political compromise regarding the provision that had been found earlier. When the legislature had discussed the abolition of the provision in 2007, it had decided to retain it. At the same time, the Prime Minister had promised that the provision would not be proactively enforced.[70] This promise had been confirmed and reinforced by the Attorney-General in 2018.[71] The Court now held that these promises had created a legitimate expectation which hindered the enforcement unless the Attorney-General explicitly pronounced that there would be a change in the policy of non-enforcement.[72] With this decision, the Court of Appeal could sidestep the sensitive issue of the criminalization of male homosexual acts, while providing some legal certainty to homosexual couples and without explicitly contradicting the government. The case may therefore indicate a cautious departure from the traditionally deferential approach.

3.3 Conclusion

The preceding analysis has shown that the Singaporean courts apply a deferential approach to the equal protection clause of the Constitution. However, this deferential approach has to be seen in context. Most of the cases that came to the courts did not involve a suspect classification. The Singaporean courts are by a long way not the only courts to apply a deferential approach when it comes to equality claims not involving a suspect classification. The rational basis doctrine of the US Supreme Court is the most prominent example.[73] When it comes to the cases involving a suspect classification, the results again do not differ radically from what other Common Law courts might have found. There are comparative examples of courts having rejected a violation of equal protection for rules favoring women over men[74] or indirect racial discrimination in death penalty cases merely because an ethnic group is overrepresented among individuals sentenced to death.[75] Only the cases regarding the criminalization of male homosexual acts in section 377A of the Criminal Code stand out because Western courts would have almost certainly come to a different result in these cases. However, it is important to consider the societal context in such cases, and one should not fail to point out that the recognition of gay equality rights is mostly a development of the last three decades even in

[70] ibid para 17.
[71] ibid para 19.
[72] ibid para 149.
[73] See Chapter 2.
[74] See eg *M v Superior Court of Sonoma County* 450 US 464 (1981); *R v Hess; R v Nguyen* [1990] 2 SCR 906 (decisions of the US Supreme Court and the Supreme Court of Canada arguing that the criminalization of men having sex with underage girls, while not criminalizing female sex with underage boys, did not violate equal protection).
[75] See *McCleskey v Kemp* 481 US 279 (1987).

the West.[76] Yet at the same time, the equality case law also represents a wider trend in the judicial review practiced by the Singapore Supreme Court. *Jaclyn Neo* and *Yvonne Lee*[77] noted in 2008 that only one legislative provision has ever been struck down by the Singapore High Court in *Taw Cheng Kong* 1998[78]—a decision that was later overturned by the Court of Appeal.[79] Consequently, despite the caveats raised in this section, the Singaporean understanding of equality seems to best fit the deferential model where courts largely defer to the legislature when it comes to defining the content of equality.[80]

4. Explanation of the doctrine

The Supreme Court's approach in specifying the meaning of the equal protection clause in the Singapore Constitution cannot be explained without considering the institutional context in which the Singaporean courts are operating in constitutional matters. The political system in Singapore is mostly dominated by the People's Action Party (PAP), which is the party of Singapore's founding father, Lee Kuan Yew, and which has been in power without interruption since Singapore's independence. This means that the judges are usually handpicked by the leadership of the PAP. Furthermore, The PAP has had a constant supermajority in parliament which allows the party to amend the Constitution in case of an unfavorable court ruling.[81] This means that Parliament can react to court decisions that are against the interest of the PAP by amending the Constitution. There is an important precedent in this respect. In *Chng Suan Tze*, the Court of Appeal ordered the release of the applicant because the government had not complied with the procedure set out in the Internal Security Act (ISA).[82] While the government formally complied with the judgment, it re-arrested the applicant after his release and made sure to

[76] cf only the several decisions of Western courts to deny claims of discrimination based on sexual orientation: BVerfGE 6, 389 (decision from 1957, arguing that the criminalization of male sex was constitutional); *Quilter v Attorney-General* [1998] 1 NZLR 523 (where the New Zealand Supreme Court refused to interpret the term marriage in a way that allowed for same-sex marriages); *Rees v UK* (1986) Series A no 106; *Schalk and Kopf v Austria* ECHR 2010-IV 409; *Joslin v New Zealand* UN Doc CCPR/C/75/D/902/1999 (HRCttee, July 17, 2002) (all arguing that same-sex marriage was not protected under the equality guarantee and the right to get married).

[77] Jaclyn L Neo and Yvonne C L Lee, "Constitutional Supremacy: Still a Little Dicey?" in Li-Ann Thio and Kevin Y L Tan (eds), *Evolution of a Revolution: Forty Years of the Singapore Constitution* (Routledge 2008) 153, 174.

[78] *Taw Cheng Kong v Public Prosecutor* [1998] SLR 943.

[79] *Public Prosecutor v Taw Cheng Kong* [1998] 2 SLR 410.

[80] See also Neo and Lee (n 77) 175–78 (generally describing the approach of the Singaporean courts as deferential).

[81] Gordon Silverstein, "Singapore: The Exception that Proves that Rules Matter" in Tom Ginsburg and Tamir Moustafa (eds), *Rule by Law: The Politics of Courts in Authoritarian Regimes* (CUP 2008) 71, 81; Neo and Lee (n 77) 155.

[82] *Chng Suan Tze v Minister of Home Affairs* [1988] SLR 132.

follow the procedure to the letter the second time.[83] More importantly, the legislature amended the Constitution to exclude appeals under the ISA.[84]

Furthermore, even though the independence of judges is guaranteed in the Singaporean Constitution, the government retains a certain level of influence even after the appointment.[85] While judges have life tenure under the Constitution, they may be retained after the age of 65 on renewable limited-term contracts. Furthermore, it is possible to remove judges from office in accordance with Article 98 of the Constitution. Finally, the government can appoint temporary judges to Singapore's top courts. These provisions have not been evidently abused in the past. In particular, temporary judges usually do not sit on constitutional cases. But it is likely that the mere existence of these pressure points influences the constitutional jurisprudence of the Supreme Court.

However, there is an alternative explanation for the deferential approach of the Singaporean courts, one that is based in the judicial culture and has been promoted by several of the Chief Justices of the Singapore Court of Appeal.[86] According to this explanation, judicial deference is due to Singapore's formalist judicial culture that avoids open conflict with the political branches. Furthermore, it is in conformity with the Confucian principle of *junzi* that emphasizes trust in government.[87] This does not necessarily mean that the judiciary would accept everything that the legislature and the executive are doing. However, the government tries to avoid conflicts with the judiciary by obtaining extensive legal advice.[88] Furthermore, courts avoid open confrontation with the legislature and the executive.[89] Instead, the court uses different means to signal potential inconsistencies of government policies with the Constitution.[90] According to this understanding of the Court's practice, the low success rate of challenges to statutes and government measures is a signal of good governance instead of extreme deference of the courts.[91]

This alternative explanation is supported by the recent repeal of the criminalization of gay sex. As we have seen, the Court of Appeal had struck a compromise in its most recent judgment of *Tan Seng Kee*.[92] While the Court left open the question

[83] Silverstein (n 81) 80.

[84] Ibid 81; Neo and Lee (n 77) 177.

[85] Silverstein (n 81) 84.

[86] See Sek Keong Chan, "Judicial Review—From Angst to Empathy" (2010) 22 Singapore Academy of Law Journal 469; Sek Keong Chan, "The Courts and the 'Rule of Law' in Singapore" (2012) 2012 Singapore Journal of Legal Studies 209; Sundaresh Menon, "The Rule of Law: The Path of Exceptionalism" (2016) 28 Singapore Academy of Law Journal 413.

[87] Jaclyn L Neo, "Autonomy, Deference and Control: Judicial Doctrine and Facets of Separation of Powers in Singapore" (2018) 5 Journal of International and Comparative Law 461, 481–82.

[88] Chan, "Judicial Review" (n 86) 475.

[89] Sundaresh Menon, "Executive Power: Rethinking the Modalities of Control" (2019) 29 Duke Journal of Comparative and International Law 277, 300–03.

[90] Menon, "The Rule of Law" (n 86) 420–21.

[91] See Chan "Judicial Review" (n 86) 475.

[92] *Tan Seng Kee* (n 20). For a more detailed analysis of the judgment, see nn 67–72 and accompanying text.

whether section 377A of the Penal Code violated the principle of equality, it argued that the government had created a legitimate expectation when it promised not to enforce the statute.[93] After the Court of Appeal had issued its judgment, the Parliament of Singapore passed a bill to renounce section 377A of the Penal Code in November 2022. The government thus showed that it had listened to and taken into account the concerns of the Court of Appeal.

Ultimately, these two explanations do not exclude each other. A non-confrontational approach may be the most that a court may achieve in the institutional position of the Singapore Court of Appeal. Therefore, it would be a matter of judicial prudence to try to influence government policies through other means than judicial confrontation. At the same time, it remains anyone's guess if the Singaporean courts would be more confrontational if they were in a stronger institutional position.

5. Conclusion

The approach of the Singapore Supreme Court to the equal protection clause is deferential. This is illustrated both by the shape of the doctrine and the results of the empirical analysis. The Court applies two different tests in equality cases depending on whether executive action or legislation is concerned. The court usually refuses to second-guess the legitimacy of the challenged distinction and merely analyzes whether there is a rational connection between measure and purpose. In its recent case law, the Court has shown tendencies toward a slightly stricter approach, advocating a more searching standard for cases "affect[ing] the appellant's life and liberty to the gravest degree."[94] However, it remains to be seen how this plays out in practice. This deferential doctrinal approach of the Court also translates into a low success rate. There has not been a single equality case in our sample in which the Court of Appeal or the High Court have struck down an executive measure or a piece of legislation because it violated Article 12 of the Singaporean Constitution. Yet, when interpreting these results, we also have to apply a caveat: The vast majority of cases did not involve a suspect classification and would probably also be subject to a rather deferential standard of review in many other jurisdictions. When it comes to the few cases involving a suspect classification, only the case concerning the criminalization of male gay sex stands out. However, one should not lose track of the societal and institutional circumstances in which the Singapore Supreme Court operates when evaluating its equality case law.

[93] *Tan Seng Kee* (n 20) para 149.
[94] *Syed Suhail bin Syed Zin* (n 14) para 63.

15
Taiwan

Wei-Ju Huang

1. Introduction

The concept of equality appears in several articles of the Constitutional Law of Taiwan (ROC). Focusing on the term literally, equality can be found at the first glance in Article 5 of the First Chapter (the General Provision), which guarantees equality among all different racial groups; Article 7 in the Second Chapter (the Charter of Human Rights and Responsibilities) stipulates that "[a]ll citizens shall be equal before the law irrespective of sex, religion, race, class, or political affiliation." Equality is mentioned again in the Additional Articles of the Constitutional Law of Taiwan (ROC) in which section 6 of the tenth additional article addresses the task of the state "to guarantee women's human dignity, to protect women's personal safety, to eliminate gender discrimination and to promote substantial equal status between the two genders."

If we extend the scope of observation further beyond the terminology, sections 7, 11, and 12 of the tenth additional article of the Constitution, which were promulgated on April 25, 2000, indicate the tasks of "supporting the physical and intellectual disabled persons, the indigenous people and the indigenous languages and cultures. The same supports are offered likewise to the citizens living in the outlying island areas Penghu, Kinmen, and Matsu," which also reveal awareness of some potential origins of social inequality. These equality-linked provisions convey a systematic impression that multiple equality and non-discrimination clauses coexist in parallel with the Constitution. However, when analyzing equality from the perspective of constitutional jurisdiction, the main emphasis lies on Article 7 of the Constitution. Article 5 of the Constitution is rather vague in content. Therefore, it is interpreted as an abstract appellation instead of a legal basis of valid claim.[1] A historical and systematic review of the origin of Article 5 also indicates that this article aims at establishing the concept of "nation" and a cross-racial political legitimacy of the newly established democracy after the Jurchen-dominated Qing Empire was

[1] Yuan-Hao Liao, "Rights of Equality: Lecture One—The Meaning of Equality in Constitution" (2008) 68 Taiwan Jurist 48, 49–50.

Wei-Ju Huang, *Taiwan* In: *Equality's Guardians*. Edited by: Niels Petersen, Oxford University Press.
 DOI: 10.1093/9780198961109.003.0015

overthrown, while both of the two concepts were unfamiliar in Eastern Asia in the early 20th century.[2] Furthermore, the tenth additional article of the Constitution is generally understood as a list of fundamental state policies, which means that the content lacks binding effect. It is instead an assignment to the Parliament, according to which the legislature shall make concrete nondiscriminatory policies based on social circumstances and therefore enjoys a large measure of flexibility.[3] Consequently, Article 7 of the Constitution is the main legal basis for the Constitutional Court of Taiwan's examination of any potential intervention of equality.[4]

Yet, the extent of the protection provided by Article 7 of the Constitution is not as clear as it seems to be. Textually, it is arguable that the qualified applicants of Article 7 should be limited because only citizens are mentioned, which might imply that foreigners were not the legal subjects of equality.[5] In Constitutional Interpretation[6] No 560, the Court examined the constitutionality of the (old) section 43(5) of the Employment Service Act, according to which the right of foreign workers to funeral payment for deceased family members paid by the labor insurance was restricted if the deceased family member did not live in Taiwan. Although the Constitutional Court justified the differential payment policy of the labor insurance on grounds of the function of social security and the different levels of economic reliance between cohabitant and separated family members, this Constitutional Interpretation still implied that foreigners are qualified claimants for equal protection. Today, there is a consensus in the legal literature that non-citizens are the subject of rights of equality in the same way as citizens.[7]

Moreover, it has been discussed whether Article 7 provides an exhaustive list of protected classifications, or whether it provides merely an exemplification.[8] These days, most legal scholars consider the categories provided by the Article 7 merely to be a non-definitive list so that additional categories can be recognized. This is also reflected in the case law of the Constitutional Court. The Court has applied

[2] Xinmin Chen, *Constitutional Law* (San Min Book Co Ltd. 2018) 150–52.

[3] Yi-Hsin Ku, "Essay on the Orientation of Fundamental National Policy in the Constitution" (2018) 106 Taipei University LR 267, 283.

[4] Liao (n 1) 50.

[5] The understanding of the nationality-based subject of equality according to the formal text was refuted by all scholars. Yet, some opinions appeal to alternative limitations of the legal subjects of equality, such as to understand the qualification as "only for the people in the territory of R.O.C." Introduction of this proposal and the opposition against it are in Hsin-Hua Wu, *Constitutional Law* (San Min Book 2021) 290 (at n 9). Another proposal is to limit the application of equality for foreigners in political area, which should be preserved to citizens with nationality. See Tzi-Yang Chen, *Constitutional Law* (Angel Publishing 2016) 649–50.

[6] "Constitutional Interpretation" is the official name of constitutional judgments before 2022.

[7] Yuan-Hao Liao, "Rights of Equality: Lecture Two—Levels of Scrutiny of the Grand Justices on Rights of Equality" (2009) 76 Taiwan Jurist 37, 37; Nian-Tsu Li, "Equal or Unequal? Foreigners in the Constitutional Interpretations" (2016) 28 DISSENT 4.

[8] Wu (n 5) 291; Chen (n 2) 153; Geng Wu and Chwen-Wen Chen, *Constitutional Theories and Governmental Systems* (San Min Book 2021) 159.

Article 7 to differential treatments based on unlisted categories, such as beneficiary status (veteran),[9] registration of domicile,[10] nationality of origin,[11] physical disability,[12] or the evaluation/appointment regulations in state examinations and public servant (including military) systems.[13]

The aforementioned examples highlight the importance of an empirical analysis of the case law even though Taiwan is known to be heavily influenced by European continental legal thought in the Japanese colonial period before the Second World War and subsequently during the Kuomintang (KMT) government.[14] Neither a pure textual interpretation nor an extensive literature review offers a comprehensive understanding of the *de facto* extent of the equality protection offered by the Bill of Rights in the Constitution. Focusing on the rights of equality, this chapter analyzes the attitude of the Constitutional Court towards equal protection. The first part focuses on the historical origin and the syntax of Article 7 of the Constitution, which provides important background information for the subsequent analysis. The second part provides a brief overview of the existing literature and summarizes the general academic understanding of equality in Taiwan. The third part presents an empirical observation of 88 constitutional interpretations related to equality from 1983 to 2021. The fourth part tries to explain the approach of the Constitutional Court. The final part concludes.

2. Equality clause of the Constitution: history, concept, and syntax

Article 7 of the Constitution was not born with the current categories of classification. The former Article 8 of the Constitutional Draft in 1936 plainly declared that "[a]ll citizens of the ROC are equal before the law." Yet, in the discussions of the Constituent Committee, equality, regardless of gender, race, religion, social class, and profession before the law, had been recognized as one of the *25 Guidelines for Founding the State*, and some categories of social classification had been acknowledged by the Committee. At that time, equality before the law was understood in a formal way, according to which the possession of the same legal treatments, rights, and duties was guaranteed.[15]

[9] Constitutional Interpretation No 485 (1999).

[10] Constitutional Interpretation No 542 (2002).

[11] Constitutional Interpretation No 618 (2006).

[12] Constitutional Interpretations No 626 (2007); 649 (2008).

[13] Constitutional Interpretations Nos 205 (1986); 341 (1994); 405 (1996); 412 (1996); 455 (1998); 526 (2001); 575 (2004); 605 (2005); 614 (2006); 682 (2010); 764 (2018); 768 (2018).

[14] Tay-Sheng Wang, "The Legal Development of Taiwan in the 20th Century: Toward a Liberal and Democratic Country" 11 Pacific Rim Law & Policy Journal 531, 533.

[15] The Advertising Committee for the Constitutional Draft of ROC (1940) 5, 12.

The criterion of profession in Article 8 of the Constitutional Draft in 1936 was removed and replaced by political affiliation in the Constitutional Draft from 1946, which can be considered as a concession of the weakening ruling party, the KMT, to the rising Chinese Communist Party (the CCP) during the political negotiations.[16] The turbulent history of constitutional development made the textual content of the Constitution full of strategic calculations and the constitutional interpretation was hardly based on a systematic thought. Besides, the understanding of equality was based on the political discourses of the revolutionist and state founder Sun Yet-Sen,[17] whose political ideology was inspired by the slogan of the French Revolution: "Liberté, Égalité, Fraternité." Specifying the text of Article 7 relied therefore mainly on the academic discourses and the constitutional jurisprudence.

3. Doctrine of equality in academic discourses

In the legal literature, there are two approaches to equal protection led by scholars with different academic backgrounds. The first one is led by scholars with a German educational background who introduced German legal thinking. This concerned in particular the concept of the prohibition of arbitrariness (*Willkürverbot*) adopted by the German Federal Constitutional Court (GFCC) in the 1950s[18] and the new functional formula adopted the GFCC[19] in the 1980s.[20] The extent of legislative discretion and the corresponding scale of judicial deference were the major issues when assessing the constitutionality of differential measures. According to this point of view, the Constitutional Court should differentiate the legislative statutes and executive action and apply different intensities of scrutiny because the legislative power is considered the core power of representative democracy, whose decisions in the form of codified statues have the strongest political support. By contrast, executive measures derive their authority from codified statutes, and their scope of application should be constrained by the rule of law and a stricter application of proportionality.[21]

A different perspective was introduced by scholars with a US educational background. This group of scholars criticized the vagueness and formalization of the

16 Yueh-Sheng Weng, "Interpretations of the Constitutional Court and the Developments of Rule of Law and Democratic Constitutionalism in Taiwan" in Dirk Ehlers, Henning Glaser, and Kittisak Prokati (eds), *Constitutionalism and Good Governance: Eastern and Western Perspectives* (Nomos 2014) 322.

17 The Advertising Committee for the Constitutional Draft of ROC (1940) 5, 12.

18 BVerfGE 1, 14.

19 BVerfGE 55, 72.

20 Chen (n 2) 160–61.

21 Ai-Er Chen, "Equality as the Discretionary Limit of Social Benefit—Comments on the Concerning Constitutional Interpretations" (2007) 32 The Constitutional Review 259, 268–80.

concept of "equality before the law (*Gleichheit vor dem Gesetz*)," and focused on the promotion of equality of disadvantaged groups in society.[22] In addition to the concept of suspect classification, scholars with a US educational background also introduced the concept of indirect discrimination and the three-tiered scrutiny model developed by the US Constitutional Court in order to replace the examination of proportionality.[23]

From the point of view of scholars with a US background, the concept of equality has a dual character: on the one hand equality and freedoms are recognized as two kinds of subjective rights different in nature; on the other hand, the test for equal protection should be different from the test of proportionality deduced from Article 23 of the Constitution. The latter was widely applied in the examination of intervention of freedom to the extent that "[t]he intervention of the listed rights of freedom could be justified only if the necessity for preventing obstacles of other freedoms or avoiding emergency, maintaining social order or promoting public welfare is proved." The formal definition of equality inherited from Aristotle that "like cases [should be] treated alike" was therefore considered as a parallel doctrine to proportionality. In the literature, the differences between equality and proportionality are summarized in that equality focuses on *which* subjects are differentiated, while proportionality focuses on *how* the subjects are treated.[24]

The philosophical difference between formal and substantive equality is often considered essential for the understanding of equality,[25] but these opposite concepts are also criticized for being too vague for legal reasoning. Instead, the philosophical distinction between formal and substantive equality rarely sheds light on the extent of equal protection in jurisdiction.[26]

In the following analysis, I will show that the Constitutional Court of Taiwan has developed a modified doctrine for equal protection, a doctrine that can be qualified as being mixed, combining elements of proportionality with tiered scrutiny, regardless of the theoretical differences between equality and liberty and the separate doctrinal approaches advocated by some scholars.

[22] Yuan-Hao Liao, "Substantive Equality" (2005) 27 Taiwan Jurist 37, 39–40; Liao (n 1) 52.

[23] Jau-Yuan Hwang, "Evolution of Equality Theory and Difficulties Concerning the Constitutional Application of the Conception of Substantive Equality" in Fu-Te Liao (ed), *Constitutional Interpretation: Theory and Practice, Vol 9* (Academic Sinica 2017) 271, 275–78.

[24] Jau-Yuan Hwang, "Choosing the Standards of Scrutiny for the Equality Right Cases: Questioning the Applicability of the Proportionality Principle" (2008) 37 National Taiwan University Law Journal 270.

[25] Chien-Liang Lee, "Introduction: Constitutionalism and Human Rights—From Ideas to Implementation" in Chien-Liang Lee (ed), *Constitutional Interpretation: Theory and Practice, Vol 9* (Academia Sinica 2017) 1, 65. This difference between formal and substantive equality was firstly mentioned in the concurring opinion of (the former) Grand Justice Tzu-Yi Lin for the Constitutional Interpretation No 571 (2004) and advocated by scholars with the US academic training experiences led by Jau-Yuan Hwang at the beginning and Yuan-Hao Liao afterwards.

[26] Lee (n 25) 76–77.

4. Empirical analysis of Article 7 of the Constitution

4.1 Research method and sampling

The empirical analysis is based on a review of all Constitutional Interpretations related to Article 7 of the Constitution before the end of 2021. All analyzed cases are published on the official website of the Taiwanese Constitutional Court[27] and were filtered by a keyword search. The two terms "Art. 7 of the Constitution" and "Equality" were searched on separately in order to compare the results and supplement them with each other. Since the arguments in the early interpretations were often simplified and the referred articles were sometimes not clearly quoted, the parallel searches ensured that all equality-related cases were found. After sampling the corresponding interpretations, all cases were manually analyzed and coded according to the general criteria developed for the project. This multi-criteria approach ensures that all analyzed Constitutional Interpretations are related to the issue of equal protection since the derivative terms of equality such as equal and equally are frequently used as modifiers in sentences and grammatically undifferentiated in Chinese.

The determination of the coding strategy is challenging, especially when the textual understanding of Article 7 of the Constitution is, as mentioned, not well integrated in Taiwan. Although Article 7 of the Constitution is understood as a general clause with exemplified categories, the selection of exemplified categories still reveals the social cognition of the members of the Constituent Committee at that time, something that should not be neglected. Furthermore, the extent of suspect classifications is controversial. A typical criticism raised is that the differentiation of political affiliation is incompatible with the general understanding of suspect criteria in a comparative perspective. However, the memberships of political parties were a result of social classification, considering the tension between the capitalist KMT and the proletariat CCP. Consequently, the differentiation according to political affiliation can also be considered as a subtype of social class difference and therefore be understood in a broader sense; that is, that the different treatment based on social class as exemplary by political affiliation should be prohibited. Besides the critique of the incompatibility of exemplified classifications with suspect criteria, the insufficient number of examples are also a key argument to support the exemplified character of Article 7 of the Constitution only covering a limited number of suspect criteria, while many conceivable suspect criteria such as skin color, age, nationality, physical conditions, and marital status etc are not mentioned. However, once the concept of suspect criteria is understood as a dynamic concept, defined by social context, the criteria necessarily have to be specified

[27] <https://cons.judicial.gov.tw/en/index.aspx> accessed January 20, 2025.

by judicial interpretations to some extent. A classic example is the broadening of the understanding of gender equality from physical to psychological, including sexual equality. From this point of view, the specified criteria of Article 7 of the Constitution comprise an incomplete list of suspect criteria.

This leaves the Court with the problem of how to identify the sources of unwritten suspect criteria. The first source is the groups mentioned in sections 6, 7, 11, and 12 of the tenth additional article: women, disabled people, indigenous people, and people residing in outlying island areas. Although the norms themselves lack strong normative effect, all these groups of people share the common characteristics of social vulnerability and thus make concrete the exemplified categories of Article 7 of the Constitution. Women are specified to be the weaker group of the two genders. At the same time, the status of indigenous people is the main source of racial difference in Taiwan, and the gap in standards of living between residents in the outlying island areas and in the main island Taiwan can lead to inequality. We can therefore assume that at least two new differentiating bases—disability and residence in remote areas—should be taken into consideration when equality is discussed at the constitutional level.

The second source of suspect criteria is international conventions relevant to equal protection and anti-discrimination. Despite the obscured political status and international recognition of Taiwan, some international conventions have been voluntarily adopted through domestic statutes. This concerns, in particular, the Act to Implement the International Covenant on Civil and Political Rights (ICCPR) and the International Covenant on Economic, Social and Cultural Rights (ICESCR), which took effect on December 10, 2009, according to which the human rights guarantees of the ICCPR and the ICESCR have equivalent effect as domestic law (Article 2) and human rights protection should be practiced by all levels of public authority (Article 4). The Act also prescribes that the interpretations of the two Conventions by the Committee on Economic, Social and Cultural Rights (CESCR) and the Human Rights Committee of the UN should be respected (Article 3). Another case is the Enforcement Act of Convention on the Elimination of All Forms of Discrimination against Women (CEDAW), which took effect on January 1, 2012 which applies the same legislative technic.

The voluntary adoption of international conventions justifies the heightened protection of vulnerable groups suffering discrimination based on skin color, language, public opinions, national or social origin, property, and birth, as depicted in the ICESCR (Article 2(2)). Hence, different treatments on the basis of exemplified categories in Article 7, sections 6, 7, 11, and 12 of the tenth additional article of the Constitution and the implied categories in the three Conventions—ICCPR, ICESCR, and CEDAW—will be coded as judgments involving suspect criteria. This concerns, in particular, distinctions based on sex (gender in broad sense), religion, race (skin color as a typical example), class (social origin, marital status),

Table 15.1 Correlation between classificatory criteria and result of judicial review

Classificatory Criteria	Total judgments	Successful judgments	Success rate
Non-Suspect classification	60	16	26.67%
Suspect classifications (all)	28	13	46.43%
Sex (Gender)	8	7	87.5%
Political affiliation	4	1	25%
Nationality	4	0	0%
Disability	3	2	66.7%
Religion	3	1	33.3%
Social class (Marriage)	2	1	50%
Residential area	2	0	0%
Age	1	1	100%
Race (Skin color)	1	0	0%
Total	88	29	32.95%

political affiliation, languages, residential area, public opinion, national origin (nationality), property, and birth.

4.2 Results

As seen in Table 15.1, the total number of cases analyzed was 88 Constitutional Interpretations. In 65 of these (73.86%), statutes were examined, while only 23 cases (26.14%) concerned executive acts. The Court declared the impugned measures unconstitutional in 29 cases, which amounts to an overall success rate of 32.95%. Of the successful cases, 26 concerned the unconstitutionality of statutes (success rate of 40%), while only 3 successful decisions were directed against unconstitutional executive acts (success rate of 13.04%). The overwhelming number of judicial reviews of statutes is the first visible character of the judicial practice of the Taiwan Constitutional Court. It can be explained by the procedural factors: The old Constitutional Court Procedure Act only allowed for judicial review of statutes. The extension of constitutional review to executive acts has remained rare and controversial. Analyzing the success rates, we can observe a significant difference regarding cases involving suspect classifications and those that did not. In the 28 cases involving a suspect classification, slightly less than half of the challenges succeeded (success rate of 46.43%). By comparison, only about a quarter of the 60 cases without suspect classification were successful (success rate of 26.67%).

4.3 Features of equal protection in Taiwan's constitutional jurisdiction

Yueh-Sheng Weng, the former president of the Judicial Yuan from 2003 to 2007 and Grand Justice of the Constitutional Court from 1972 to 2007, once highlighted the characteristic features of the constitutional jurisprudence in Taiwan. Focusing on the contribution to the development of democratic constitutionalism, Weng divided the Constitutional Interpretations before the end of 2010 into six chronological phases. In each phase, the Court functioned differently and the influence of the constitutional interpretations gradually grew.[28] Weng pointed to specific historical events to delimit the different phases. The first were the abolishment of martial law on July 14, 1987 and the termination of the Period of Mobilization for Suppressing the Communist Rebellions (the status of emergency) on May 1, 1991. Subsequently, the function of judicial power became normalized, and the Court started emphasizing the protection of human rights.[29] The second event were the continuous amendments of the Grand Justices Council Adjudication Act. As a result, the judicial independence was strengthened and the procedural requirements for constitutional adjudication were liberalized.[30] The amendments also changed the appointment of the Grand Justices to the Constitutional Court. Consequently, the geographic ancestral origins of the candidates were no longer taken into consideration.[31] Weng also indicated that the indirect influence of the German jurisprudence that can be observed after 2003 was due to the fact that more than half of the Grand Justices had obtained their PhD degrees (seven seats) or carried out short-term research stays in Germany (two seats). Yet, the number of the Grand Justices with a US educational background was only slightly lower (six seats).[32]

It is interesting to note that the (Chinese) migration background has lost its influence on the internal differences in the Court over time, as the Chinese immigrant jurists were continuously replaced by new generations. Since the sixth session (1994–2003) of the Court, the Grand Justices have overwhelmingly been domestic jurists who were born and received legal training in Taiwan. It can therefore be expected that the differences in legal opinions due to cognitive and political identities should reduce over the time. As a result, the jurisprudential education

28 Weng (n 16) 325–31.
29 ibid 327.
30 ibid 328.
31 ibid 328.
32 ibid 331.

in either Germany or the United States played an increasing role in explaining the changing attitude of the Court toward equal protection.

On the basis of this classification, we can observe that the doctrine for equal protection evolved over time. From the test of reasonableness applied in the early Constitutional Interpretations, the reception of the doctrine of proportionality in the late 1990s to the blended doctrine with tiered scrutiny in the early 21st century, the development of the equal protection doctrine can be divided into three stages.

4.4 Transforming doctrines of equal protection

4.4.1 From the 1980s to the 1990s: dominance of approach of reasonableness

Although the Court had noticed the rigidity of the general clause of equal protection and the necessity of a substantive understanding of Article 7 of the Constitutional Law between the early 1980s and mid-1990s, the early judgments were rarely based on coherent and persuasive argumentation. Although the Court referred to the purpose and necessity of the involved measures in some cases, the reasoning of the Court was oversimplified and inconsistent. In the landmark cases, the Court simply relied on a doctrine based on reasonableness. It emphasized the comparison between the existing social reality and factual necessity of a legal amendment and maintaining the differential treatment. The evaluation of this factual necessity was not based on evidential support but merely on the intuition of the judges.

This form of legal argumentation contributed to the general understanding of equality. For example, the Court argued that "Article 7 of the Constitution does not prohibit differential legal treatment if the legal differentiation is reasonable."[33] Furthermore, it claimed that "[t]he pursued equality of the Court was substantial equality, which means that the purpose and factual necessity justify the differential treatment as long as it is appropriate/reasonable."[34] These doctrinal formulas were reiterated in most of the constitutional interpretations, but the two quotations also reveal an obscure understanding of formal and substantive equality by the Court. By developing the two vague concepts of "reasonable" and "appropriate," the Constitutional Court created a vague standard of judicial review. This led to legal uncertainty because the developed doctrine of equality did not give guidance on how to decide individual cases. As a result, the understanding of equality displayed in the early constitutional interpretations seems to be underdeveloped.[35]

33 Constitutional Interpretation No 179 (1983).
34 Constitutional Interpretations No 205 (1986); 211 (1986).
35 Weng (n 16) 95–96.

Classic examples are the early Constitutional Interpretations dealing with gender differentiation. In Constitutional Interpretation No 365, the Court declared that the (old) Article 1089 of the Civil Code, according to which the father's parental rights trumped the mother's if no consensus was reached, should be amended within two years since the traditional and historical context of the legislation had changed.[36] This conclusion was not supported by any empirical evidence regarding the extent of social changes. Instead, the Court made the decision after declaring an ambiguous justification for the gender differentiation: "The different treatment based on gender is constitutional in exceptional constellations, to which the treatment was justified due to the physical differences between males and females and the thereafter derivative functional roles of the gender in social life."[37] This criterion not only lacked logical connection to the conclusion of the judgment but it also constructed a controversial justification of gender differentiations based on physical condition and the corresponding social expectations.

4.4.2 Reception of doctrine of proportionality since 1990s

In Taiwan, the doctrine of proportionality was first introduced by the scholarly discussion in administrative law and afterwards prescribed in Article 7 of the Administrative Procedure Act as a multistage test composed of three subprinciples. According to this test, an administrative measure has to be appropriate, necessary, and reasonable.[38] In the constitutional jurisprudence, the doctrine was first mentioned in Constitutional Interpretation No 414 without substantial explanation. But in later decisions, the doctrine of proportionality was commonly applied as a tool of constitutional review concerning the potential infringement of human rights.

In the context of equal protection, the doctrine of proportionality was officially acknowledged as the leading approach in Constitutional Interpretation No 438, in which it was read into Article 23 of the Constitution. In this case, the challenged differentiation in the taxation of entrepreneurs based on the percentage of overseas commissions paid in domestic currency was considered to be proportionate and equal. Meanwhile, the purpose and necessity of different legal treatments due to the balance of interests discussed in the early reasonableness-based examinations did not vanish. As a result, the two tests served as parallel doctrines of constitutional review. However, the application of the two doctrines was irregular so that it is difficult to identify a clear pattern.

An interesting question is whether the introduction of the doctrine of proportionality led to a qualitative enhancement of equal protection. On the one hand, the number of constitutional interpretations increased dramatically in the 1990s,

[36] Constitutional Interpretation No 365 (1994).
[37] ibid.
[38] Weng (n 16) 340–41.

which indicates a higher level of judicial accessibility and an increased willingness of the Court to protect human rights.[39] On the other hand, the progress of the equal protection jurisprudence in this period is not only due to the introduction of the doctrine of proportionality. While the latter contributed to formulating legal arguments and enhancing the quality and predictability of decisions, it did not necessarily promote results in favor of socially disadvantaged individuals. Furthermore, proportionality was, at that time, predominantly applied in the context of liberty rights. In cases in which a preferential treatment was clearly identified, the Court preferred to resort to the traditional reasonableness approach. This concerns, *inter alia*, gender inequality. Two examples are the household registration rule in the old Civil Code, according to which the wife had to register at the place of her husband's habitual residence if the spouses did not agree on a different habitual residence,[40] or the limitation of the cession of veteran's land use rights to the veteran's male inheritor.[41] In both cases, the Court pointed out that gender differentiation was either incompatible with the social reality or irrelevant for the purpose of the impugned policy. When the equal protection of the minority and the personal freedoms of the majority conflict, the Court tends to rely exclusively on the proportionality test.[42] As a consequence, the proportionality test was merely a formalized test, which was mostly restricted to the early, superficial steps of examining the legislative purpose and necessity, but rarely touched the core element of proportionality: the balance of competing interests.

One typical example for this tendency is Constitutional Interpretation No 490, in which the compulsory military service for male citizens and the limited possibilities of exemption in the (old) Act of Military Service System were challenged. The applicant, a member of Jehovah's Witnesses, had complained about insufficient alternatives to military service. Nevertheless, the Court deemed the impugned measures to be justified because of the vital state interest of national security and the difference in physical capacity, which served to justify the gender differentiation and the restriction of freedoms of belief and religion.[43]

[39] Weng (n 16) 328.

[40] Constitutional Interpretation No 452 (1998).

[41] Constitutional Interpretation No 457 (1998).

[42] See Jau-Yuan Hwang, "Judicial Review of the Cases Involving Competing Claims of Equality and Liberty Rights: Comments on J.Y. Interpretation No 649" (2009) 7 Journal of New Perspectives on Law 17, 37–38 (criticizing that the Constitutional Court examined the constitutionality of prohibition by defining it as both an intervention to rights of profession of the public and a measure of equal protection for the vision-impaired people but applied different levels of scrutiny of constitutional review to the two dimensions. As a result, the stricter scrutiny of constitutional review applied to the intervention of rights of profession overruled the concern of equal protection, especially the necessity of affirmative action to social disadvantageous groups.); see Yuan-Hao Liao, "The Better Protected Lays in Comparison to the Visually Impaired Groups?—Critic on the Robust Constitutional Interpretation No 649 for the Obtuseness on Power Relations" (2009) 123 Taiwan Law Journal 187, 193 (criticizing the decision for its formal neutrality that the public's rights of freedom are better protected than the substantive equality of vision-impaired people).

[43] Constitutional Interpretation No 490 (1999).

The Court also applied the same logic to other cases. The 10-year duration of naturalization as additional qualification for public servants, which had been specified for migrants from mainland China, was ruled constitutional in order to guarantee the stability of democracy.[44] Furthermore, the enrollment policy of the Central Police University which excluded color-blind applicants was justified because the quality of police system was an important state interest and the legislative discretion had to be respected.[45] The (old) Article 37(1) of the Act for Protecting Rights of People with Physical and Mental Disabilities, according to which any person without visual impairment was prohibited from conducting a massage business, was, by contrast, ruled unconstitutional because of the disproportionate infringement of the freedom of profession. This finding rejected the affirmative action policy for visually impaired people as a justification.[46] In these judgments, the Court rarely paid attention to the legitimacy of the differential policy. Neither the classified criteria nor the indirect after-effect for the targeted groups were taken into consideration when the constitutionality of the impugned legal measures were examined. Instead, the Court tended to be deferential when any imaginable state interest existed. Even if the content of the state interest was ambiguous and not implied in the statutory text, the Court was deferential to the legislative power.

4.4.3 Tiers of scrutiny as supplement of proportionality since early 2000s

In the early 2000s, the Court started introducing an analysis of the appropriate tiers of constitutional scrutiny in most cases. There were two tiers of constitutional scrutiny prevalent in the Taiwanese constitutional jurisdiction. A case could either be examined through rational basis review or intermediate (also known as "the stricter") scrutiny, depending on the significance of the legal purpose and the social status of the claimants. Subsequently, the Court required different burdens of proof and justification. The simplified model echoed the three-tiered scrutiny model developed by the US Supreme Court and revealed a transformation of the constitutional jurisprudence. Since then, the doctrine of proportionality and the tiered scrutiny doctrine have merged in most Constitutional Interpretations. While the doctrine of proportionality provides the framework of legal argumentation, the tiered scrutiny of constitutional review functions as a sorting tool, roughly attributing the material findings and required burden of proof to two different levels in the constitutional jurisprudence.

The sorting criteria for the tiers is inspired by the concept of suspect criteria developed by the US constitutional jurisprudence.[47] The choice of the tier of scrutiny is—with few exceptions—largely decisive for the results of the judicial decisions. Generally speaking, if a different legal treatment is based on a suspect criterion

[44] Constitutional Interpretation No 618 (2006).
[45] Constitutional Interpretation No 626 (2007).
[46] Constitutional Interpretation No 649 (2008).
[47] See Chapter 2.

and if vulnerable groups of people are involved, the Court tends to adopt the intermediate level of scrutiny and imposes a higher burden of proof and justification. According to this heightened standard, the purpose of the impugned legal measure has to be linked to an important public interest and the legal effects should further an important public interest in substance. Based on this standard, the impugned statute is often declared unconstitutional and invalid.

The link between the concept of suspect criteria and intermediate scrutiny was finally made explicit in the recent Constitutional Interpretation No 807, while this correlation had not been clearly indicated in the past Constitutional Interpretations. In this case, the Court declared that Article 49(1) of the Labor Standards Act, which generally prohibited women from working at night unless the employer offered women exclusive safety and hygiene facilities, transportation services, or accommodation, was unconstitutional. The Court argued that these provisions were not only ineffective to lift the stereotype of gender difference and to promote health and safety cares of all workers regardless of genders but also irrelevant to fulfill concrete demands of individual female workers.[48] This argumentation, which emphasizes the motivation of the legislature and the symbolic effect for society, sheds light on the shifted attitude and argumentative strategy of the Court when the latter deals with the tension between the equal protection of the minority and the freedom of the majority. This tendency also explains why the prohibition to charge a fee to an international marriage agency in Article 58(2) of the Immigration Act was justified even though it restricted the freedom of contract because it contributed to preventing the objectification of immigrants for marriage.[49]

Gender equality is enduringly the most prevalent subject of equal protection. Although the Court rejected the challenge against Article 4(1) of the Act for the Ancestor Worship Guild in Constitutional Interpretation No 728 and acknowledged the constitutionality of the male-dominated membership of the ancestor worship guilds that had been established before the Act came into effect, this is the only case where a general concern of private autonomy and legal stability took precedence over gender equality. In other cases, in which statutes explicitly included gender differentiations (such as the patriarchal dominance of paternal custody, residence and marital property management in the old Civil Code),[50] the Court consistently considered them as violations of Article 7 of the Constitution. Similarly, the Court also found violations in cases of indirect discrimination where the gender differentiation was hidden behind a legal text that is on its face neutral, such as in the case of a partial administrative penalty imposed on prostitutes in the illegal sex service because of its *de facto* negative effect to the socio-economically disadvantaged female sex workers.[51]

[48] Constitutional Interpretation No 807 (2021).
[49] Constitutional Interpretation No 802 (2021).
[50] Constitutional Interpretations No 365 (1994); 410 (1996); 452 (1998).
[51] Constitutional Interpretation No 666 (2009).

However, while cases involving a suspect classification usually lead to a violation of Article 7, a differentiation is not *per se* justified if no suspect criterion is detected. In fact, many legal differentiations in the area of tax law were declared unconstitutional since the authority did not provide any reasonable explanation for the design of the tax base and the differential burdens on different groups of taxpayers.[52] In addition, the Court was willing to contribute to overturning the social structure and to instruct the legislature to make particular legal amendments when the applicants sought judicial remedies for sensitive political issues. A classic example is Constitutional Interpretation No 748, in which the Court extended the concept of gender equality to sexual orientation and held that the exclusive definition of marriage as an intimate community between one man and one woman given by the Civil Code constituted a violation of gender equality. The Court obliged the legislature to protect the homosexual right of marriage either by amending the Civil Code or by enacting a new specified statute within two years. This Constitutional Interpretation prompted the issuing of the Act for Implementation of Constitutional Interpretation No 748 announced on May 22, 2019, which allowed for same-sex marriage in substance.

Furthermore, Constitutional Interpretations No 791 and No 793 convey the impression of a politicized Constitutional Court. In the former judgment, the Court supported the decriminalization of adultery and annulled the (old) provision of section 239 of the Code of Criminal Procedure, according to which the married spouse of the adulterers could partially withdraw the application for criminal charges against his or her married spouse, while the application against the other adulterer remained. The preferential procedural effect of this provision on the spouse was, in the view of the Constitutional Court, not only ineffective to maintain the marriage but also used marital status as an irrelevant differentiating factor even though the offenders had committed the same crime. In Constitutional Interpretation No 793, the Court declared that the Act Governing the Settlement of Ill-gotten Properties by Political Parties and Their Affiliate Organizations and the compulsory clearing process of specified political parties, which really only affected the KMT and its affiliates, did not violate Article 7 of the Constitution because of the dominant political status of KMT in the past and the significance of transitional justice.

The chronological progress is summarized in Table 15.2. The periods mark different stages of development of the constitutional equality doctrine. The boundaries between these stages are delineated by the following landmark judgments: the Constitutional Interpretations No 179 in 1983 (the first judgment based on Article 7), No 438 in 1997 (the first judgment that adopted the proportionality test), and No 626 in 2007 (the first judgment that adopted the merged test).

Table 15.2 shows an increasing number of equality-related judgments, which indicates the willingness of the Court to address the issue of equality. Although the success

[52] Constitutional Interpretations No 722 (2014); 745 (2017); 779 (2019).

Table 15.2 Successful judgments in individual periods

	Period 1 1983–1996		Period 2 1997–2006		Period 3 2007–2021	
Number of Cases	11		32		45	
Violation of Article 7	Yes	No	Yes	No	Yes	No
	4	7	7	25	18	27
Success Rate	36.4%		21.9%		40%	

rate of equality challenges varies in each period, the success rate in the second period is lower than those in the other two periods. Furthermore, it seems that the success rate has increased from the second to the third period when the tiered scrutiny model was merged with the proportionality test.

4.5 Influential factors of the development of equal protection

It should be remembered that the chronological phases of constitutional jurisprudence discussed in the previous section cannot be neatly separated from each other, and the exact turning points between each period cannot be clearly identified. Rather, it is a progressive evolution. Deviant judgments with literary styles that differ significantly from the associated period inevitably exist. Furthermore, institutional factors such as the repeatedly modified length of tenure of the grand justices from nine to ten to the current eight years, the staggered sessions of the Court, and the anonymous majority opinions make a definitive explanation of the strategy of judicial policymaking difficult, but the political context still explains the changing judicial behaviors.

The most important factor is the democratization process that occurred from the late 1980s. From this period, the Court started to exercise judicial power independently instead of acting as a rubber stamp bestowing legitimacy on deficient executive measures and statutes in the martial law period. This move to judicial independence did not come easily and it prompted the Court to define itself as the guardian of human rights and constitutionalism against autocracy.[53] This characteristic is similar to many courts in young democratic countries.[54]

However, the Court's effectiveness in controlling the political branches was diminished before the ruling party in parliamentary and presidential elections changed. A fundamental reason is that the appointment of Grand Justices is based on the

[53] Weng (n 16) 326.

[54] The politicized tendency of the constitutional courts for the function to secure the unstable institutional structures and human rights protection in young democracies. See Martin Schulz, "Verfassungsgerichtsbarkeit im globalen Kontext" (GIGA Focus Global Working Paper 2010) <https://nbn-resolving.org/urn:nbn:de:0168-ssoar-276766> accessed January 20, 2025.

president's nomination and parliamentary confirmation. Consequently, the political preferences of the President and the parliamentary majority play a decisive role with regards to the composition of the Court. Generally, the Court focused more on technical issues such as tax legislation during the period of the KMT regime, while the Court was bolder in the period of the Democratic Progressive Party government, taking on more political issues and rendering legal opinions on highly controversial issues.

The self-identification as a progressive political actor turns the Constitutional Court, to some extent, into a supplementary legislature to correct legislative omissions. This was acknowledged in a speech of the current president of the Judicial Yuan, Tzong-Li Hsu in 2017. In his speech, Hsu claimed that political engagement of the Constitutional Court was acceptable according to comparative legal studies and was justified by the supplementary nature and the self-restraint of judicial power in individual procedures.[55]

Historical and political factors alone are not sufficient explanations. Rather, the personal perspectives of the Grand Justices have been a second influential factor. The recent paradigm shift from proportionality to the mixed model with tiered scrutiny reveals the increasing influence of Anglo-American jurisprudence since the number of Grand Justices with a US educational background has increased and matched those with a European educational background.

This diversity of educational backgrounds is a double-edged sword for Taiwanese jurisprudence. On the one hand, the introduction of legal concepts from Europe and the United States has brought new awareness of social phenomena and improved the quality of constitutional review. On the other hand, the diverse academic perspectives from different legal cultures also complicate the discussion and increase the risk of losing focus. This results in variable argumentative techniques and inconsistent results in constitutional adjudication, which also limit the pooling size of our sample judgements. Once the major opinion defines a fact as the application of freedom, the judgment will be decided by different considerations from equality and therefore be omitted by our research framework, even though it could possibly be deemed as a case of equal protection in substance.

5. Conclusion

Overall, the case law of the Taiwanese Constitutional Court largely follows the equality as reasonableness model. While the success rate for suspect classifications is higher than the success rate for non-suspect classifications, the latter is still significant. Furthermore, the total number of successful cases is slightly higher

[55] Tzong-Li Hsu, "Taiwan Constitutional Court as a Positive Legislator" (2019) 25 Academia Sinica Law Journal 1, 29–33.

for cases not involving a suspect classification than for those involving a suspect classification. This shows that the review in non-suspect classification cases goes beyond a mere subsidiary arbitrariness test. To the contrary, the pattern is quite similar to the pattern that we have observed in jurisdictions in continental Europe that follow the equality as reasonableness model.

It is interesting to note that the rather high success rate for cases not involving a suspect classification persists and even increases in the post-2007 era of the Court, after the introduction of a bifurcated, tiered standard of review. In this period, the success rate of cases not involving a suspect classification amounted to 35.48% (11 out of 31 cases), while the success rate for cases involving a suspect classification was slightly higher at 46.67% (7 out of 15 cases).

Furthermore, the Taiwanese approach to equal protection is influenced by multiple factors, such as the domestic political situation in Taiwan and the personalities of the Grand Justices affected by their individual life experiences, especially their academic training in Germany and the United States. In particular, the German influence might explain the high success rate of cases not involving a suspect classification.

An important legal reform is the new Act of Constitutional Adjudication, which entered into full force on January 4, 2022. Besides reorganizing the Constitutional Court from the joint Committee of the Grand Justices and renaming the decisions from constitutional interpretation to constitutional judgement in order to emphasize the judicial nature of constitutional adjudication, the main substantial adjustment of the new Act is the introduction of the individual complaint procedure (*Verfassungsbeschwerde*), modeled after the German constitutional jurisdiction.[56] This newly implemented constitutional remedy in Taiwan is likely to focus more on the protection of individual subjective rights, instead of examining the textual compatibility of subordinated norms to constitutional law.[57]

[56] See the comparative table of the old and new acts and the illustrations, especially point 1 (for the renaming reason) and point 3 of art 1 of the new act (for the revision of constitutional procedures).

[57] A brief introduction of the old Taiwanese constitutional procedures in comparison to the German constitutional procedures and the critics of the insufficient protection of subjective rights of the old mechanism of constitutional complaints. See Tzu-Hui Yang, "Der taiwanesische Verfassungsprozess im Lichte richterlicher Rechtsfortbildung" (2009) 57 Jahrbuch des öffentlichen Rechts der Gegenwart 711, 719–20.

16
New Zealand

Niels Petersen

1. Introduction

The New Zealand Bill of Rights Act (NZBORA) was enacted in 1990 after the tenure of former Prime Minister Robert Muldoon had exposed the brittleness of the informal constitutional arrangements in New Zealand.[1] The Bill of Rights Act is an example of weak-form judicial review.[2] It does not give courts the power to strike down legislation.[3] The Courts can only interpret statutes in conformity with the constitution[4] or issue a declaration of inconsistency.[5] The NZBORA does not contain a general equality provision. However, it has a non-discrimination guarantee in section 19 NZBORA, according to which "[e]veryone has the right to freedom from discrimination." For the grounds of discrimination, the provision refers to section 21 of the Human Rights Act (HRA). The latter contains an extensive list of prohibited grounds, including sex, religious belief, race, age, and sexual orientation. However, unlike in most human rights documents, the list is not indicative but exhaustive. By establishing an exhaustive list of grounds of discrimination, the drafters of the Bill of Rights sought to limit judicial power.[6]

Our analysis will focus on the case law of the Court of Appeal and the Supreme Court regarding the interpretation of section 19 NZBORA. However, even if we

[1] Claudia Geiringer, "When Constitutional Theories Migrate: A Case Study" (2019) 67 AJCL 281, 292.

[2] On the concept, see Mark Tushnet, "Alternative Forms of Judicial Review" (2003) 101 Michigan LR 2781; Mark Tushnet, *Weak Courts, Strong Rights: Judicial Review and Social Welfare Rights in Comparative Constitutional Law* (Princeton University Press 2008); Rosalind Dixon, "The Core Case for Weak-Form Judicial Review" (2017) 38 Cardozo LR 2193. On the related concept of Commonwealth Constitutionalism, which also implies some form of weak-form judicial review, see Stephen Gardbaum, "The New Commonwealth Model of Constitutionalism" (2001) 49 AJCL 707; Stephen Gardbaum, *The New Commonwealth Model of Constitutionalism* (CUP 2013). For a defense of the New Zealand approach, see Grant Huscroft and Paul Rishworth, "'You Say You Want a Revolution': Bills of Rights in the Age of Human Rights" in David Dyzenhaus, Murray Hunt, and Grant Huscroft (eds), *A Simple Common Lawyer: Essays in Honour of Michael Taggart* (Hart Publishing 2009) 123.

[3] S 4 NZBORA.

[4] S 6 NZBORA.

[5] *Attorney-General v Arthur William Taylor* [2018] NZSC 104.

[6] Grant Huscroft, "Freedom from Discrimination" in Paul Rishworth and others (eds), *The New Zealand Bill of Rights* (OUP 2003) 366, 367; Geiringer (n 1) 313.

Niels Petersen, *New Zealand* In: *Equality's Guardians*. Edited by: Niels Petersen, Oxford University Press.
 DOI: 10.1093/9780198961109.003.0016

look at both courts, we find very few cases.[7] In the following, we will first look at the doctrine that the New Zealand courts have established to operationalize the non-discrimination guarantee of the Bill of Rights Act (Section 2). Then, we will turn to our empirical analysis that provides a systematic analysis of all non-discrimination cases that were decided by the Court of Appeal or the Supreme Court under section 19 NZBORA (Section 3). The analysis will show that New Zealand courts follow an equality as non-discrimination model. The following section will explain this result, arguing that the observation is mostly due to the particular norm structure of the NZBORA (Section 4). The final section (5) concludes.

2. The equality doctrine of the New Zealand courts

In the landmark case of *Atkinson*, the Court of Appeal established that the non-discrimination analysis under the NZBORA consists of three steps.[8] First, the court has to establish whether there is "differential treatment between groups or persons . . . in . . . comparable situations on the basis of a prohibited ground of discrimination."[9] Second, the analysis turns to whether this differential treatment has a discriminatory impact.[10] Third, the court analyzes whether the discrimination can be justified under section 5 NZBORA.[11]

The main emphasis of the first step often lies in finding the right comparator group to the applicant claiming discrimination.[12] For example, the judgment in *Atkinson* contained a lengthy discussion of the comparator group. The case concerned a policy regarding the care of disabled children. The state only paid for this care if the parents were not able or willing to provide it and it was provided by professional caregivers instead. However, if parents provided the care themselves, they were not compensated. The Court argued that the parents had to be compared to the professional caregivers who were compensated so that the non-compensation resulted in a difference in treatment based on family status, which is a prohibited ground in section 21 HRA.[13] In other cases, the Court of Appeal has denied the comparability of the groups put forward by the applicant. For example, in *GB as Executor of the Estate of EB of Whangarei*, the Court argued that a married couple

[7] See also Andrew Butler and Petra Butler, *The New Zealand Bill of Rights Act: A Commentary* (2nd edn, LexisNexis NZ 2015) para 17.9.22.
[8] *Ministry of Health v Atkinson* [2012] NZCA 184, para 55.
[9] ibid para 55.
[10] ibid.
[11] ibid para 143.
[12] On this issue, see Butler and Butler (n 7) para 17.10. For a critique of the courts' comparator approach, see Asher Gabriel Emanuel, "To Whom Will Ye Liken Me, and Make Me Equal? Reformulating the Role of the Comparator in the Identification of Discrimination" (2014) 45 Victoria University of Wellington LR 1.
[13] *Atkinson* (n 8) paras 60–74.

was not in a comparable position to a single person when it came to making wealth assessment deductions.[14]

The second step focuses on discriminatory impact. The Court of Appeal argues that a differential treatment has a discriminatory impact if it "imposes a material disadvantage on the person or group differentiated against."[15] The Court rejects a "material" disadvantage if the disadvantage suffered by a group is only minor or "trivial."[16] The application of this test is usually straightforward, and there are few cases in which the courts have denied material disadvantage. One exception is the case of *Ngaronoa*.[17] The applicants in that case argued that a voting ban for prisoners constituted an indirect racial discrimination because Māori individuals were vastly overrepresented in the prisoner population. The Court of Appeal rejected this argument. It held that if one compared the Māori voting population to the general voting population, the disadvantage caused by the voting ban was immaterial:

> However, in terms of the overall number of voters, the difference is not significant. Less than one percent of either group, Māori or non-Māori, is in prison. Therefore, the impact of the prohibition on Māori as a group, affecting as it does less than one percent, is so small that there is no material disadvantage to Māori resulting from the enactment of s80(1)(d).[18]

The final step is the justification analysis under section 5 NZBORA. The New Zealand courts usually apply a proportionality test in the justification analysis.[19] In *Atkinson*, the Court of Appeal confirmed this approach also with regards to the non-discrimination guarantee.[20] There are several cases in which the courts found a differential treatment with a discriminatory impact but nevertheless deemed the measure to be justified.[21] A recent discussion of the justification analysis can be found in the Supreme Court decision in *Make It 16*.[22] The case concerned the question of whether a minimum voting age of 18 years was a proportionate restriction of the prohibition of age discrimination. The Supreme Court argued that the restriction was disproportionate because the Attorney-General had not offered a justification for the restriction, beyond arguing that the latter was justified because it was within the "range of reasonable alternatives."[23] Furthermore, the available

[14] *GB as Executor of the Estate of EB of Whangarei v the Chief Executive of the Ministry of Social Development* [2013] NZCA 410, para 39.
[15] *Atkinson* (n 8) para 55.
[16] ibid para 136.
[17] *Ngaronoa v Attorney-General* [2017] NZCA 351.
[18] ibid para 148.
[19] *Hansen v R* [2007] NZSC 7, para 104.
[20] *Atkinson* (n 8) para 143.
[21] See eg *Melanie Trevethick v Ministry of Health* [2008] NZCA 397; *Child Poverty Action Group (CPAG) v Attorney-General* [2013] NCZA 402.
[22] *Make It 16 Inc v Attorney-General* [2022] NZSC 134.
[23] ibid para 43.

evidence indicated that individuals of 16 years of age did not lack the maturity to vote.[24]

Although the concept of indirect discrimination has been recognized by section 65 HRA, the New Zealand courts have not developed a specific approach to indirect discrimination or disparate impact claims in the context of section 19 NZBORA. While they do not deny the possibility of indirect discrimination in principle, it appears that they do not make a doctrinal difference between direct and indirect discrimination claims. If one wants to find an implicit doctrinal difference, it seems that the requirement of "material disadvantage" is most relevant in indirect discrimination cases. It is difficult to imagine direct discrimination cases where the courts find a disadvantage but deny the "material" character of the disadvantage. However, in indirect discrimination cases, it is conceivable that disadvantages of a particular group are deemed immaterial by the Court. The most salient example is the already mentioned *Ngaronoa* case, which dealt with the question of whether a voting ban for prisoners constituted an indirect discrimination of Māoris.[25] As discussed, the Court argued that the disadvantage suffered by Māoris was immaterial because prisoners only formed a small proportion of the Māori voting population.[26]

The lack of distinction between direct and indirect discrimination may sometimes lead the courts to treat the challenge posed by disparate impact cases rather superficially.[27] For example, the applicant in *B v Waitemata District Health Board* had argued that a smoking ban policy in a healthcare institution imposed an indirect discrimination based on disability because patients in intensive care units (ICUs) were not allowed to leave the grounds and thus were unable to smoke.[28] The Supreme Court rejected this argument because the smoking ban was a "neutral rule" and the negative impact was caused by a different, "legitimate" policy that confined the applicant in the ICU.[29] While the smoking ban itself was certainly neutral, it definitely had a disparate impact on individuals who were restricted to ICUs. The appropriate place to discuss the issue would have been the justification analysis. In other cases, the Court of Appeal refused to recognize a discrimination in disparate impact cases because of the wide-reaching consequences that such a finding would have for the institution in question.[30] For example in *Ngaronoa*, the Court argued that finding in favor of an indirect discrimination would open up all sorts of follow-up issues because it would concern all prison-related disadvantages.[31] Furthermore, Māori were not the only group overrepresented in the

[24] ibid paras 52–57.
[25] *Ngaronoa* (n 17).
[26] See n 17 and accompanying text.
[27] See Huscroft (n 6) 387–88 (discussing the case of *Lal v Residence Appeal Authority*).
[28] *B (SC 60/2016) v Waitemata District Health Board* [2017] NZSC 88.
[29] ibid para 99.
[30] See eg *Hester and Others v Commissioner of Inland Revenue* [2005] NZLR 172, para 106; *Ngaronoa* (n 17) para 138.
[31] ibid para 138.

prisoners' population. This was also true for young persons and males—indicating indirect discrimination based on age and sex.[32] Again, this argument does not deny the existence of a disparate impact but it would have been more appropriate to discuss this in the justification analysis.

3. Empirical analysis of the equality case law

3.1 Generating and analyzing the sample

The empirical analysis focused on decisions of the New Zealand Court of Appeal and the New Zealand Supreme Court regarding the antidiscrimination provision in section 19 of the New Zealand Bill of Rights until the end of August 2023. It did not include antidiscrimination claims that were brought under other statutes, such as the Employment Relations Act or the HRA. The sampling strategy thus excluded some important non-discrimination cases, such as *McAlister*, a case brought by an Air New Zealand pilot based on age discrimination.[33] However, it is consistent with the research design for the other analyzed jurisdictions, which limited the analysis to constitutional equality provisions. The sample for the empirical research was generated through a search in the Westlaw NZ database. It included all cases of the New Zealand Court of Appeal and the New Zealand Supreme Court. The search term was "19" in the same sentence as "NZBORA" or "Bill of Rights." This search generated slightly more than 50 hits. The sample then had to be cleaned manually because many cases did not include a substantive discussion of section 19 NZBORA but only mentioned the provision in passing or in a footnote. Furthermore, I also excluded cases in which the deciding court left open the question of whether section 19 was violated.[34] Finally, if a case was decided in substance both by the Court of Appeal and the Supreme Court, only the Supreme Court decision was analyzed to avoid double-counting. The final sample contained 14 cases. Eleven of these cases were decided by the Court of Appeal and three by the Supreme Court. The first case in the sample is *Quilter v Attorney-General* on the prohibition of same-sex marriage from July 29, 1994.[35] The last case is *Make It 16 Inc. v Attorney-General* on the minimum voting age from November 21, 2022.[36]

32 ibid.
33 *McAlister v Air New Zealand Ltd* [2009] NZSC 78.
34 See eg *Kearns v R* [2017] NZCA 51.
35 *Quilter v Attorney-General* [1998] 1 NZLR 523.
36 *Make It 16* (n 22).

3.2 The results of the analysis

The overall sample only contains two successful cases—1 case, which formally found a discrimination based on family status, involving parents caring for their disabled children,[37] and 1 case finding that establishing a minimum voting age at 18 years constituted age discrimination for children of at least 16 years of age.[38] The first successful case was *Atkinson*, where the Court of Appeal had to deal with a policy that did not pay parental caregivers who cared for their disabled children, while it provided funds for a professional caregiver if family members were not willing or able to provide adequate care.[39] The Court argued that this policy discriminated based on family status and that this discrimination was not justified.

The decision was criticized in the literature because it found a discrimination based on a characteristic that cannot be truly described as suspect.[40] Even if family status is explicitly mentioned in section 21(1) lit. l HRA, there is no history of discrimination against the core family which would make the latter a vulnerable group. If at all, family status can only be regarded as a suspect characteristic if the individuals targeted by a measure do not belong to a traditional family, such as, for example, when measures are aimed at extramarital children. However, Janet McLean has pointed out that there is a different issue lurking in the background in *Atkinson*, which was not addressed directly by the Court of Appeal.[41] This is the issue of disability. If the real problem was, as McLean suggests, a chronic underfunding of the disability assistance scheme, then the non-payment of parental caregivers could instead be classified as an indirect discrimination based on disability.[42]

The second successful decision, *Make It 16*, concerned a challenge of the minimum voting age of 18 years in New Zealand.[43] The Supreme Court found that there was indeed a differentiation based on age and that this differentiation could not be justified.[44] There was one specificity in the normative material of New Zealand human rights law that might have guided some of the considerations in this case: section 21(1) lit. I HRA prohibits discrimination based on age commencing with the age of 16 years. Therefore, the Supreme Court did not have to enter into the difficult discussion of where effectively to draw the line.

[37] *Atkinson* (n 8).
[38] *Make It 16* (n 22).
[39] *Atkinson* (n 8).
[40] Julia Adams, "Breaking the Constitution: Discrimination Law, Judicial Overreach and Executive Backlash After *Ministry of Health v. Atkinson*" (2016) 2016 NZLR 255, 266.
[41] Janet McLean at a lecture honoring Nicholas Smith's book *Basic Equality and Discrimination* (Routledge 2011) (unpublished manuscript, on file with the author).
[42] ibid.
[43] *Make It 16* (n 22).
[44] ibid. See also n 22–24 and accompanying text.

Yet, most of the discrimination cases that came to the Court of Appeal and the Supreme Court under section 19 NZBORA were unsuccessful. A couple of them concerned non-suspect characteristics. In *R v King*, the applicants had claimed that they were discriminated based on their criminal history. But the Court of Appeal dryly rejected the claim, arguing that "discrimination on the basis of criminal history is not a listed ground."[45] Similarly, the Court of Appeal did not accept a discrimination claim in *Audrey Bredmeyer*, in which the applicant faced more stringent requirements for claiming certain social benefits because she was an Australian resident. The Court rejected the claim, noting that "residence" was not a ground of discrimination "in terms of s 19 of the Bill of Rights."[46]

Half of the unsuccessful cases concerned indirect discrimination claims.[47] In some of these, the courts did not find sufficient evidence for an indirect discrimination. For example, in *R v McMillan*, the defendant claimed that he had received a heavier sentence for sexual abuse of minors because one of his victims was male. The Court of Appeal swiftly rejected this argument: "There is no evidence to support the contention that Mr. McMillan's sentence was heavier because one of his victims was male."[48]

Other cases involved more complicated issues. In the already mentioned case of *Ngaronoa*, the Court of Appeal rejected the claim that a voting ban on prisoners constituted indirect racial discrimination against Māoris due to the latter's overrepresentation in the prisoners' population.[49] The case of *Trevethick* involved a claim regarding indirect discrimination based on disability.[50] The applicant had converted her car because of a disability that she had due to an illness. She argued that the costs of converting her car would have been reimbursed under New Zealand Accident Compensation scheme (ACC) if her disability had been caused by an accident. In essence, the applicant claimed an extension of positive state benefits that existed in other domains to her situation. However, the Court rejected this claim and argued that the differentiation was justified.[51] The ACC had been established to pre-empt private compensation claims for torts. Therefore, it was a legitimate policy choice not to extend all the benefits of this scheme to the general health insurance system because it only provided individuals with what they would have received under tort law from the person responsible for the accident if the ACC did not exist.[52]

[45] *R v King* [2008] NZCA 79, para 36.
[46] *Audrey Bredmeyer v the Chief Executive of the Ministry of Social Development* [2008] NZCA 557, para 63.
[47] See *Lal v Residence Appeal Authority*, CA53/97 (1999) 5 HRNZ 11; *Hester* (n 30); *R v McMillan* [2007] NZCA 394; *Trevethick* (n 21); *Ngaronoa* (n 17); *B (SC 60/2016) v Waitemata District Health Board* [2017] NZSC 88.
[48] *McMillan* (n 47) para 41.
[49] *Ngaronoa* (n 17).
[50] *Trevethick* (n 21).
[51] ibid para 18.
[52] ibid.

Finally, there are four unsuccessful cases, which arguably involve a direct differentiation on a suspect characteristic. In *Quilter*, the Court of Appeal had to deal with the question of whether the prohibition of same-sex marriage constituted a discrimination based on sexual orientation.[53] The majority of the Court argued that the legislation did not constitute discrimination. The main obstacle to finding a discrimination seems to have been section 4 NZBORA, which bars courts from repealing a legislative provision if it is inconsistent with a guarantee of the Bill of Rights because all Justices agreed that it was the clear intention of the New Zealand legislature establishing the marriage act that marriage should only be open to heterosexual couples. Justice Keith argued that

> Parliament would not have effected such a major change to a fundamental institution in our society and legal system with a great number of consequential changes (where the law depends on marital status) in such an indirect way. Rather, to make such a change, Parliament would be expected to act in a direct way by expressly changing the definition of marriage or by making particular incidents attaching to marriage more widely available.[54]

Justices Thomas and Tipping argued in their dissents that the restriction of marriage to heterosexual couples constituted discrimination based on sexual orientation. Justice Thomas added that this discrimination could not be justified under section 5 NZBORA,[55] but he also refused to interpret the marriage in a way that was consistent with the Bill of Rights and argued that the matter should be left to be resolved by the legislature.[56]

In *M v Minister of Immigration*, the applicant was a Romanian national who sought to acquire the status of a refugee in New Zealand.[57] When his wife and children wanted to visit him in New Zealand, they could not rely on a family privilege for obtaining a visa because this privilege was not applicable to individuals whose application for refugee status was still pending. The applicant claimed that this practice discriminated against him on the basis of ethnic or national origin. However, the Supreme Court rejected this claim. When comparing the applicant to New Zealand nationals, the Court argued that the difference between them was the right to residence so that the two groups were not even comparable.[58] This is

[53] *Quilter* (n 35).
[54] ibid 555 (per Keith J).
[55] ibid 535–41 (per Thomas J dissenting).
[56] ibid 543.
[57] *M v Minister of Immigration* [2013] NZSC 9.
[58] ibid para 50.

hardly a surprising result considering that most countries give their nationals preferential treatment when it comes to the visa application of family members.

In *Child Poverty Action Group (CPAG)*, the Court of Appeal dealt with a tax credit for poor families with three or fewer children.[59] This tax credit was only available for persons who did not receive income-tested social benefits and who worked at least a certain number of hours per week against remuneration. The appellant maintained that these two exclusions constituted discrimination based on employment status. The Court found a differential treatment between two groups in comparable situations. Nevertheless, it held that the difference in treatment was justified. It argued that the exclusions served as a means to incentivize low-income earners to pursue gainful employment.[60] While it acknowledged that the issue of child poverty was a serious one, it argued that the restriction was a proportionate response to the incentive problem that lay within the discretion of the legislature.[61]

Finally, the case of *GB as Executor of the Estate of EB of Whangarei* concerned a distinction based on marital status.[62] The applicants were a married couple that had made gifts of 27,000 NZD each to a trust over several years. They argued that these gifts reduced their wealth for the purpose of calculating their eligibility for a residential care subsidy. However, the administration only recognized a gift to the amount of 27,000 NZD per year for the married couples, instead of 27,000 NZD for each individual (ie 54,000 NZD for the couple). The applicants argued that this amounted to discrimination based on marital status because their gifts would have been recognized separately had they not been married. However, the Court of Appeal rejected this argument. It held that couples can pool their assets and financial activities so that their financial position is different from that of a single person.[63] For this reason, couples are not in a comparable situation to single individuals.[64]

Despite the low success rate, the New Zealand case law best fits the equality as non-discrimination approach. There are no plausible cases of race or sex discrimination in the New Zealand case law, while these categories often drive the high success rate of discrimination cases in other jurisdictions. The one plausible case revolving around sexual orientation, *Quilter*, is largely unsuccessful because of the specifics of weak-form judicial review as expressed by section 4 NZBORA.[65] Cases concerning age discrimination or disability are highly context dependent and, therefore, often also have lower success rates in other jurisdictions. Furthermore, it

59 *CPAG* (n 21).
60 ibid para 77.
61 ibid para 152.
62 *GB as Executor of the Estate of EB of Whangarei* (n 14).
63 ibid para 39.
64 ibid.
65 On the concept of weak-form judicial review, see n 2.

is not uncommon to make distinctions based on nationality when it comes to immigration matters. Finally, some of the unsuccessful cases concern the extension of positive benefits, which would rather fall into our positive-equality category. For these reasons, it seems appropriate to classify New Zealand as non-discrimination jurisdiction.

4. Explanation of the doctrine

When we try to explain the jurisprudential pattern in New Zealand, two factors seem particularly relevant. The first is the norm structure. Section 19 NZBORA establishes a non-discrimination guarantee and refers to the grounds of discrimination in section 21 HRA. However, while most jurisdictions have an open-ended list of prohibited grounds of distinction, the list in New Zealand is exclusive and cannot be amended through judicial interpretation. This is most obvious in *Audrey Bredmeyer*, a case concerning a distinction based on residence, which in some contexts can arguably be considered to be a suspect classification.[66] The Court rejected a possible discrimination simply by referring to the fact that residence was not mentioned as a prohibited ground in section 21 HRA.[67] Furthermore, the New Zealand judges have been influenced by the Canadian approach to non-discrimination. Even if they do not copy the Canadian doctrine, they often refer to the Canadian case law in their jurisprudence.[68] We have seen that Canada also adheres to a rather restrictive non-discrimination model.[69] Even if the New Zealand courts do not go as far as the Canadian Supreme Court in restricting the scope of possible discriminations, it seems hardly surprising that the pattern in New Zealand looks similar to the one in Canada.

5. Conclusion

The New Zealand case law on equality and non-discrimination under the NZBORA is rather limited in quantity. We have identified 14 cases in which either the Court of Appeal or the Supreme Court took a substantive decision on section 19 NZBORA. Furthermore, the success rate is rather low. Only 2 of the 14 cases

[66] *Audrey Bredmeyer* (n 46).
[67] ibid para 63.
[68] See eg *McAlister* (n 33), para 134 (per Elias CJ and Blanchard J); *Malcolm Bruce Moncrief-Spittle v Regional Facilities Auckland Ltd* [2022] NZSC 138, paras 82, 87, 89 (per Ellen France J). See also Geiringer (n 1) 293 (arguing that the drafters of the NZBORA were influenced by the Canadian Charter of Rights and Freedoms).
[69] See Chapter 3.

were successful. Yet, despite the low success rate, we would still characterize the New Zealand case law as following the non-discrimination model. The low success rate is instead due to the nature of cases that have come to the Court. The two successful cases—extending social benefits for family caregivers of disabled children and lowering the minimum voting age to 16 years—can hardly be described as expressing of a deferential approach.

17

African Court on Human and Peoples' Rights

Helina Stiphanos Teka

1. Introduction

The Protocol establishing the African Court on Human and Peoples' Rights (the Protocol) was adopted in 1998.[1] However, it took nearly six years for the African Court on Human and Peoples' Rights (AfrCtHPR) to become operational and over a decade to issue its first decision<. The Court's jurisdiction includes interpreting and applying the Charter,[2] the Protocol, and any human rights instrument ratified by the states concerned.[3] Thus, the right to equality can be derived from various legal instruments. However, the Court primarily relies on the Charter's provisions to resolve disputes. Accordingly, Articles 2 and 3 of the Charter remain the main guarantees of the right to equality before the Court. This chapter analyzes the AfrCtHPR's equality jurisprudence in five steps. Section 1 explains the Court's understanding of Articles 2 and 3. Section 2 discusses the equality tests applied by the Court. Section 3 analyzes the empirical results. Section 4 discusses the factors explaining the practice of the Court discussed. The last section concludes the chapter with brief remarks.

2. Equality as a right

The Charter contains both a non-discrimination as well as a general equality guarantee. Article 2 prohibits discriminations based on suspect grounds, such as race, ethnic group, color, sex, language, or religion. By protecting against discriminations based on "other status," the Charter provides an illustrative list, giving the Court flexibility to extend the list of protected grounds of distinction. Article 3

[1] Organization of African Unity, Protocol to the African Charter on Human and People's Rights on the Establishment of an African Court on Human and People's Rights (June 10, 1998).

[2] Organization of African Unity, African Charter on Human and Peoples' Rights (Banjul Charter) (June 27, 1981).

[3] Art 3(1) Protocol African Court on Human and People's Rights (n 1).

Helina Stiphanos Teka, *African Court on Human and Peoples' Rights* In: *Equality's Guardians*. Edited by: Niels Petersen, Oxford University Press. DOI: 10.1093/9780198961109.003.0017

contains a general equality guarantee, providing for "equality before the law and equal protection of the law."

The AfrCtHPR recognized that Articles 2 and 3 of the Charter are interrelated in the *Tanganyika Law Society* case, which was the Court's first judgment on the merits.[4] The case concerned a constitutional amendment in Tanzania requiring any candidate in presidential, parliamentary, and local government elections to be sponsored by a political party. The applicants argued that this requirement discriminated against independent candidates. The Court found violations of Articles 2 and 3(2) and highlighted the relationship between the two provisions.[5] In a separate opinion, Judge Fatsah Ouguergouz clarified that the principle of non-discrimination was limited to rights guaranteed under the Charter while equality extended beyond such rights.[6] The Court acknowledged this in a subsequent decision where it identified Article 2 as "imperative" for all other rights.[7]

3. The equality test

The AfrCtHPR generally applies a two-step assessment for identifying a breach. First, it analyzes whether there is differentiation and identifies the grounds of distinction. Secondly, it examines a potential justification for the differentiation. The formulas of the Court in the justification analysis vary slightly. In some cases, the Court analyzes whether the distinction was "objective and reasonable."[8] In other cases, it uses elements of proportionality and requires the measure to be "necessary and proportional."[9] In cases concerning judicial procedures, the Court asks whether the procedure in question was "unfair."[10] The burden of proof lies with the applicants. They have to establish the ground of discrimination and provide sufficient evidence to prove a violation.

In principle, this test is used to determine the violation of both the non-discrimination and equal protection clauses. However, in cases concerning Article 3, the Court does not always undertake a justification analysis. Instead, it makes the determination whether the equal protection guarantee was violated in one single step. One example is *APDH*, a case against Côte d'Ivoire.[11] The case concerned the establishment of an Independent Electoral Commission. This Commission had a

[4] *Tanganyika Law Society and the Legal and Human Rights Centre v Tanzania; Reverend Christopher R. Mtikila v Tanzania* (2011) 1 AfCLR 32.

[5] ibid para 119.

[6] *Tanganyika Law Society* (n 4) para 36 (Separate Opinion Judge Fatsah Ouguergouz).

[7] *African Commission on Human and Peoples' Rights v Kenya* (2017) 2 AfCLR 9, para 137.

[8] ibid para 139.

[9] ibid.

[10] *Isiaga v Tanzania (merits)* (2018) 2 AfCLR 218, para 85; *Kemboge v Tanzania* (2018) 2 AfCLR 369, para 52.

[11] *Actions Pour La Protection Des Droits De L'Homme v Côte d'Ivoire* (2016) 1 AfCLR 668.

Central Committee where different government officials, including the President of the Republic, were represented. The Court found that this composition violated equal protection of the law. It reasoned that the composition placed the President or anyone affiliated with him in a better position than other candidates if they were to run in an election.[12] After this analysis, the Court refrained from undertaking a justification analysis.

Equality does not amount to identical treatment in all instances. Hence, mere differential treatment is insufficient for a violation. In a 2014 case against Burkina Faso, the families of an investigative journalist who was murdered alleged that the government failed to act as expeditiously in their case as it did in another case.[13] The AfrCtHPR argued that the length of investigations could vary due to the particular complexity of each case without necessarily resulting in a violation of Article 3.[14]

In finding a violation, the Court analyzes the actual practice and looks beyond a state's black-letter commitments. In the *Ogiek* case, the African Commission on Human and Peoples' Rights brought the case on behalf of an indigenous community in Kenya that faced forced eviction from their ancestral land.[15] The Ogieks could not benefit from land ownership due to colonial laws that did not recognize the community's tribal status. Despite Kenya's legislative amendment which covered the Ogieks under "marginalized community," the Court still found a violation because the state's practice was not in line with the letters of its constitution.[16]

4. Empirical analysis of the equality case law

4.1 Generating and analyzing the sample

The sample was established from the official website of the AfrCtHPR.[17] The search terms "discrimination," "non-discrimination," "equality," "inequality," "article 2," and "article 3" were used and only judgments on merits were analyzed. The period of analysis ranges from the beginning of the Court's judicial activity on June 14, 2013, when the first judgment on merit was issued, to the end of 2022. In total, 36 cases were identified and analyzed.

[12] ibid paras 149–151.

[13] *Beneficiaries of Late Norbert Zongo, Abdoulaye Nikiema Alias Ablasse, Ernest Zongo and Blaise Ilboudo and the Burkinabe Human and Peoples' Rights Movement v Burkina Faso* App no 013/2011 (March 28, 2014).

[14] ibid paras 167–169.

[15] *AfrCommHPR v Kenya* (n 7).

[16] ibid paras 143–144.

[17] <https://www.african-court.org/cpmt/decisions> accessed January 20, 2025.

4.2 Results of the analysis

The vast majority of the cases coming to the AfrCtHPR did not concern distinctions based on a suspect classification. According to our coding, only the already mentioned *Ogiek* case concerned such a distinction. In this case, the Court found a distinction based on ethnicity and ultimately a violation of Article 2 of the Charter.[18] All other cases concern non-suspect distinctions. While the Court also found a violation of Article 2 of the Charter in *Tanganyika Law Society*, the Court does not really distinguish between Articles 2 and 3 in its analysis.[19] The case concerned an electoral provision in Tanzania prohibiting independent candidates from standing in elections. The Court argued that the provision "*might* be related to a distinction based on 'political or any other opinion,'"[20] without taking a clear position because it found a violation of equality regardless.[21] Therefore, we coded this case as not involving a suspect classification.

If we look at all cases not involving a suspect classification, we find a success rate of 14.29% (5 out of 35).[22] The majority of the successful cases concern provisions that aim at skewing the political playing field. In the *Tanganyika Law Society* case, the government tried to decrease political competition by prohibiting independent candidates from standing in elections.[23] In *APDH*, the supposedly "Independent" Electoral Commission in Côte d'Ivoire had been filled with members of the current government.[24] In *Kambole*, the Court found a violation by a constitutional provision in Tanzania that excluded any judicial remedies against the declaration of a winner in presidential elections by the electoral commission.[25]

The two remaining cases concern procedural fairness. In *Ajavon*, the Court found a violation of the principle of equality of arms in criminal procedures because findings of the Public Prosecutor's Office to the detriment of defendants could not be appealed, while decisions in favor of defendants were subject to appeal.[26] In *Munthali*, the AfrCtHPR argued that the failure of the judiciary to grant the applicant a right to compensation despite a clear violation of his right to property amounted to a violation of the principle of equal protection before the law.[27]

Overall, the case law of the African Court of Human and Peoples' Rights adheres to the equality as non-discrimination model. Cases involving a suspect

[18] *AfrCommHPR v Kenya* (n 7) para 142.
[19] *Tanganyika Law Society* (n 4).
[20] ibid para 119.
[21] ibid.
[22] The successful cases are *Tanganyika Law Society* (n 4); *APDH v Côte d'Ivoire* (n 11); *Ajavon v Benin (merits)* (2019) 3 AfCLR 130; *Kambole v Tanzania* (2020) 4 AfCLR 460; *Munthali v Malawi* App No 022/2017 (June 23, 2022).
[23] *Tanganyika Law Society* (n 4) paras 116–119.
[24] *APDH v Côte d'Ivoire* (n 11) paras 108–151.
[25] *Kambole* (n 22) paras 63–83.
[26] *Ajavon* (n 22) paras 224–225.
[27] *Munthali* (n 22) paras 80–84.

classification have a success rate of 100%, even though the sample size is very small. Cases not involving a suspect classification have a success rate of slightly less than 15%. This is in line with other courts adhering to the same model. Furthermore, all cases correcting non-suspect classifications can reasonably be classified as corrections of arbitrary state action. They either concerned measures in electoral law giving the ruling party a clear advantage or procedural provisions, which either violate the principle of equality of arms or clearly seem arbitrary.

5. Explanation of the doctrine

5.1 Institutional context

A major factor in explaining the shape of the AfrCtHPR's case law is the institutional context in which the Court operates. In Africa, the idea of a regional court was entertained as early as 1961 but states were unwilling to submit themselves to a court's jurisdiction because they did not want to relegate their sovereignty to a supranational institution.[28] Instead, the African Commission on Human and Peoples' Rights was established in 1986. The Commission only had the power to make recommendations. The establishment of the Commission provided for a compromise. It introduced a human rights framework similar to Europe and the Americas while safeguarding states' interests. However, after the end of the Cold War, external and internal actors, including the Commission, called for a court.[29] The Commission had remained largely ineffective in achieving human rights protection, strengthening the need for an effective regional mechanism.[30]

Therefore, a Protocol establishing the AfrCtHPR was adopted in 1998, and the Court was established in 2004. The Court's jurisdiction extends to the adjudication of claims against states that have ratified the Protocol.[31] However, it can only receive cases from individuals and nongovernmental organizations (NGOs) when their states file a declaration accepting the Court's competence to do so.[32] While 34 member states of the African Union have ratified the Protocol, only eight of them

[28] Martin Faix and Ayyoub Jamali, "Is the African Court on Human and Peoples' Rights in an Existential Crisis?" (2022) 40 Netherlands Quarterly of Human Rights 56, 63; Rowland J V Cole, "The African Court on Human and Peoples' Rights: Will Political Stereotypes Form an Obstacle to the Enforcement of its Decisions?" (2010) 43 The Comparative and International Law Journal of Southern Africa 23, 24.

[29] Gina Bekker, "The African Court on Human and Peoples' Rights: Safeguarding the Interests of African States" (2007) 51 Journal of African Law 151, 159–64 (for extensive discussion on the various platforms where calls for a court were made).

[30] ibid 157–59.

[31] Art 3(1) Protocol African Court on Human and People's Rights (n 1).

[32] Art 34(6) Protocol African Court on Human and People's Rights (n 1).

have filed a declaration of acceptance under Article 34(6).[33] Furthermore, four states that had originally filed a declaration have withdrawn their declarations. These states are Benin, Côte d'Ivoire, Rwanda, and Tanzania. Save for Tanzania, which stated that the declaration was against its Constitution, the states explicitly blamed the Court for their withdrawal from the declaration.[34]

Furthermore, the African Union General Assembly decided to merge the AfrCtHPR and the African Court of Justice, an organ of the African Union, to create a new court.[35] The Protocol on the African Court of Justice and Human Rights[36] was adopted on July 1, 2008. However, as of April 2024, only 8 of the required 15 states have ratified the Protocol, delaying the actual merger of the ACtHPR and the African Court of Justice.[37]

These developments underline the precarious institutional context in which the AfrCtHPR is operating. If the Court is too bold it faces backlash by the states, which is facilitated by the ability to withdraw the acceptance of the Court's jurisdiction and exemplified by the withdrawal of Benin, Côte d'Ivoire, Rwanda, and Tanzania. The 4 countries that have withdrawn their declarations accounted for 77.77% of the adjudicated equality cases (28 of 36). Tanzania was a respondent in 24 of them. Benin and Côte d'Ivoire each received a violation verdict while Tanzania received two. Thus, a more assertive Court could give the already low number of states an excuse to withdraw. Moreover, it might scare off new ratifications of the Protocol and declaration. At the same time, the Court would undermine its own legitimacy if it applied a standard that is too deferential, even accepting clearly arbitrary state action or discriminations based on suspect grounds. For this reason, we can observe a rather deferential approach with the Court intervening only in exceptional cases.

5.2 Foreign influences

As a more recent regional human rights court, the ACtHPR draws upon the experiences of other human rights institutions.[38] For example, the Court cited both

[33] The eight countries that have made a declaration accepting the competence of the Court to receive cases from individuals and NGOs are Burkina Faso, the Gambia, Ghana, Guinea Bissau, Malawi, Mali, Niger, and Tunisia.

[34] For a detailed discussion on why the states withdrew their declarations, see Segnonna Horace Adjolohoun, "A Crisis of Design and Judicial Practice? Curbing State Disengagement from the African Court on Human and Peoples' Rights" (2020) 20 African Human Rights LJ 1; Oliver Windridge, "Assessing Rwexit: The Impact and Implications of its Article 34(6) Declaration before the African Court on Human and Peoples' Rights" (2018) 2 African Human Rights Yearbook 243.

[35] Assembly/AU/Dec 45 (III) Rev 1, para 4.

[36] African Union, Protocol on the Statute of the African Court of Justice and Human Rights (July 1, 2008).

[37] The countries that have ratified the Protocol are Angola, Benin, Burkina Faso, Congo, the Gambia, Libya, Liberia, and Mali.

[38] See also Niels Petersen, "Equality and International Law" in Neha Jain and Mila Versteeg (eds), *Oxford Handbook on Comparative Human Rights Law* (OUP forthcoming 2025).

the European and the Inter-American Courts of Human Rights extensively when establishing its approach to the justification analysis in *Tanganyika Law Society*.[39] In the *Ogiek* case, the AfrCtHPR used the formula of "objective and reasonable" justification[40] that the ECtHR had developed in the *Belgian Linguistics* case.[41] Additionally, the Court has engaged with the Committee on the Elimination of Racial Discrimination regarding indirect discrimination. It cited the latter when noting that the prohibition against discrimination included both direct and indirect discrimination.[42] Finally, the ACtHPR has incorporated legal standards established by other tribunals outside the realm of human rights. In particular, it referred to the International Criminal Tribunal for the former Yugoslavia in establishing that the burden of proof for discriminatory treatment should be with the applicant.[43]

5.3 Lack of resources for litigation

Considering that the implementation of the rule of law is lacking in many states on the African continent, the comparatively low success rate of cases before the AfrCtHPR is rather surprising. Next to the precarious institutional position of the Court, this may also be due to the quality of cases that come before it. A considerable number of non-violation judgments were due to the lack of specific submissions or evidence.[44] Parties often lack the funds to organize qualified legal representation. Legal aid could, therefore, help to tackle such gaps.

Consequently, the Court has set up a legal aid program to assist individual applicants lacking economic resources in line with Article 10(2) of the Protocol and Rule 31 of the Rules of the Court. In 2022, four cases were approved for assistance.[45] The Court also produced simplified forms, including for contentious proceedings, in various languages, to facilitate access.[46] However, less than half of the African population has access to the Internet.[47] This could hurt the effectiveness of the Court's effort to facilitate access. Still, all of these are recent initiatives so they

[39] *Tanganyika Law Society* (n 4) paras 106.2–107.1.
[40] *AfrCommHPR v Kenya* (n 7) para 139.
[41] *Certain Aspects of the Laws on the Use of Languages in Education in Belgium v Belgium* (1968) Series A no 6.
[42] *Kambole* (n 22) para 70.
[43] *Abubakari v Tanzania* App no 007/2013 (June 3, 2016) para 153.
[44] See eg *Emile v Côte D'Ivoire* App no 044/2019 (July 15, 2020), paras 243–246; *Mariko v Mali* App no 029/2018 (March 24, 2022) paras 104–108; *Machera v Tanzania* App no 035/2017 (22 Sept. 2022), para 82.
[45] Report of the African Court on Human and Peoples' Rights (2022) para 28.
[46] ibid paras 22–23.
[47] International Telecommunication Union, *Measuring Digital Development—Facts and Figures 2022* (ITU Publications 2022) 1.

did not have a significant effect on our sample, and may only show results in the future.

5.4 Institutional set-up of the Court

The lack of resources does not only concern the parties. It also concerns the AfrCtHPR itself. Article 15(4) of the Protocol requires all the judges except for the President to work on a part-time basis. This leaves the Court with a substantial case load that needs to be covered within a limited time period.[48] This could be a factor in the lack of detailed substantive discussions in some equality judgments. Particularly, decisions of non-violation are often very brief, which is an obstacle in the development of a stable doctrine.

6. Conclusion

The overall number of cases that come to the AfrCtHPR is small. Furthermore, the success rate is rather low. Overall, we have qualified the Court as adhering to the equality as non-discrimination model. It corrects discriminations based on suspect classifications but is rather reluctant to intervene when a distinction is not based on a suspect classification. The cases in which it finds violations can be described as corrections of arbitrary state action. There are multiple reasons that explain this observation. On the one hand, the Court is probably sensitive to political pressure and thus applies a rather deferential approach. On the other hand, the lack of resources for victims of human rights violations might lead to low-quality applications that get rejected by the court even though they might have been successful with better counsel. Despite these challenges, the ACtHPR's engagement with foreign jurisprudence and effort to improve access are steps in the right direction.

[48] Markus Löffelmann, "Protection of Human Rights in Theory and Reality: The Case of the African Court on Human and People's Rights" (2010) 85 Konfliktregion Afrika 161, 163.

18

South Africa

Helina Stiphanos Teka

1. Introduction

The South African interim Constitution marked a significant milestone in the country's transition from apartheid to constitutional democracy. During apartheid, the systemic discrimination of Black South Africans was legalized, while the small white minority controlled the political, social, and economic landscapes of the country. Inequality in South Africa was also rooted in colonialism and cultural attitudes that embraced patriarchy. These factors contribute to a still profoundly unequal society, even 30 years after the transition.

With apartheid as the immediate backdrop, equality was a central guarantee of the interim Constitution.[1] Building on the foundation laid by the interim Constitution, the final South African Constitution (Constitution), which came into force in 1997, recognizes equality as one of the nation's founding values.[2] In doing so, it highlights it as a value that all the remaining provisions are inherently tangled with. Additionally, equality is incorporated as a legally enforceable right in itself.[3] This chapter explores how the Constitutional Court has operationalized this right. It proceeds in four steps. The first section of the chapter briefly describes the elements of section 9. It also touches upon the limitation clause in the context of equality. The second section of this chapter evaluates the doctrine which the Constitutional Court uses to examine equality cases. It explains the tests developed by the Court to identify violations of equal protection and non-discrimination. The chapter's third section discusses the empirical results of the Court's equality cases and explores the factors that might have influenced the Court's equality doctrine. The last section concludes.

[1] Constitution of the Republic of South Africa, No 200 (1993).
[2] Constitution of the Republic of South Africa, No 108 (1996), s 1.
[3] ibid s 9.

Helina Stiphanos Teka, *South Africa* In: *Equality's Guardians*. Edited by: Niels Petersen, Oxford University Press.
 DOI: 10.1093/9780198961109.003.0018

2. Right to equality under the South African Constitution

The South African Constitution incorporates both an equal protection and a non-discrimination clause. Section 9(1) of the South African Constitution provides: "Everyone is equal before the law and has the right to equal protection and benefit of the law." The non-discrimination clause, provided under section 9(3) of the Constitution, enumerates several grounds of non-discrimination. The provision's phrasing indicates that the list is non-exhaustive. While there is a presumption of unfair discrimination for distinctions made based on the characteristics explicitly listed in section 9(3), such a presumption does not exist for non-listed grounds. Section 9(5) provides that only discrimination which is unfair is prohibited. This provision shifts the burden of justification to the respondent when a distinction is based on one of the listed grounds. The non-discrimination clause has both a vertical and horizontal effect. The prohibition of unfair discrimination concerns both the state (vertical) and private individuals (horizontal).[4] It further entails a positive obligation of the state to prevent or prohibit unfair discrimination by private actors. This obligation requires the state to enact national legislation targeting unfair discrimination.[5] The equality provision also authorizes positive discrimination as section 9(2) serves as basis for legislative and other measures aimed at uplifting disadvantaged groups of society. Finally, the right to equality is not an absolute right. It is subject to a general limitation provision found under section 36 of the Constitution, which requires any limitation against the Bill of Rights to be reasonable and justifiable.[6]

3. Equality doctrine of the Constitutional Court of South Africa

3.1 The basic test

The Constitutional Court laid the groundwork for its interpretation of equality and non-discrimination in the three cases of *Hugo*,[7] *Prinsloo*,[8] and *Harksen*.[9] In particular, *Harksen* provided a comprehensive outline of the Court's approach, which has been the basis for the subsequent equality doctrine of the Court. The Court applies a two-stage test to assess the violation of the general equality clause

[4] ibid s 9(3) and (4).
[5] ibid s 9(4).
[6] ibid s 36(1).
[7] *The President of the Republic of South Africa v Hugo* [1997] ZACC 4. The case concerned a Presidential Act which granted pardon to three categories of prisoners one of which was mothers of minors under 12 years. A father who had a minor child challenged the Act for discriminating against him based on sex or gender. The Court did not find a violation.
[8] *Prinsloo v van der Linde and Another* [1997] ZACC 5.
[9] *Harksen v Lane N.O. and Others* [1997] ZACC 12.

and a multitiered test to determine the existence of unfair discrimination. The two are related, as the multi-tiered non-discrimination test builds on the two-stage test if the latter did not result in a violation of equality. This test applies to cases concerning direct as well as indirect discrimination.[10]

The Court starts by analyzing the general equality clause in section 9(1) of the Constitution. First, the Court analyzes whether there is a differentiation between people or categories of people.[11] In a second step, it asks if there is a rational connection between the differentiation and a legitimate government purpose.[12] In *Prinsloo*, the Court specified this requirement, arguing that "[t]he purpose of this aspect of equality is, therefore, to ensure that the State is bound to function in a rational manner."[13] If the Court finds a rational connection, the general equality clause is not violated.

However, the Court continues with the analysis of a potential violation of section 9(3).[14] Here, the Court analyzes whether the identified differentiation amounts to unfair discrimination. If the ground of distinction is explicitly mentioned in section 9(3), the unfairness of the discrimination is presumed, but the contrary may be established by the respondent.[15] By contrast if the ground is not explicitly mentioned, the Court has to establish the unfairness of the discrimination.[16] When considering the unfairness of a discrimination, the Court considers several factors.[17] Most importantly, it asks whether the discrimination "has led to an impairment of their fundamental human dignity or constitutes an impairment of comparably serious nature."[18]

If the Court finds an infringement of the general equality clause or an unfair discrimination, it undertakes a justification analysis under section 36 of the Constitution. Discrimination can only be justified if it is "*justifiable in an open and democratic society*."[19] The Court applies this test by evaluating the purpose and effect of the legal act vis-à-vis the extent of its infringement of the right.[20] This is an integral part of the tests as the presumption of unfair discrimination can be rebutted. However, this last stage requires a law of general application. Accordingly, in *Jacques Charl Hoffmann*'s case, where the applicant was denied employment as a cabin crew because of his HIV/AIDS status, the Court found a violation of section 9. A justification was not possible because of the lack of a law of general application.[21]

10 *City Council of Pretoria v Walker* [1998] ZACC 1, para 35.
11 *Harksen* (n 9) para 42.
12 ibid.
13 *Prinsloo* (n 8) para 25.
14 *Harksen* (n 9) para 44.
15 ibid para 45. This is now codified in s 9(5) of the Constitution.
16 *Harksen* (n 9) para 45.
17 ibid para 51.
18 ibid.
19 Constitution (n 2) s 36(1).
20 *Harksen* (n 9) para 52.
21 *Hoffmann v South African Airways* [2000] ZACC 17, para 41.

3.2 Substantive equality and restitutionary measures

The South African Constitutional Court advances a substantive understanding of equality in lieu of a mere formal understanding. This requires assessing the conditions of peoples' lives and the actual effect of actions.[22] In *National Coalition for Gay and Lesbian Equality*, the Court held that sodomy laws that criminalized sexual activity between consenting males violated the equality right.[23] It emphasized the need to focus on context, impact, and the point of view of the affected person to guarantee substantive equality.[24] In doing so, it evaluated the systemic harm of differentiation. One mechanism for promoting substantive equality is restitutionary measures. These measures are explicitly recognized by section 9(2) of the Constitution. In *Van Heerden*, the Constitutional Court has developed three conditions, under which a restitutionary measure is not considered to be an unfair discrimination.[25] According to the Court, a positive measure is justified if it targets groups disadvantaged by unfair discrimination, if its aim is to protect and advance such persons or categories of persons, and if the measure promotes the achievement of equality.[26] One important consideration when analyzing the second and third prongs of the test is the consistency of the measure. In a 2018 judgment, the Court struck down a restitutionary measure because it only partially promoted groups disadvantaged in the past, while imposing a burden on other disadvantaged groups.[27]

4. Empirical analysis of the case law

4.1 Identifying relevant cases

Our sample comprises all equality cases since the South African Constitutional Court started reviewing cases in 1995 until the end of 2021. This also includes a few cases decided under section 8 of the interim Constitution that was in force when the Constitutional Court was established. The cases were accessed from the Southern African Legal Information Institute site.[28] The keywords "section 8," "section 9," "equality," "non-discrimination," and "discrimination" were used to filter

[22] Anne Smith, "Equality Constitutional Adjudication in South Africa" (2014) 14 African Human Rights LJ 609, 613.
[23] *National Coalition for Gay and Lesbian Equality and Another v Minister of Justice and Others* [1998] ZACC 15.
[24] ibid para 126.
[25] *Minister of Finance and Another v Van Heerden* [2004] ZACC 3, para 36.
[26] ibid para 37.
[27] *Minister of Justice and Constitutional Development and Another v South African Restructuring and Insolvency Practitioners Association and Others* [2018] ZACC 20.
[28] <http://www.saflii.org/za/cases/ZACC/> accessed January 20, 2025.

Table 18.1 Success rates based on specific suspect criteria

Suspect Criteria	Total Cases	No of Violations	Success Rate (%)
Sex/Gender	13	11	84.6
Marriage	10	9	90
Race/Ethnic Origin/Color	8	8	100
Sexual orientation	8	8	100
Nationality/Citizenship	5	4	80
Religion	4	2	50
Birth	2	2	100
HIV/AIDS status	1	1	100
Birth	1	1	100
Employment	1	1	100
Not suspect	29	9	31.03

Note: Cases with multiple discrimination were counted several times so that the total number is higher than the overall number of cases in our sample. For example, a case where the Court found unfair discrimination on the grounds of race and sex is counted towards each suspect criterion.

the relevant decisions. For this period, 69 relevant cases were identified. Eleven of these cases were decided under the interim Constitution. The cases were analyzed and coded according to the general coding scheme described in the introduction of this book.[29]

4.2 Results of empirical study

Overall, equality cases have a high success rate. The South African Constitutional Court found violations of equality in 42 of 69 cases (60.8%). In cases not involving a suspect classification, the success rate was 33.33% (10 out of 30 cases), and in cases involving a suspect classification, it was 82.05% (32 out of 39 cases). Table 18.1 shows the success rates depending on the suspect classification.

4.2.1 Violations of cases with suspect criteria

In its equality jurisprudence, the South African Constitutional Court has put a strong emphasis on recognition and social inclusion.[30] This is underlined by the

[29] See Chapter 1, section 4.2.

[30] Catherine Albertyn, "Contested Substantive Equality in the South African Constitution: Beyond Social Inclusion Towards Systemic Justice" (2018) 34 South African Journal on Human Rights 441, 455.

results in Table 18.1. Many of the cases address gender inequality, inequalities of non-married individuals, racial equality, equality of different sexual orientations, and the systemic exclusion of foreign nationals. In all these categories, the success rate is at or above 80%. In particular, cases regarding distinctions based on race and sexual orientation have a perfect success rate.[31] The two unsuccessful sex discrimination cases are controversial. In *Hugo*, the applicant challenged a presidential act that pardoned all imprisoned mothers with children under the age of 12 years.[32] The applicant was a father with a child under 12 years of age whose mother had died. The majority of the Court thought that the sex discrimination inherent in the presidential act was justified because women were the primary caregivers of children.[33] In *Jordan*, the applicants challenged a criminal norm that punished the selling of sex by prostitutes but did not punish the clients buying the sexual services.[34] They argued that this constituted an indirect discrimination based on sex. However, the majority of the Court rejected this argument, reasoning that distinctions between dealer and customer were quite common in other contexts.[35]

4.2.2 Intersectional discrimination and restitutionary measures

One feature of the South African case law is the focus on intersectional discrimination. First coined by Professor Kimberlé Crenshaw,[36] intersectionality acknowledges the interaction of power structures, individual and group experiences, and political marginalization in shaping identities and agency.[37] As intersectionality is an evolving concept and rarely has universal criteria, only those cases in which intertwined identities were recognized by the Court were coded as such.

The leading case is *Mahlangu*,[38] in which the Court explicitly recognized the prohibition of intersectional discrimination for the first time. Ms. Mahlangu drowned in her employer's pool, where she was a domestic worker. Her daughter approached the Department of Labour but was informed she could get neither compensation nor unemployment insurance benefits under the Compensation for Occupational Injuries and Diseases Act 1993 (COIDA). In addressing unfair discrimination, the Court pointed out the still-existing intersectional disadvantage of

[31] For a nuanced discussion of the Constitutional Court's case law regarding sexual orientation, see James Fowkes, *Building the Constitution: The Practice of Constitutional Interpretation in Post-Apartheid South Africa* (CUP 2016) 156–87.

[32] *Hugo* (n 7).

[33] ibid para 37.

[34] *S v Jordan and Others* [2002] ZACC 22.

[35] ibid para 10.

[36] Kimberlé W Crenshaw, "Demarginalizing the Intersection of Race and Sex: A Black Feminist Critique of Antidiscrimination Doctrine, Feminist Theory, and Antiracist Politics" [1989] University of Chicago Legal Forum 139.

[37] Patricia Hill Collins, *Intersectionality as Critical Social Theory* (Duke University Press 2019) 26. For a detailed discussion on how the Court treats multi-ground discrimination, see Shreya Atrey, *Intersectional Discrimination* (OUP 2019) 118–38.

[38] *Mahlangu and Another v Minister of Labour and Others* [2020] ZACC 24.

domestic workers due to apartheid.[39] In *Mahlangu*, the Court used intersectionality as a general interpretive device, focusing on Black women working as domestic workers injured at work and their dependents.[40] In doing so, it was able to focus on the unique vulnerability of Black women working as domestic workers. The Court even based the retrospective invalidation of the challenged statute on the intersectional nature of the unfair discrimination.[41]

While the Constitutional Court has recognized the justifiability of positive, restitutionary measures, challenges to such measures have only played a marginal role in the Court's case law. Only one case in our sample—the case of *Van Heerden*—dealt with such a measure.[42] The landmark decision concerned a differentiated scheme of employer benefits for members of parliament. This scheme mostly treated new members of parliament who joined after 1994 in an advantageous way. The Court found that the measure was justified because it predominantly benefited a group of parliamentarians who had previously been excluded because of their race, political affiliation, or belief.[43]

4.2.3 Violations with no suspect criterion

While the success rate for cases not involving a suspect criterion, at about a third of all cases, is significantly lower than that of cases involving a suspect criterion, it is still substantial. In particular in international comparison, a success rate of more than 30% is higher than for most other jurisdictions in our sample. If we look at the concrete successful cases, it is difficult to find a uniform pattern. All successful cases in our sample were decided on the basis of section 9(1). Many of these concerned criminal procedure law.[44] For example, in *Phaahla*, the Constitutional Court held that the retroactive application of a more onerous criminal procedure norm depending on the date of the conviction was arbitrary.[45] In *Centre for Child Law*, the Court argued that a distinction between child victims who have now passed into adulthood and accused and witnesses who were still under 18 years of age for protectionary measures in the criminal procedure was not rationally connected to a government aim.[46]

[39] ibid paras 96–100.
[40] See Shreya Atrey, "Beyond Discrimination: Mahlangu and the Use of Intersectionality as a General Theory of Constitutional Interpretation" (2021) 21 International Journal of Discrimination and the Law 168, 172.
[41] *Mahlangu* (n 38) para 128.
[42] Technically, *BEADICA 231 CC and Others v Trustees for the time being of the Oregon Trust and Others* [2020] ZACC 13 also dealt with s 9(2) of the Constitution. However, the Court found that the claim of the applicants that the provision was violated was not sufficiently substantiated. Furthermore, in *Solidarity v Department of Correctional Services* [2016] ZACC 18 the Court interpreted the Employment Equity Act (EEA) in light of s 9(2) of the Constitution (ibid para 42).
[43] *Van Heerden* (n 25) paras 38–44.
[44] *S v Ntuli* [1995] ZACC 14; *Mhlongo v S, Nkosi v S* [2015] ZACC 19; *Phaahla v Minister of Justice and Correctional Services and Another* [2019] ZACC 18; *Centre for Child Law and Others v Media 24 Ltd and Others* [2019] ZACC 46.
[45] *Phaahla* (n 44).
[46] *Centre for Child Law* (n 44) paras 29–35.

The remaining cases concerned various issues.[47] In *Nyathi*, the Constitutional Court, for example, struck down a provision that prohibited the execution of a court judgment into state property because it differentiated a creditor obtaining a judgment against the state and a creditor obtaining a judgment against private debtors.[48] In *Ngewu*, the Court argued that the different treatment of divorcees of members of different public pension funds amounted to a violation of equality.[49] The decision in *Sarrahwitz* concerned a distinction between buyers making a one-off payment for buying property and those that made payments in several installments with regards to the protection in bankruptcy proceedings.[50]

The discussion shows that while the Constitutional Court has developed a rather deferential formula to make section 9(1) of the Constitution operational, it does not always apply a deferential standard in practice. It seems that the Court is often driven by concerns of individual justice. While many of the distinctions challenged before the court seem unjust in the individual case, the legislative characterization in the abstract often does not seem indefensible. Consequently, the Court seems to review the rationality of legislative decision-making rather closely, granting a rather low level deference to the legislature.

4.2.4 Assessment

The empirical analysis shows a quite diverse pattern. On the one hand, the Court puts a strong emphasis on substantive equality. This is underlined by the high success rate of cases involving suspect classifications. In particular, cases concerning race and sexual orientation have, so far, a perfect success rate. This is also a consequence of the historical, social, and economic situation of South Africa after the end of apartheid. Furthermore, the Court has recognized indirect and intersectional discrimination. Yet, despite this focus on substantive equality, there has been a controversial debate on whether the Court has gone far enough. While it is acknowledged that the Court has promoted inclusion, it has been criticized for the lack of transformative impact.[51] The case law has a strong focus on inclusiveness.

[47] Next to the cases mentioned in the following footnotes, see also *Print Media South Africa and Another v Minister of Home Affairs and Another* [2012] ZACC 22, paras 79–82 (concerning a distinction between newspapers and magazines for an exceptional provision); *Herbert N.O. and Others v Senqu Municipality and Others* [2019] ZACC 31, paras 29–38 (concerning a distinction between different types of rights against a trust).

[48] *Nyathi v Member of the Executive Council for the Department of Health, Gauteng and Another* [2008] ZACC 8.

[49] *Ngewu and Another v Post Office Retirement Fund and Others* [2013] ZACC 4, para 17.

[50] *Sarrahwitz v Maritz N.O. and Another* [2015] ZACC 14.

[51] Cathrine Albertyn, "Substantive Equality and Transformation in South Africa" (2007) 23 South African Journal on Human Rights 253, 263; Pierre De Vos, "The Inevitability of Same-Sex Marriage in South Africa's Post-Apartheid State" (2007) 23 South African Journal on Human Rights 432, 457; for a more nuanced evaluation, see Dennis M Davis and Karl E Klare, "Transformative Constitutionalism and the Common and Customary Law" (2010) 26 South African Journal on Human Rights 403. The term "transformative constitutionalism" goes back to Karl E Klare, "Legal Culture and Transformative Constitutionalism" (1998) 14 South African Journal on Human Rights 146.

The recognition of the right of homosexuals to marry, which the South African Constitutional Court recognized as one of the first courts, is a good example.[52] Moreover, the Court has taken steps to recognize an individual way of being, as is demonstrated by the recognition of the "right to be different" in respect of gay/lesbian rights.[53] By contrast, transformation requires understanding law as a product of social relations that can be re-inscribed with transformative ends.[54] Despite its rhetoric, the Court has not devised remedies with a transformative character. In particular, it has so far refrained from imposing positive duties derived from equality on the legislature. This is in contrast to some Latin American courts, such as the Inter-American Court of Human Rights or the Brazilian Federal Supreme Court, which have derived positive duties from equality norms.

Finally, it has to be noted that the case law also displays a considerable success rate for cases not involving a suspect classification. These cases do not, contrary to what the doctrinal formula suggests, only correct clearly arbitrary state measures. Instead, they show a rather low level of deference. Overall, the South African case law is hybrid when it comes to the classification according to our equality models. It shows signs of both the equality as non-discrimination model and the equality as reasonableness model.

5. Explanation of the doctrine

5.1 Historical and political context

The Constitution was a reaction to the apartheid era that was characterized by the oppression of Black people and significant social inequality. The structural and systemic nature of the inequality that resulted from apartheid, as well as colonialism, patriarchy, ableism, and similar factors, fueled the urge to challenge the state.[55] Specifically, there was a long struggle to address the structural underpinnings of racial as well as gender inequalities. This history of exclusion and racial struggle led to a substantive understanding of equality and the concept of an inclusive, non-racial, and non-sexist democracy. This anti-discriminatory stance also translated into support for fighting against discrimination based on sexual orientation.[56] The most salient expression of this development is the inclusion of sexual orientation among the suspect grounds in section 9(3). This historical context explains why the Court, from early in its history, placed a strong emphasis on dignity

[52] *Minister of Home Affairs and Another v Fourie* [2005] ZACC 19.
[53] *National Coalition for Gay and Lesbian Equality* (n 23), para 22; *Fourie* (n 52), para 60.
[54] Albertyn, "Substantive Equality and Transformation in South Africa" (n 51) 258.
[55] Albertyn, "Contested Substantive Equality" (n 30) 460.
[56] Fowkes (n 31) 156–63.

and recognition as the lack of recognition of the majority of the population was very present during the days of apartheid.

The internal political set-up is another factor that influences South Africa's equality jurisprudence. During the period of analysis, the African National Congress (ANC) was the dominant political player in South African politics. Despite criticisms of unfulfilled promises and corruption scandals during its 30-year rule, the ANC maintains broad public support. This has created a certain uneasy relationship between the Court and the ANC as judgments that would have been politically too costly for the government might have led to backlash.[57] The Court has sometimes been able to exploit the political context to make decisions based on constitutional principles.[58] This is highlighted by the focus of the South African Constitutional Court on recognition as this is in line with the political priorities of the post-apartheid ANC. Arguably, the decisions on equality of sexual orientation were in line with the views held by key members of the ANC elite.[59] At other times, the Court was less progressive and resorted to the "separation of powers doctrine" to avoid confrontation with the legislature.[60] Furthermore, it has a strong focus on procedure that takes precedence over sweeping substantive rulings.[61] Consequently, the Court has not unequivocally adopted a more expansive progressive jurisprudence, but rather tried to find a balanced approach that combines interpretative, value-based, and institutional elements.[62]

5.2 Foreign influence

The Constitutional Court was the first of its kind in South Africa when formed in 1993. Established during a significant transition, it had to look elsewhere to lay the groundwork for interpreting the right to equality. The Constitution allows the Court to take into account international and foreign law for the interpretation of the Bill of Rights.[63] In line with this, the Court has referred to foreign legal instruments and judgments in interpreting the equality clause, especially during its early years.[64] The Court has referred in particular to Canadian

[57] Theunis Roux, "Principle and Pragmatism on the Constitutional Court of South Africa" (2009) 7 I.CON 106, 118–33. For an extended and refined version of the argument, see Theunis Roux, *The Politics of Principle: The First South African Constitutional Court, 1995–2005* (CUP 2013).

[58] Roux, "Principle and Pragmatism" (n 57) 118–33.

[59] See Fowkes (n 31) 164–65.

[60] Roux, "Principle and Pragmatism" (n 57).

[61] See Susan Rose-Ackerman, Stefanie Egidy, and James Fowkes, *Due Process of Lawmaking: The United States, South Africa, Germany, and the European Union* (CUP 2015) 158–59. See also the account of Fowkes (n 31) 169–70 on the decision of the Constitutional Court to involve parliament in the implementation of the *Fourie* decision.

[62] See, seminally, Fowkes (n 31).

[63] Constitution (n 2) s 39(1)(b) and (c).

[64] See eg *Prinsloo* (n 8) para 32; *National Coalition for Gay and Lesbian Equality* (n 23) para 23; *Walker* (n 10) paras 40–44; *Brink v Kitshoff N.O.* [1996] ZACC 9, paras 34–38. For a comprehensive

jurisprudence.[65] For example, the reference to dignity in interpreting the non-discrimination clause of section 9(3) of the Constitution seems to have been inspired by the Canadian example.[66] Furthermore, the Constitutional Court's approach of assessing the impact on the complainant to determine unfairness on unspecified grounds is close to one of the approaches that Justice *L'Heureux-Dubé* advocated in Canada.[67]

6. Conclusion

The analysis of the South African equality case law shows a hybrid picture. The Constitutional Court displays a strong rhetorical commitment to a substantive understanding of equality. This is evidenced by the doctrine that the Court has developed to operationalize section 9 of the Constitution and the high success rate of cases involving a suspect classification. At the same time, the Court mostly focuses on recognition. The case law lacks a substantive, transformative character that we see in Latin American jurisdictions where courts impose positive obligations derived from equality on legislature and executive. However, the Court is also engaged in correcting individual injustices. This is evidenced by the comparatively high success rate in cases not involving suspect classifications. While the doctrine seems to be rather deferential, its application is not. The strongest explanation of the shape of the Court's equality case law points to the political context in which the Court is operating. Because of the dominance of the ANC in the political process, the Court has limited room for maneuver. On the one hand, the focus on recognition is in line with the preferences of the elites of the ANC. On the other hand, a more progressive approach might have led to political backlash. The focus on correcting individual injustices, finally, bolsters the popular legitimacy of the Court with ordinary citizens without imposing a significant cost on the government or the legislature.

analysis, see Christa Rautenbach, "The Influence of Foreign Judgments on the Development of Post-Apartheid Constitutional Law in South Africa: Judicial Law-making in Action?" (2020) 7 Journal of International and Comparative Law 99.

65 ibid 115–18.

66 See Chapter 3.

67 Peter W Hogg, "Canadian Law in the Constitutional Court of South Africa" (1998) 13 Southern African Public Law 1, 13.

19
UN Human Rights Committee

Niels Petersen

1. Introduction

The International Covenant on Civil and Political Rights (ICCPR) contains several equality guarantees. The main equality norm is contained in Article 26 ICCPR, which encompasses both a general equality guarantee as well as a non-discrimination guarantee. Furthermore, the Covenant also contains an accessory prohibition of discrimination in Article 2 ICCPR, which guarantees that the provisions of the Covenant can be enjoyed free of discrimination based on certain specific criteria. Finally, the Covenant contains several specific equality and non-discrimination guarantees. These are the equality of men and women (Article 3 ICCPR), equality before courts and tribunals (Article 14 ICCPR), a prohibition of discrimination concerning children (Article 24 ICCPR) and in political affairs (Article 25 ICCPR).

These norms form part of a larger ecosystem of equality rights under the UN human rights system. In particular, there are specific treaties targeting discriminations based on sex and race—the Convention on the Elimination of All Forms of Racial Discrimination (CERD) and the Convention on the Elimination of All Forms of Discrimination against Women (CEDAW). The practice of the CERD and the CEDAW Committees will sometimes be referred to as points of comparison. However, the analysis will focus predominantly on the practice of the UN Human Rights Committee (HRCttee) under the ICCPR. In this practice, Article 26 ICCPR is, by far, the most important guarantee so that this chapter will mostly focus on this norm. The analysis will proceed in three steps. First, we will examine the doctrine that the HRCttee has developed to specify Article 26 ICCPR. Second, we will analyze the empirical pattern that emerges from the analysis of the individual communications of the HRCttee related to equality and non-discrimination. The final chapter will seek an explanation.

Niels Petersen, *UN Human Rights Committee* In: *Equality's Guardians*. Edited by: Niels Petersen,
Oxford University Press. © Niels Petersen 2025. DOI: 10.1093/9780198961109.003.0019

2. The equality doctrine of the UN Human Rights Committee

2.1 Development of the doctrine

The HRCttee implements the equality norm via a two-step test.[1] In the first step, the Committee asks whether there has been a difference in treatment. The second step offers the opportunity for a justification if the differentiation identified in the first step was based on "reasonable and objective criteria."[2] The HRCttee has never consistently specified the terms "reasonable and objective criteria."[3] Sometimes the Committee uses elements of proportionality.[4] In other individual communications, one gets the impression that the HRCttee seeks to weed out intentional discrimination.[5] However, such specifications can only be found in individual cases and are not employed consistently.

Moreover, the HRCttee does not consistently attribute a special role to suspect criteria in its doctrinal formulae.[6] In its early case law, the Committee referred to its standard formula regardless of whether suspect criteria were involved or not.[7] For the first time, the Committee explicitly discussed the issue in *Müller and Engelhard*.[8] It argued that "treatment based on one of the specific grounds enumerated in article 26, clause 2 of the Covenant . . . places a heavy burden on the State

[1] For detailed accounts on the interpretation of art 26 ICCPR, see Bertrand G Ramcharan, "Equality and Nondiscrimination" in Louis Henkin (ed), *The International Bill of Rights: The Covenant on Civil and Political Rights* (Columbia University Press 1981) 246; Christian Tomuschat, "Equality and Non-Discrimination under the International Covenant on Civil and Political Rights" in Ingo von Münch (ed), *Staatsrecht—Völkerrecht—Europarecht: Festschrift für Hans-Jürgen Schlochauer zum 75. Geburtstag am 28. März 1981* (Walter de Gruyter 1981) 691; Torkel Opsahl, "Equality in Human Rights Law with Particular Reference to Article 26 of the International Covenant on Civil and Political Rights" in Manfred Nowak (ed), *Fortschritt im Bewusstsein der Grund- und Menschenrechte: Festschrift für Felix Ermacora* (NP Engel 1988) 51; Manfred Nowak *U.N. Covenant on Civil and Political Rights: CCPR Commentary* (2nd edn, NP Engel 2015) art 26. On the practice of the HRCttee, see also Anne F Bayefsky, "The Principle of Equality or Non-Discrimination in International Law" (1990) 11 Human Rights LJ 1; Carla Edelenbos, "The Human Rights Committee's Jurisprudence Under Art. 26 of the ICCPR: The Hidden Revolution" in Gudmundur Alfredsson and others (eds), *International Human Rights Monitoring Mechanisms: Essays in Honour of Jakob Th. Möller* (Martinus Nijhoff 2009) 77; Niels Petersen, "The Implicit Taxonomy of the Equality Jurisprudence of the UN Human Rights Committee" (2021) 34 Leiden Journal of International Law 421. The test was established in *LG Danning v the Netherlands* CCPR/C/OP/2, 205 (April 9, 1987) and has not undergone major changes.

[2] *Danning* (n 1) para 13.

[3] See *General Comment No 18: Non-discrimination* HRI/GEN/1/Rev 1, 26 (HRCttee, November 10, 1989) para 13, which merely repeats that the criteria for a differentiation have to be "reasonable and objective" and adds that the distinction has to achieve a legitimate purpose in order to be justified.

[4] See eg *Jacobs v Belgium* CCPPR/C/81/D/943/2000 (July 7, 2004) para 9.5, where the HRCttee held that a gender quota for judges did not "amount to a disproportionate restriction of candidates' right of access."

[5] See *Järvinen v Finland* CCPR/C/39/D/295/1988 (July 25, 1990) para 6.4, where the Committee finds that the challenged measure is justified because "[t]he legislation . . . had no discriminatory purpose."

[6] See more in detail Petersen (n 1) 428–29.

[7] ibid.

[8] *Müller and Engelhard v Namibia* CCPR/C/74/D/919/2000 (March 26, 2002).

party to explain the reason for the differentiation."[9] In other cases, the Committee rejected a violation of Article 26 ICCPR because the challenged distinction was "neither discriminatory by reference to any of the grounds mentioned in article 26 of the Covenant, nor arbitrary."[10] However, this line of jurisprudence has not been applied consistently. Instead, the Committee often reverts to the old formula without making an explicit distinction between distinctions based on suspect classifications and other distinctions.[11]

2.2 Indirect discrimination and positive measures

In its initial case law, the Committee did not address the problem of indirect discriminations.[12] It acknowledged the problem for the first time in *Althammer*, which concerned a potential age discrimination.[13] The Committee argued that "a violation of article 26 can also result from the discriminatory effect of a rule or measure that is neutral at face value or without intent to discriminate."[14] However, in the concrete case, the Committee held that the challenged legislation was justified.[15] The Committee's subsequent practice has been inconsistent.[16] The Committee did not mention the concept in a number of future cases, where the problem would have merited a discussion. For example, *Prince* concerned the lack of an exception for the use of cannabis for religious purposes in South Africa.[17] The Committee argued that the regulation "affects all individuals equally" and was thus not discriminatory without discussing whether there was a potential indirect discrimination based on religion.[18] Similarly, in *Oulajin and Kaiss*, the authors of the individual communication had argued that the denial of child benefits for foster

[9] ibid para 6.7.

[10] *Pohl et al. v Austria* CCPR/C/81/D/1160/2003 (July 9, 2004) para 9.3. See, similarly, *Jongenburger-Veerman v the Netherlands* CCPR/C/85/D/1238/2004 (November 1, 2005) para 7.2; *O'Neill and Quinn v Ireland* CCPR/C/87/D/1314/2004 (July 24, 2006) para 8.4.

[11] See *Conçalves et al v Portugal* CCPR/C/98/D/1565/2007 (March 18, 2010) para 7.5; *Alekperov v Russia* CCPR/C/109/D/1764/2008 (October 21, 2013) para 9.10; *Whelan v Ireland* CCPR/C/119/D/2425/2014 (March 17, 2017) para 7.12.

[12] See eg *Ballantyne et al. v Canada* CCPR/C/47/D/359/1989 (March 31, 1993) para 11.5, where the Committee did not see a problem in a requirement to advertise only in French in Quebec because the requirement concerned Francophones and Anglophones in the same way. On the HRCttee's approach to indirect discrimination, see also Daniel Moeckli, "Equality and Non-Discrimination" in Daniel Moeckli, Sangeeta Shah, and Sandesh Sivakumaran (eds) *International Human Rights Law* (OUP 2013) 157, 165.

[13] *Althammer et al. v Austria* CCPR/C/78/D/998/2001 (August 8, 2003).

[14] ibid para 10.2.

[15] ibid.

[16] Sarah Joseph, Jenny Schultz, and Melissa Castan, *The International Covenant on Civil and Political Rights* (2nd edn, OUP 2004) para 23.32. For a detailed discussion of the indirect discrimination cases of the HRCttee, see also Paul M Taylor, *A Commentary on the International Covenant on Civil and Political Rights: The UN Human Rights Committee's Monitoring of ICCPR Rights* (CUP 2020) 739–42.

[17] *Prince v South Africa* CCPR/C/91/D/1474/2006 (October 31, 2007).

[18] ibid para 7.5.

children living outside the Netherlands constituted a discrimination of migrant workers.[19] The Court denied an indirect discrimination, arguing that the authors had not substantiated why the challenged provision affected migrant workers more severely than Dutch foster parents.[20] More recently, however, the HRCttee acknowledged indirect discrimination in *F.A. v France* where the author, a Muslim woman, was dismissed because she refused to discontinue wearing a headscarf.[21]

In contrast to the mixed record of the HRCttee, both the CERD and the CEDAW Committees put a strong emphasis on indirect discriminations. The CERD Committee, in many cases, finds violations of the CERD for police or prosecutorial failures to investigate or judicial failures to correctly appreciate instances of racial discrimination.[22] Similarly, the CEDAW Committee has often found violations of the CEDAW in cases of indirect discrimination. This concerns the failure to protect women against domestic violence,[23] the failure of judicial authorities to prosecute violence against women,[24] the failure to adopt a gender-sensitive approach for female prisoners,[25] the lack of adequate care for women in the healthcare system,[26] or the failure of courts adequately to appreciate sex discrimination.[27]

The case law of the HRCttee regarding positive measures is not very extensive but the Committee principally recognizes that positive measures, supporting a vulnerable group, can be justified even if they treat members of supposedly non-vulnerable groups less favorably.[28] The only individual communication where this has become relevant to date is *Jacobs v Belgium*.[29] The case concerned a gender quota for non-justice members at the High Council of Justice in Belgium. Half of the members of the High Council had to be justices and half of them non-justices. For the non-justices, the regulation in force required there to be at least four members of each sex out of eleven non-justice members of each linguistic college. The author claimed that this latter requirement amounted to sex discrimination.

19 *Oulajin and Kaiss v the Netherlands* CCPR/C/46/D/406/1990 (October 23, 1992).
20 ibid para 7.5.
21 *FA v France* CCPR/C/123/D/2662/2015 (July 16, 2018).
22 See *Ahmad v Denmark* CERD/C/56/D/16/1999 (March 13, 2000); *B.J. v Denmark* CERD/C/56/D/17/1999 (March 17, 2000); *Jewish Community of Oslo v Norway* CERD/C/67/D/30/2003 (August 15, 2005); *Durmic v Serbia and Montenegro* CERD/C/68/D/29/2003 (March 6, 2006); *Gelle v Denmark* CERD/C/68/D/34/2004 (6 March 2006); *Dawas and Shava v Denmark* CERD/C/80/D/46/2009 (March 6, 2012); *TBB v Germany* CERD/C/82/D/48/2010 (February 26, 2013); *VS v Slovakia* CERD/C/88/D/56/2014 (December 5, 2015); *Gabaroum v France* CERD/C/89/D/52/2012 (May 10, 2016); *Belemvire v Molodova* CERD/C/94/D/57/2015 (November 24, 2017).
23 See eg *Goekce v Austria* CEDAW/C/39/D/5/2005 (August 6, 2007); *Vienna Intervention Centre v Austria* CEDAW/C/39/D/6/2005 (August 6, 2007); *VK v Bulgaria* CEDAW/C/49/D/20/2008 (July 25, 2011); *Jallow v Bulgaria* CEDAW/C/52/D/32/2011 (July 23, 2012).
24 See eg *SVP v Bulgaria* CEDAW/C/53/D/31/2011 (October 12, 2012).
25 See eg *Abramova v Belarus* CEDAW/C/49/D/23/2009 (July 25, 2011).
26 See eg *Lourdes da Silva Pimentel v Brazil* CEDAW/C/49/D/17/2008 (July 25, 2011); *TPF v Peru* CEDAW/C/50/D/22/2009 (October 17, 2011).
27 See eg *RKB v Turkey* CEDAW/C/51/D/28/2010 (February 24, 2012).
28 Joseph, Schultz, and Castan (n 16) para 23.59.
29 *Jacobs* (n 4).

However, the Committee rejected the argument because the measure was necessary to promote "awareness of gender-relevant issues"[30] and constituted no "disproportionate restriction of candidates' right of access" so that the distinction was justified.[31]

3. Empirical analysis of the equality case law

3.1 Generating and analyzing the sample

The empirical analysis concerns all individual communications of the UN Human Rights Committee regarding equality until the end of 2022. The sample analyzed was constructed by using the document search of the Office of the High Commissioner for Human Rights,[32] selecting the CCPR as the treaty body and the relevant articles (CCPR-2-1. CCPR-3, CCPR-14-1, CCPR-24-1, CCPR-26). The sample was then narrowed down manually to filter out all cases in which the Committee did not make a pronouncement on the merits regarding a violation of equality or non-discrimination. The sample contains a total of 102 cases. The first case is *Aumeeruddy-Cziffra v Mauritius* from April 9, 1981,[33] and the last is *J.S.K.N. v Denmark* from October 25, 2022.[34] Repeat cases involving the same issue and the same respondent were only counted once in order to avoid an inflated case count. For example, there are several cases against the Czech Republic regarding expropriations in the Communist era[35] or against Russia regarding the prohibition of assemblies promoting issues of sexual identity.[36] After the construction of the sample, all cases contained therein were analyzed. The variables were coded according to the coding scheme introduced in the introductory chapter.[37]

The study did not analyze the concluding observations (COBs) of the HRCttee on periodic country reports. Neither did it systematically analyze the individual communications of the CERD or the CEDAW Committees.[38] While this would

30 ibid para 9.4.
31 ibid para 9.5.
32 <https://juris.ohchr.org/search/documentstable> accessed January 20, 2025.
33 *Aumeeruddy-Cziffra v Mauritius* CCPR/C/OP/1, 67 (April 9, 1981).
34 *Genero v Italy* CCPR/C/128/D/2979/2017 (March 13, 2020).
35 See eg *Simunek v Czech Republic* CCPR/C/54/D/516/1992 (April 4, 2002); *Adam v Czech Republic* CCPR/C/57/D/586/1994 (July 23, 1996); *Des Fours Walderode v Czech Republic* CCPR/C/73/D/747/1997 (October 30, 2001); *Malinosky v Czech Republic* CCPR/C/130/D/2839/2016 (November 6, 2020).
36 See *Nepomnyashchiy v Russia* CCPR/C/123/D/2318/2013 (July 17, 2018); *Alekseev v Russia* (No 1) CCPR/C/130/D/2727/2016 (October 16, 2020); *Alekseev v Russia* (No 2) CCPR/C/130/D/2757/2016 (November 5, 2020); *Ivanov v Russia* CCPR/C/131/D/2635/2015 (March 18, 2021); *Alekseev et al. v Russia* CCPR/C/134/D/2943/2017 (March 14, 2022); *Savolaynen v Russia* CCPR/C/135/D/2830/2016 (July 19, 2022).
37 See Chapter 1, section 4.2.
38 For more general accounts on equality and discrimination in international law see Egbert Willem Vierdag, *The Concept of Discrimination in International Law* (Nijhoff 1973); Marc J Bossuyt,

have probably given a more complete picture of the equality conception prevailing in the UN human rights system, the choice was made to ensure comparability of the study with other international human rights courts, such as the IACtHR or the ECtHR, and the constitutional courts that are included in the comparative study and that do not have parallel institutions comparable to the COBs of the HRCttee.

3.2 Results of the analysis

While the doctrinal formulae of the HRCttee suggest that the Committee interprets Article 26 ICCPR as a general equality clause, the empirical results of our analysis point into a different direction. Even through there are a few cases in which the Committee found a violation in the absence of a suspect classification, most cases in which it came to the conclusion that Article 26 ICCPR was violated involved a distinction based on a suspect classification. Furthermore, the probability for a challenge to succeed was four times higher for challenges against distinctions involving a suspect classification (67.6%) than for a distinction not involving a suspect classification (16.1%). A detailed classification of success rates based on the type of suspect classification can be found in Table 19.1.

If we look closer at the different categories, we see that there are some categories without successful cases. These are age, marriage, and place of residence. For all three categories, we can debate whether they should actually be classified as suspect categories. Marriage is a social institution that often comes with social prestige. The flipside of the coin is that unmarried women often suffer from social stigma.[39] But whether marriage is actually a problematic criterion of distinction is highly context dependent. In the cases decided by the HRCttee, the Committee considered whether or not to be married to be a choice of the couple, which justified that societies treated married couples more favorably than unmarried ones. Similarly, place of residence is also a criterion of distinction that is context-dependent. It may be

L'interdiction de la discrimination dans le droit international des droits de l'homme (Bruylant 1976); Matthew Craven, "Non-Discrimination and Equality" in Matthew Craven (ed), *The International Covenant on Economic, Social and Cultural Rights: A Perspective on Its Development* (Clarendon Press 1995) 153; Natan Lerner, *Group-Rights and Discrimination in International Law* (2nd edn, Kluwer 2003); Wouter Vandenhole, *Non-Discrimination and Equality in the View of the UN Human Rights Treaty Bodies* (Intersentia 2005); Kristin Henrard, "The Protection of Minorities Through the Equality Provisions in the UN Human Rights Treaties: The UN Treaty Bodies" (2007) 14 International Journal on Minority and Group Rights 141; Jarlath Clifford, "Equality" in Dinah Shelton (ed), *The Oxford Handbook of International Human Rights Law* (OUP 2013) 420; Moeckli (n 12).

[39] See *General Comment No 28: Article 3 (The equality of rights between men and women)* HRI/GEN/1/Rev 9 (HRCttee, March 29, 2000) para 27, which stresses the necessity to respect various forms of families on an equal basis.

Table 19.1 Success rate based on suspect classification

Criterion	Violation	No violation	Violation pct	Total
Not suspect	5	26	16.1	31
Race	3	1	75	4
Sex	18	4	81.8	22
Nationality	4	3	57.1	7
Extramarital birth	1	0	100	1
Residence	0	1	0	1
Religion	6	5	54.5	11
Disability	2	0	100	2
Sexual identity	5	1	83.3	6
Property	1	0	100	1
Marriage	0	4	0	4
Political opinion	8	2	80	10
Age	0	2	0	2
Total	53	49	52	102

used to exclude outsiders,[40] but it may also be a legitimate requirement, for example in the context of voting rights.[41] Finally, age is often considered to be a suspect criterion of distinction,[42] but distinctions based on age may also be necessary in certain contexts.

Some categories have a particularly high success rate. These are sex, sexual identity, and political opinion (each 80% or more). The unsuccessful sex discrimination cases mostly concerned technicalities of the Dutch social benefits legislation.[43] One case was a case of positive discrimination where the HRCttee upheld a quota that required that each sex had to have a certain minimum number of seats in the Belgian High Court of Justice.[44] The one unsuccessful sexual identity case

[40] See *General Comment No 20: Non-Discrimination in Economic, Social and Cultural Rights (Art. 2, para 2, of the International Covenant on Economic, Social and Cultural Rights)* UN Doc E/C.12/GC/20 (CESCR, 2009) para 34 (classifying residence as a suspect criterion).

[41] See *Gillot et al. v France* CCPR/C/75/D/932/2000 (July 15, 2002).

[42] See *Love et al v Australia* CCPR/C/78/D/983/2001 (March 25, 2003) para 8.2, where the Committee argues that age is a status of distinction under art 26 ICCPR.

[43] *Vos v the Netherlands* CCPR/C/66/786/1997 (July 26, 1999); *Cavalcanti Araujo-Jongen v the Netherlands* CCPR/C/49/D/418/1990 (October 22, 1993); *Pepels v the Netherlands* CCPR/C/51/484/1991 (July 15, 1994). For a critique of *Vos*, see Bayefsky (n 1) 15.

[44] *Jacobs* (n 4).

concerned same-sex marriage,[45] a politically sensitive issue in which the HRCttee probably did not want to get involved and in which it took a stance similar to the one taken by the European Court of Human Rights (ECtHR).[46]

If we look at the successful cases that did not involve suspect classifications, they mostly concern arbitrary state action.[47] In *Fábryova*, the Committee held that a decision denying the author restitution for expropriation during communist rule violated Article 26 ICCPR because other individuals in comparable situations had actually received compensation.[48] *Blaga* concerned a decision of the Romanian Supreme Court that had overturned a decision of the Court of Appeals even though the latter had already become final.[49] Finally, in *Kavanagh*, the Committee found a violation in an Irish legislation that gave the public prosecutor unfettered discretion regarding the appropriate forum for criminal procedures in terrorism cases.[50]

If we look at the bigger picture, the Human Rights Committee follows the non-discrimination model of equality. Cases only have a significant chance of success if a suspect classification is involved. Cases not involving suspect classifications are only successful in exceptional circumstances. At the same time, for cases involving a suspect classification, the chances of success are very high, in particular if one takes into account that some of the unsuccessful challenges concerned positive measures supporting vulnerable groups or indirect discrimination cases.

4. Explanation of the doctrine

The non-discrimination model is a rather common model for courts to adopt. In the international realm, the ECtHR also largely follow the same model. One of the reasons is arguably the institutional position of international courts. It is now largely recognized that domestic and international courts face similar institutional constraints regarding the implementation of their decisions.[51] Nevertheless, there are differences in degree. International courts are usually in a weaker position because they will often enjoy less public support than domestic constitutional or supreme courts. The general public often knows less about international courts than about their domestic counterparts and is also less familiar with their decisions.

[45] *Joslin v New Zealand* CCPR/C/75/D/902/1999 (July 17, 2002).

[46] See *Rees v UK* [1986] Series A no 106; *Schalk and Kopf v Austria* ECHR 2010-IV 409 (arguing that the ECHR did not contain a right to same-sex marriages).

[47] See Edelenbos (n 1) 80–81; Petersen (n 1) 437–38.

[48] *Fábryová v Czech Republic* CCPR/C/73/D/765/1997 (October 30, 2001).

[49] *Blaga v Romania* CCPR/C/86/D/1158/2003 (April 24, 2006).

[50] *Kavanagh v Ireland* CCPR/C/71/D/819/1998 (April 4, 2001).

[51] Jeffrey K Stanton and Will H Moore, "Judicial Power in Domestic and International Politics" (2011) 65 International Organization 553; Tom Ginsburg, "Political Constraints on International Courts" in Cesare Romano, Karen Alter, and Yuval Shany (eds), *The Oxford Handbook of International Adjudication* (OUP 2014) 483, 486.

Decisions that are discussed in the generalist media occur less often than in the case of domestic courts. Therefore, international courts are usually in a weaker institutional position than many constitutional or supreme courts. For this reason, it would probably weaken their legitimacy if they adopted the less deferential consistency model that often second-guesses the rationality of legislative decisions. Instead, the non-discrimination model seems to be the more balanced option. It pays more deference to the legislature than the consistency model but nevertheless tries to protect vulnerable groups and to correct structural injustice.

A second factor influencing the concrete form of the doctrine of the HRCttee is the influence by other international courts and tribunals. This concerns, in particular, the ECtHR. Some of the judges of the ECtHR courts have also served on the HRCttee before or after their tenure in Strasbourg, and most experts of the Committee will be familiar with the regional human rights case law. Certainly, the HRCttee largely refrains from citing the case law of regional human rights courts or other quasi-judicial bodies. Yet, this is mostly due to the position of the HRCttee as a universal institution. If it were to cite, say, the ECtHR frequently, this might raise doubts concerning its impartiality. Nevertheless, one can see traces of influence of the regional human rights courts. This concerns, in particular, the general doctrinal formula that the HRCttee adopted in *Danning v the Netherlands*.[52] The reasonable and objective criteria formula of the HRCttee closely resembles the objective and reasonable justification formula that the ECtHR developed in the *Belgian Linguistics* case.[53] Even though the HRCttee did not cite the Strasbourg court, we can assume that it was aware of the latter's landmark case.

5. Conclusion

This chapter has shown that cases involving a suspect classification have a much higher success rate than cases in which the differentiation is not based on a problematic criterion. It is rather the exception that the HRCttee finds a violation of Article 26 ICCPR in the latter type of cases. Consequently, the equality model of the HRCttee can be qualified as a non-discrimination model. There are two possible explanations for this development. The main factor is the weaker position of the HRCttee when the latter confronts national parliaments and governments, if compared to many domestic courts, correcting human rights violations. As courts cannot implement their own decisions, they rely on public support and institutional cooperations as a source of power to confront the executive and the legislature. However, public support for international courts is usually weaker than

[52] *Danning v the Netherlands* (n 1) 205.

[53] *Case Relating to Certain Aspects of the Laws on the Use of Languages in Education in Belgium v Belgium* [1968] Series A no 6.

for domestic courts because less people know about their activity. Therefore, it is not surprising that international courts choose the more deferential non-discrimination model over the general equality model, which is often considered more intrusive with respect to the prerogatives of parliament and the executive. On the other hand, the influence of other international courts and tribunals arguably also plays a role. The doctrinal formula developed by the HRCttee is close to the one established by the ECtHR in its landmark *Belgian Linguistics* case. Even though the HRCttee did not cite the latter in its decisions, it can be assumed that the experts serving on the Committee were aware of the most important of the latter's cases.

20
The Diversity of Judicial Conceptions of Equality

Niels Petersen

The chapters in this book have shown that the judicial operationalization of equality is a diverse phenomenon. Different courts have different answers to Peter Westen's challenge of equality as an "empty idea."[1] They give the concept different interpretations, and the social problems that are dealt with under the heading of equality vary from jurisdiction to jurisdiction. This chapter will take stock of these different approaches. We will first conduct a mapping of the equality doctrines of the different analyzed jurisdictions and see how the various doctrines fit the models sketched in the introductory chapter (Section 1). In a second step, we will look at some individual doctrinal issues and discuss the different solutions that the analyzed courts have found to the related problems—this concerns the role of suspect classifications, indirect discriminations, and positive measures (Section 2). Finally, we will identify the reasons why courts adopt specific doctrines. We will see that there is not one single factor explaining the whole picture. Instead, a complex interplay of different factors emerges (Section 3).

1. Mapping of equality models

In the introduction, we hypothesized that the narrative of a "global model of constitutional rights"[2] does not provide a good description for the judicial operationalization of equality. Instead, we observe more diversity. The analysis in the jurisdictional chapters in this book has confirmed that the equality case law of apex courts can roughly be classified into four different models. This section will summarize and compare these results. First, I will briefly discuss the methodology of how we classified the different jurisdictions in the various models (1.1).

[1] Peter Westen, "The Empty Idea of Equality" (1982) 95 Harvard LR 537. On this challenge, see Chapter 1, section 1.
[2] Kai Möller, *The Global Model of Constitutional Rights* (OUP 2012).

Niels Petersen, *The Diversity of Judicial Conceptions of Equality* In: *Equality's Guardians*. Edited by: Niels Petersen, Oxford University Press. © Niels Petersen 2025. DOI: 10.1093/9780198961109.003.0020

Subsequently, I will analyze the different models. The predominant model is—unsurprisingly—the equality as non-discrimination model. This model is prevalent mostly in common law jurisdictions and international human rights courts and tribunals (1.2). Another prominent model is the equality as reasonableness model which can be found mostly in continental Europe (1.3). The positive equality model is the prevailing model in Latin America (1.4). Finally, there is the deferential approach to equality, which we observed in Singapore (1.5).

1.1 The methodology of classifying jurisdictions

The different models that we used to classify the equality case law of the analyzed courts and that were introduced in the introductory chapter[3] are descriptive models that show the patterns that emerge from the courts' case law. These patterns are identified according to the "output" of the case law instead of the doctrinal "input."[4] Consequently, the starting point for classifying the different jurisdictions was the success rates that we identified for cases involving suspect classifications and cases not involving suspect classifications in each jurisdiction. Then we used qualitative clustering to group jurisdictions together that share similar characteristics.[5] Success rates are certainly only a crude measure influenced by many different factors. These include the type of cases coming to the court or chosen by the judges for a decision if the latter have control over their docket.[6]

Consequently, a low success rate may merely be an indication of a mature legal system where the most problematic cases do not make it to the courts because the situation has already been resolved by the political process. The cases that do come to the judiciary often involve complex trade-offs that may be resolved in better ways by the political system than by the courts. Furthermore, challenges of affirmative action measures will usually be less successful than challenges of measures imposing a disadvantage on a suspect group, and indirect discrimination cases will be less successful than direct discrimination cases. Therefore, the success rate for a court seeing lots of affirmative action or indirect discrimination cases will usually be lower than for a court that deals with plenty of direct discrimination cases.

[3] See Chapter 1, section 2.

[4] For an excellent and comprehensive framework of judicial deference focusing rather on the "input," see Cora Chan, *Deference in Constitutional Adjudication* (OUP 2024) (who identifies six devices for exercising deference: burden of proof, standard of proof, standard of review, giving of weight to views, choice of interpretation, and choice of remedy).

[5] On qualitative clustering see eg Laura Macia, "Using Clustering as a Tool: Mixed Methods in Qualitative Data Analysis" (2015) 20 The Qualitative Report 1083.

[6] On this problem see George L Priest and Benjamin Klein, "The Selection of Disputes for Litigation" (1984) 13 Journal of Legal Studies 1; Tonya L Putnam, "Courts without Borders: Domestic Sources of U.S. Extraterritoriality in the Regulatory Sphere" (2009) 63 International Organization 459, 472–73.

For this reason, the success rate is only a starting point for our analysis. We also looked at additional factors. One factor that we deemed important for the classification of jurisdictions in the equality as reasonableness category is the absolute number of successful cases not involving a suspect classification. If we observe a high number of cases not involving a suspect classification coming to court, this indicates that the parties bringing these cases assume a reasonable chance of success and feel encouraged by the court's previous case law. Furthermore, we also looked at the difference in success rates between cases involving a suspect classification and cases not involving a suspect classification. As this difference concerns the same court, the selection effect will presumably be less pronounced. A less considerable difference was an indication that the respective jurisdiction could rather be classified as adhering to the equality as reasonableness model than the equality as non-discrimination model.

Finally, we also went beyond the numbers and analyzed the types of corrections that a court made in its case law. If a court predominantly corrected clearly arbitrary state action in its equality cases not involving a suspect classification, this was an indication that it followed the equality as non-discrimination model. By contrast, if it made a more intensive review of the overall rationality of legislation, this was an indication that the court followed the equality as reasonableness model. Moreover, the classification into the positive equality model mostly depended on a qualitative assessment of the case law regarding the extent to which courts imposed positive obligations on the legislature.

1.2 Equality as non-discrimination

The equality as non-discrimination model is the predominant approach in the sample of analyzed courts. Half of the courts that we studied follow this approach; this is particularly the case for courts from common law systems. The US Supreme Court is the most prominent example, but we also found similar patterns in the case law of the Supreme Court of Canada, the UK Supreme Court, the Supreme Court of New Zealand, and the Supreme Court of India. Another group of courts that predominantly fits into the equality as non-discrimination category are international and supranational courts and tribunals. This concerns the European Court of Human Rights (ECtHR), the Court of Justice of the European Union (CJEU), the UN Human Rights Committee (UN HRCttee), and the African Court of Human and Peoples' Rights (AfCtHPR).

The case law of these courts shares certain characteristics, but it also reveals differences, illustrating that the equality as non-discrimination model is a large tent rather than an exact blueprint. The results are shown in Table 20.1. Primarily, the success rate of cases not involving a suspect classification is rather low. Furthermore, the overall number of successful cases is significantly lower than for cases involving a suspect classification. In all jurisdictions classified under this model, the success rate for non-suspect classifications was below 20%. This ranged from the total lack of successful cases for Canada and New Zealand or one exceptional case in the United Kingdom to jurisdictions where cases not involving a suspect classification are rarely successful, but where the court has used equality to weed out occasional arbitrary state actions. This concerns the ECtHR, the CJEU, the HRCttee, the AfrCtHPR, the US Supreme Court, and the Supreme Court of India.

We also observe some significant differences in the success rates for cases involving a suspect classification (see Table 20.1). Half of the courts have case success rates over 50%. These are the AfrCtHPR, the CJEU, the HRCttee, and the US Supreme Court. Other courts have been more reluctant to find violations of the prohibition of non-discrimination even in cases involving a suspect classification. These are the Supreme Court of India, the UK Supreme Court, the Supreme Court of Canada, and the Supreme Court of New Zealand.

As indicated in the previous section, the success rates are influenced by many different factors. The comparatively high success rate of cases not involving a suspect classification in the US Supreme Court is likely to be influenced by the Court's ability to control its own docket. Furthermore, the overall low success rate in some of the commonwealth jurisdictions might be an indication for a mature legal system where cases coming to the highest courts involve complex trade-offs. Nevertheless, it appears that the commonwealth courts of the United Kingdom, Canada, and New Zealand are, overall, more deferential than their judicial counterparts in other jurisdictions belonging to the equality as non-discrimination model. This is not only suggested by the comparatively low success rate of cases involving a suspect classification but also by the near total absence of successful

Table 20.1 Success rates of within the equality as non-discrimination model

Court	**Non-suspect classifications**	**Suspect classifications**
AfrCtHPR	14.29% ($N = 35$)	100% ($N = 1$)
HRCttee	14.3% ($N = 28$)	62.71% ($N = 59$)
CJEU	11.82% ($N = 203$)	67.14% ($N = 140$)
US Supreme Court	15.93% ($N = 113$)	58.71% ($N = 155$)
Supreme Court of India	17% ($N = 171$)	44.4% ($N = 55$)
UK Supreme Court	5.88% ($N = 17$)	43.75% ($N = 32$)
Supreme Court of Canada	0% ($N = 6$)	32.7% ($N = 55$)
New Zealand SC and CoA	0% ($N = 2$)	16.67% ($N = 12$)

cases not involving a suspect classification. While most courts exercise at least a subsidiary review of arbitrariness in these cases, the courts of the United Kingdom, Canada, and New Zealand almost completely defer to the legislature. In Canada and New Zealand, such cases are not even brought to the highest courts anymore—at least they are not framed as equality cases—because of the complete lack of success in resolving them. This is indicated by the low overall number of decided cases not involving a suspect classification.

Finally, we can also see differences with regards to the treatment of positive measures. The Supreme Courts of Canada, the United Kingdom, and New Zealand largely defer to the legislature in such cases. This does not only concern the legality of the positive measure as such but also the determination of the beneficiaries of these positive measures.[7] By contrast, the US Supreme Court and the Indian Supreme Court are much less deferential in this respect. It is well known that the US Supreme Court applies strict scrutiny to affirmative action cases,[8] but the Indian Supreme Court too often strikes down positive measures designed to support certain backward castes.[9]

1.3 Equality as reasonableness

The second model with widespread appeal is the equality as reasonableness model. The model can predominantly be found in continental Europe. In our sample, all continental European courts, that is, the constitutional courts of Germany, France, and Poland, adhere to the model. However, it has also spread to other parts of the world, as the example of the Constitutional Court of Taiwan demonstrates. The model is mostly characterized by the comparatively high success rate of cases not involving a suspect classification, a high overall number of such cases and a comparatively small difference in the success rates of cases involving a suspect classification, and those not involving a suspect classification.

The success rate of cases not involving suspect classifications ranges from 15.7% for France to 37.97% for Poland. With the exception of France, this rate is significantly higher than in the jurisdictions adhering to the equality as non-discrimination model (see Table 20.2). At the same time, the success rate for cases involving a suspect classification while higher than for cases not involving a suspect classification is consistently below 50%. The difference in success rates is always below 20 percentage points.

[7] See eg *Alberta v Cunningham* [2011] SCR 670, 690–91; *Ermeskin Indian Band and Nation v Canada* [2009] 1 SCR 222, 283–86 (both Canada); *Melanie Trevethick v Ministry of Health* [2008] NZCA 397 (New Zealand).

[8] See Chapter 2, section 2. The latest case was the recent *Students for Fair Admissions, Inc v President and Fellows of Harvard College* 600 US 181 (2023).

[9] See Chapter 13, section 3.2.

Table 20.2 Success rates of within the equality as reasonableness model

Court	Non-suspect classifications	Suspect classifications
German Federal Const. Court	25.07% (*N* = 758)	39.55% (*N* = 134)
French Conseil constitutionnel	15.7% (*N* = 1,074)	19.7% (*N* = 191)
Polish Constitutional Tribunal	37.97% (*N* = 495)	49% (*N* = 53)
Const. Court of Taiwan	26.67% (*N* = 60)	46.43% (*N* = 28)

Finally, the *absolute number* of cases is, in most of these jurisdictions, far higher for cases not involving a suspect classification than for cases involving one. This indicates that the doctrines developed by these courts and the jurisprudential patterns invite lots of challenges of measures not involving a suspect classification. In particular, in France, Germany, and Poland, the number of challenges to measures not involving a suspect classification dwarfs the number challenges to measures involving a suspect classification. This effect is more modest in Taiwan.

These numbers suggest that the courts following an equality as reasonableness approach exercise far less deference towards the legislature and executive than the courts following an equality as non-discrimination approach. This is not only suggested by the statistics but also by the kinds of corrections that these courts impose on the legislature on the basis of equality. For example, the German Federal Constitutional Court struck down a measure which treated differently the taxation of pensions under the pension scheme for public servants and under the general pension scheme for employees.[10] Similarly, the Polish Constitutional Tribunal had to decide about the extent of a special pension regime for Police officers and other uniformed officials.[11] It held that the exclusion of custom officials from this pension scheme violated the equality guarantee because the latter were deemed similar to policemen.[12] Finally, in Taiwan, the Constitutional Court found a provision of the income tax statute incompatible with equality because it allowed a tax deduction for medical expenses paid to certain specifically appointed medical institutions, while denying the deductibility of expenses paid to common medical institutions.[13] The correction of tax legislation in these examples is quite far-reaching, but at the same time typical for courts following the equality as reasonableness model. One will be hard-pressed to find such types of corrections in jurisdictions following the equality as non-discrimination model.

10 BVerfGE 105, 73.
11 Case K 39/13 (PCT, March 3, 2015).
12 ibid.
13 Constitutional Interpretation No 701 (Constitutional Court of Taiwan, 2012).

As in the equality as discrimination category, we also see some internal variations within the equality as reasonableness model. On the one hand, France has a lower success rate for cases not involving suspect classifications than the other courts in this category. Nevertheless, the overall characteristics still seem similar. On the one hand, France has a high absolute number of successful cases concerning non-suspect classifications, which is in line with the observations regarding the Polish Constitutional Tribunal and the German Federal Constitutional Court. Furthermore, France also has the highest overall number of equality cases, suggesting that the *Conseil constitutionnel* might have less control over the cases it selects and publishes than, for example, the German Federal Constitutional Court. If we had access to all cases decided by the latter, the success rate would most probably decrease. Furthermore, the share of successful cases involving a suspect classification is considerably lower than for most jurisdictions in the equality as non-discrimination model. In particular, the difference in success rates—just 4 percentage points—is much less in France than in all jurisdictions following the equality as non-discrimination model.

1.4 Positive understanding of equality

The positive approach to equality can predominantly be found in Latin America. All Latin American courts in our sample, the IACtHR, the Brazilian Federal Supreme Court (STF), and the Constitutional Court of Colombia, can be classified as adhering to this model. Furthermore, we also classified the South African Constitutional Court in this category even though it does not share all the traits of the other three courts. If we only look at the success rates, the courts following the positive equality model show characteristics similar to the equality as reasonableness model. This is, in particular, the case for the Brazilian STF and the Constitutional Court of Colombia, where the overall number of cases not involving a suspect classification is greater than the number of cases involving a suspect classification (see Table 20.3). A striking difference is the much higher success rate for cases involving a suspect classification. With the exception of Brazil, these are all above 70% and thus even higher than in most courts following the equality as non-discrimination model.

Furthermore, the three Latin American courts also have an extensive jurisprudence regarding positive measures that we have not observed to the same extent in the jurisdictions that we classified in the other three models. This is particularly the case for the IACtHR, where 41.5% of the cases in our sample concern positive obligations of the state that the IACtHR derived from equality. One prominent example is the *Fireworks Factory* case, where the IACtHR held that Brazil had violated Article 24 of the American Convention on Human Rights (ACHR) because it had failed to adopt positive measures to support a historically marginalized group

Table 20.3 Success rates within the positive equality model

Court	Non-suspect classifications	Suspect classifications
IACtHR	28.6% (*N* = 14)	89.74% (*N* = 39)
Brazilian STF	47.6% (*N* = 170)	52.25% (*N* = 89)
Const. Court of Colombia	28.7% (*N* = 129)	70.19% (*N* = 52)
Const. Court of South Africa	32.26% (*N* = 31)	82.05% (*N* = 39)

in a situation of structural poverty.[14] In Brazil, many decisions of the STF also concern positive measures. The Court has mostly reaffirmed and expanded existing positive measures, but in individual cases also created new positive obligations for the state. For example, in *ADO 26*, the Court argued that the legislature had violated the equality guarantee of the Brazilian constitution by not criminalizing homophobia and transphobia and thus failing to protect the victims of these acts.[15] Finally, the Colombian Court has shown a propensity to emphasize positive measures even though this dimension is weaker than for the IACtHR or the STF. Unlike the latter two courts, the Colombian Constitutional Court has not independently imposed positive duties on the legislature. However, it had to assess positive measures adopted by the legislature several times, and it usually either upheld or even expanded the scope of these measures.[16]

The South African Constitutional Court is an outlier in this respect. While the Court has shown a strong rhetoric in favor of substantive equality and the transformative character of the Constitution,[17] the transformative rhetoric is stronger than the transformative character of the judicial practice.[18] In particular, the South African Constitutional Court has not imposed positive obligations on the legislature and executive that it derived from the concept of equality. However, this

[14] *Workers of the Fireworks Factory in Santo Antônio de Jesus and their Families v Brazil* (IACtHR, July 15, 2020).

[15] *ADO 26/DF* (STF, June 13, 2019).

[16] See eg T-025/04 (Constitutional Court of Colombia, January 22, 2004); T-192/14 (Constitutional Court of Colombia, April 1, 2014).

[17] The concept of transformative constitutionalism goes back to Karl E Klare, "Legal Culture and Transformative Constitutionalism" (1998) 14 South African Journal on Human Rights 146.

[18] See Catherine Albertyn, "Contested Substantive Equality in the South African Constitution: Beyond Social Inclusion Towards Systemic Justice" (2018) 34 South African Journal on Human Rights 441 (arguing that the South African Constitutional Court has put a greater emphasis on equality of recognition than on redistribution). See also the academic criticism labelling the fundamental rights jurisprudence of the Constitutional Court as too minimalist: Alfred Cockrell, "Rainbow Jurisprudence" (1996) 12 South African Journal on Human Rights 1; Patrick Lenta, "Judicial Restraint and Overreach" (2004) 20 South African Journal on Human Rights 544. For a more nuanced assessment, see Dennis M Davis and Karl E Klare, "Transformative Constitutionalism and the Common and Customary Law" (2010) 26 South African Journal on Human Rights 403.

might also be due to the strong emphasis on social rights in the South African Constitution, which might crowd out positive equality cases.[19] Considering the high success rate of cases involving a suspect classification and the strong rhetoric regarding positive equality, it seems that the jurisprudence of the South African Constitutional Court is more comparable to the Latin American equality case law than to case law of the courts following the equality as reasonableness model.

In the introductory chapter, we argued that a court embracing positive measures for the protection of vulnerable groups did not necessarily also have to adopt a non-deferential approach towards non-suspect classifications. Conceptually, we can distinguish these two categories. However, our results show that the four courts in this model often correct measures concerning non-suspect classifications. This is, in particular, the case for the Brazilian STF and the Constitutional Court of Colombia. Both Courts show high success rates for non-suspect classifications, which are in line with what we saw for the equality as reasonableness courts. Furthermore, the overall number of cases not involving suspect classifications are higher than the number of cases involving suspect classifications, signaling an openness of the respective courts to review these challenges. The situation is slightly different for the IACtHR and the South African Constitutional Court where the number of cases involving suspect classifications surpasses the number of cases not involving a suspect classification. Nevertheless, the success rate for the latter category is also high, which is a characteristic of a rather non-deferential approach. These observations suggest that courts imposing positive measures on the legislature and the executive generally apply a low level of deference. This does not only concern measures affecting vulnerable groups but the review of acts of state authority in general. As a result, it appears that, in practice, the positive equality model is the least deferential of all four models.

1.5 Deferential approach to equality

The final model in our categorization is the deferential approach that predominantly leaves questions of equality for the legislature to decide. We have seen that some courts in the equality as non-discrimination category, such as the Supreme Court of Canada or the Supreme Court and the Court of Appeal of New Zealand, are rather deferential in their equality jurisprudence, but they still fit into the former category. The only court that squarely fits into the deferential model is the Supreme Court of Singapore. In the period of analysis, the Court of Appeal and the High Court, which together form the Supreme Court, have not found a single violation of equality. Certainly, this might not entirely be due to the Court's

[19] See David Bilchitz, *Poverty and Fundamental Rights: The Justification and Enforcement of Socio-Economic Rights* (OUP 2007) on social rights in the South African Constitution.

Table 20.4 Distribution of jurisdictions across equality models

Equality as non-discrimination	**Equality as reasonableness**
US Supreme Court Supreme Court of Canada UK Supreme Court Supreme Court of New Zealand Supreme Court of India Human Rights Committee European Court of Human Rights Court of Justice of the European Union African Court of Human and Peoples' Rights	German Federal Constitutional Court French Conseil Constitutionnel Polish Constitutional Tribunal Constitutional Court of Taiwan
Deferential approach to equality	**Positive equality**
Supreme Court of Singapore	Inter-American Court of Human Rights Brazilian Supremo Tribunal Federal Corte constitucional de Colombia Constitutional Court of South Africa

approach but also to the type of cases that have come to the Court. Only very few of these concerned differentiations based on suspect classifications. Nevertheless, the Court's approach can only be described as deferential.[20]

1.6 Conclusion

In a descriptive sense, the study underlying this book has largely confirmed our hypothesis: there is no uniform global model of equality rights. Instead, we have seen that courts largely follow the four different models of equality that we introduced in the introduction.[21] These models appear in different frequencies (see Table 20.4). The prevailing model is the equality as non-discrimination model, which also dominates the scholarly discourse about equality. However, the equality as reasonableness and the positive equality models are present in quite a few jurisdictions—the former predominantly in continental Europe, the latter in Latin America and South Africa. Finally, the deferential approach is rather exceptional as a categorical approach. However, it is important to emphasize that we cannot generalize these patterns. They are heavily dependent on the choice of the sample. If we had chosen different jurisdictions, that is, fewer common law jurisdictions and more jurisdictions from continental Europe, Asia, or Africa, we might have found a different distribution.

[20] For a detailed discussion, see Chapter 14, section 3.3.
[21] See Chapter 1, section 2.

What the analysis demonstrates, however, is that the four models correlate with different degrees of deference. The deferential approach is—as the name already indicates—the most deferential of the four models. The equality as non-discrimination approach is expression of a medium level of deference where courts only intervene when suspect classifications are involved, while they largely defer to the legislature in cases that do not involve suspect classifications. The equality as reasonableness approach is more searching because the courts following this approach also correct measures that differentiate on non-suspect grounds. The least deferential approach is the positive equality approach. Courts falling into this category usually share the inclination to correct measures even if they do not involve a suspect classification. But in addition, they also frequently impose positive duties on the legislature and the executive that they derive from equality.

These findings have implications for the broader comparative discussion. On the one hand, they confirm our initially voiced assumption that there is no uniform global model for constitutional equality guarantees. Even though the formulation of equality guarantees is fairly similar across different constitutions and international human rights treaties, we do not observe a doctrinal convergence in their implementation. Instead, the judicial operationalization of equality differs quite significantly across jurisdictions and legal traditions.

On the other hand, it also has implications for our understanding of the relationship between common law and civil law jurisdictions. In their excellent book *Comparative Constitutional Reasoning*, András Jakab, Arthur Dyevre, and Giulio Itzcovich tried to cluster constitutional orders based on certain pre-identified characteristics.[22] They found that the distinction between common law and civil law is much less pronounced in constitutional law than is generally assumed.[23] However, this finding is not reflected in our results. While the common law courts in our sample—with the exception of Singapore—all follow the equality as non-discrimination model, applying a certain level of deference, the only non-common law courts falling under this model are international courts and tribunals. All other domestic apex courts adhere to one of the other three models. They apply less deference to legislature and executive than the common law courts.

Furthermore, the results of the cluster analysis of Jakab, Dyevre, and Itzcovich[24] are not strongly reflected in our findings. While a strong connection between Canada and the United Kingdom can also be observed in our results, the similarities of other courts described by Jakab, Dyevre, and Itzcovich are less clear in our analysis. For example, the similarity of the UK and Canadian Supreme Courts to Germany or the similarities of the CJEU and Taiwan or the ECtHR and South Africa cannot be observed in our results. Certainly, our findings do not discredit

[22] András Jakab, Arthur Dyevre, and Giulio Itzcovich, "Conclusion" in András Jakab, Arthur Dyevre, and Giulio Itzcovich (eds), *Comparative Constitutional Reasoning* (CUP 2017) 761.
[23] ibid 768–82.
[24] See ibid 778.

the results of Jakab, Dyevre, and Itzcovich. To the contrary; our study focused on a much narrower issue—equality—while taking a much more in-depth perspective. We not only focused on landmark judgments but a representative sample of the issue in question. Instead, if both the findings of Jakab, Dyevre, and Itzcovich as well as our results hold, it might suggest that equality follows a different logic than fundamental rights in general.

2. In-depth analysis of cross-cutting issues

The last section tried to draw a general picture of the equality case law across the different jurisdictions of our sample. In this section, we focus on an in-depth analysis of certain cross-cutting issues that are subject to intensive debates in the international discourse on equality and non-discrimination. First, we want to look at the role of suspect classifications (Subsection 2.1). As we have seen in the introduction, there is a controversial debate on how to identify classifications to be considered as suspect. In this section, we will focus on the judicial practice—which classifications do judges treat as suspect? Second, we will analyze the different courts' approaches to indirect discrimination. Again, there is no agreement in the literature on the reason why indirect discrimination is problematic nor on how courts should approach the issue. Therefore, we will look at the courts' strategies in practice (Subsection 2.2). The final part of this section deals with positive measures and their assessment by courts (Subsection 2.3).

2.1 Role of suspect classifications

As we have seen in the introduction, there is a prominent debate on the characteristics of a suspect criterion of distinction.[25] For courts, the interest of this theoretical debate is more limited. If they interpret a non-discrimination norm, they do not have to justify why a specific characteristic is suspect if it is explicitly mentioned in the norm. A greater effort of justification could, in theory, be expected if courts want to expand the list of explicitly mentioned characteristics, but in practice, the identification of analogous grounds of distinction is often not accompanied by an elaborate reasoning. For example, when the ECtHR qualified sexual orientation as an "other status" in the sense of Article 14 ECHR, it simply argued that sexual orientation was "a concept which is undoubtedly covered by Article 14 of the Convention. The Court reiterates in that connection that the list set out

[25] See Chapter 1, section 2.2.1.

in that provision is illustrative and not exhaustive, as is shown by the words 'any ground such as.'"[26]

Courts sometimes touch on the issue when they want to justify a heightened or reduced level of deference or burden of justification. For example, the UK Supreme Court argued that nationality was "not a particularly 'suspect' classification" in the "context of immigration"[27] or that residence was not a suspect classification because it was a matter of choice.[28] Furthermore, in its famous footnote 4 of the *Carolene Products* decision, the US Supreme Court referred to "prejudice against discrete and insular minorities" as a justification for a "more searching judicial inquiry",[29] but this statement came in an *obiter dictum*. When it comes to the justification of attributing concrete levels of scrutiny to specific kinds of classifications, the Supreme Court is usually much less explicit. When it introduced the standard of intermediate scrutiny for sex discriminations in *Craig v Boren*, for example, Justice Brennan, writing for the Court, only referred to the Court's precedence in *Reed*[30]—notwithstanding that *Reed* had been decided on the basis of rational basis review.[31]

Consequently, it appears more fruitful to analyze the results of our empirical analysis to get a sense of which differentiations courts are actually considering to be suspect in their judicial practice. The picture that emerges is quite diverse and complex. One criterion of distinction that is consistently regarded as suspect by almost all courts is the criterion of sex or gender. In most jurisdictions, this criterion draws a considerable number of challenges and usually has a rather high success rate, but there are a few exceptions. In the United Kingdom, gender discrimination only plays a minor role in the case law of the Supreme Court, and all cases that have been brought to the Court have been unsuccessful. We hypothesized that this might be due to the kinds of cases that have come to the Court and that many of the issues have been crowded out by the jurisdictions of the CJEU.[32] In Brazil, the success rate is also rather low, but this has again been explained by the specific cases that have come to the Court.[33] A rather astonishing jurisdiction is India, where the Supreme Court has only decided two cases concerning gender distinctions that were contained in our sample.[34] There are studies that suggest a significant gender bias in the Indian judiciary.[35] This might explain the low number of gender

[26] *Salgueiro da Silva Mouta v Portugal* ECHR 1999-IX 309.
[27] *R (Ali) v Secretary of State for the Home Department* [2015] UKSC 68, para 57 (per Lady Hale).
[28] *R (Carson) v Secretary of State for Work and Pensions* [2005] UKHL 37, para 58 (per Lord Hoffman).
[29] *United States v Carolene Products Co* 304 US 144 (footnote 4) (1938).
[30] *Craig v Boren* 429 US 190, 197 (1976).
[31] *Reed v Reed* 404 US 71, 75–77 (1971).
[32] See Chapter 6, section 3.2.
[33] See Chapter 12, section 4.2.
[34] See Chapter 13, section 3.2.
[35] See in particular Nirvikar Jassal, "Does Victim Gender Matter for Justice Delivery? Police and Judicial Responses to Women's Cases in India" (2024) 118 APSR 1278.

discrimination cases in the Indian Supreme Court. Finally, there has not been a single successful gender discrimination case in Singapore.[36]

Another suspect classification that is recognized almost consistently across jurisdictions is sexual orientation. While there are usually not as many cases as with regards to gender, these cases usually have a high success rate. But there are again a few jurisdictions where sexual orientation cases are either absent or not successful: Poland, Singapore, and India.

When it comes to race or ethnicity, we observe more diversity. In some jurisdictions, race is the dominant characteristic, featuring in the majority of cases of discrimination. This is obviously the case for the US Supreme Court, where the demand for heightened scrutiny in race cases has been at the origin of the Court's tiered scrutiny doctrine.[37] Therefore, it is not surprising that a relative majority of cases involving a suspect classification before the US Supreme Court concern direct or indirect distinctions based on race.[38] Similarly, race is the suspect classification with the highest number of successful cases before the ECtHR.[39] The cases before the Strasbourg Court predominantly concern discrimination against Sinti and Roma. Two further courts where distinctions based on race or ethnicity play a considerable role in the case law are the IACtHR and the South African Constitutional Court. In particular, in South Africa, the Court's sensitivity to race-based distinctions is not surprising, considering that the Court emerged as part of the post-apartheid constitutional order. Finally, in Brazil, race is equally an important factor in equality cases. However, the cases usually do not challenge negative race discrimination, but positive measures that favor disadvantaged groups, which have all been unsuccessful before the STF.[40]

However, in all other jurisdictions, race-related cases only play a marginal role. This is not primarily because these cases are not successful, but because there are very few of them (if at all). For example, our sample of the case law of the German Federal Constitutional Court does not contain a single case dealing with a race-based distinction. We can only speculate about the reasons.[41] Some of the societies that are subject to our analysis are ethnically more homogenous than others so race-based distinctions might traditionally have been less likely to occur. However, it seems unlikely that such distinctions are totally absent. Furthermore, we also have more pluralist societies like Canada or New Zealand where distinctions

[36] See Chapter 14, section 3.2.

[37] See Robert M Cover, "The Origins of Judicial Activism in the Protection of Minorities" (1982) 91 Yale LJ 1287; Michael Klarman, "An Interpretive History of Modern Equal Protection" (1991) 90 Michigan LR 213; Richard H Fallon, "Strict Judicial Scrutiny" (2007) 54 UCLA LR 1267.

[38] See Chapter 2, section 3.3.

[39] See Chapter 4, section 3.2.2.

[40] See Chapter 12, section 4.2.

[41] For a thorough analysis of potential reasons for the absence of racial discrimination cases in the EU, see Gráinne de Búrca and Virginia Passalacqua, "The Curious Absence of Race Discrimination Litigation in EU Law" (conference paper at the 2024 I.CON conference, on file with the author).

based on race are outside the focus of the judiciary. A more plausible explanation concerns the access to courts. There is often a correlation between race and social class. Racial minorities often come from social groups where distrust of the formal court system is widespread and information about potential legal remedies is lacking.[42] In the United States, organizations like the National Association for the Advancement of Colored People (NAACP) have been crucial for bringing racial discrimination cases to the Supreme Court.[43] However, such organizations are often lacking in states where racial discrimination is less salient.[44]

Furthermore, there may be procedural obstacles to bringing race discrimination cases. Today, racial discrimination is often indirect and due to implicit biases. However, in many cases, such discrimination is difficult to prove. Finally, it might also be that there are different mechanisms to deal with issues of race and ethnicity. For example, in New Zealand, issues concerning the Māori population are often dealt with under the Treaty of Waitangi and not under the prohibition of discrimination of the Bill of Rights Act.[45] This would certainly be an interesting issue to explore in further research.

Some characteristics are important in some jurisdictions but not in others. For example, discrimination against children whose parents have not been married at the time of birth have been subject to a significant number of cases in the United States, the ECtHR, Germany, and Colombia, while the issue seems to be marginal in other jurisdictions. Disability is a concern in the majority of jurisdictions analyzed. Cases concerning disability have a rather high success rate, but the overall number of cases brought is usually low. Similarly, distinctions based on marriage or family status have drawn strict judicial scrutiny in jurisdictions such as the United Kingdom, Germany, Colombia, Brazil, Taiwan, New Zealand, and South Africa, while they are largely absent in other jurisdictions. Distinctions based on age and residency status have seen different treatment by various courts. While age cases have seen a significant measure of success before the CJEU and the IACtHR, as well as in Colombia, Brazil, Taiwan, and New Zealand, there were other courts with a considerable number of age-related cases with a rather low success rate, such as Canada, Germany, and Poland. With regards to distinctions based on residence, such cases were rather successful in the United States, Poland, Colombia,

[42] See Sara Sternberg Greene, "Race, Class, and Access to Civil Justice" (2016) 101 Iowa LR 1263.

[43] On the NAACP, see Patricia Sullivan, *Lift Every Voice: The NAACP and the Making of the Civil Rights Movement* (New Press 2010).

[44] See also de Búrca and Passalacqua (n 40) who observe an absence of institutional support for racial discrimination cases and a lack of networks between lawyers and activists and victims of racial discrimination.

[45] This was suggested in a discussion by my colleague Janet McLean. For example, a case on COVID-19 vaccine priority, which could have been framed, as a discrimination case was treated by the Waitangi Tribunal instead, see *Haumaru: The covid-19 Priority Report*, WAI 2575 (Waitangi Tribunal Report 2021) <https://www.waitangitribunal.govt.nz/> accessed January 20, 2025.

and Brazil, while they have seen less success in Germany, the United Kingdom, Taiwan, and India.

Finally, we have some characteristics that are treated as a concern in individual jurisdictions but that do not resonate in the majority of jurisdictions in our sample. The most obvious example is caste, which is a dominant preoccupation of the Indian Supreme Court but of no concern outside India. Another example is poverty or economic status. Challenges of direct or indirect distinctions based on economic status have been particularly successful in Latin America: The IACtHR, the Constitutional Court of Colombia, and the Brazilian Supreme Court have decided a sizeable number of cases related to economic status, and these cases have had success rates of 100% for the IACtHR, of 75% for the Constitutional Court of Colombia, and of 50% for the Brazilian Supreme Court. In the case of Brazil, the relatively "low" success rate is explained by the fact that unsuccessful cases usually target positive measures that aim to improve the position of economically vulnerable groups. This is not surprising, considering the strong emphasis that they have put on positive duties derived from equality and the strong focus on eradicating poverty in the respective constitutions. Outside Latin America, the only court where economic status has played a substantial role is Poland, where the Constitutional Tribunal has decided eight cases related to economic status, with a success rate of 50%.

2.2 Indirect discrimination

A mere focus on direct discrimination without also targeting indirect discrimination would be ineffective.[46] Once distinctions based on certain suspect criteria become prohibited and the prohibition is implemented, the practice usually fades. In our post-1970 sample of the US Supreme Court, only four cases concern direct racial discrimination—a significant reduction compared to the 1950s and 1960s. However, this does not necessarily mean that the intentional disadvantaging of vulnerable groups also ceases. Instead, actors intending to discriminate often resort to apparent neutral distinctions that are correlated with the suspect distinction.[47] In the case of race, these may be education or identity requirements. Correspondingly, our post-1970 sample of the US Supreme Court shows a considerable number of indirect race discrimination cases.[48] Therefore,

[46] Hugh Collins and Tarunabh Khaitan, "Indirect Discrimination Law: Controversies and Critical Questions" in Hugh Collins and Tarunabh Khaitan (eds), *Foundations of Indirect Discrimination Law* (Hart 2018) 1, 4.

[47] For an elegant elaboration of this point, see Reva Siegel, "Why Equal Protection No Longer Protects: The Evolving Forms of Status-Enforcing State Action" (1997) 49 Stanford LR 1111.

[48] See Chapter 2, section 3.3.

it is commonly accepted that distinctions that intend to discriminate are discriminatory regardless of whether they are explicitly based on a suspect criterion or only have a disadvantageous effect on a vulnerable group. However, the question of whether disparate impacts are problematic beyond intentional discrimination is controversial.[49]

In *Griggs*, a case decided under the Civil Rights Act 1964, the US Supreme Court initially indicated a broader conception of indirect discrimination. It argued that measures disparately impacting ethnic minorities had to be reasonably related to a legitimate aim.[50] However, the Court significantly restricted the scope of indirect discriminations in its later jurisprudence on the constitutional equal protection clause. In *Washington v Davis*, the Court held that a mere disparate impact was not sufficient for triggering strict scrutiny for racial discrimination.[51] Instead, strict scrutiny required the proof of discriminatory intent.[52] This requirement of discriminatory intent for heightened scrutiny has been confirmed several times in the later jurisprudence.[53] While the absence of discriminatory intent does not automatically exclude discrimination, it leads to the application of the rational basis test. In practice, there is not a single indirect discrimination case that has been successful when decided under the rational basis test.[54]

This strict approach of the US Supreme Court is almost universally rejected outside of the United States. Most courts argue explicitly that intentional discrimination is not required for a finding of indirect discrimination.[55] Some courts are explicitly or implicitly influenced by the US Supreme Court decision in *Griggs* without engaging with the post-*Washington v Davis* restriction of the doctrine.[56] The concept of indirect discrimination has played a very prominent role in the jurisprudence of the CJEU.[57] In the late 1970s, the Court started to develop an indirect discrimination doctrine with regards to discriminations based on nationality and

[49] See the discussion in Chapter 1, section 2.2.2.
[50] *Griggs v Duke Power Co* 401 US 424, 436 (1971).
[51] *Wash v Davis* 426 US 229 (1976).
[52] ibid 239.
[53] See in particular *McCleskey v Kemp* 481 US 279, 292 (1987).
[54] See Chapter 2, section 3.3.
[55] See eg *Law Society of British Columbia v Andrews* [1989] 1 SCR 143, 174; *Fraser v Canada (Attorney General)* 2020 SCC 28, para 69; Case 170/84 *Bilka-Kaufhaus* [1986] ECR 1607; *D.H. v Czech Republic* [GC] ECHR 2007-IV 241, para 184; *Althammer et al. v Austria* CCPR/C/78/D/998/2001 (HRCttee, August 8, 2003) para 10.2. See also Barbara Havelková, "Judicial Scepticism of Discrimination at the ECtHR" in Hugh Collins and Tarunabh Khaitan (eds), *Foundations of Indirect Discrimination Law* (Hart 2018) 83 (arguing that it might be less confrontational for courts to find an indirect discrimination instead of discriminatory intent).
[56] See eg *British Columbia (Public Service Employee Relations Committee) v BCGSEU* [1999] 3 SCR 3, 19; *Quebec (Attorney General) v A* [2013] 1 SCR 61, 219; *Kahkewistahaw First Nation v Taypotat* [2015] 2 SCR 548, 557–58; *Fraser v Canada (Attorney General)*, 2020 SCC 28 paras 32–38, 53–55, 70–71.
[57] See Chapter 5, section 2.2.

sex.[58] But the concept has also been adopted by other international courts, such as the ECtHR[59] and the IACtHR,[60] and by domestic apex courts.[61]

If courts have developed a specific doctrine for indirect discrimination, they usually apply a two-step test. First, they ask whether there is a disparate impact, and second, whether there is a reasonable justification for this disparate impact. Both steps are not without problems. The first step requires a measure for what counts as a disparate impact. Often parties will cite statistical effects to support their case. However, it is unclear whether a statistically significant difference between the "dominant" and the vulnerable group is sufficient or whether this effect has to be of a certain magnitude.[62] In the justification stage, not every legitimate aim *per se* justifies a disparate impact. Therefore, the question of justification ultimately comes down to a balancing between the aim of the measure and the prevention of its negative effects. However, it is unclear from where we can derive standards for such balancing, and the analyzed courts do not openly discuss this question.

The most convincing approach focuses on whether the disparate impact is due to structural reasons.[63] The disparate impact of differentiations between part-time and full-time employees on women would be based on structural reasons because women are more likely to work part-time because they disproportionately bear the burden of childcare in most societies. By contrast, if a difference in effect is merely accidental, it does not constitute an indirect discrimination. The line between these two categories will be difficult to draw in many cases, however our analysis has shown that the judicial discussion on indirect discrimination is often superficial and has, thus far, only scratched the surface of the problem.

2.3 Positive measures

When it comes to positive measures, courts can follow two approaches, in principle. Either they can interpret equality asymmetrically or they can treat the positive measure as a *prima facie* interference and discuss the violation of equality on

[58] See Case 43/75 *Defrenne (No 2)* [1976] ECR 456, para 18; Case 61/77 *Commission v Ireland* [1978] ECR 417, para 79.

[59] See *D.H.* (n 55). For an excellent discussion of indirect discrimination in the case law of the ECtHR, see Havelková (n 55).

[60] See *Artavia Murillo et al. ("in vitro fertilization") v Costa Rica* (IACtHR, November 28, 2012).

[61] See eg *R (JS) v Secretary of State for Work and Pensions* [2015] UKSC 16, para 61 (per Lord Reed); BVerfGE 97, 35, 43–44; *RE 500.171-7* (STF, August 13, 2008).

[62] For a discussion of this problem, see eg *R v Secretary of State for Employment ex p. Seymour-Smith (No 2)* [2000] UKHL 12.

[63] See Anna Katharina Mangold, *Demokratische Inklusion durch Recht* (Mohr Siebeck 2021) 242–46. See also Gerald L Neuman, "Questions of Indirect Discrimination on the Basis of Religion" (2021) 34 Harvard Human Rights Journal 177 (arguing that the potential justification of indirect discriminations should depend on the normative reason for which we consider non-intentional indirect discriminations to be problematic).

the justification stage. The asymmetric interpretation of equality is often advocated in the academic discussion of equality.[64] However, in judicial practice, it is rather rare. The court that has shown an asymmetric approach most clearly is the Supreme Court of Canada. It requires that a distinction perpetuates prejudice or stereotyping to constitute a discrimination. Therefore, positive measures usually do not even get to the justification stage because they fail to constitute a *prima face* discrimination.[65] Furthermore, Latin American courts have also been guided by an asymmetric approach to equality, where positive measures do not engage equality on a *prima facie* level.[66]

By contrast, most other courts in our sample deal with the question of positive measures on the justification stage. Here, courts show different levels of accommodation towards positive measures. While the majority of courts show a rather high level of deference towards the legislature and generally accept the constitutionality of positive measures, some courts are less deferential. This concerns most prominently the US Supreme Court. While the latter has accepted in principle that positive measures—or in the terminology of the court: affirmative action—can be justified, it applies the standard of strict scrutiny to such affirmative action measures.[67] Consequently, about half the challenges of affirmative action are successful. While the doctrinal approach of the US Supreme Court is unique, the skepticism towards positive measures is not. This issue cuts across our different models of equality. For example, the Indian Supreme Court has struck down about half of all the affirmative action measures that it has reviewed.[68] Similarly, the CJEU has restricted the use of quotas on women in the hiring process.[69] At the same time, skepticism towards positive measures can also be observed in jurisdictions following the equality as reasonableness model. Most notably, the French *Conseil constitutionnel* has declared women's quotas in politics to be incompatible with the French Constitution on two occasions.[70]

[64] See Owen M Fiss, "Groups and the Equal Protection Clause" (1976) 5 Philosophy & Public Affairs 107; Kenji Yoshino, "Assimilationist Bias in Equal Protection: The Visibility Presumption and the Case of 'Don't Ask, Don't Tell'" (1998) 108 Yale LJ 485; Tarunabh Khaitan, *A Theory of Discrimination Law* (OUP 2015) 61–62.

[65] See Chapter 3, section 2.2.

[66] See Chapters 10, 11, and 12.

[67] See *Wygant v Jackson Bd of Education* 476 US 267, 274 (1986); *Richmond v JA Croson Co* 488 US 469, 493 (1989); *Adarand Constructors v Pena* 515 US 200, 222 (1995); *Gratz v Bollinger* 539 US 244, 257 (2003); *Grutter v Bollinger* 539 US 306, 321 (2003); *Parents Involved in Cmty Sch v Seattle Sch Dist No 1* 551 US 701, 720 (2007); *Fisher v Univ of Tex* 570 US 297 (2013); *Fisher v Univ of Tex II* 579 US 365 (2016); *Fair Admissions, Inc v President and Fellows of Harvard College* 600 US 181 (2023).

[68] See Chapter 13, section 3.2.

[69] Case C-450/93 *Kalanke* [1995] ECR I-3051, para 22; Case C-409/95 *Marschall* [1997] ECR I-6363, para 33; Case C-407/98 *Abrahamsson and Anderson* [2000] ECR I-5539. For a discussion of the CJEU's approach, see Uladzislau Belavusau and Kristin Henrard, "A Bird's Eye View on EU Anti-Discrimination Law: The Impact of the 2000 Equality Directive" (2019) 20 German LJ 614, 632–33; Mark Bell, "EU Anti-Discrimination Law: Navigating Sameness and Difference" in Paul Craig and Gráinne De Búrca (eds), *The Evolution of EU Law* (OUP 2021) 651, 658–60.

[70] Decision no 82-146 DC (French CC, November 18, 1982); Decision no 98-407 DC (French CC, January 14, 1999). See Chapter 8, section 4.2 for a more detailed discussion.

On the other side of the spectrum, some courts do not only approve positive measures that have been enacted by the legislature or implemented by the executive but even impose them on executive and legislature if the political branches fail to act. The classical example is the protection of women against gender-based violence. This violence is often not exercised directly by the state but by private individuals. However, courts attribute the violence to the state by imposing positive duties of protection against gender-based violence on the legislature and the executive.[71] In most jurisdictions, such positive duties are derived from equality only in exceptional cases. However, in the Latin American jurisdictions in our sample, the imposition of positive duties can be found more often and it spans a wider range of different issues.[72]

3. Reasons for the different models

While the previous two sections have described the state of the equality case law across the analyzed jurisdictions, this section seeks to explain the picture that has emerged. Why have specific courts favored one approach to equality over another? Why have they differed in their approaches and not converged to the same extent that we see in other areas of fundamental rights? Certainly, the wording of constitutional norms matters. If the constitution contains a general equality clause, the court will be more likely to adopt a less deferential approach than if it only contains a non-discrimination clause. For example, the focus of the CJEU on antidiscrimination seems to be shaped to a significant extent by the highly specific wording of the EU antidiscrimination norms.[73] But the differences in the wording of equality norms cannot be the only explanation for the divergences that we have observed. Instead, the following analysis will focus on five different factors that are partly interrelated. First, we analyze how the authority of courts influences their equality doctrine (Subsection 3.1). Second, we will examine the historical context in which the system of judicial review was established and how this founding narrative impacted the courts' approach towards equality (Subsection 3.2). Furthermore, we will discuss the role of legal tradition (Subsection 3.3) and political ideology (Subsection 3.4), before, finally, tracing the influence of foreign and international courts on the development of the equality doctrine (Subsection 3.5).

[71] See eg *Goekce v Austria* CEDAW/C/39/D/5/2005 (August 6, 2007); *Opuz v Turkey* ECHR 2009-III 107; *Gónzalez et al. ("Cotton Field") v Mexico* (IACtHR, November 16, 2009); *Purna Maya v Nepal* CCPR/C/119/D/2245/2013 (HRCttee, March 17, 2017); *X v Sri Lanka* CCPR/C/120/D/2256/2013 (HRCttee, July 27, 2017).

[72] See earlier, section 1.3.

[73] See Chapter 5, section 4.

3.1 The authority of courts

The effectiveness of courts cannot be assumed *per se*. Courts lack the power to implement their own decisions and their competences may be restricted by the legislature.[74] For this reason, the effectiveness of courts depends on their authority.[75] The greater the legitimacy of a court, the more the non-implementation of its judgments or the restriction of its powers can hurt political actors because they have to fear backlash.[76] Therefore, we hypothesized that the authority of a court is correlated with the level of deference that it applies. A court that has a rather precarious institutional position will tend to be more deferential toward the legislature or the executive because it might fear political backlash if it applies a more searching level of scrutiny.

Our analysis provides some evidence for this hypothesis. The Courts that apply less deferential approaches usually enjoy a high level of legitimacy. The German Federal Constitutional Court is a widely respected authority within the German constitutional system and enjoys broad popular support.[77] Therefore, it seems unsurprising that the Federal Constitutional Court applies a less deferential approach to equality. Similarly, the Brazilian STF has a strong role within the Brazilian institutional system. The hearings of the court are streamed live on public television and the judges are household names—unlike in most other legal systems.[78] Consequently, it seems fitting that the STF shows probably the most

[74] See Heinz Klug, "Introducing the Devil: An Institutional Analysis of the Power of Constitutional Review" (1997) 13 South African Journal on Human Rights 185, 189; Helmuth Schulze-Fielitz, "Das Bundesverfassungsgericht in der Krise des Zeitgeists—Zur Metadogmatik der Verfassungsinterpretation" (1997) 122 Archiv des öffentlichen Rechts 1, 27; Roland Lhotta, "Das Bundesverfassungsgericht als politischer Akteur: Plädoyer für eine neo-institutionalistische Ergänzung der Forschung" (2003) 9 Swiss Political Science Review 142, 143; Andrej Lang, "Wider die Metapher vom letzten Wort: Verfassungsgerichte als Wegweiser" in Dominik Elser and others (eds), *Das letzte Wort* (Nomos 2014) 15.

[75] Georg Vanberg, *The Politics of Constitutional Review in Germany* (CUP 2005) 49–53; Walter F Murphy and Joseph Tanenhaus, "Publicity, Public Opinion, and the Court" (1990) 84 Northwestern University LR 985; Lee Epstein, Jack Knight, and Olga Shvetsova, "The Role of Constitutional Courts in the Establishment and Maintenance of Democratic Systems of Government" (2001) 35 Law & Society Review 117, 125; Christoph Engel, "Delineating the Proper Scope of Government: A Proper Task for a Constitutional Court?" (2001) 157 Journal of Institutional and Theoretical Economics 187, 213; Clifford James Carrubba, "A Model of the Endogenous Development of Judicial Institutions in Federal and International Systems" (2009) 71 Journal of Politics 55, 65; Sascha Kneip, *Verfassungsgerichte als politische Akteure* (Nomos 2009) 199; Silvia von Steinsdorff, "Verfassungsgerichte als Demokratie-Versicherung? Ursachen und Grenzen der wachsenden Bedeutung juristischer Politikkontrolle" in Klemens H Schrenk and Markus Soldner (eds), *Analyse demokratischer Regierungssysteme: Festschrift für Wolfgang Ismayr zum 65. Geburtstag* (VS Verlag für Sozialwissenschaften 2010) 479, 492; Lang (n 74) 27.

[76] Vanberg (n 75) 74.

[77] Hans Vorländer and André Brodocz, "Das Vertrauen in das Bundesverfassungsgericht: Ergebnisse einer repräsentativen Bevölkerungsumfrage" in Hans Vorländer (ed), *Die Deutungsmacht der Verfassungsgerichtsbarkeit* (VS Verlag für Sozialwissenschaften 2006) 259.

[78] See Diana Kapiszewski, "How Courts Work: Institutions, Culture, and the Brazilian *Supremo Tribunal Federal*" in Javier Couso, Alexandra Huneeus, and Rachel Sieder (eds), *Cultures of Legality: Judicialization and Judicial Activism in Latin America* (CUP 2010) 51, 66. Regarding the widespread recognition of the judges in the general public, see also the following study by a Brazilian law

non-deferential approach of all courts within our sample. Finally, the Colombian Constitutional Court is also known to be a respected court that has set limits to powerful political actors, while also applying a non-deferential positive equality approach.[79]

On the flipside, the position of Singaporean courts vis-à-vis politics is rather weak because of the *de facto* one-party rule in Singapore. Therefore, the Singaporean courts prefer a very deferential approach. Similarly, most of the international human courts in our sample also apply a rather deferential equality as non-discrimination approach. As international courts, they have to be even more mindful of the implementation of their judgments and the safeguarding of their institutional position than domestic courts. For example, the ECtHR has often been challenged by member states for perceived interference in political affairs.[80] Some member states discuss leaving the Convention or have strategies to nominate more deferential justices to the court.[81] The Court, therefore, has to strike a fine balance between ensuring political acceptance and avoiding irrelevance by failing to protect the Convention rights. The equality as non-discrimination model seems to represent exactly this balance. Similarly, the UN Human Rights Committee faces many of the same issues as the ECtHR and applies a comparable doctrinal approach.[82]

However, judicial authority does not explain all the observations of our study. For example, all the common law courts in our sample adhere to a rather deferential equality as non-discrimination model even though these courts do not lack legitimacy or institutional respect. On the flipside, the IACtHR is institutionally a rather weak court. As an international court, it shares many of the same challenges as the ECtHR or the UN HRCttee, has a limited budget, and is often challenged by domestic constitutional courts.[83] Nevertheless, it shows a very non-deferential

school: FGV Direito SP, relatório ICJ Brasil 2021, <https://repositorio.fgv.br/items/c50527f9-8183-46ae-b152-f3bb0737a03c> accessed January 20, 2025.

[79] See Vicente Fabian Benitez-Rojas, "We the People, They the Media: Judicial Review of Constitutional Amendments and Public Opinion in Colombia" in Richard Albert, Carlos Bernal and Juliano Zaiden Benvindo (eds), *Constitutional Change and Transformation in Latin America* (Bloomsbury 2019) 143.

[80] For a detailed analysis of pushback against the ECtHR, see Dana Burchardt, *The Authority of International Courts* (Habilitation thesis, University of Bonn 2023) 450–79. See also Courtney Hillebrecht, *Saving the International Justice Regime: Beyond Backlash against International Courts* (CUP 2021) 133–57.

[81] See Ed Bates, "The UK and Strasbourg: A Strained Relationship—The Long View" in Katja S Ziegler, Elizabeth Wicks and Loveday Hodson (eds), *The UK and European Human Rights: A Strained Relationship?* (Hart 2015) 39; David Aronofsky, "Brexit Human Rights Issues: It's Time to Play E.U. Hardball" (2018) 53 Texas International LJ 177; Hillebrecht (n 80) 2.

[82] For a comparison of the different legitimating narratives of the ECtHR and the UN HRCttee, see Yuval Shany, "Can Strasbourg be Replicated at a Global Level? A View from Geneva" in Helmut Philipp Aust and Esra Demir-Gürsel (eds), *The European Court of Human Rights – Current Challenges in Historical and Comparative Perspective* (Edward Elgar 2020) 71.

[83] See René Uruena, "Double or Nothing? The Inter-American Court of Human Rights in an Increasingly Adverse Context" (2018) 35 Wisconsin International LJ 398, 405–08; Thomas M

approach that goes as far as imposing positive duties on member states that are derived from the equality guarantees of the ACHR. Consequently, judicial authority is not the only factor in play explaining the doctrinal choices of the judiciary regarding equality.

3.2 Historical context and founding narrative

A second factor that influences courts can broadly be described as historical context. This refers to the originally intended role—the "founding narrative"—both of the equality provision and the court interpreting this provision. For example, the equal protection clause of the Fourteenth Amendment of the US Constitution was clearly intended to give African Americans equal legal status after the Civil War.[84] This was one of the reasons why the US Supreme Court introduced heightened scrutiny for racial distinctions in the 1950s.[85] It also partially explains why immutability seems to be a necessary element of a suspect characteristic triggering heightened scrutiny. But it cannot explain the whole US equal protection doctrine. It cannot explain why suspect classifications are extended beyond race or the position of the US Supreme Court on indirect discrimination or affirmative action cases. It only provides one piece of the larger puzzle.

The historical context of section 15 of the Canadian Charter of Rights and Freedoms also shaped the case law of the Canadian Supreme Court. Subsection 2 of the provision explicitly empowers the legislature to adopt measures that ameliorate the conditions of disadvantaged individuals or groups. This subsection was adopted as a clear response to the restrictive affirmative action case law of the US Supreme Court. As we have discussed in the chapter on the Canadian equality case law, the Supreme Court of Canada often seeks to differentiate its own jurisprudence from the one of its counterpart south of the border.[86] This does not only concern affirmative action but also the basic construction of the equality doctrine or the approach to indirect discrimination.

However, it is not only the founding narrative of equality provisions that shapes the equality doctrine in different jurisdictions but also the founding context of the courts themselves. Many courts in our sample were established or at least remodeled after a transition from an authoritarian or otherwise morally compromised regime to a constitutional democracy. This concerns the establishment of the

Antkowiak, "The Americas" in Daniel Moeckli, Sangeeta Shah, and Sandesh Sivakumaran (eds), *International Human Rights Law* (OUP 2022) 445, 446.

[84] John P Frank and Robert F Munro, "The Original Understanding of 'Equal Protection of the Laws'" (1950) 50 Columbia LR 131, 136–42.
[85] See Chapter 2, section 4.1.
[86] See Chapter 3, section 4.

German Federal Constitutional Court after the Second World War and the defeat of the Nazi regime in Germany, the Polish Constitutional Tribunal after the end of communism in Poland, and the Constitutional Court of South Africa after the end of apartheid.[87] It is also the case for the extension of judicial authority of the Brazilian STF after the military dictatorship, or the greater *de facto* independence of the Constitutional Court of Taiwan after the end of the Kuomintang dictatorship. One of the central tasks of these courts was to prevent the fallback of the newly emerging democracies into a dictatorship or an authoritarian regime. In other words, they were tasked with policing failures of the political process.[88]

This may have prompted the courts to adopt a less deferential approach. It might also have been necessary because the rationality of the reviewed legislation could not *per se* be assumed. Germany after the Second World War and South Africa in the post-apartheid transition did not and could not abolish all pre-transition legislation. For this reason, a closer scrutiny of such legislation seemed a logical consequence. Similarly, the IACtHR was established in a period when military regimes in Latin America were widespread. One of the main functions of the IACtHR was to control and restrict these authoritarian regimes. This led to the idea of the Court as a motor of transformative constitutionalism.[89] This transformative self-understanding of the Court also explains a more interventionist role of the IACtHR.

3.3 Legal tradition

A third factor influencing the shape of equality doctrines is the legal tradition.[90] We have seen that the approaches of common law and civil law courts to equality

[87] On the influence of the founding context in the case of the German Federal Constitutional Court see the nuanced analysis of Michaela Hailbronner, *Traditions and Transformations: The Rise of German Constitutionalism* (OUP 2015). On post-apartheid South Africa see Theunis Roux, *The Politics of Principle: The First South African Constitutional Court, 1995–2005* (CUP 2013); James Fowkes, *Building the Constitution: The Practice of Constitutional Interpretation in post-apartheid South Africa* (CUP 2016). On constitutional courts in post-communist jurisdictions see Wojciech Sadurski, *Rights before Courts: A Study of Constitutional Courts in Postcommunist States of Central and Eastern Europe* (Springer 2005).

[88] The idea that courts police failure of the political process goes back to John Hart Ely, *Democracy and Distrust: A Theory of Judicial Review* (Harvard University Press 1980). For a comparative application, see Stephen Gardbaum, "Comparative Political Process Theory" (2020) 18 I.CON 1429. But also see Michaela Hailbronner, "Political Process Review: Beyond Distrust" (2020) 18 I.CON 1458 (warning of the dangers of using the vague notion of "failure" to legitimize judicial interventions).

[89] See Armin von Bogdandy and René Uruena, "International Transformative Constitutionalism in Latin America" (2020) 114 AJIL 403. The concept of transformative constitutionalism comes, however, from South Africa, see Klare (n 17). See also Michaela Hailbronner, "Transformative Constitutionalism: Not Only in the Global South" (2017) 65 AJCL 527 (demonstrating the diversity and proliferation of the concept).

[90] On the concept of legal tradition, see eg H Patrick Glenn, *Legal Traditions of the World: Sustainable Diversity in Law* (5th edn, OUP 2014); Jaakko Husa, *Legal Culture vs. Legal Tradition—Different Epistemologies* (Maastricht European Private Law Institute Working Paper No 2012/18).

are quite distinctive. While the former mostly adhere to the equality as non-discrimination model, the latter adopt less deferential approaches. There are two possible explanations for this difference. One explanation focuses on differences in societal context and values. The openness of common law legal systems to non-discrimination law is explained by the greater diversity of these societies because of their colonial history or their historical status as immigrant nations.[91] By contrast, a focus on forging a common identity in many continental European states might emphasize formal equality over the specific protection of vulnerable groups because the latter has the danger of making sub-societal group identities more salient.[92]

Another explanation focuses on the different narratives for legitimizing the judiciary in common law and civil law jurisdictions. In civil law courts, the legitimation of judicial review through expertise plays a crucial role.[93] According to this understanding, courts have the power to review the acts of the legislature because their review is limited to the legal realm and does not encroach the political dimension.[94] It is therefore the belief in legal expertise that justifies judicial review. By contrast, the political role of courts is more salient in common law legal systems.[95] This concerns, in particular, legal systems that have traditionally adhered to the doctrine of parliamentary sovereignty, such as the United Kingdom, Canada, and New Zealand. According to this doctrine, courts do not have the ability to review legislation.[96] While the strictures of the doctrine have been relaxed to varying degrees in recent decades, the concept is still prominent.[97] In the United States, intellectual

[91] Dagmar Schiek, Lisa Waddington, and Mark Bell, "A Comparative Perspective on Non-discrimination Law" in Dagmar Schiek, Lisa Waddington, and Mark Bell (eds), *Cases, Materials and Text on National, Supranational and International Non-Discrimination Law* (Hart 2007) 15–17; Jule Mulder, "Cultural Narratives and the Application of Non-Discrimination Law" in Barbara Havelková and Mathias Möschel (eds), *Anti-Discrimination Law in Civil Law Jurisdictions* (OUP 2019) 31, 32.

[92] Barbara Havelková and Mathias Möschel, "Introduction: Anti-Discrimination Law's Fit into Civil Law Jurisdictions and the Factors Influencing It" in Havelková and Möschel (eds) (n 91) 1, 16.

[93] See Mirjan R Damaška, *The Faces of Justice and State Authority: A Comparative Approach to the Legal Process* (Yale University Press 1986) 36–38.

[94] See Ernst-Wolfgang Böckenförde, "Demokratie als Verfassungsprinzip" in Josef Isensee and Paul Kirchhof (eds), *Handbuch des Staatsrechts der Bundesrepublik Deutschland. Band II: Verfassungsstaat* (C.F. Müller 2004) 429, para 24; Matthias Jestaedt, *Demokratieprinzip und Kondominialverwaltung* (Duncker & Humblot 1993) 295.

[95] See Damaška (n 93) 42–43; Denise G Réaume, "Of Pigeonholes and Principles: A Reconsideration of Discrimination Law" (2002) 40 Osgoode Hall LJ 113, 119.

[96] See Jeffrey Goldsworthy, *The Sovereignty of Parliament: History and Philosophy* (OUP 1999) 1–8. The concept goes back to Albert Venn Dicey, *Introduction to the Study of the Law of the Constitution* (Macmillan 1885).

[97] See Anthony Bradley, "The Sovereignty of Parliament—Form or Substance?" in Jeffrey Jowell and Dawn Oliver (eds), *The Changing Constitution* (7th edn, OUP 2011) 35; Mark Elliott, "The Principle of Parliamentary Sovereignty in Legal, Constitutional, and Political Perspective" in Jeffrey Jowell, Dawn Oliver, and Colm O'Cinneide (eds), *The Changing Constitution* (8th edn, OUP 2015) 38 (for the UK); Vanessa MacDonnell, "The New Parliamentary Sovereignty" (2016) 21 Review of Constitutional Studies 13 (for Canada); Matthew S R Palmer, "New Zealand Constitutional Culture" (2007) 22 New Zealand Universities LR 565, 582–86; Janet McLean, "The Unwritten Political Constitution and its Enemies" (2016) 14 I.CON 119, 133.

movements like legal realism and critical legal studies have undermined the belief in the guiding function of legal doctrine.[98] For these reasons, judicial review of legislation is viewed with much more skepticism in many common law jurisdictions than in civil law jurisdictions.[99] As a consequence of this skepticism, courts adopt a more deferential equality as non-discrimination model, trying to diffuse the impression of political activism. By contrast, civil law courts whose legitimacy is built on legal expertise can afford to adopt a less deferential approach because the suspicion of political activism is less evident.

But legal tradition plays a role beyond the explanation of the divide between civil law and common law. This is most evident in Singapore. The chapter on the Singaporean equality case law has shown that the rather weak institutional position of the Singapore Supreme Court vis-à-vis a *de facto* one-party state is not the only reason for the deferential approach of the Singaporean courts.[100] It is part of the judicial tradition in Singapore to avoid open conflicts with the legislature and the executive. Instead, the courts use subtle signaling to induce a self-correction of the political process.

3.4 Political ideology

In some jurisdictions, the political ideology of judges has been a powerful driver behind the shape of the equality doctrine. This is most obvious with regards to the equal protection doctrine of the US Supreme Court.[101] The tiered scrutiny doctrine with heightened scrutiny for distinctions based on certain suspect characteristics took shape during the Warren Court, which is usually perceived as a progressive era of the Court.[102] By contrast, the conservative turn from the 1970s onward led to rather restrictive developments of the equal protection doctrine. This concerns, for example, the requirement of discriminatory intention for strict scrutiny in indirect discrimination cases or the application of strict scrutiny in affirmative action cases.

In other jurisdictions, the influence of political ideology is less salient. This is not necessarily because it is less important. In jurisdictions where court decisions are published as *per curiam* decisions without disclosing the votes of individual judges, the influence of ideology is much more difficult to observe. But even in jurisdictions following a *seriatim* style, there is usually less research on the influence

[98] Kristoffel Grechenig and Martin Gelter, "The Transatlantic Divergence in Legal Thought: American Law and Economics vs. German Doctrinalism" (2008) 31 Hastings International and Comparative LR 295.

[99] This skepticism is expressed in a representative fashion in Jeremy Waldron, "The Core of the Case Against Judicial Review" (2006) 115 Yale LJ 1346. See also McLean (n 97) 123 (for New Zealand).

[100] See Chapter 14, section 4.

[101] See Chapter 2, section 4.3.

[102] See Fiss (n 64); Yoshino (n 64); Khaitan (n 64) 61–62.

of political ideology on judicial decision-making than in the United States.[103] Nevertheless, our study gives some indications. In India, we have seen, for example, that most of the Justices on the Supreme Court did not come from backward classes. Their skepticism of affirmative action measures for backward castes might thus not only have been driven by genuine concerns about the design of the measure but also by general hostility towards the idea of affirmative action that might—in their view—water down the quality of accepted candidates.[104]

Finally, there are some jurisdictions where the equality doctrine has been shaped by specifically influential judges whose value system was thus infused into the equality doctrine. This has been most obvious in the case of the IACtHR where the former president, Antônio Augusto Cançado Trindade, played a crucial role in the development of the Court's approach.[105] Cançado Trindade was a strong supporter of the *pro homine* principle and his approach was heavily influenced by natural law concepts.[106] However, from a natural law perspective, there is little institutional role for judicial deference so that it is not surprising that the IACtHR adopted a non-deferential approach, imposing positive obligations on legislatures and executives.

3.5 Influence of other courts

Another important factor for the shape of equality doctrines is the influence of foreign courts. In the realm of equality, the dominant court of reference is the US Supreme Court. The jurisprudence of many courts in our sample shows the influence of the Supreme Court's three-tiered scrutiny model. Nevertheless, there has been no court that has copied the US doctrine exactly. Instead, the US example has shaped equality doctrine in other jurisdictions in more subtle ways. Some courts have adopted a tiered model of scrutiny. For example, we can find allusions to different tiers of scrutiny in Colombia, Taiwan, and Germany. However, these courts have established different numbers of tiers or composed the tiers differently. For example, the Colombian Constitutional Court has equally developed a three-tiered model of scrutiny but uses different trigger criteria and different tests within the tiers.[107] Furthermore, we see a fusion of approaches of different courts. For

[103] See Niels Petersen and Konstantin Chatziathanasiou, "Empirische Verfassungsrechtswissenschaft: Zu Möglichkeiten und Grenzen quantitativer Verfassungsvergleichung und Richterforschung" (2019) 144 Archiv des öffentlichen Rechts 501, 521–25 (with further references).

[104] See Chapter 13, section 4.

[105] See Chapter 10, section 4.3.

[106] See Augusto Antônio Cançado Trindade, *International Law for Humankind: Towards a New Jus Gentium* (2nd edn, Martinus Nijhoff 2010).

[107] See Chapter 11, section 4.1.

example, the Constitutional Courts of Colombia and Taiwan have merged US-style tiered scrutiny with German-style proportionality.[108]

Other courts have an even more complex relationship with the US model. This is particularly the case for the Supreme Court of Canada.[109] The Justices of the Supreme Court have been influenced by some of the earlier decisions of their US counterpart. For example, footnote 4 of the *Carolene Products* decision has played a prominent role in the development of the Canadian doctrine.[110] Furthermore, the Canadian Supreme Court referred to *Griggs v Duke Power*[111] when developing its indirect discrimination jurisprudence.[112] However, the current US equality doctrine rather serves as an anti-model in Canada. The skepticism of the US Supreme Court towards affirmative action has led the drafters of the Canadian Charter to include an explicit authorization of the practice into section 15 of the Charter, and many of the doctrinal choices of the Canadian Supreme Court can be understood as an attempt to avoid the perceived aberrations of the US doctrine.

Another influential court is the CJEU. The Court has been particularly influential in its jurisprudence on indirect sex discrimination. Here, the CJEU has taken the opposite approach of the US Supreme Court and argued that a disparate impact without discriminatory intention is sufficient for a finding of discrimination.[113] This has resonated with courts in EU member states. To a certain extent, this is to be expected because of the principles of primacy and direct effect of EU law.[114]

[108] See Silvana Insignares-Cera and Viridiana Molinares-Hassan, "Juicio integrado de constitucionalidad: Análisis de la metodología utilizada por la Corte Constitucional Colombiana" (2012) 124 Vniversitas 91, 102–04; Carlos Bernal Pulido, *El principio de proporcionalidad y los derechos fundamentales* (Universidad Externado 2014) 1021 et seq (regarding Colombia); Chin-Chie Lin, "Proportionality in Taiwan: American-German Fusion" in Po-Jen Yap (ed), *Proportionality in Asia* (CUP 2020) 60 (regarding Taiwan). It is interesting to note, though, that proportionality—while dominant in the German fundamental rights approach in general—has initially only played a marginal role in the equality case law of the German Federal Constitutional Court, see Konrad Hesse, "Der Gleichheitssatz in der neueren deutschen Verfassungsentwicklung" (1984) 109 Archiv des öffentlichen Rechts 174; Rudolf Wendt, "Der Gleichheitssatz" (1988) 7 Neue Zeitschrift für Verwaltungsrecht 778; Jost Pietzcker, "Der allgemeine Gleichheitssatz" in Detlef Merten and Hans-Jürgen Papier (eds), *Handbuch der Grundrechte. Band V: Grundrechte in Deutschland: Einzelgrundrechte II* (C.F. Müller 2013) 883; Lerke Osterloh, "Der Gleichheitssatz zwischen Willkürverbot und Grundsatz der Verhältnismäßigkeit" in Claudio Franzius and others (eds), *Beharren. Bewegen: Festschrift für Michael Kloepfer zum 70. Geburtstag* (Duncker & Humblot 2013) 139; Niels Petersen, "Gleichheitssatz und Einzelfallgerechtigkeit: Eine Rekonstruktion der Dogmatik von Art. 3 GG im Vergleich zur US-amerikanischen *equal protection* Doktrin" (2018) 57 Der Staat 327.

[109] See Chapter 3, section 4.

[110] See eg *R v Turpin* [1989] 1 SCR 1296, 1333 (per Wilson J); *Rudolf Wolff & Co v Canada* [1990] 1 SCR 695, 702 (per Cory J); *R v Généreux* [1992] 1 SCR 259, 275 (per Lamer CJ).

[111] *Griggs v Duke Power Co*, 401 US 424 (1971).

[112] See *British Columbia (Public Service Employee Relations Committee) v BCGSEU* [1999] 3 SCR 3, 19; *Quebec (Attorney General) v A* [2013] 1 SCR 61, 219; *Kahkewistahaw First Nation v Taypotat* [2015] 2 SCR 548, 557–58; *Fraser v Canada (Attorney General)*, 2020 SCC 28, paras 32–38, 53–55, 70–71.

[113] See eg *Bilka-Kaufhaus* (n 55). For a more detailed analysis, see Chapter 5, section 2.2.

[114] On primacy, see Monica Claes, "The Primacy of EU Law in European and National Law" in Anthony Arnull and Damian Chalmers (eds), *The Oxford Handbook of European Union Law* (OUP 2015) 178; Fulvio Maria Palombino, *Duelling for Supremacy: International Law vs. National Fundamental Rights* (CUP 2019); Niels Petersen and Konstantin Chatziathanasiou, *Primacy's*

However, the influence often went beyond the areas directly affected by EU law and also concerned the interpretation of constitutional equality provisions. For example, the German Federal Constitutional Court changed its approach regarding sexual orientation after a respective ruling of the CJEU.[115] Even beyond the EU, the CJEU has proved to be influential. The Court's approach regarding indirect discrimination, focusing on disparate impact instead of discriminatory intent, has become dominant outside the United States.[116] While we cannot prove the direct influence of the CJEU, it is likely that its approach has provided some inspiration.

Another Court that has been influential is the ECtHR. On the one hand, the Court has influenced the equality jurisprudence of other international human rights courts and tribunals.[117] All other human rights bodies in our sample have either explicitly referred to the ECtHR or implicitly adopted its concepts in parts of their equality jurisprudence.[118] On the other hand, the ECtHR has also had influence on the equality case law of domestic courts. This is most obvious in the case of the UK Supreme Court, which is also applying Article 14 ECHR and thus frequently refers to and discusses the case law of the Strasbourg Court. But other member states of the ECHR occasionally refer to the ECtHR too. Finally, some domestic courts have exercised a certain measure of influence. We have already seen that elements of the doctrinal approach of the German Federal Constitutional Court have been adopted in Colombia or Taiwan even if they are used differently in these jurisdictions. Furthermore, the Supreme Court of Canada is influential among Commonwealth courts. But these courts do not come close to the importance of the US Supreme Court when it comes to shaping the equality case law around the world.

3.6 Conclusion

The discussion in this section shows that the reasons why courts adopt specific doctrines are quite complex. They do not simply depend on the wording of the

Twilight? On the Legal Consequences of the Ruling of the Federal Constitutional Court of 5 May 2020 for the Primacy of EU Law (European Parliament 2021).

[115] See Chapter 7, section 4.
[116] See earlier, section 2.2.
[117] See Niels Petersen, "Equality and International Law" in Neha Jain and Mila Versteeg (eds), *Oxford Handbook of Comparative Human Rights Law* (OUP forthcoming 2025).
[118] See eg Advisory Opinion, *Proposed Amendments to the Naturalization provision of the Constitution of Costa Rica*, OC-4/84 (IACtHR, January 19, 1984), para 56; *Tanganyika Law Society v Tanzania; Mtikila v Tanzania* App nos 009/2011 and 011/2011 (AfrCtHPR, June 13, 2013) paras 106.2–107.1. Regarding the HRCttee, see Chapter 19, section 4. However, while the ECtHR is the most influential of the international courts, it is not the only one who has exercised influence. Both the UN HRCttee and the IACtHR are sometimes cited by other international courts, see eg *Tanganyika Law Society* ibid paras 106.2–107.1; *Opuz v Turkey* (n 71) paras 85–86. For a more detailed discussion of the cross-influence of the different international human rights bodies, see Petersen (n 117).

norm or the drafting history, even though these are certainly influencing the doctrinal choices of the judges. Instead, there are multiple factors that influence why courts adopt specific doctrines. The strength of these factors varies by jurisdiction. These factors are predominantly the authority of the court, the historical context and the founding narrative of the equality norm and the court, and the legal tradition. Moreover, the political ideology of the judges and the influence of foreign or international courts also play a role.

Two results are particularly notable. In the descriptive part we have seen that the approaches of common law and civil law courts differ quite significantly. This was, *prima facie*, surprising because of the increasing similarity of the two traditions.[119] But there are significant differences between common law and civil law courts when it comes to understanding the role of judges. A final observation concerns the role of the US Supreme Court. The practice of the Court is often coined by the phrase "American exceptionalism"[120] because it does not fit the "global model" of constitutional rights.[121] However, we have seen in the descriptive findings that the global model narrative does not fit the equality case law. Instead, the range of models that we find is much more diverse than the narrative suggests. Interestingly, the US Supreme Court plays a crucial role in this process. On the one hand, the Court's three-tiered scrutiny and its equality practice is a constant reference point for a great number of jurisdictions. However, it has not simply been copied but is only taken as an inspiration. Some jurisdictions have adopted a modified version of a multitiered scrutiny. Others have only made terminological allusions, while some jurisdictions have taken the US experience as counter-model in developing their own doctrines.

4. Conclusions

The insights that have emerged from this study concern two different academic discourses. On the one hand, the comparative analysis of equality doctrines gives us food for thought for the general comparativist discussion in constitutional law. It demonstrates that the narrative of a "global model" of constitutional rights has its limits. It does not apply to equality, where we have failed to observe a significant

[119] See Jakab, Dyevre, and Itzcovich (n 22); Günter Hager, *Rechtsmethoden in Europa* (Mohr Siebeck 2009) 109–15.

[120] See Steven G Calabresi, "'A Shining City on a Hill': American Exceptionalism and the Supreme Court's Practice of Relying on Foreign Law" (2006) 86 Boston University LR 1335; Lorraine Eisenstat Weinrib, "The Postwar Paradigm and American Exceptionalism" in Sujit Choudhry (ed), *The Migration of Constitutional Ideas* (CUP 2006) 84. See also Frederick Schauer, "Freedom of Expression Adjudication in Europe and the United States: A Case Study in Comparative Constitutional Architecture" in Georg Nolte (ed), *European and US Constitutionalism* (CUP 2005) 49 (specifically regarding freedom of expression).

[121] Möller (n 2).

convergence. It has also shown that the common law–civil law divide is more persistent than is often assumed in the constitutional law discourse. It might be worth conducting further research into whether these phenomena are limited to the field of equality or whether they can also be observed in other areas of fundamental rights on closer inspection. Finally, our study has added additional context to the discussion on the "migration of constitutional ideas"[122] by demonstrating how such ideas are customized in the recipient jurisdictions and how they may even serve as counter-model from which courts try to distance themselves.

On the other hand, the results of our study also provide lessons for the discourse on equality. Peter Westen famously described the idea of equality as "empty."[123] This book has shown that the judicial conceptualization and operationalization of equality is not empty but that it displays a considerable diversity. We have identified four models of equality that differ regarding the level of judicial deference that courts apply toward the legislature. In the introduction, we have seen that each of these models, in normative terms, has specific advantages and drawbacks. For this reason, a relative normative assessment or even a ranking of the normative desirability of these different models seems difficult. There is not one model that suits all jurisdictions and legal traditions equally well. Instead, the models have to be understood as the result of the specific institutional and cultural contexts in which the courts operate. This concerns, in particular, the legal tradition and the legitimizing narrative of constitutional review in this legal tradition, the security of the court's position in the institutional framework, and the historical context in which the court and/or the constitutional equality guarantee emerged. This does not suggest that a comparative normative assessment of these models is fruitless, but any normative evaluation will have to take into account the context in which these models emerged.

[122] On this concept, see Frederick Schauer, "On the Migration of Constitutional Ideas" (2005) 37 Connecticut LR 907; Sujit Choudhry, "Migration as a New Metaphor in Comparative Constitutional Law" in Sujit Choudhry (ed), *The Migration of Constitutional Ideas* (CUP 2006) 1.

[123] Westen (n 1). See the discussion on Westen in Chapter 1, section 1.

Annex: Code Book of Variables

Year: Year when the case was decided.

Majority opinion: Which judge was the author of the majority opinion (please assign one number to each judge; zero if there was a decision of the whole bench or a plurality opinion with no clear author; please delete this column for jurisdictions where the author of an opinion cannot be identified).

Violation of equality norm: Did the court find a violation of the equality norm?

Criterion binary: Did the court discuss a violation based on a suspect criterion (yes = 1/no = zero)? You have discretion to decide what is a suspect criterion; as a rule of thumb, a suspect criterion is a characteristic which identifies vulnerable groups that suffer from a disadvantage gap. The characteristic has to be either immutable or a fundamental choice (eg race, sex, religion, origin, disability, age, birth out of wedlock, etc).

Criterion class: If no suspect criterion was discussed, please mark zero; if one was discussed, please mention the criterion; the list that is already contained in the file is not exhaustive; please feel free to amend it.

Factual rejection: Did the court discuss a suspect criterion (eg race) but decided that there was no (indirect) discrimination based on this criterion because of factual grounds? If so, please mention the suspect criterion in the previous column and enter a 1 in this column. If the court did not discuss a suspect criterion at all or if it found that there was indeed a discrimination based on factual grounds, please enter a zero (Example: In the US, strict scrutiny is only applicable if an intentional racial discrimination can be proven; assume that the court finds that there was no intentional discrimination based on race; in this case, please enter 1 in Crit binary, 2 in Crit class, and 1 in factual rejection).

Subject area: What is the subject area in which the discrimination takes place? You can take broad categories; again, the list is not exhaustive, so please feel free to add categories that seem important in your jurisdiction; please only add new categories if there are several cases, otherwise please just note "other."

Statute: Did the court review the constitutionality of a statute in its decision?

Judiciary: Did the court review a judicial decision? Please only note 1 here if there was no other underlying executive decision. Most challenges to executive action do not come directly to an apex court but are first reviewed by courts in lower instances. Therefore, if the real issue of a reviewed court decision is the review of a legislative act or of executive action, then please code zero here; Only code 1 if the reviewed decision neither reviews executive nor legislative action (eg decision of a criminal court or dispute between private parties).

Indirect discrimination: Did the court find that there was an indirect discrimination (zero if no, 1 if yes)? This is only relevant if the court discusses a suspect criterion. If there is no suspect criterion, please mark zero.

Affirmative action: Was the underlying measure that was reviewed a measure of affirmative action, in other words a measure that intended to benefit a vulnerable group which was subject to a disadvantage gap in the past (eg measure to support Black individuals or women or disadvantaged castes, etc).

Political participation: This variable concerns all cases, which deal with political representation and the functioning of the political system (1—political system is concerned, zero—it is not concerned), that is, cases on access to the ballot, equal weight of votes, party financing, campaign financing and campaign ads, gerrymandering, minimum quotas for representation in parliament, etc.

Index

For the benefit of digital users, indexed terms that span two pages (e.g., 52–53) may, on occasion, appear on only one of those pages.

Tables are indicated by an italic *t* following the page number.